Caribbean Culture

Caribbean
Culture

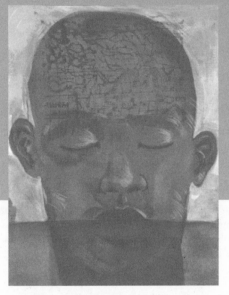

Soundings on
Kamau Brathwaite

Edited by Annie Paul

University of the West Indies Press
Jamaica • Barbados • Trinidad and Tobago

University of the West Indies Press
7A Gibraltar Hall Road   Mona
Kingston 7   Jamaica
www.uwipress.com

11 10 09 08 07   5 4 3 2 1

Caribbean culture: soundings on Kamau Brathwaite / edited by Annie Paul.

p. cm.

Papers presented to the Second Conference on Caribbean Culture held at
the University of the West Indies (Mona, Jamaica), January 2002.

Includes bibliographical references.

ISBN: 978-976-640-150-4

1. Brathwaite, Kamau, 1930– 2. Caribbean Area – Civilization.   3. Caribbean Area –
Intellectual life. 4. Popular culture – Caribbean Area. 5. Caribbean Area – Social life
and customs. 6. Caribbean literature. 7. Caribbean Area – History. I. Brathwaite,
Kamau, 1930– II. Paul, Annie. III. Conference on Caribbean Culture (2nd: 2002:
Kingston, Jamaica)

PR9230.9.B68 Z63 2002   811.54

Cover illustration: Christopher Cozier, *Around and Submerged*
(ink on paper, 9 x 7 inches), from the series *Tropical Night* (2005)

Book and cover design by Robert Harris.

Set in Stone Serif 9/14 x 24

Printed in Canada.

Contents

Introduction

Nadi **Edwards** |

I

The Second Conference on Caribbean Culture, which was held at the Mona campus of the University of the West Indies in January 2002, paid tribute to the work of Kamau Brathwaite, the noted Caribbean poet, historian, cultural critic and man of letters. Over a period of two days, various scholars and cultural practitioners presented papers and participated in discussions on the work of this leading anglophone Caribbean intellectual who had pioneered theoretical and methodological innovations in Caribbean studies, and transformed the region's literary canon with his poetic excavation of the fragmented histories of diaspora and his formal innovation in terms of the use of vernacular "nation language" and African-diaspora musical cultures. In honouring Kamau Brathwaite, the University of the West Indies fittingly, albeit belatedly, recognized the signal importance of this Caribbean "man of words" who exemplifies Edward Said's description of the intellectual as a figure "with a vocation for the art of representing. . . . And that vocation is important to the extent that it is publicly recognizable and involves both commitment and risk, boldness and vulnerability."[1]

1

After five productive decades of highly innovative and provocative creative and scholarly writings, Brathwaite's penchant for risk taking has resulted in his status as a pathfinder, the author and founder of an intellectual tradition and methodology that articulates an influential conceptual and theoretical approach to Caribbean studies. Like C.L.R. James, whose work represents the attempt to synthesize various intellectual and creative engagements with the Caribbean, Brathwaite's enterprise emanates from and converges on a common site – the awareness of the need for a postcolonial Caribbean epistemology that is opposed to what Sylvia Wynter defines as the "regulatory metaphysics" and the "normalizing discourses . . . of the globally dominant Western-European bourgeoisie".[2] His central contributions to Caribbean literature, historical and cultural studies are grounded in this categorical necessity to articulate what he punningly designates as an *alter/native* to the master narratives of colonialist historiography and aesthetics. Like many other Caribbean writers and scholars, his point of departure is the fragmented genesis of Caribbean history, and the kaleidoscopic vision of its creolized and native futures. His assertion at the end of his first poetic trilogy, *The Arrivants*, of the need to fashion "something torn and new" from the "broken ground" of Caribbean history, signals a restorative philosophy of history and art which takes fragmentation, catastrophe and trauma as both the beginnings of and routes towards new languages of culture, place, nation and identity. Language, in fact, is central to Brathwaite's prolific *oeuvre*; it is coterminous with culture, nation and identity, and a sense of language as naming and renaming, language as steeped in the exteriority of what Said dubs "worldliness", underpins all of his projects. This worldliness is a confluence of historical and cultural specifics: Caribbean social history; creolization, hybridity and syncretism; African diasporic cultural continuities; the relation of the Caribbean subject to Africa; and the politics and poetics of cultural and linguistic decolonization.

Brathwaite's prolific and varied output defies easy categorization, but it is possible, for analytical purposes, to divide his work into three categories: poetry and creative prose; literary and cultural criticism; and social history. His reputation as a poet has overshadowed his roles as critic, historian and cultural analyst, although, as Edward Baugh observes, his criticism outweighed his poetry prior to the publication of *Rights of Passage* in 1967.[3] In the latter text, as well as *Masks* (1968) and *Islands* (1969), Brathwaite boldly elaborated the epic and diasporic dimensions of Afro-Caribbean experience in the syncopated cadences of the musical registers of black globality: African drum rhythms; African-American jazz, blues, spirituals, field shouts and tin pan alley; Caribbean mento, calypso and Rasta "grounation" rhythms. Later collections of poetry such as *Mother Poem* (1975), *Black and Blues* (1976), *Other Exiles* (1977), *Sun Poem* (1982), and *X/Self* (1987) revealed Brathwaite's deepening exploration of the layered histories of cultural encounters, conquest, racial slavery, trauma, psychological alienation, displacement, self-construction, the relation to place, the excavation of submerged cultural memories, the peregrinations of diasporic and globalizing processes, and the verbal and sonic mapping of the archipelago. His increasingly eclectic and idiosyncratic poetic output has veered towards both hybrid confluences of prose narrative and intense metaphorical ellipsis, as in the prose poems of *Dreamstories* (1994), and the nightmarish realism of recontextualized newspaper accounts, radio transcripts and meditations in *Trench Town Rock* (1996). In the elegiac and poignant autobiographical statements of *The Zea Mexican Diary* (1993), Brathwaite unveils his own personal loss and anguish as he mourns the death of his first wife in a heartfelt narrative that is steeped in all the pain and power of poetic expression. More recently, his 2000 collection, *Words Need Love Too*, forges dreamlike celebrations of the word out of the fragments, the linguistic and cultural detritus of New World vernacular expressions.

Brathwaite's poetic output and his critical essays have had enormous impact on younger Caribbean writers and critics, who have found in his work an exemplary model of a Caribbean aesthetic. The flowering of dub and rapso poets in Jamaica and Trinidad, respectively, certainly owes a lot to Brathwaite's use of Caribbean Creole languages and musical forms in his poetry, as well as his theoretical injunctions regarding the need for Caribbean writers to ground their aesthetics in the region's vernacular resources. Brathwaite's interventions also took the form of editorial and institutional support in his role as one of the founding members of the Caribbean Artists' Movement and its house journal, *Savacou*, which offered a forum for younger writers to publish works that reflected the cultural nationalist zeitgeist.

While the vagaries of poetic influence are subject to debate, there is little doubt about the nature and scope of the impact of Brathwaite's scholarly work in the realm of historical and cultural studies. In his ground-breaking works, *The Development of Creole Society in Jamaica, 1770–1820* (1971) and *Contradictory Omens: Cultural Diversity and Integration in the Caribbean* (1974), Brathwaite cogently conceptualized Caribbean sociocultural and historical formations in terms of the process of creolization, which he defines as operating at two related levels: "ac/culturation, which is the yoking (by force and example, deriving from power/prestige) of one culture to another (in this case the slave/African to the European); and inter/culturation, which is an unplanned, unstructured but osmotic relationship proceeding from this yoke".[4] Creolization, Brathwaite argues, is the result of the above, and it is a process that becomes "the tentative cultural norm of the society", a norm which has been historically constituted as fragmented and ambivalent, and hence lacking wholeness and solidity. Acculturation posits a Euro-creole norm: interculturation enables the emergence of "a more truly creole norm: not white but black/white: mulatto; the 'white' and 'black' still locked in competition for ascendancy" (*Omens*, 6). Creolization is thus a conflictual process with regard to the nature of the cultural order of the society, and Brathwaite's acknowledgement of its mulatto or hybrid nature accords so far with the claims of his fellow poet, Derek Walcott. Brathwaite's model, however, emphasizes Africa as the "submerged mother" of the creole system, and the primacy of the African/European encounter which forms the basal creole matrix that must be adjusted to by more recent waves of Asian immigrants. The colonial relation, within which creolization occurs, informs the latter process with several dichotomies:

> Creole society is the result therefore of a complex situation where a colonial polity reacts, as a whole, to external metropolitan pressures and at the same time to internal adjustments made necessary by the juxtaposition of master and labour, white and non-white, Europe and colony, European and African (mulatto creole), European and Amerindian (mestizo creole), in a culturally heterogenous relationship. (*Omens*, 10–11)

The concept of creolization outlined above has had a significant impact on Caribbean historiography and cultural studies, and Verene Shepherd and Glen Richards note that it "is now undeniably the dominant intellectual construct in the fields of Caribbean and Atlantic World history and informs all the historical presumptions of the leading historians in these fields today".[5] But history is only one of the disciplines that have been reconceptualized by Brathwaite's interventions, since anthropology, sociology, cultural studies and literary criticism have all had to engage with the theoretical and methodological implications of his creolization thesis. In fact, given his sustained and systematic contributions to literary and cultural criticism, Brathwaite is best described as a cultural theorist whose theoretical propositions elaborate a

Caribbean poetics that Silvio Torres-Saillant defines as "a counter-discourse that constantly questions the norms and assumptions of the hegemonic culture. . . . a discrete, sociohistorically specific, regional manifestation of the poetics of the marginal".[6] The majority of Brathwaite's essays have in fact been concerned with articulating a Caribbean aesthetic, and they reveal the dynamic evolution of an intellectual enterprise wedded to constructing categorical modes of exploring, describing and defining Caribbean cultural practice in relation to language, history, community and hybridity.

A theoretical audit of Brathwaite's critical writings reveals two distinct phases: the period 1957–1969 that begins with "Sir Galahad and the Islands" (1957) and ends with "Caribbean Critics" (1969); the second phase, 1970–1984, initiated by "Timehri" (1970) and capped by *History of the Voice: The Development of Nation Language in Anglophone Caribbean Poetry* (1984).[7] The central concern of the first phase is that of establishing the problematic and the thematic of West Indian literature in terms of the relationship between the artist and the community, a relationship which is increasingly mapped onto a plane of dichotomous analogies and correspondences: oracy/literacy, creole/metropolitan, Prospero/Caliban.[8] This concern devolves into a cultural politics which seeks to describe, in Lamming's words, "the historic novelty of our situation",[9] but Brathwaite goes beyond the description and the pinpointing of Caribbean modernity by his incessant efforts to outline the discursive archive of that modernity. The essays which span the first decade of independence constitute literary criticism, in the conventional sense, because of their focus on selected texts and authors, and their charting of the major thematic and stylistic aspects of West Indian literature. These studies also focus on fiction, and this generic bias shapes the nature of Brathwaite's early critical formulations, which tend to posit the novel as the Caribbean text par excellence.[10] The approach is reflectionist, as the novel is seen as the quintessential representation of society: "Novels are essentially the expression of a society, they reflect the individual toil *within* a society".[11] If the aesthetics of the first phase are couched in terms of the problems of resolving the divide between artist and community, individual fragment and communal whole, then it is no accident that "Jazz and the West Indian Novel" is the major manifesto of this period, and its emphasis on dialogical counterpointing and rhythms accurately describes the tonal and rhythmic structures of Brathwaite's first trilogy, *The Arrivants*.

"Timehri" marks a cognitive break with the mode of conventional literary

criticism and a movement into the realm of cultural archaeology and genealogy that results in Brathwaite's work being marked by disciplinary and discursive convergence. The second-phase studies are best described in terms of
cultural studies rather than literary criticism;[12] they synthesize his historical
research on the dynamics of Caribbean creolization, his interest in African
diasporic cultures, and his ongoing poetic experimentation with language
with his attempts to adumbrate a Caribbean aesthetic. Thus the apparently
"literary" essays of this period such as "Creative Literature of the British West
Indies during the Period of Slavery" (1970), "The African Presence in
Caribbean Literature" (1974), "The Love Axe/l: Developing a Caribbean
Aesthetic, 1962–1974" (1977–78), and *History of the Voice* (1984) have to be
read alongside the historical and cultural works on creolization, African cul-
tural continuities and putative models of Caribbean studies: *The Development
of Creole Society in Jamaica, 1770–1820* (1971), *Contradictory Omens: Cultural
Diversity and Integration in the Caribbean* (1974), "Caribbean Man in Space and
Time" (1974), "Caliban, Ariel and Unprospero in the Conflict of Creolization:
A Study of the Slave Revolt in Jamaica in 1831–32" (1977), "Kumina: The
Spirit of African Survival in Jamaica" (1978), and "Caribbean Culture: Two
Paradigms" (1983). Both sets of texts share the same conceptual methods and
vocabularies, and these are in turn disseminated throughout Brathwaite's
post-*Arrivants* poetry. The cross-fertilization of history, cultural criticism and
poetry results in an increasingly idiosyncratic *oeuvre* that is characterized by
the virtual invention of its conceptual field, as Brathwaite coins terms, categories, sets of relations and structural models. This process of epistemological
invention is used to incrementally revise his concept of creolization, formu-
lated in *The Development of Creole Society in Jamaica* and *Contradictory Omens,*
and utilized as an interpretive principle in "Creative Literature of the British
West Indies during the Period of Slavery". This essay traces the genealogy of
colonial mimicry in the pre-emancipation British West Indies by analysing
the relationship of an imported model of literary style and language to the
particulars of place. Thus the failure of pre-emancipation white expatriate and
creole writers to achieve "West Indianness" is attributed to their total acquiescence to the dominant European norms that categorize the region and its
nonwhite population as inferior:

> To have produced "West Indian" literature at this period, the writers concerned
> would have had to have possessed a far greater knowledge of and interest in the

society they were writing about. They would have had, above all, to have come to terms with the institution of slavery; they would have had to have had an interior knowledge of the life of the slaves.[13]

"Creative Literature in the British West Indies" is to some extent an example of the kind of critical method that Brathwaite advocates in "Caribbean Critics", his polemical review essay of *The Islands in Between*. "Caribbean Critics" takes issue with the critical premises and methodologies of most of the essays in the first book-length collection of essays on West Indian literature.[14] The piece points to the absence, in *The Islands in Between*, of a set of definite propositions regarding the nature of West Indian literature. Brathwaite further contends that "West Indian" is conceived by the editor of *The Islands in Between* in "terrifyingly simple and Eurocentric" terms that offer a monolithic definition of culture which excludes West Indian heterogeneity.[15] The Caribbean, he argues, is not simply an outpost of European culture since "in spite of the operation upon it of the European system, in spite of – indeed, because of – 'the peculiar circumstances' of its history, [it] contains within itself a 'culture' different from, though not exclusive of Europe" ("Critics", 114).

In opposition to the monolithic, universalizing model of culture espoused by Cameron King and Louis James, Brathwaite asserts the creolized heterogeneity of Caribbean culture:

> The use of the word "culture" by King and James assumes "it" to be some kind of unified, articulate system with a clearly defined and identifiable "voice", coming out of a fully developed set of institutions. But this, surely, is an "establishment" view of culture – culture as an agreed on and imposed pattern. In the case of the West Indies, which is a (post-) colonial society without recognized autochthonous centres of its own, this definition can only lead to the discovery of no West Indian culture. Only Europe appears to be present. But what happens if we define culture as a complex of voices and patterns held togeher by geography, political force and social interaction? Under these terms, the concept of exclusiveness is ruled out, or at any rate is seen to be a operative only when a particular culture is static or dead. In a dynamic, working sense, each culture becomes definitive not only in itself, but in relation to others on which it impinges. West Indian culture, from this point of view, is identifiable in relation to the culture, say, of Latin America, of North America, of West Africa, of Western Europe; but it also exists as West Indian in terms of its social structures, its politics, its deposits of history and the life of its *peo-*

ple as seen to be persisting separately, often, from the life of the elite. There will be no "one West Indian voice", because there *is* no "one West Indian voice". ("Critics", 114–15)

Brathwaite's polemic is informed, as his references in "Caribbean Critics" indicate, by his ongoing research into creolization, and the formulation of a model that extrapolates from the ethnological work of several scholars on African continuities in the Caribbean. It is this "broadly ex-African base" which functions as the matrix of interacting cultural traditions and forms, but Brathwaite avoids the trap of reducing Caribbean culture to its African component. His vision of West Indian culture as a polyvocal conversation that "must be defined in terms of the process of creolization" ("Critics", 116), accords with Mikhail Bakhtin's conclusions regarding social discourses as dialogized heteroglossia. Culture, in this reading, is structured like a language which contains a "multitude of concrete worlds, a multitude of bounded verbal-ideological and social belief systems",[16] and Brathwaite, in fact focuses on language as the representational locus of culture. Thus he asserts the centrality of "the speech of the folk – dialect" in shaping the thematic and formal designs of the West Indian novel. Dialect becomes the representation of the folk community, the tradition which is engaged with by the writers in their attempt to "liberate the consciousness of the submerged folk" ("Critics", 117).

This liberatory *telos* is used by Brathwaite to differentiate West Indian writing from modern European and American literature: the former is communally oriented in contrast to the alienated individualism of the latter, hence any critical approach (such as that adopted by the contributors of *The Islands in Between*) which does not factor the communal and creole concerns of the writers into its analysis is doomed to reproduce a set of critical statements that can only place West Indian writing in relation to European literature. It is the mimicry of the critics which enables them to construct West Indian texts as tropical derivations of the Great Tradition, a relationship of filiation which ignores other ancestries as well as the immediacy of the local. This misplacing of critical paradigms results in

> the strange situation where the work of a body of writers, mainly concerned with the communal values of their creole society, is examined in a more or less "academic" fashion by a body of critics trained to respond almost exclusively to European influences, and whose main concerns are with "the artist" and "the individual". ("Critics", 117)

Critical relevance, on the other hand, demands an awareness of not only "[the] authors' use of European elements, but their use and transformation of their own local raw material" (p. 116).

"Caribbean Critics" inveighs against the uncritical application of metropolitan critical norms to West Indian literature, but it also seeks to establish guidelines for a local critical practice which is informed by non-European and non-establishment perspectives on the folk. Brathwaite notes the presence of the Prospero/Caliban dichotomy in the treatment of Africa and African influence, and the manner in which Caliban/Africa "comes off rather badly", at best as survival, at worst as "shame and shambles" ("Critics", 119, 121). He maintains the dichotomy in his own theorizing, but he revalues the significance of the African presence by arguing that the majority of West Indian writers, contrary to the assertions of Eurocentric West Indian criticism, validate this presence by making it the communal heartbeat and groundswell of their work. Local theories, he concludes, emerge out of the creative attempts of writers to construct "an *alternative*" paradigm – a poetics of "dialect, rather than 'standard' speech, 'folk' rather than middle class characters" (pp. 125–26). There is a developmental logic that links his conclusions in this essay to the exploratory work of the earlier essays, especially the elaboration of an *alternative* aesthetic in "Jazz and the West Indian Novel" that uses dialectal counterpointing and improvisation as primary concepts; however, "Caribbean Critics" engages the issues of competing cultural and critical paradigms, and it also unmasks the ethnocentrism, and the historical and cultural relationships of power, that parade behind the banner of the universal.

The *alternative*, in its alterity and nativism, begins to take on increasing importance as the theoretical object of Brathwaite's essays, an object that is produced within an increasingly occulted conjunction of cultural archaeology, the history of creolization as an eccentric reading of *The Tempest*, and the polemical assertion of the creole "nation languages" and oral traditions as root and matrix of Caribbean aesthetics. In "The African Presence in Caribbean Literature" Brathwaite explores African continuities in Caribbean literature in terms of a fourfold taxonomy: rhetorical; the literature of African survival; the literature of African expression; and the literature of reconnection. The essay charts a hierarchy of Afrocentric signification that ranges from the nominal aspects of rhetorical invocations of a romanticized Africa, the Africanisms of the folk tradition, and the deliberate transformation of the folk tradition (the *hounfort*)[17] into formal literature, to the pan-Africanist and diasporic evocation of historical and cultural linkages between Africa and the Americas. "The African Presence" recalls "Jazz", and anticipates *History of the Voice,* in its programmatic outlining of a Caribbean creole aesthetics that is produced at the interface of African and European linguistic and cultural systems, at the edge of writing and speech, between hounfort and text.

Language, specifically Caribbean "nation language", becomes increasingly central to Brathwaite's theorizing as both object and tool of inquiry. In fact, the procedural and taxonomic features of "The African Presence" and *History of the Voice* are essentially organized around varieties and modes of language use. As repositories of national identity, creolization and creole languages constitute "contradictory omens", a contested futurity that defies the neat linear and horizontal unfolding of national history. This temporal disruption, this "process in its historical continuum of movement and interruption" (*Omens,* 63) requires the kind of secular interpretation that Bhabha, echoing Said, calls for: a recognition of "a kind of 'doubleness' in writing; a temporality of representation that moves between cultural formations and social processes without a 'centred' causal logic".[18]

Unlike Bhabha, Brathwaite's advocacy of "doubleness" does possess a causal logic, the historical process of creolization which produces cultural formations that are always "other than" their parental components. Creolization defies the schema of genealogy; it is not a composite, but instead a new whole, a sociocultural continuum that is shaped by the differential tensions of integration and separatism. The latter processes derive from the historical relationships of power between Europeans and Africans during the period of slavery, relationships marked by confrontation, friction, and also creativity. Creolization becomes the sign of Caribbean difference, and it holds forth the possibilities of cultural autonomy and political independence which white West Indians failed to grasp because they were "blinded by the need to justify slavery". This abortion of nationalism accounts for the tenacity of colonial mimicry, since the white elite "preferred a bastard metropolitanism – handed down to the society in general after Emancipation – with its consequence of dependence on Europe, to a complete exposure to creolization and liberation of their slaves".[19]

"The African Presence in Caribbean Literature" is thus a necessary supplement to "Creative Literature in the British West Indies", as it outlines the differential play of the energies of African continuities on the force field of Caribbean literature. Brathwaite also takes issue with the notion that the

Middle Passage signifies an irrecoverable loss, a total cultural catastrophe that allows for no connections between Africa and the New World. Instead of cultural amnesia, Brathwaite advocates cultural transference and creative adaptation. He asserts the methodological and cognitive necessity of defining African culture in terms of its religious focus – "that, in fact, it is within the religious network that the entire culture resides", hence religion functions as the "form or kernel or core of the culture".[20] Thus despite the "depredations and fragmentations" of slavery and the plantation system, African culture survived, and is signalled in the modalities of the Afro-Caribbean religious complex: performative and possession-centred worship; rites of passage; divinatory, healing and occult practices. This cultural core was threatened after emancipation as a result of Christianization and colonial education, on the one hand, and the colonial legislation that deprived the ex-slaves of the franchise, curtailed their "socio-economic mobility", and banned Afro-Caribbean popular cultural practices ("Shango, cumfa, kaiso, tea-meeting, susu, jamette-carnival" ["African Presence", 197]). The erasure of the African presence is thus a feature of post-emancipation assimilation rather than a logical outcome of the trauma of the Middle Passage, and its recuperation requires a "revolutionized value system" (p. 200) that will redefine the concepts of "culture" and "literature" in terms of diversity and orality respectively:

> Until, therefore our definition of "culture" is re-examined in terms of its totality, not simply its Europeanity, we will fail to discover a literature of negritude and with it, a literature of authenticity. Likewise, the African presence in Caribbean literature cannot be fully or easily perceived until we redefine the term "literature" to include the nonscribal material of the folk/oral tradition, which, on examination, turns out to have a much longer history than our scribal tradition, to have been relevant to the majority of our people, and to have had unquestionably wider provenance. ("African Presence", 204)

These redefinitions underscore Brathwaite's cultural archaeology, which restores the fragments of African culture within the organic force field of the hounfort. Oral traditions, folk culture and the resonances of Africa within the diaspora thus constitute the critical referents for Brathwaite's discussion of Caribbean aesthetics. The relationship of the individual artist to the folk, that perpetual dynamic of Brathwaite's criticism, is reiterated as a canonical and critical principle which assigns typological and evaluative status to texts based on their incorporation and transformation of "the art of the hounfort" into the art of their respective genres ("African Presence", 236).

The major concepts outlined in "The African Presence" are essentially a more nuanced Afro-Caribbean ethnological refashioning of Brathwaite's advocacy of a jazz aesthetic, outlined in "Jazz and the West Indian Novel", as well as a precursor of the more extensive typologies of the nation-language aesthetics of *History of the Voice*. These concepts also underline Brathwaite's polemical overview of the development of a Caribbean aesthetic in the first decade after independence, "The Love Axe/l: Developing a Caribbean Aesthetic, 1962–1974". All of these essays are concerned with creating new critical terminologies and conceptual fields. Naming and taxonomy are definitive features of Brathwaite's second-phase criticism, and "The African Presence" introduces some of his primary concepts such as *hounfort, nommo, nam, loa, marronage, nation language,* and *groundation*. These constitute the alter/native Calibanic and creole poetics that enable Caribbean subjects to "become ourselves, truly our own creators, discovering word for object, image for the word".[21] Representational and figural politics underscore this conceptual process which yokes social history, anthropology and literary criticism to produce what Gordon Rohlehr calls an aesthetic of energy.[22]

Naming, as theoretical praxis, is crucial to Brathwaite's cultural poetics. Lamming's description of a young girl dancing in the tonelle, in *Season of Adventure,* is taken by Brathwaite as a stellar example of the transformation of Caribbean literature "into a new species of original art" ("African Presence", 235) which is redolent with "a certain kind of attitude to the *word,* the atomic core of language" (p. 236). Brathwaite defines this attitude in terms of the Dogon concept of *nommo,* the word seen as creative and transformative force, as conjuration and ontogenetic principle. This concept of *nommo* is evident in an entire range of black Atlantic vernacular rhetorical practices: "our love of courtroom scenes (both factual and fictional), the rhetoric of yard quarrels, 'word-throwings', tea-meetings and preacher/political orations", calypso, indeed the entire "sociology of nation-language" (pp. 240–42).

The term "nation-language" makes its first appearance in "The African Presence", and it becomes the primary conceptual tool of Brathwaite's major theoretical work, *History of the Voice.* The latter work is a sustained exploration of the emergence of the submerged orality of the Caribbean, the inner movement of this trace of the African presence working within writing to release the energies of *nommo* and *nam* that disrupt the constraints of the iambic pentameter (Brathwaite's umbrella term for metropolitan languages and literary conventions). But it is in "The African Presence" that nation language is first deployed and classified according to its range of techniques and modes. These techniques are essentially the same as those described in "Jazz and the West Indian Novel", except that the taxonomic procedures are more rigorous and less impressionistic than in the earlier essay, which identifies *nommo*, rhythm and improvisation as constitutive aspects of the jazz aesthetic. "The African Presence" adds the elements of *nam*, possession, icon and kinesis to the mix (with improvisation being subsumed under rhythm).[23]

Nam is one of Brathwaite's neologisms, and it is integrally related to naming and the politics of identity.[24] It is an unapologetically essentialist concept: an "irreducible kernel that holds the essence of Caribbean culture or any emerging culture".[25] While relatively undefined in "The African Presence" and *History of the Voice, nam* is explained at length in "Caribbean Culture: Two Paradigms" as an "ikon cymbel symbol beyond sentences" which is the disguise of man, an anagrammatic camouflaging of name and identity.[26] Brathwaite casts *nam* in an etymology that points to an intransigent core, an ontological horizon: "seed if you like. or soul. dry and reduced and irreducible and green: the utter inner self. Like when you eat the flesh you cannot eat the fetish. the irreversible and loveliest numen of your *nam*" ("Caribbean Culture", 37). Nam emerges from the debris of conquistadorial cannibalizing of culture and identity, and Brathwaite constructs an eccentric etymology that functions both as a sign of Caliban's linguistic inventiveness and as a linguistic allegory of the strategies of cultural and psychological marronage of enslaved and colonized peoples: "Nam / is the name reduced. survival nomen. oppression eats the e (or eye) and yet the a (or alpha) is protected by that n and m: dark consonants. deep boulders of the continent. cool sound . . . so even if you lose your name . . . your nam (e) . . . you cannot lose your nam" (p. 37).

Like the hounfort, *nam* is a metaphor of the cultural alter/native, and of the submerged folk traditions which have acted as cultural conservators despite fragmentation and catastrophe. *Nam* is the energizing force behind cultural/psychic marronage, and the icon of the maroon becomes increasingly important in Brathwaite's later poetry and cultural criticism. Indeed, his later work posits the need for a reclamation of the "submerged mothers" of Caribbean history and culture: hence the movement in *Mother Poem* towards a poetics of Sycorax, Caliban's mother, and the engendering of a post-

Gutenberg (post-modem "writing in light") aesthetics of Stark (Caliban's sister, Brathwaite's most recent "writing beyond the ending" of Shakespeare's *Tempest*).[27] The concepts of *nommo* and *nam* thus link Brathwaite's poetics to George Lamming's recognition of the relationship between power and naming; Derek Walcott's Adamic imperative to (re)name the New World; and Wilson Harris's exploration of the state of Namless (the enabling condition of ab-original namelessness) in novels such as *Black Marsden* and *The Eye of the Scarecrow*.

It is this poetics of *nam,* the irreducible kernel of Calibanic culture, that Brathwaite affirms as the constitutive paradigm of Caribbean nation language. *History of the Voice* attempts to describe and define Caribbean poetry in terms of an emergent orality. The history of the emergence of this orality is coterminous with that of Caribbean nationalism. The conflated trajectories signal the real intent of Brathwaite's project: the articulation of a nationalist discourse, an aesthetics that is simultaneously an ethics and politics of national becoming. Brathwaite's basic thesis is similar to Fanon's assertions that national culture cannot be conceived of outside the crucible of nationhood since "culture is first the expression of a nation" and "national consciousness . . . is the most elaborate form of culture".[28] Nation language thus functions as a mode of agency that transforms the politics of the present: "The word becomes a pebble stone or bomb and dub makes sense (or nonsenseness) of politics demanding of it life not death, community not aardvark, new world to make new words and we to overstand how modern ancient is".[29] The transformative power of nation language lies in its capacity to implode and explode the scribal by a rhythm-driven orality; the resulting oral/scribal configuration gains its unsettling power from its location at the edge, its mutual displacement of speech and writing. This is what Brathwaite asserts in his description of nation language as "person-centred, fluid/tidal rather than ideal/structured nature", as continuum rather than static structure. Nation language, marked with the hybridity of European and African languages, is defined by linguistic marronage – "the submerged area of that dialect which is much more closely allied to the African aspect of experience in the Caribbean" – and explosive sonic errancy: "an English which is like a howl, or a shout or a machine-gun or the wind or a wave. And sometimes it is English and African at the same time" (*Voice*, 13).

Brathwaite's rendering of nation language as primal scream, as the vocables of sensation and the limit/horizon of ontological plenitude, apparently goes against the grain of contemporary postmodernist disparaging of the "meta-physics of presence" and the essentializing of the voice.[30] But Brathwaite's stance does not exclude difference, as nation language's efficacy depends on its ability to set in motion the differential play of meaning in a process of tidal expansion and contraction that Brathwaite defines as "tidalectics", a tidal dialectics which abandons the narrative of linear advance for the ebb and flow, the pulsions of cross-currents. The pulsions of nation language radiate from the sonic detonations of *explosure* and *implosure*: the former defined as "the uncurled bloom of light, rather than exposure (colonial subordination to the light)"; and the latter as the "firm but subtle feeding to the stem of ori-gins, in distinction to imposure (imprint of the rule and ruler: imperson/per-sonator)" (*Omens*, 61). Explosure and implosure are also the forces that constitute the intercultural dynamic of creolization, hence nation language has the same strategic import as creolization in Brathwaite's aesthetics.

Brathwaite's later essays and poetry reveal a marked convergence of theory and practice in relation to nation language. Conventional academic discourse is either mixed with poetic passages and nation-language interventions ("Caribbean Man in Space and Time"; "Caliban, Ariel and Unprospero"; "Proem for Hernan Cortez"; *History of the Voice*; "The Love Axe/l"), or it is eschewed completely for a hybridized poetic polemic that combines perform-ance, shamanistic deployment and decipherment of Brathwaite's Calibanic/Sycoraxic idiolect ("Caribbean Culture: Two Paradigms"). Nation language becomes the force that implodes and explodes the syntactical, lexical, phono-logical and semantic structures of English; it erodes the very shape of the word and reconfigures the page by subverting the directional axes (left to right, top to bottom) of the margins. Writing, for Brathwaite, is both alphabetic and hieroglyphic; it is simultaneously a representation of sonic vibrations and a graphic image. It is this conflation of sound and sight that enables his puns, word-play, neologisms, syntactical variation, heterodox line breaks and the format of text on the page. The text is "othered" by the disruptive agency of Caribbean nation language, which makes its presence felt not only in Brathwaite's use of the vernacular but also in his use of Standard English where, as Nathaniel Mackey observes, "he takes his cue from the vernacular, subjecting words to bends, breaks, deformation, reformation – othering".[31]

Linguistic othering is also achieved by Brathwaite's use of the inventive speech of Rastafari with its semantic inversions, word-play and neologisms. Rastafarian dread talk is put into effect in Brathwaite's work as a technique of occultation and opacity. The strategies of opacity signal the ethnocultural difference of nation language rather than the vertical differentiation of dialect and standard.[32] Brathwaite's assertion of the slave's "(mis-)use" of language as the most effective form of rebellion, and of the creativity of language in the folk tradition, signals an awareness of the antihegemonic role of linguistic subversion, the radical propriety of malapropisms, and the "creative chaos" of the detonated word.

Brathwaite's idea of nation language is marked by certain simplifications, and a terminological fuzziness, that derive from his propensity towards metaphor and generalizations. The pentameter and the dactyl are used as metaphors for Standard English and Caribbean Creoles respectively, but their sweeping applications result in the eliding of crucial distinctions between syntactical variation and linguistic/cultural difference. Nation language, for Brathwaite, is also conceptualized in terms of a racial and cultural solidarity that excludes non-African elements: "Nation language is the language which is influenced very strongly by the African model, the African aspect of our New World/Caribbean heritage" (*Voice*, 13). The theoretical shortcomings of Brathwaite's work do not, however, obviate the importance of the conceptual paradigm of nation language for Caribbean aesthetics in general and Brathwaite's *oeuvre* in particular. Nation language, as Brathwaite points out, is akin to Edouard Glissant's description of the "forced poetics" of language as camouflage and evasion. Brathwaite's assertion of the integral relationship "between native musical structures and the native language" (p. 16) has the same valency as Glissant's declaration: "It is nothing new to declare that for us music, gesture, dance are forms of communication just as important as the gift of speech. This is how we first managed to emerge from the plantation: esthetic form in our cultures must be shaped from these oral structures".[33] Brathwaite's model of nation language moves away from textuality towards what Paul Gilroy describes as "dramaturgy, enunciation, and gesture – the pre- and anti-discursive constituents of black metacommunication".[34]

The emphasis on the voice counters the valorization of writing in European discourse, but Brathwaite has a balanced awareness of the dangers of fetishizing orality as the *sole* feature of Caribbean literature. Despite his unequivocal commitment to the aesthetics of nation language, he warns against investing in a model which privileges only one mode, whether oral or scribal. Calibanic models of criticism must eschew Prospero's limiting taxonomies because "to confine our definitions of literature to written contexts in a culture that remains ital in most of its people proceedings, is as limiting as its opposite: trying to define Caribbean literature as essentially orature" (*Voice*, 49).

Brathwaite's project is thus more than an essentialist attempt to re-place writing with speech; it is instead a challenge to reinvent and reimagine the word by confronting the monumentality of Standard English with the polyrhythmic flux of Caribbean nation language. Brathwaite's paradigms result in a poetic practice that privileges semantic and linguistic decentring, a "broken speech" which simultaneously encodes the silencing of dominated subjects and their vernacular utterances, which destabilize and change the very order of the imperial language itself. His historical and cultural studies are also animated by this principle of ontological and epistemological innovation, which deploys a recuperative archaeological procedure of excavating the fragmented and catastrophic terrain of Caribbean history in order to "refashion futures like a healer's hand".[35] This is his continuing legacy to Caribbean studies, his insistence on seeing the fragments whole, but even more importantly, on challenging us to rethink and renew our disciplinary languages, methodological frameworks and modes of imagining.

II

This collection is a tribute to Brathwaite's formidable legacy, and it builds on and supplements the necessary work done by previous collections edited by Stewart Brown (*The Art of Kamau Brathwaite*), Tim Reiss (*For the Geography of a Soul*), and Verene Shepherd and Glen Richards (*Questioning Creole: Creolisation Discourses in Caribbean Culture*) respectively.[36] It combines the literary-critical emphasis of *The Art of Kamau Brathwaite* and *For the Geography of a Soul* with the multidisciplinary perspectives of *Questioning Creole*. Unlike its predecessors, it engages with concerns of globalization and subalternity, and the relationship between Caribbean creolization, historiography, orature and aesthetics, and other regional cultures. In its wide-ranging treatment of Brathwaite and other subjects, it reflects the conjunctural impact of globalization, the anxieties of sovereignty, and the impact of discourses of gender and sexuality on notions of culture, citizenship and identity.

The twenty-two essays in this volume encompass disciplinary and methodological perspectives that range from literary and cultural criticism to histori-

ography, gender studies, popular culture, citizenship, and discourses of globalization. Some of these essays directly engage Brathwaite's poetry, criticism
and historical studies, or utilize, reframe and interrogate his concepts and
methodologies, while others are imbued with the spirit of his intellectual project, which he cogently describes in "Caribbean Man in Space and Time" as an
attempt to re-map Caribbean studies by excavating the resources of the "inner
plantation".

The collection is divided into seven sections that cohere around shared
thematic concerns, intellectual questions and methodological procedures.
Part 1, "Ceremonies of the Word", consists of five essays that address the
issues of orature and performance, the formal and structural practices that
shape oral performance, the language of myth, and the presence of these features in Brathwaite's poetry. In the first three essays, by Kofi Anyidoho,
Maureen Warner-Lewis and Ted Chamberlin, Brathwaite's concerns with
nation language and the crafting of an oral-based aesthetic are related to various collective contexts of oral expression. Kofi Anyidoho, in "Atumpan:
Kamau Brathwaite and the Gift of Ancestral Memory", analyses Brathwaite's
use of African orature and places him in the venerable tradition of African
diaspora men of words who fuse the functions of priest and griot: "a Fon/
Haitian **hougan**, an Asante **okyeame**, a Mande **djeli**, a Zulu **mbongi**, a Yoruba
babalawo, an Ewe **awuno bokono**, a **Logosu** of the Yewe Mystical Order".
Brathwaite's relation to Africa is cast in terms of literal and imaginative diasporic peregrinations that evoke the poet's experience of Africa and the ontological value of the word. Anyidoho rightly sees Brathwaite's Ghanaian
sojourn as a profoundly catalytic factor in his intellectual, critical and creative
formation, one that enables a salient ontological and epistemological transformation in his understanding of Africa and the Caribbean. Brathwaite as a diasporic African-Caribbean subject thus invents and reinvents his relationship
to the word by informing it with the particulars of history, language and
place. His acts of reinvention are profoundly concerned with using language
as a tool to rethink history and culture, and to challenge and undermine the
inherited colonial language with the explosive orality of African diasporic languages and musical forms. The latter, epitomized in the complex polyrhythms
of African drum poetics, serve to ground Brathwaite's poetry in a diasporic
network of ancestral memory and submerged histories.

While Anyidoho highlights Brathwaite's relation to African orality,
Maureen Warner-Lewis, in "The Rhythms of Caribbean Vocal and Oral-Based

Texts", stresses his equally important relation to the Caribbean, and Ted Chamberlin, in "Keeping Your Word: Contracts, Covenants and Canticles", points to the shared concerns of memory, language and narrative that link Brathwaite's work to Native and ethnic Canadian traditions of storytelling and praise singing. All three critics facilitate our understanding of Brathwaite's relation as "a man of words" to the local, the diasporic and the global. Where Anyidoho and Warner-Lewis delineate the vernacular poetics of African and Afro-Caribbean orature and performance modes that appear in Brathwaite's poetry, Chamberlin weaves a web of stories about stories and storytelling that constitute collective contracts, covenants and modes of negotiating encounters between peoples, places and cultures. By turns anecdotal, reflective and scholarly, Chamberlin's contribution reminds us of the elemental power of the word, and of the part that it plays in the Americas, its function in defining a relationship to place, its articulation of belonging and exile, its vision of the past, its problematic and contradictory oscillations between doubt and belief, between representation and nonrepresentation. Brathwaite, Chamberlin proclaims, "has given all of us in the Americas, of which the Caribbean is like a tuning fork, a sense of what an imaginative vision of the past and of the place might be like, of the deep contradictions that will inevitably be at its heart, and of the dangerous confusions that it will foster". Chamberlin provides an unsurpassable description of Brathwaite's project as being "simply an ancient dedication to ceremonies of the word", and his felicitous phrasing captures the ritualistic and performative ethos of Brathwaite's poetry, its elemental sense of awe, imaginative wonder and incantatory belief in the world-creating power of the word.

Warner-Lewis offers a magisterial exposition of the mechanics of orality in Caribbean poetry, with finely tuned readings of rhythms from a variety of Caribbean oral genres. In tracing the dialectic of sound and sense, speech and writing, Standard English and Caribbean Creoles, Warner-Lewis synthesizes linguistics, literary history, musicology and literary criticism into a model of precise cultural analysis. She unpacks the syllabic, tonal and accentual modes of Caribbean orature in an incisive demonstration of the artfulness and the formal regularities of seemingly unstructured Caribbean performances. As she argues, "investigating the syllable quantities of indigenous lyrics provides a platform from which to appreciate the technical characteristics of art forms we hardly think of in terms of shape and structural coherence". In showing the relationship between "folk-music prosody and some of the anglophone

Caribbean's twentieth-century poetic styles", Warner-Lewis locates Brathwaite's own creative and critical practice in relation to his understanding of the word as "a site for explosion and revisioning of our collective and personal experiences, in physical, phonological and semantic senses". His idiosyncratic and idiolectal penchant for neologisms, puns and semantic subversion is thus in line with the modalities of Caribbean nation language.

The issues of orality and performance are also discussed in Hubert Devonish's "When Form Becomes Substance: Discourse on Discourse in Two Calypsos", which examines the metadiscursive nature of calypso performance. Devonish alerts us to the self-reflexive nature of the calypso as a performance speech act, and the symbiotic and instrumental relationship between form and content. He analyses the two winning calypsos sung by Adrian Clarke, the 2001 Pic-O-De-Crop Calypso Monarch for Barbados, in terms of their strategic rhetorical and performative effects. What emerges in Devonish's refreshingly lucid reading is an awareness of the sophisticated poetics of performance, the knowledge of speech genres, and the layered artifice that cunningly plays on audience expectations and knowledge to frame form and content in ways that reinforce each other for the strategic purpose of winning a song competition.

Jeanne Christensen's "A Language of Myth" resonates with Anyidoho's and Chamberlin's recognition of the numinous and communally oriented nature of orality. The language of myth is different from that of Enlightenment scientific rationality, but it has its own logic and rationale. Myth, unlike logic, does not separate the word from the world but sees the one as inextricably entwined with the other. The mythic conception sees the word as world-creating. This is the force of language in the oral tradition, the power to name reality and call it into being. Christensen contextualizes Brathwaite's work within a universal schema of myth and archetype, and she offers another interpretive framework for understanding his approach to language.

Part 2, "Jah Music and Dub Elegy: Soundings on Kamau Brathwaite and Mikey Smith", consists of three essays: the first two address the seminal influence of music in Brathwaite's poetry and intellectual thought, and the third is an elegiac retrospective of the life and work of the late Jamaican dub poet, Michael "Mikey" Smith. In "The Music of Kamau Brathwaite", Lilieth Nelson briskly and lucidly analyses Brathwaite's formal and thematic deployment of musical elements and motifs in his poetry. Nelson draws persuasive analogies between musical scores and Brathwaite's verbal compositions, in a manner that enables her to catalogue the poet's use of antiphonal structures, repetition and rhythm, syncopation, melody, tempo, and harmony. Nelson's meticulous exegesis balances Donette A. Francis's finely nuanced reading of the importance of jazz in Brathwaite's intellectual formation. In many ways, while Nelson analyses the poetry as informed by a musical sensibility, Francis carefully charts the biographical and conjunctural factors that resulted in Brathwaite's exposure to jazz and its subsequent impact on his creative and critical work. Francis's thesis, in " 'Travelling Miles': Jazz in the Making of a West Indian Intellectual", is an unequivocal statement that jazz "laid the foundation for Kamau Brathwaite's work on Caribbean culture, since it was through jazz that he first discovered an aesthetics of dissonance that enabled him to conceive of an alternative to Eurocentric culture and aesthetics". Francis's essay is an exemplary instance of intellectual history that positions diasporic and transatlantic routes, sites and cultural practices as instrumental to the formation of Caribbean intellectuals. In asserting the cosmopolitan and diasporic nature of Brathwaite's formative cultural experiences, Francis also complicates "the dominant narrative about the radicalization of West Indian intellectuals", by arguing that the local exposure to a diasporic cultural form rather than the metropolitan experience of racism served as the catalyst for Brathwaite's intellectual radicalization. Jazz, in her reading, provides Brathwaite with an idiom for translating the meaning of race and the pathos of racism to his colonial context, and for discussing ontological and representational politics. Francis essentially positions jazz as an intellectual archive that is simultaneously both the content and the medium of its transmission, a fluid modality of diasporic cultural exchange and black cosmopolitan modernism that provides the tonal and conceptual palettes for the portrait of the subaltern artist as a young man.

In "Remembering Michael Smith (Mikey, Dub and Me)", Linton Kwesi Johnson, himself a world-renowned practioner of the genre of reggae/dub performance poetry, memorializes the late Jamaican dub poet via a succinct synthesis of concrete biographical details, and the sociopolitical and cultural contexts that birthed dub poetry in general and Mikey Smith's art in particular. Johnson's dispassionate exposition provides the necessary detachment for understanding the passion and power of Mikey Smith's expression as well as the tragic nature of his demise, and he adds to our understanding of the affinities and affiliations between himself, Smith and Jamaican popular culture. Apropos of his subject, Johnson recognizes Brathwaite's "seminal influence"

on the major dub poets, a fact reiterated in his citing of Brathwaite's insightful comment on Mikey Smith's stellar deployment of nation language. In a
sense, Brathwaite's unremitting indigenist cultural politics is a sort of subtext
in Johnson's tribute to Mikey Smith, since the latter's work exemplified many
of the theoretical propositions articulated in Brathwaite's aesthetic manifestos
on nation language, and vernacular culture and performance.

   The articles in part 3, "The Sea Is History: Tidalectics, Middle Passages and
Migrant Crossings", examine Brathwaite's relation to the non-anglophone
Caribbean through his use of aquatic metaphors to represent history, his concern with migrancy and displacement, and his engagement with Haiti both in
terms of its contemporary political and social crises and its symbolic status in
black revolutionary iconography. Elizabeth DeLoughrey, in "Routes and
Roots: Tidalectics in Caribbean Literature", remarks on the parallels between
Brathwaite's trope of tidalectics, the Calibanic opposite of Hegel's dialectic,
and the theories of Edouard Glissant and Antonio Benítez-Rojo. Tidalectics,
the cyclical oscillation of the ripples caused by skimming a stone on water, the
skipping irregularity of pebble cleaving foam and spray in an arc that evokes
the Caribbean archipelago, has functioned in recent years as a powerful concept in Brathwaite's poetics. Its inventive etymology is derived from *tidal,*
dialectic and *dialect,* thus wrapping in one neologism a triple reference to the
sea and ocean, historical progression, and language. DeLoughrey argues that
Brathwaite, Glissant and Benítez-Rojo use this and related aquatic tropes to
posit a regional rather than national identity, while at the same time preserving the sociocultural, linguistic and national difference. She frames their "sea
cartography" in terms of an antiessentialist privileging of fluvial indeterminacy, rhizomatic routes and transversal relations, in the Glissantian sense,
rather than fixed sites and identities. In this reading "the sea is history" and
Caribbean realities are diasporic and migratory. DeLoughrey applies the
tidalectical tropes of Brathwaite, Glissant and Benítez-Rojo to narratives by
Edwidge Danticat and Ana Lydia Vega to reveal the problematic status of the
Caribbean region: its relative powerlessness in the face of imperial territorialization and surveillance, and its tenuous position between openness and closure. The contemporary voyages of migrants and refugees recall the trauma of
the historical Middle Passage and the multiple dislocations of diasporas. Adrift
on the sea, there is no possibility of configuring identity in relation to land
and national sovereignty.

   Marie-José Nzengou-Tayo's "Kamau Brathwaite and the Haitian Boat

People: *Dream Haiti* or the Nightmare of the Caribbean Intellectual" is a close reading of one of Brathwaite's "dreamstories", *Dream Haiti,* as a representation of Brathwaite's engagement with and empathy for the plight of the Haitian boat people, who suffered the travails of perilous crossings and the indignities and humiliations of incarceration and repatriation back to their tragic homeland. Nzengou-Tayo sees the poem as an augury of the future of the Caribbean, indicated in the shifting narrative perspectives and the indeterminate positioning of voice and address. The dream framework of the poem functions as a mode of both dealing with trauma and complicating meaning, as it allegorizes the present as omen of past and future catastrophes. In the end, the poem highlights the conflicted stance of the Caribbean writer, the sense of powerlessness before imperial power and neocolonial retrogression, and the haunting evocation of Haiti as both nightmare and dream, a revelation of "the ambiguity of artistic creation".

Part 4, "Creolization, Historiography and Subalternity", contains articles that engage Brathwaite's historical scholarship, his creolization thesis, conceptual premises, conclusions, procedures and discursive style in the context of general questions of Caribbean and New World historiography. Cecil Gutzmore, in "Whose World View Rules? Sublated Contradictions of African and Creole in the Caribbean Historiography of Kamau Brathwaite", argues that the conceptual schema of creolization and its cognates is epistemologically and ontologically problematic, undertheorized, conceptually derivative, and subject to the error of misnaming African as creole. While appreciative of Brathwaite's contributions to the rethinking of Caribbean historiography, Gutzmore nonetheless asserts that creolization discourse has "tended 'objectively' to exclude several Caribbean communities, especially Asians but also Amerindians, Maroons, Jews, Portuguese and others". Gutzmore proceeds to accuse creole discourse of "a tendency to de-Africanize and inferiorize Caribbean and continental Africans. Indeed, some practitioners of creole discourse appear quite uncomfortable with the well-attested fact of African folk/popular cultural centrality within the expressive arts of the Caribbean region". This constitutes a "contradiction within Caribbean historiography", evidenced in the cognitive disconnect between the etymology of the term and its usage by contemporary historians. For Gutzmore, the inadequacies of creole discourse in Caribbean historiography result from the failure by its practitioners to pay adequate attention to historical theory, hence the lack of attention to the fact that Brathwaite's seminal contributions to creolization

theory take the form of sublating familiar terms from the "creole ideas cluster
to the level of first-order analytical concepts in his historiography and cultural criticism". Sublation has resulted in a conceptually shaky theoretical
apparatus, as the concepts lack the categorical and theoretical *gravitas* to go
beyond the epistemological horizon of earlier theories such as M.G. Smith's
plural society model. The epistemological and ontological contradictions that
underpin creolist discourse are adduced by Gutzmore as evidence of
Brathwaite's "strong tendency towards sociocultural totalization and the cultural resolution of issues".

Glen Richards's "Kamau Brathwaite and the Creolization of History in the
Anglophone Caribbean" is a synoptic overview of Brathwaite's contributions
to Caribbean historiography. Richards proffers a succinct and lucid exposition
of the evolution of Caribbean historiography, from the plantocratic and colonialist histories of Bryan Edwards and Edward Long, the racist imperial histories of J.A. Froude and Lowell Ragatz, to the emergence of a nationalist
anglophone Caribbean historiography represented by such figures as C.L.R.
James, Eric Williams, Douglas Hall and Elsa Goveia. He deftly sketches the
intellectual contexts and foundations established by Brathwaite's intellectual
precursors, such as the historians listed above as well as nonhistorians such as
the anthropologists Melville and Frances Herskovits, whose works had a lasting impact on Brathwaite's scholarly approach to the history of the African
diaspora. Richards, like Gutzmore, defines Brathwaite's primary contribution
to Caribbean historiography in terms of his theoretical development of the
already existing concept of creolization, and his deployment of it to counter
the intellectual pessimism of M.G. Smith's plural society model. Brathwaite's
theoretical and conceptual innovations are praised, but Richards also levels
criticism at the limitations of Brathwaite's creolization model, particularly as
expressed in later essays which evince an Afrocentric essentialism and a
propensity for overly rigid systemic schema that exclude nonblack groups
from the ambit of creolization.

Ileana Rodríguez's "Creolization, Hybridity, Pluralism: Historical
Articulations of Race and Ethnicity" and Leah Rosenberg's "The Prose of
Creolization: Brathwaite's *The Development of Creole Society* and Subaltern
Historiography" are intelligent and insightful models of comparative readings
of postcolonial and subaltern intellectual projects that raise interesting questions about comparative intellectual genealogies, and the ways in which critical concepts and languages can travel, evade translation, or recur within

different contexts that subject them to sublation or elision. In Rodríguez's case, this means foregrounding concepts such as creolization and creole in order to trace, as she puts it, "the genealogy of the postmodern discussions of hybridity and multiculturalism". In a fascinating counterpointing of Latin American signifiers of hybridity such as *mestizo* and *mestizaje* with the Caribbean cognates of *creole* and *creolization,* Rodríguez teases out points of convergence and divergence, notes the tactical and strategic advantages of creole relative to mestizo, and posits its radical epistemological and ontological potential, its organic oppositionality and its thoroughly historicized subaltern semiotic field:

> *Creole* presented itself as the most salient description of a social formation, as a possible structure of organic governance from below . . . it was the real thing, a historically produced condition out of which sets of discursive chains, clusters and fields of meaning could be worked out for the benefit of society at large.

Creolization in Rodríguez's eloquent exploration is invested with the utopian potential for articulating a Gramscian politics of ethnicity as positionality, of a historically contingent articulation of race that divests itself of the essentialist baggage inherent in concepts such as *mestizaje*. Rodríguez's comparative reading of New World articulations of race, culture and identity is a profligate feast of interwoven, braided concepts – mestizaje, creolization, transculturation, hybridity, heterogeneity, subalternity – that are subtended by a divisive logic of language, "the confrontation between the voice and the letter". In essence, Rodríguez's essay is an eloquent unpacking of Latin American and African diasporic negotiations of the slippery terrain of cultural difference and encounter, the liminal spaces that evade the rigor mortis of cognitive and cultural absolutes, the conjunction of alterities that energize the process of creolization.

In Leah Rosenberg's "The Prose of Creolization: Brathwaite's *The Development of Creole Society* and Subaltern Historiography", the parallels drawn are between Brathwaite's work and that of Ranajit Guha, associated with the influential Subaltern Studies group. Guha's important essay, "The Prose of Counterinsurgency", and Brathwaite's *The Development of Creole Society* are informed by the same intellectual *telos*: "Both seek to address the hierarchy and inequality of post-independence society and culture through a revision of history that situates the disenfranchised majorities as the centre of historiography". Rosenberg carefully outlines their respective similarities and differences: the shared predicament of retrieving the history of the dominated via the imperial archive; the belief that the archive could be read against the grain; the hostility of Guha to nationalist elites compared to Brathwaite's participation in cultural nationalism; and their different approaches to the colonial archive – Guha's investment in an explicit critique of his sources, versus Brathwaite's "performative" placing of "the reader in the position of historian by deluging her with citations, sometimes contradictory or unlabelled". Guha's inventive appellation of the hegemonic discourses as "a prose of counterinsurgency" is mirrored in Brathwaite's interpretive inversions of the normative consensus of colonialist narratives. Rosenberg makes the salient point that both Guha and Brathwaite fail to pay adequate critical attention to the contradictory and ambivalent nature of colonialist discourse, even though their subversive readings are dependent on the existence of such ambiguities and slippage. Decoding is the operative reading strategy for both men, but Brathwaite also employs a subversive imitation of colonial discourse by reproducing its rhetorical and taxonomic excess, its exaggerated details of the particulars of slaves, and its citational apparatus to demonstrate the internal contradictions, evidentiary quagmires and ultimate "impossibility of using such sources to produce a straightforward history". Rosenberg's comparative reading is an object lesson in broadening the discussion of creolization and historiography beyond the ethnic, cultural and national confines of the Caribbean region, but it is also a nuanced and surgical exegesis of historical discourse that calls attention to the methodological and conceptual limitations of reading against the grain, given the ambiguities and contradictions of colonial discourse.

The essays in part 5, "Resurrecting the Human Face from the Archive", attempt to put in practice many of the theoretical issues raised in the preceding section regarding the voices and agency of the dominated, the capacity for the subaltern to speak, and the historical status of marginalized texts. Verene A. Shepherd's "Resisting Representation: Locating Enslaved and Indentured Women's Voices in the Colonial Caribbean" raises the problematic issue of retrieving the subaltern voices of enslaved and indentured women from the colonial archive, particularly in light of the absence of autobiographical narratives and testimonies. Shepherd advocates the strategies that characterize Ranajit Guha's and Kamau Brathwaite's reading against the grain. She posits inversion and an explicit, self-conscious critical approach to reading as the *modus operandi* of retrieving women's voices from the imposed silence of colonial subjugation and the force multipliers of racial and sexual othering. Like Brathwaite, she also argues for a widening of the archive to include genres such as novels in addition to historical narratives and official documents, and she adopts a strategy of heightened critical attention to how enslaved and indentured women's voices are ventriloquized. Shepherd's position is that the female subaltern can speak through others, but only through a process of symptomatic reading alert to the fissures, contradictions and ambiguities in the texts. Representation of the subaltern female voice is thus a mediated reconstruction which can only ever be partial, dependent on redefinition of the archive and problematizing the distinction between fact and fiction.

Whereas Shepherd mulls over the problem of the paucity of subaltern discourse, Douglas B. Chambers identifies discursive excess, the multilingual competence of Brutus, young Jamaican slave fluent in two African languages, as a forensic clue that troubles accepted conceptions of creolization. In "The Links of a Legacy: Figuring the Slave Trade to Jamaica", Chambers argues that the disquieting linguistic competencies of Brutus unsettle both Brathwaite's and Sidney Mintz's models of the plantation and the slave ship, respectively, as the sites of creole formation. Chambers suggests instead that Africa is the generative site of creolization, and that we need to pay attention to the particulars of African ethnic identities and the demographic and spatial distributions of enslaved Africans in order to position Africa as a central site in the history of creolization, rather than a null point. Chambers buttresses his argument with statistical extrapolation from empirical data of the number of slaves imported into Jamaica from 1655 to 1810, and he advocates a movement away from a single linear developmental model of African arrival in Jamaica towards a recognition of sequential waves of Africans, clusters of ethnicities and concomitant cultural influences based on demographics. According to Chambers, the statistical data produce alternative explanations that challenge the dominant creolization thesis and its related assumptions about cultural and linguistic practices and continuities. Chambers posits an interesting multilayered "mental geography" of Jamaica, in which African identity is variegated, layered and inside rather than outside the process of creolization.

Yacine Daddi Addoun and Paul E. Lovejoy add another thread to the tapestry of creolization in Jamaica in their synoptic commentary, "The Arabic Manuscript of Muhammad Kabā Saghanughu of Jamaica, c.1820". In this article they use the archival document to engage in what Kamau Brathwaite has defined as the task of a decolonizing historiography: to resurrect the human face from the archive. The impressive reconstruction of Kabās life, habitat, background and community of fellow Muslims struggling to maintain their Islamic heritage in a hostile setting certainly accords with the practice of a social history that focuses on those below. Addoun and Lovejoy offer a detailed accounting of the contingencies and exigencies faced by enslaved Muslims, and their experience of creolization in its two modes of acculturation and interculturation. The article is a richly textured narrative of accommodation and survival, resistance and compromise, and of the importance of language and literacy in maintaining identity. One notes, with a wry irony, the aliases that proclaim the slave's vulnerability to loss of identity and social death as well as the sustaining power of camouflage. After all, as Addoun and Lovejoy point out, Kabā and his fellow Muslims "successfully maintained a sense of community as Muslims, communicating in writing, even as they had to disguise their Muslim identity through the use of Christian names, hiding behind the cloak of evangelical missionary Christianity". But what is really interesting, from the point of view of creolization theory, is that the linguistic ideology that underpins creole discourse is inverted in the case of the Muslim slaves, who use their literacy in Arabic to resist denigration and loss of identity. The clash between writing and orality is configured here in terms of a reversal of attributes: "They used the spoken word to convey a message of accommodation and adherence to Christianity, while they used written Arabic and identifying symbols, such as names, to claim their religious autonomy and spiritual superiority as Muslims". In short, Addoun and Lovejoy force us to rethink the trajectories and modalities of creolization by alerting us to the complex interplay of religion, language, literacy and identity that fostered affinities and affiliations between enslaved Muslims in the Caribbean.

Addoun and Lovejoy describe a religious community that resists through artful compromise, but Veront M. Satchell, in "Religion and Sociopolitical Protest in Jamaica: Alexander Bedward of the Jamaican Native Baptist Free Church, 1889–1921", narrates an account of the rise and fall of militant religious resistance to the colonial Jamaican state. The Native Baptist preacher Alexander Bedward inherited the radical mantle of predecessors such as Sam Sharpe and Paul Bogle and became the most vocal spokesman for the black majority; his charismatic leadership transformed his Jamaica Native Baptist Free Church into "a mass politico-religious movement" that anticipated subsequent nationalist and political movements. Satchell's reading of Bedward's movement is unabashedly revisionist, and steeped in the conceptual frame-work of the creole-society model that Brathwaite uses with remarkable effi-cacy in *Nanny, Sam Sharpe and the Struggle for People's Liberation.*[37] Satchell casts the radical preacher as a charismatic and messianic figure, whose appeal derived from his syncretic blending of Christian and African rituals and sym-bols. Bedward's conflation of religious deliverance and racial redemption con-stituted a subversive prophetic politics that led to conflict with the colonial authority. Subjected to surveillance, arrested for treason and sedition, and twice consigned to the lunatic asylum, Bedward was eventually silenced by the overwhelming power of the establishment, but he left a legacy of "new historical awareness". Satchell's article is conceptually grounded in a nation-alism intrinsic to the creolization thesis, hence his forceful reframing of Bedward as "a politico-religious nationalist, a political priest" who used reli-gion to challenge entrenched colonial and white minority interests.

In part 6, "Creole Bodies, Dancehall Style: Gender, Sexuality and Representation in Jamaican Popular Culture", Donna P. Hope and Rachel Moseley-Wood turn the spotlight on contemporary popular culture and mass media. Hope and Moseley-Wood reference Brathwaite's discussion of creole society and his injunction regarding Caribbean aesthetics, respectively, and these references allude to the persistence of the creolization model in Caribbean cultural theorizing. Hope's " 'Love Punaany Bad': Negotiating Misogynistic Masculinity in Dancehall Culture", while ostensibly grounded in the conceptual categories of gender studies, reads contemporary postcolo-nial Jamaican gender conflicts in terms of the dysfunctional legacies of colo-nial histories of slavery, and the resultant racial and sexual hierarchies that constructed certain functional stereotypes of black sexuality. For Hope, these stereotypes are the result of "the creolization of gender in a racialized class system" that spins out local variants of the madonna/whore syndrome such as the middle-class *browning* and the *trang* (strong) lower-class black woman. Hope outlines a schema of sexuality organized around creolized pathological norms of hypermasculinity subscribed to by marginalized males whose penury prevents them from wielding power over their women, and survival-ist polygamous relationships that women have with powerful men in the community. In this milieu dancehall masculinity is hypermasculinity, coded as incessant sexual conquest of women and unquenchable thirst for the vagina (*punaany*). Dancehall masculinity is apparently misogynistic, and the love of punaany is really a sublimated fear of women, but Hope also points out the contradictions in this sphere, since mothers are revered in the lyrics of dancehall deejays. Misogyny is contingent on sexuality and sexual conquest, economic and social variables, hence it would be wrong to label all masculine performances in the dancehall space as misogynistic. Instead, Hope points to the "creative negotiation of multiple masculinities as part of the lived realities of the actors in the dancehall dis/place". The dancehall, it appears, is overdetermined by the structural forces of creolized postcolonial Jamaica that engender masculinities in need of validation.

Moseley-Wood examines the Jamaican film *Dancehall Queen* within the context of a call for a Caribbean film aesthetic that can discard the stereotypes of Hollywood cinematic representation, particularly those of the exotic, picturesque native, or the mute, servile type. Echoing Brathwaite, she advocates a decolonization of cinematic form and language analogous to Brathwaite's forceful injunction in *History of the Voice* for Caribbean writers to reject the uncreative mimicry of imported literary models and cultivate instead indigenous aesthetic forms. Brathwaite's advocacy of nation language as the submerged repository of a Caribbean aesthetic is redeployed by Moseley-Wood in the context of Jamaican film. But Moseley-Wood also raises the problematic issues of gender and sexuality which complicate the indigenizing of Caribbean film. She zeroes in on the contradictions between *Dancehall Queen*'s instrumental appropriation of Jamaican popular music (which constitutes the nation language in the filmic text) and its continuing indebtedness to a visual vocabulary that is dominated by Hollywood conventions that privilege the male gaze. The film's representation of the body is fractured and ambivalent, simultaneously interrogating "conventional ways of seeing the female body and female sexuality, as well as conventional attitudes towards the display of sexualized images of the female body" and reproducing "the perspectives and concerns of dominant cinema". Moseley-Wood's critique combines theoretical insights from contemporary cultural studies, gender studies and film studies with detailed analysis of *Dancehall Queen*'s visual narrative, to convincingly make her case that the liberatory performance of female eroticism in the dancehall space is framed within the voyeuristic visuality of patriarchal codes.

The final section, part 7, "Jamaican Identities and Globalization: Citizenship, Subalternity and Cyberspace", consists of two essays which raise interesting and provocative questions about the construction of Jamaican identity and citizenship in the current conjuncture of globalization and digital information technology. In "Citizenship and Subalternity of the Voice within Globalization: Dilemmas of the Public Sphere, Civil Society and Human Rights in the Periphery", Robert Carr updates Brathwaite's concerns with submerged and subaltern voices by engaging with the political and juridical issues pertaining to the exclusion of certain groups from the public sphere. Carr seeks "to raise questions about the politics of the constitution of the public sphere in its history, identity, ethnicity, class, nation, and in relationships to the state, state-formation and the international division of labour", and he reminds us that these questions underlie the creolized construction of Caribbean societies along the axes of class, ethnicity and ideology. Carr's interrogation unfolds as a critique of the contemporary Jamaican state's abrogation of the human rights of its marginalized underclass. The violence of the state is thus predicated on the domination of the subaltern, but Carr's provocative thesis really begins to take shape in his assertion that "under globalization creole culture from below takes on brutal incarnations". The latter, he argues, are constructs of a subaltern and underclass hypermasculinity that destructively mirrors the state's own gender assumptions. The question of the public sphere in Jamaica is thus intrinsically aligned to "male gender identity formation" which is articulated in terms of race, class, colour and sexuality. The hegemonic masculinity of the state and dominant social classes suppresses underclass men, hence the latter construct masculinity via the gangsterism of the "don" system, a nihilistic criminality which threatens the very state itself. For Carr, the crucial issue is the way in which both dominant and subaltern masculinist ideologies have effectively denied citizenship and human rights to various *untermenschen*: "prisoners, gay men and persons who are HIV-positive". The exclusion of these groups is symptomatic of the brutal fall-out of neoliberal globalization and the retreat of the nation state, but it also signifies the very threat to the state itself of the violence endemic to the pathological masculinism of Jamaican male gender identity formation.

Bernard Jankee, like Carr, is interested in the question of Jamaican identity in the context of globalization, but where Carr is concerned with the confluence of the debilitating effects of globalization's economic fall-out and creole hypermasculinity in denying citizenship and rights to certain groups, Jankee explores the ways in which the Internet and digital information technologies have been deployed in constructing a Jamaican national identity. Jankee's "The Word in Cyberspace: Constructing Jamaican Identity on the Internet" explicitly references Brathwaite's concept of nation language to argue that Jamaicans in the "transnational, transborder realms of existence" use cyberspace to rearticulate local identities in terms of a repertoire of cultural and linguistic references that constitute a "nation language". Jankee examines the issues of identity and representation as manifested in three web sites, and his engaging, albeit brief, case studies reveal a debate about the nature of Jamaican identity, as the various constructions are predicated on different discourses and languages of affiliation and affinity. "Identities", Jankee concludes, "are constructed around words and word-images that are owned or co-opted by particular communities of interest". This is an insight that squares with Kamau Brathwaite's relentless insistence on language as both cornerstone and stumbling block of Caribbean culture, both pebble and seed, pathway to the past and the future, a medium of discovery and creation.

In his keynote address at the conference which was the occasion for these essays, Brathwaite urged participants to think of the event as a "golokwati", a meeting place of ideas, a crossroads of difference, debate and exchange. Like so many of Brathwaite's terms, the word is both old and new; it is the name of a Ghanaian market town, but in his redeployment it assumes an ecumenism of thought and intellectual inquiry that is present in these essays. In their scholarship and their concerns, they constitute a fitting tribute to one of the intellectual giants of the Caribbean. This book is a golokwati for Kamau Brathwaite, and it enjoins you to enter, sit down and join the reasoning.

Notes

1. Edward Said, *Representations of the Intellectual* (New York: Vintage, 1996), 13.
2. Sylvia Wynter, "On Disenchanting Discourse: Minority Literary Criticism and Beyond", *Cultural Critique* 7 (Fall 1987): 208.
3. Edward Baugh, "Edward Brathwaite as Literary Critic: Some Preliminary Observations", *Caribbean Quarterly* 28, nos. 1–2 (March–June 1982): 66–75.
4. Edward Kamau Brathwaite, *Contradictory Omens: Cultural Diversity and Integration in the Caribbean* (Kingston, Jamaica: Savacou Publications, 1974), 6. Hereafter cited in the text.
5. Verene A. Shepherd and Glen L. Richards, introduction to *Questioning Creole: Creolisation Discourses in Caribbean Culture* (Kingston, Jamaica: Ian Randle; Oxford: James Currey, 2002), xiii.
6. Silvio Torres-Saillant, *Caribbean Poetics: Towards an Aesthetic of West Indian Literature* (Cambridge: Cambridge University Press, 1997), 12–13.
7. I have used *History of the Voice* as a terminus rather than "Metaphors of Underdevelopment: A Proem For Hernan Cortez" (*New England Review and*

Breadloaf Quarterly 7, no. 4 [1985]) or "World Order Models: A Caribbean Perspective" (*Caribbean Quarterly* 31, no. 1 [1985]), and *Barabajan Poems* (Kingston, Jamaica and New York: Savacou North, 1994). The former is essentially Brathwaite's explication of poetic work in progress (which resulted in *X/Self* [Oxford and New York: Oxford University Press, 1987]), while "World Order Models" is an application of the theoretical paradigms of "Caribbean Culture: Two Paradigms" (in *Missile and Capsule*, ed. Jurgen Martini [Bremen: distributed by Universität Bremen, 1983]) in order to elaborate a Caribbean epistemology. *Barabajan Poems* essentially reiterates prior theoretical arguments and does not offer much in terms of theoretical innovation.

8. Partha Chatterjee's discussion of the problematic and the thematic as modal concepts in nationalist discourse provides a way of placing Brathwaite's work within the larger context of nationalist thought. See Chatterjee's *Nationalist Thought and the Colonial World: A Derivative Discourse?* (London: Zed Books, 1986).

9. George Lamming, "The Occasion for Speaking", in *The Pleasures of Exile* (1960; reprint, Ann Arbor: University of Michigan Press, 1992), 38.

10. Brathwaite does discuss West Indian poets and poetry in some of these early essays. "Sir Galahad and the Islands" (*Bim* 25 [1957]; reprinted in Brathwaite, *Roots* [Havana: Casa de las Américas, 1986]) is evenly balanced in its discussion of fiction and poetry, and "The Controversial Tree of Time" (*Bim* 30 [1960]) is one of the earliest assessments of Wilson Harris's *Eternity to Season*. Gordon Rohlehr describes Brathwaite's essay on Harris as a "lucid analysis . . . which was to remain for years the clearest statement to be made on that artist" (Rohlehr, *Pathfinder: Black Awakening in* The Arrivants *of Edward Kamau Brathwaite* [Tunapuna, Trinidad: G. Rohlehr, 1981], 13). Fiction, however, is the genre that occupies most of his critical attention, and it constitutes the object of his aesthetic paradigm in his major essay of this period, "Jazz and the West Indian Novel" (first published in 1967–68; reprinted in *Roots*).

11. Brathwaite, "Roots", in *Roots,* 54.

12. I use the term "cultural studies" to refer to interdisciplinary and transdisciplinary investigations of the symbolic and material domains of culture. See Raymond Williams, *Culture* (London: Fontana, 1981); and Lawrence Grossberg, et al., eds., *Cultural Studies* (London and New York: Routledge, 1992).

13. Brathwaite, "Creative Literature of the British West Indies during the Period of Slavery", in *Roots,* 129. Hereafter cited in the text.

14. Brathwaite, "Caribbean Critics", in *Roots*; hereafter cited in the text. This review article first appeared in *Southern Review* 5, no. 3 (1969), revised *New World Quarterly* 5, nos. 1–2 (1969), and *Critical Quarterly* (Autumn 1969). Brathwaite's response to *The Islands in Between* is not a singular event, as the latter text gener-

ated critical responses from Edward Baugh ("Towards a West Indian Criticism", *Caribbean Quarterly* 14, nos. 1–2 [1968]) and Sylvia Wynter ("We Must Learn to Sit Down Together and Talk about a Little Culture: Reflections on West Indian Writing and Criticism", parts 1 and 2, *Jamaica Journal* 2 [December 1968]: 23–32; 3 [March 1969]: 27–42]) which called for the development of a West Indian criticism.

15.   Brathwaite's response is particularly directed to certain comments made by Cameron King and Louis James on the poetry of Derek Walcott, to the effect that West Indian culture is essentially an outgrowth of European culture since the latter is universal and transcends the confines of nationalism. "The 'literature of England' ", King and James pronounce, "reaches backwards and outwards to the cultures of Greece, Rome and medieval France. It touches the thought and civilization of Europe, the new world, even Asia and Africa. Its preoccupation is with man as a human being, and for this reason a culture that becomes isolationist and inward-looking can paradoxically cut itself off from the means of knowing itself. It is not simply chance that the greatest nationalist writers in French and Spanish as well as English, in modern Africa as well as the West Indies, have been those who have been able most fully to come to their own predicaments through mastery of the European literary experience" (Cameron King and Louis James, "In Solitude for Company: The Poetry of Derek Walcott", in *The Islands in Between,* ed. Louis James [London: Oxford University Press, 1968], 90).

16.   M.M. Bakhtin, *The Dialogic Imagination: Four Essays,* ed. Michael Holquist, trans. Caryl Emerson and Michael Holquist (Austin: University of Texas Press, 1981), 288.

17.   The *hounfort* is one of Brathwaite's central theoretical concepts that is borrowed from Haitian *vodoun.* It has the same literal and metaphorical meanings as the tonelle of Lamming's *Season of Adventure,* a sacralized communal space which is the focus of performative worship and the immanence of possession by the *loas.* The hounfort, for Brathwaite, signifies the cultural core of the folk; it is a site of creativity as well as resistance to the hegemonic colonial order.

18.   Homi Bhabha, "DissemiNation: Time, Narrative, and the Margins of the Modern Nation", in *Nation and Narration,* ed. Homi Bhabha (London and New York: Routledge, 1990), 293.

19.   Both quotes from Brathwaite, *The Development of Creole Society in Jamaica, 1770–1820* (Oxford: Clarendon Press, 1971), 307. Hereafter cited in the text.

20.   Brathwaite, "The African Presence in Caribbean Literature", in *Roots,* 194. Hereafter cited in the text.

21.   Brathwaite, "Timehri", *Is Massa Day Dead?,* ed. Orde Coombs (New York: Anchor-Doubleday, 1974), 42.

22.   Gordon Rohlehr, "The Problem of the Problem of Form", *Caribbean Quarterly* 31, no. 1 (1985): 4. This fine essay is a comprehensive and insightful application of the creole continuum model (derived from linguistics) to West Indian literature in order to demonstrate aesthetic code switching between the poles of literary modernism and performative orality. Rohlehr's work is itself influenced by his study of Brathwaite's poetry, essays and ongoing research in creolization.

23.   I owe this schematic classification of Brathwaite's aesthetic concepts to Rex Nettleford's discussion of the former in the context of negritudinist aesthetics. See Rex Nettleford, "The Aesthetics of *Négritude*: A Metaphor for Liberation", in *Intellectuals in the Twentieth-Century Caribbean*, vol. 1, ed. Alistair Hennessey (London: Macmillan, 1992), 92.

24.   In *X/Self,* Brathwaite calls these neologisms "calibanisms", thus indicating his self-conscious subversion of Prospero's language by appropriating Caliban's linguistic profit.

25.   Nettleford, "The Aesthetics of *Négritude*", 92.

26.   Brathwaite, "Caribbean Culture: Two Paradigms", 36. Hereafter cited in the text.

27.   I adapt Rachel Blau Duplessis's concept of women writing beyond the ending of canonical discourse to Brathwaite's postcolonial inventions of Caliban's female kin. The concept of "writing in light" comes from the poem "X/Self's Xth Letters from the Thirteen Provinces", in which the Caliban persona writes a letter to his mother, Sycorax, describing writing on the computer as "chiss/ellin darkness writin in light" (*X/Self*, 87). For a graphic illustration of Brathwaite's post-modem videotext style, see *The Zea Mexican Diary, 7 Sept 1926–7 Sept 1986*, with a foreword by Sandra Pouchet Paquet (Madison: University of Wisconsin Press, 1993), *Dreamstories* (Harlow: Longman, 1994), and *Barabajan Poems* (1994).

28.   Frantz Fanon, *The Wretched of the Earth*, trans. Constance Farrington (New York: Grove Press, 1965), 244, 247. A national culture, for Fanon, is not a fixed artefact, frozen in the past; it is a future project that is coeval with the liberation of the nation: "To fight for national culture means in the first place to fight for the liberation of the nation, that material keystone which makes the building of a culture possible" (p. 233). Fanon also explicitly differentiates culture from custom: "culture has never the translucidity of custom; it abhors all simplification. In its essence it is opposed to custom, for custom is always the deterioration of culture" (p. 224).

29.   Brathwaite, *History of the Voice: The Development of Nation Language in Anglophone Caribbean Poetry* (London and Port of Spain: New Beacon Books, 1984), 50. Hereafter cited in the text.

30.   Jacques Derrida's extensive critique of Jean-Jacques Rousseau's *Essay on the Origin of Languages* (trans. and ed. John T. Scott [Hanover, N.H.: University Press of

New England, 1998]) inveighs against the latter's privileging speech over writing and thus subscribing to the metaphysics of presence, which posits the word as signifier of a transcendental signified (Derrida, *Of Grammatology*, trans. Gayatri Chakravorty Spivak [Baltimore: Johns Hopkins University Press, 1998]). Brathwaite's investment in the concepts of *nommo* and *nam* certainly ensure that his approach to language will be heavily slanted towards a metaphysics of presence. The operative questions are, however: Whose metaphysics? And whose presence?

31.   Nathaniel Mackey, "Other: From Noun to Verb", in *Discrepant Engagement: Dissonance, Cross-Culturality, and Experimental Writing* (Cambridge: Cambridge University Press, 1993), 272.

32.   Brathwaite's strategies of "othering" constitute a theory and practice of indigenization. Ian Adam sees the latter as a mode of counter-discursivity which "moves *towards* a discourse of utter difference" ("Breaking the Chain", in *Past the Last Post,* ed. Ian Adam and Helen Tiffin [Calgary: University of Calgary Press, 1990], 80). For a Caribbean discussion of indigenization, see Sylvia Wynter's critical interventions, especially "Jonkonnu in Jamaica: Towards the Interpretation of Folk Dance as a Cultural Process", *Jamaica Journal* 4, no. 2 (1970): 34–38, and "Creole Criticism: A Critique", *New World Quarterly*, no. 5 (1973): 12–36. Brathwaite acknowledges the importance of Wynter's critical work in his essay, "The Love Axe/l: Developing a Caribbean Aesthetic, 1962–1974" (parts 1–3, *Bim* 16, no. 61 [1977]: 53–65; no. 62 [1977]: 100–106; no. 63 [1978]: 181–92), and praises her essay "We Must Learn to Sit Down Together and Talk about a Little Culture" as "one of our great critical landmarks: a major essai in literary ideas" ("Love Axe", 101).

33.   Edouard Glissant, *Caribbean Discourse: Selected Essays,* trans. J. Michael Dash (Charlottesville: University Press of Virginia, 1989), 248–49.

34.   Paul Gilroy, *The Black Atlantic: Modernity and Double Consciousness* (Cambridge, Mass.: Harvard University Press, 1993), 75.

35.   Brathwaite, "Negus", in *Islands,* in *The Arrivants: A New World Trilogy* (Oxford: Oxford University Press, 1973), 224.

36.   See Stewart Brown, ed., *The Art of Kamau Brathwaite* (Bridgend, Wales: Seren, 1995); Timothy J. Reiss, ed., *For the Geography of a Soul: Emerging Perspectives on Kamau Brathwaite* (Trenton, N.J.: Africa World Press, 2001); and Verene A. Shepherd and Glen L. Richards, eds., *Questioning Creole: Creolisation Discourses in Caribbean Culture – In Honour of Kamau Brathwaite* (Kingston, Jamaica: Ian Randle; Oxford: James Currey, 2002).

37.   Brathwaite, *Nanny, Sam Sharpe, and the Struggle for People's Liberation* (Kingston, Jamaica: Published by API for the National Heritage Week Committee, 1977).

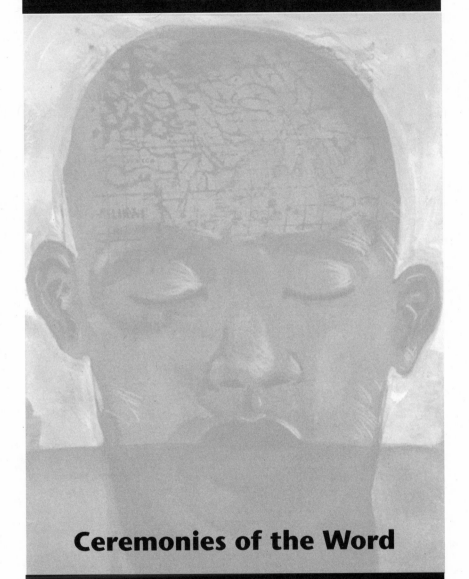

Ceremonies of the Word

1

Atumpan

Kamau Brathwaite and the Gift of Ancestral Memory

Kofi **Anyidoho** |

The Power of Words

Be skilled in words that you may be strong –
> the king's tongue is his mighty arm;
Words are more powerful than any fighting,
> and none encircle the resourceful man.
The ignorant sit on their mats,
> but wisdom is the bulwark of a leader;
Those who know his knowledge do not test him,
> nor do mishaps happen during his time.
Truth comes to him distilled
> like counsels spoken by the sages of old times.
Do better than your fathers and your forefathers;
> work for a like success through learning.
See how their words endure in the Writings!
>> Unroll them, read them, and surpass the wise!
>> Each sage was once a wide-eyed pupil.[1]

It is Fergusson who, like an Ashanti *okyeame*, kept the memory of the ancestral dead alive with his interminable rehearsal of the tale of Cuffee Ned, the slave rebel. Cuffee Ned becomes the ancestor of the whole village, and it is his memory and the whole African tradition which depends on it, that keeps these people inviolate.[2]

Invocation

Kamau Brathwaite: True sun/son of the Bajan, with your long, stretched limbs, you could have been a Fon/Haitian *hougan,* an Asante *okyeame,* a Mande *djeli,* a Zulu *mbongi,* a Yoruba *babalawo,* an Ewe *awuno bokono,* a *Logosu* of the Yewe mystical order.

Kamau Brathwaite: True historian of the Afro-Caribbean xperience of fragmentation, re/vision, re/memory, you could have been Isanusi the Pathfinder, SoulGuide and peerless Fundi of "a knowledge of the craftsmanship of the soul".[3] You whose voice whose words led us from Axum through Ouagadougou through Chad through Timbuktu searching searching forever searching for mythical "Naderina, of which the / the sages speak"; you whose "imagination / rose on wide unfolded wings" across the timelessness of a million agonies.

Kamau Brathwaite: *Odomankoma Kyerema,* Divine Drummer, slowly and patiently, you beat the restless drums of affliction, the relentless drums of memory, the polyphonic drums of ancestral wisdom:

> Our path has crossed the river
> The river has crossed our path
> But which is the elder?

> Their path has crossed the ocean
> The ocean has crossed their path
> Which is the elder?

> We cut our path and found the river.
> They cut their path and found the ocean.
> The river is from long ago.
> The ocean is from long long ago.
> The river-ocean is from the Ancient Creator of the Universe.[4]

Kamau Brathwaite: pathfinder, divine drummer, master in the art of eloquence: Once upon a forgetful time, you came back home to the land of the sahel, the land of the savannah, the land of the sahara and of the kalahari; you returned to the land of the Tano, of the Prah, and of the Volta, the land of the Niger, the land of the Congo, the Gambia, the Zambezi, land of the premordial Nile. You gathered a harvest of ancestral voices and memories, the gift of song, the gift of *nam,* of *nommo.* But you who were born of the multitudinous ocean, you could not forever settle for the dust-laden clouds of the desert, you could not find lasting solace in the misty vapours of rivers. So you had to return. Once more

> Exiled from [Africa]
>
> to seas
>
> of bitter edges,
>
> whips of white worlds[5]

But like Paule Marshall's Fergusson, ancestral man of "the chosen place / the timeless people", you returned to Bajan with an abiding sense of metaphor, the gift of "historical depth and cultural possibility".

Brathwaite and the Ancestral Heritage

A comprehensive theory of verbal art in Africa may very well have to begin with a proper appreciation of the ontological value of *the word,* not merely as a semiotic fact, but, above all, as a natural cosmic force with a potential for creative and destructive ends.[6] In both his theoretical/scholarly and his creative work, Kamau Brathwaite more than demonstrates a deep faith in the ancestral legacy of *The Word as Energy.* Of particular relevance here is his description of *the Word* as "the atomic core of language" and his recognition that "the word (*nommo* or name) is held to contain secret power".[7] By his own testimony, this faith in the power of *the Word* is founded on solid foundations of personal experience of the ancestral legacy, initially traced to his eight-year stay in Ghana followed by a shorter but equally significant stay in Kenya. As pointed out by Fabian Adekunle Badejo,

> For Brathwaite, it was a re-connection, a re-education, even a re-baptism in ancestral waters. After eight years of immersion in those waters, he re-emerged a new person with a first-hand knowledge of African ancestry and returned home, to the Caribbean. His memory of his roots now rekindled in a renewed self-knowledge, he could give us *Masks* (1968), not as a romantic, idealized vision of Africa, but as an existential testament to the continuity that had been truncated by slavery and colonialism.[8]

Against the reality of the imposition of a foreign language and its claims as the only legitimate medium of expression, there is almost always an option for the continental African, the option of a mother tongue and its own traditions of artistic expression. However, in looking globally at African literature in its historical and contemporary relations with what have been called the totalizing claims of imperial/colonial discourse, it is important that we should never forget the peculiar location of the African diaspora writer. Ali Mazrui reminds us of the important distinction that needs to be made today between two African diasporas – the diaspora of slavery and the diaspora of colonialism. On the question of African-heritage writers and the logic of imperial discourse, the historically most significant lessons are offered by writers and communities of the diaspora of slavery. It is this understanding that leads us now to a consideration of the extreme case of the silencing of the tongue and re/invention of mother tongues under transatlantic slavery.

Of the exceptional ones among the diaspora returnees to Africa for whom the ancestral language may hold the key to the memory lock, we must single out Kamau Brathwaite for special attention. I do so now, despite his own warning that there is a grave danger of oversimplification in attempts at looking too readily at his work as that of "an **African-oriented** writer – a person involved mainly with Africa (I lived in Ghana for 10 years) certainly with the African Diaspo/ra which is true & nothing but the truth but not, however, all of it".[9] It is instructive to keep in mind Brathwaite's insistence

> that 60% or more – the
> core & kernel – of my output – remains firmly rooted – as you would/
> shd xpect – in where I come from – in how I walk talk & think Barbaj
> (n).[10]

And Bajan culture, Brathwaite defines for us, is that "shared collective xperience on a rock of coral limestone, half-way from Europe, half-way (?back) to Africa . . .)".[11] That is Barbados, the Caribbean island closest, they say, to Africa.

This important insistence by Brathwaite recalls for us the words of a younger Caribbean poet whose work shares many points of intersection with that of Brathwaite, M. NourbeSe Philip:

> For the poet the primary and most important relationship is with the word. As important a relationship is that between poet and place, and bonding with place is as essential to the poet's development as bonding between parent and infant is to the development of humans.
>
> That certain location in time and space where historical, social, cultural and geographical forces coalesce and/or collide to produce an individual is how I define place. . . . If the poet is truly bonded with place, it then forms the matrix of her

work: place remains within the poet, although she be in exile or never write a word about it. A rooting in place would, however, of necessity, preclude the latter alternative.

True poetry – a poetry of truth – depends very much upon such a rooting in place, despite the forces of displacement and alienation that prey upon most poets today. . . .

For displaced poets the struggle and search is for that place – psychic, psycho-logical, spiritual, economic, geographical, cultural or historical – that is theirs by rightful belonging.[12]

A displaced poet's struggle and search is for his or her place in history, his or her place in the universe, a place from which s/he has been exiled into "seas / of bitter edges, / whips of white worlds". This is a most appropriate way of defining Brathwaite's achievement in his first trilogy, *The Arrivants*. In *Masks,* especially, the struggle and search are for the reclamation of his ances-tral heritage and restoration to himself of not only a sense of belonging to an ancestral place, but indeed to the human race, even at the dawn of history.

Ngugi recalls how, as a young lecturer visiting at the University of Nairobi, Brathwaite "saw no barriers between geography, history, and literature. What formed the African and Caribbean sensibility could not be divorced from the landscape and the historical experience."[13] For anyone with even the most casual familiarity with African oral traditions in poetry, especially such as may be found among the Akan, the convergence of history, geography and poetry is a constant cultural factor. And to history, geography and poetry, we must also add religion and the general philosophy of life. In an earlier comparative study of Brathwaite and the Ghanaian poet Atukwei Okai, I draw attention to the many ways in which both poets have drawn on the Akan archetypal poet – *Odomankoma Kyerema,* the divine drummer.

In the Akan tradition, the *Odomankoma Kyerema* is a highly accomplished poet-musician with heavy social and sacred responsibilities/burdens. He is his-torian and custodian of sacred truths of life and of death; he is myth maker and translator of the will of the gods; he is ritual and prayer specialist through whose performances society's fears and hopes arrive at the doorstep of the gods. The primal drum, probably mankind's oldest device for codifying thought and emotion, is uniquely suited to this multidimensional poetics. The vision of reality captured in drum-based poetry is one marked by life per-ceived as energy in a constant state of flux, life defined by an intricate system of interrelationships. This dynamic handling of physical and metaphysical reality is a dominant feature of the poetry of Brathwaite and Okai. My suggestion elsewhere regarding Okai's poetry is equally true of the poetry of Brathwaite: theirs is a universe of constant motion and great energy, often bordering on a clash of wills but never degenerating into total chaos.[14] It is also a universe of natural, human, mythic and psychic forces, often apprehended in postures of confrontation and in modes of invocation and prayer.

Even a casual look at the titles of Brathwaite's poems in *The Arrivants,* especially in *Masks,* confirms how well he has absorbed the techniques and the symbolic world/codes of the Akan divine drummer, who often begins his performance with a prelude containing the plea "I am learning, let me succeed":

> He then addresses in turn the components of the drum: the wood of the drum, the drum pegs, strings, the animal that provides the hide of the drum: the elephant or duyker.
>
> Next he addresses the Earth god, the witch, the cock and the clock bird, ancestor drummers, and finally the god Tano, saying:
>
> The path has crossed the river.
> The river has crossed the path.
> Which is the elder?
> We made the path and found the river.
> The river is from long ago.
> The river is from the Creator of the universe. . . .[15]

Brathwaite's *Masks* as a whole may be seen as a re-enactment of a six-part historical drama in which the leading role is played by the poet as divine drummer. As is typical of many African musical events, the "Prelude" of part 1 ("Libation") is presented as song, opening with:

> Gong-gongs throw pebbles in the routed pools of silence: . . .[16]

Then comes the drum's voice in the lines

> Beat heaven
> of the drum, beat
> the dark leaven
> of the dungeon
> ground where buds are wrapped
> twist-
> ed round dancing roots. White
> salt crackles at root lips, bursts like a fist

and beats out this
prayer:[17]

In the choice of ". . . beats out this / prayer", we find a poet who clearly sees himself as a divine drummer. The next scene, "The Making of the Drum", confirms Nketia's observations, as the drummer-poet addresses in turn the skin, the barrel, the two curved sticks of the drummer, the gourds and rattles, and the gong-gong. In the final section of this scene, "The Gong-Gong", the poetic text captures for us the central role of this particular percussion instrument in African musical performance tradition:

god is dumb
until the drum
speaks.

The drum
is dumb
until the gong-gong leads
it. Man made,

the gong-gong's
iron eyes

of music
walk us through the humble
dead to meet

the dumb
blind drum
where Odomankoma speaks.[18]

As timekeeper and standard reference point for all the various sounds and voices and dance movements of the musical drama, the gong-gong is identified as the central regulative force in the complex rhythmic texture of the performance.[19] In the strong plosive sounds that dominate Brathwaite's text above, we can hear the regulative beats often carried by the very instrument the lines invoke so well.

The final section of part 1 presents the sounds of the Atumpan, the Akan talking drums. With the opening lines

Kon kon kon kon
Kun kun kun kun[20]

the poet establishes the contrasting tonal identities of the two drums: the first line with the lower-pitched vowel /o/ represents the male drum; the second line with its higher-pitched vowel /u/ is for the female drum. Nketia informs us, "Of all the elements of speech reproduced in surrogate languages, undoubtedly tone is the most important. When this is combined with rhythm, identification of linear units is greatly facilitated."[21] A sense of symmetry and rhythmic balance is apparent in the original Akan text with which the piece opens. The rest of the poem is a skilful transposition into English of this Akan original.

The strong presence of the drum and other percussion instruments that marks part 1 of *Masks* gives way in the next four parts to a focus on the human drama of the historic migratory journeys for African peoples, from Axum through the desert regions of North Africa, through the sahel/savannah belts into the dense tropical forest zone down to the sea coast, the point of arrival and of departure into the Middle Passage. In the final part, "Arrival", we once again return to the dominant presence of the drum. Appropriately, the drum returns not with a fury of sounds, but with the slow rhythms of the funereal march of those

> Exiled from here
> to seas
> of bitter edges,
> whips of white worlds. . . .

Brathwaite's closing piece, "The Awakening", is in fact a major recasting of key lines from the famous Akan drum prelude, *Anyaneanyane* (Awakening), usually played by the divine drummer to usher in the Adae festival.[22] Of particular significance here is the fact that Brathwaite's sequence *ends* with the drum *prelude*. Judging from the symbolic patterning of Brathwaite's poetry, S.O. Asein has observed that there is "a constant emphasis which the poet places on his underlying belief in the circularity of civilization and human experience through time and space".[23] The original Akan drum prelude captures this principle in its opening lines, where the path crosses the river and the river crosses the path. In Brathwaite's piece the principle is re-enacted in the dual presence of the dark path and of "*akuko* the cock". In the crowing of the cock at dawn, day and night cross each other's path and give hope to the returned and now departing orphan, stranger/son of the soil who must once again walk the night into the terrors of the seas of bitter edges and white whips.

We note also that Brathwaite's return to his ancestral land is far from being a romantic one. He certainly returns seeking his birth cord among the ruins left by a turbulent history. He leaves us in no doubt that he finds more than his birth cord. But he also discovers some of the reasons for the fragmentation of that ancestral heritage. That is why his sense of joy is constantly qualified by a recurring sense of dis-ease, to be seen in a series of queries for the gods and the elders. The exiled stranger/son now returns with questions so profound not even the wisest and most knowledgeable elder can offer completely satisfactory answers: "Whose ancestor am I?"[24]

In his comments on Brathwaite's first trilogy (*The Arrivants*) as a whole, J. Michael Dash observes in *Masks* "a contrast to the first [*Rights of Passage*] in that it is an evocation of serenity and reverence totally absent in the violated New World".[25] However valid this contrast between the two sequences may be, it is important to note that the world of *Masks* is, in fact, not as uniformly serene as the statement suggests. The central mythical symbol of the journey it explores is marred/marked by moments of apprehension, agony and terror. Perhaps the migratory journeys down to the coast in search of more fertile and restful homes may not surpass the Middle Passage in agony and terror. But the migratory journeys of the first phase of African fragmentation have known their own particular sorrows. In Axum we experience the pillage of towns and temples, and taste the "splattered / blood in the corn". In Ouagadougou we hear the screams of children and search in vain for "the dancers, / the flutes' reed voices / cut from the river . . .". Sometimes we are guilty of errors that make us too soft, "too ready for peace and for terror".[26] And so we watch the camels carry away Timbuktu's gold and glory to lands beyond the surrounding dust, beyond our time and place.

The point, then, is that even this stage of our history's flow may be likened to the drum's rhythmic flow. It is not an endless sequence of soothing sounds, but moments of hard, rapid and groaning beats and whips, alternating with welcome stretches of modulated tension sometimes giving way to soft, liquid vowels. Moments of silence and rest alternate with periodic clashes of sounds. This is the essence of the poetry of conflict and resolution on the edge of chaos. The final calm we experience at the end of *Masks* is all the more satisfying because it brings to a close a long season of storms. But our present joy is immediately qualified with reminders of other storms rising beyond the horizon.

Thus no single moment or experience is ultimate, but must be seen against the backdrop of other moments and experiences, for this is the world of inter-relations. The divine drummer assures us that although the path has crossed the river and the river has crossed the path, it is only the river that is from long ago, from the ancient Creator of the universe. Our final consolation, then, is that we are made to perceive a higher order of historical reality in which the river shall outlast all paths of human civilization. The ultimate vision of reality borne by this poetic drama is one of enduring hope and of regeneration. Like the divine drummer, this poet reactivates our memory into a historical consciousness and projects our hope beyond present, even recurrent sorrows.

In "The African Presence in Caribbean Poetry", Brathwaite recalls the persistent claim that the trauma of the Middle Passage almost completely destroyed the culture of Africans who were transported across it. And he reminds us of how "modern research is pointing to a denial of this showing, that African culture not only crossed the Atlantic, it crossed, survived, and creatively adapted itself to its new environment. Caribbean culture was therefore not 'pure' African, but an adaptation carried out mainly in terms of African tradition."[27]

Later in his article Brathwaite admits that he "cannot maintain that African continuities are as easily traced in our literature as in the socio/ideological world. . . . [But this] does not mean there is no African presence in Caribbean/New World writing". To be able to see the literary continuities more easily, he advises that we redefine the term "literary" to include the "nonscribal material of the folk/oral tradition".[28] His own poetry more than proves the point for us, in its extensive use of techniques and principles of composition and even the symbolic language of the folk/oral tradition of drum poetics. Robert Fraser demonstrates other aspects of Brathwaite's drum poetics, concluding, "Throughout *Masks*, poetry is seen as being an analogous art to drumming."[29]

There is more than ample evidence here that a true African-heritage poetry, even though written in English, may be governed by aesthetic principles beyond the scope of traditional English verse structure and form. For this poet, as for at least a few others, an ideal model is provided by the drum, especially in their search for *total art*. Perhaps the heritage of drum-based poetics is shared by many more African-heritage poets than we so far have recognized. Wilfred Cartey makes a substantial case for the widespread use of drum poetics among négritude poets from Africa and the Caribbean. Cartey's words are clearly applicable to the work of Kamau Brathwaite, not only in *Masks,* but in much of his later poetry as well:

> The poet will not only summon the word, but as if postulating that timbre and music of any kind have their own vital restorative power, he turns to the rhythm of the drums and melodies of the flute. . . . for the poet, the drum becomes an ancient heirloom, resurrecting memories. . . . It not only awakens emotions, but has the power to infuse vitality and movement into lifeless form.[30]

There is an essential sense in which the poet as drummer cannot be confused with the drum as an energizing force. Scientists who study the physical properties of sound suggest that once a sound is generated, the waves, as its essence, continue to travel through space and time long after they are lost to human ears. Perhaps, on a metaphysical level, the sounds and rhythms generated by drum-based poetry do not necessarily die with the performance or even the performer. They may linger on, either as echoes or, at least, as memories. They evoke various times, places, things, people, all of which become enduring aspects of the world we know and the world we dream.

It is not for nothing that the drum, the primal drum, has been humankind's most faithful codifier of thought and emotion since the dawn of civilization.[31] Because its sounds and rhythms touch our total being in ways and with an intensity that no graphic symbol can surpass, their symbolic value transcends space and time. The single drumbeat is often an echo of the past, a record of the present, a dream of the future. It activates the memory of humankind and calls up visions of future time. It has been suggested that "the drum's pristine significance resides in its symbolic embodiment of the existing patterns of social and cosmogonic phenomena, in its comprehensiveness as metaphor for the community's self-definition in time and space".[32]

It is important to remind us all that the arguments so far made here for an African drum poetics as an essential creative and analytical model for Brathwaite's work, in particular, must be seen only as a necessary point of departure. His total creative universe offers many other particular challenges that can only be fruitfully accounted for with reference to the totality of the Caribbean experience. As so well demonstrated by Gordon Rohlehr (in *Pathfinder*) and by Nana Wilson-Tagoe, for *Masks,* indeed for *The Arrivants* as a whole, it is important that we see Brathwaite's creative project as one that is fully grounded in the submerged history of the Caribbean.[33] Brathwaite himself has also given us a crucial direction we need to follow. As indicated in his statement quoted earlier in this presentation, we must see his work as a uniquely Caribbean cultural production, done not as a "pure" African, but "an adaptation carried out mainly in terms of African tradition". In my analysis here, I have drawn most of my illustrations from Brathwaite's earlier work, which was most fully grounded in African, especially Akan, tradition. It is a matter of common knowledge to students and critics of his vast corpus that a great deal of his later work draws not so much on the particular models provided by the Akan *Odomankoma Kyerema,* but on such African-heritage models of the diaspora as found in the kaiso, jazz and blues. If I am unable to focus on any such illustrations, it is because, like Kamau Brathwaite, I have learned a very fundamental lesson from the divine drummer: slowly and patiently, I am only now learning the complexities of these new traditions of the diaspora. Until I succeed in mastering the technical resources of the kaiso, of jazz, of the blues, I should be glad to leave these aspects of Kamau Brathwaite's vast legacy to those better qualified to handle them. Fortunately, there is no shortage of competent Brathwaite specialists. It has been my privilege to share the experience of this conference, this Festival of the Word, with many whose works on Brathwaite's Words I have found most illuminating. I must, even at the risk of offending many, pay special respects to Gordon Rohlehr, whose work, especially *Pathfinder*[34] and several other essays, I have found particularly enlightening.[35]

Re-Invocation

Kamau Brathwaite: you who once upon a drought nursed thoughtseeds among the cane/cottonfields of our history, behold your harvest of words, your harvest of songs flowing like springwaters across deserts into cane/painfields of the land of the Taino and the Arawak.

Kamau Brathwaite: Mythmaker, you who

... dare to remember

the paths we shall never remember

again:[36]

see how your voice, like the curved drumsticks of the *Atumpan,* beats the dance back into the crippled gait of our gods; see how the gods still walk the narrow lanes of our countless shanty towns, dressed in words, moved by the counter-rhythms of the kaiso, playing hide-and-seek among our nightmares, among our dreamstories, slowly taming the thunder in the howl of hurricanes, whispering words of solace into storm fields of this endless archipelago of fragmented hopes/voices.

Kamau Brathwaite: Word Making Man, Mender of Broken Dreams, GreatGrandChild of Kweku Ananse Kokoroko, Original Owner of DreamStories; you who once prayed the gods to be

> . . . given words to shape [your] name
> to the syllables of trees
>
> [to be] given words to refashion futures
> like a healer's hand[37]

We invite we invoke you now to rise gently slowly patiently ever so gently and so slowly to stretch your limbs and step gently but firmly upon your trembling Earth stretch forth your limbs your voice across the Bay the Day of Pigs to your comrade and friend Nicolas Guillén on his Ancestral Isle of Youth. Come claim "the vast splendour of the sunshine & the sunflower & the stars".[38]

Come. Come join us now in this Festival of Hope. This Ceremonial Dance of Ancestral Voices. This Festival of The Word.

Notes

1. "The Instruction for Merikare", composed by Khety, the King of Upper and Lower Egypt, for his Royal Son, Merikare. See *Ancient Egyptian Literature: An Anthology,* trans. John L. Foster (Austin: University of Texas Press, 2001), 193.
2. Edward Kamau Brathwaite, "The African Presence in Caribbean Literature", in *Roots* (1986; reprint, Ann Arbor: University of Michigan Press, 1993), 256–57.
3. See Ayi Kwei Armah, *Two Thousand Seasons* (Nairobi: East African Publishing House, 1973), 139.
4. An adaptation, based on the Akan original as translated by J.H. Kwabena Nketia in his article "Akan Poetry", in *Introduction to African Literature,* ed. Ulli Beier (Evanston: Northwestern University Press, 1967), 23–33.

5. Brathwaite, *Masks* (London: Oxford University Press, 1968), 70.

6. For an elaboration on this statement, see Kofi Anyidoho, "Oral Poetics and Traditions of Verbal Art in Africa" (PhD diss., University of Texas at Austin, 1983).

7. Brathwaite, "The African Presence", 236.

8. Fabian Adekunle Badejo, introduction to *Words Need Love Too,* by Kamau Brathwaite (Philipsburg, St Martin: House of Nehesi, 2000), xi.

9. Brathwaite, *Barabajan Poems* (Kingston, Jamaica, and New York: Savacou North, 1993), 22.

10. Ibid., 23.

11. Ibid., 21.

12. M. NourbeSe Philip, *A Genealogy of Resistance and Other Essays* (Toronto: Mercury Press, 1997), 57–58.

13. *Ngugi wa Thiong'o,* "Kamau Brathwaite: The Voice of African Presence", *World Literature Today* 68, no. 4 (Autumn 1994): 677.

14. Anyidoho, "Atukwei Okai and His Poetic Territory", in *New West African Literature,* ed. Kolawole Ogungbesan (London: Heinemann, 1979), 56–57.

15. Nketia, "Akan Poetry", 29–30.

16. Brathwaite, *Masks,* 3.

17. Ibid., 4.

18. Ibid., 10.

19. A.M. Jones, *Studies in African Music,* vol. 1 (London: Oxford University Press, 1959); also Jones, "African Metrical Lyrics", *African Music* 3, no. 3 (1964): 6–14; Anyidoho, "Musical Patterns and Verbal Structures: Aspects of Prosody in an African Oral Poetry", *Black Orpheus* 6, no. 1 (1986): 27–44.

20. Brathwaite, *Masks,* 11.

21. Nketia, "Surrogate Languages of Africa", in *Current Trends in Linguistics,* vol. 7, *Linguistics in Sub-Saharan Africa,* ed. Thomas A. Sebeok (The Hague: Mouton, 1971), 718.

22. Nketia, "Akan Poetry", 29; also Kofi Awoonor, *The Breast of the Earth* (New York: Doubleday, 1975), 102.

23. S.O. Asein, "Symbol and Meaning in the Poetry of Edward Brathwaite", *World Literature Written in English* 21, no. 1 (1981): 96–104.

24. Brathwaite, *The Arrivants: A New World Trilogy* (London: Oxford University Press, 1973), 125.

25. J. Michael Dash, "Edward Kamau Brathwaite", in *West Indian Literature,* ed. Bruce King (London: Macmillan, 1979), 219.

26. Brathwaite, *The Arrivants,* 103, 104.

27. Brathwaite, "The African Presence", 191–92.

28. Ibid., 204.

29. Robert Fraser, *A Critical Review on Edward Brathwaite's* Masks. The British Council Nexus Books (London: Rex Collins, 1981), n.p.
30. See Wilfred Cartey, introduction to *Négritude: Black Poetry from Africa and the Caribbean,* ed. and trans. Norman R. Shapiro (New York: October House, 1970), 20–21.
31. See Femi Osofisan, *The Nostalgic Drum: Essays on Literature, Drama and Culture* (Lawrenceville, N.J.: Africa World Press, 1999).
32. Osofisan, "The Nostalgic Drum: Oral Literature and the Possibilities of Modern African Poetry", in *The Nostalgic Drum,* 313.
33. See Nana Wilson-Tagoe, "Edward Brathwaite and Submerged History: The Aesthetics of Renaissance", in *Historical Thought and Literary Representation in West Indian Literature* (Gainesville: University Press of Florida; Kingston, Jamaica: The Press University of the West Indies; Oxford: James Currey, 1998), 182–222.
34. Gordon Rohlehr, *Pathfinder: Black Awakening in* The Arrivants *of Edward Kamau Brathwaite* (Tunapuna, Trinidad: G. Rohlehr, 1981).
35. I should also draw attention to June D. Bobb's very valuable work *Beating a Restless Drum: The Poetics of Kamau Brathwaite* (Trenton, N.J.: Africa World Press, 1998), as well as the particularly rich collections of essays edited by Stewart Brown and Timothy J. Reiss, respectively, *The Art of Kamau Brathwaite* (Bridgend, Wales: Seren, 1995), and *For the Geography of a Soul: Emerging Perspectives on Kamau Brathwaite* (Trenton, N.J.: Africa World Press, 2001). Yet another major collection of essays, *Questioning Creole: Creolisation Discourses in Caribbean Culture* (eds. Verene A. Shepherd and Glen L. Richards [Kingston, Jamaica: Ian Randle; Oxford: James Currey, 2002]), was formally launched as part of the Second Conference on Caribbean Culture.
36. Brathwaite, *The Arrivants,* 13.
37. Ibid., 223–24.
38. Brathwaite, *Middle Passages* (New York: New Directions Books, 1992), 7.

2

The Rhythms of Caribbean Vocal and Oral-Based Texts

Maureen **Warner-Lewis** |

Kamau Brathwaite's important monograph, *History of the Voice: The Development of Nation Language in Anglophone Caribbean Poetry* (1984), elaborates his ideas regarding the intersection of poetry and sound in anglophone Caribbean literature. As such, the work addresses the properties of orality in West Indian poetry. My comments here set out to extend that topic by explicating orality and its connection with orature, pointing to some of the phonological and grammatical features of Caribbean Creoles, and eventually examining the devices of rhythm and syllable quantification which appear to underlie certain Caribbean song genres and which are selectively incorporated in anglophone Caribbean poetry.

Orality stands in a relationship of tension with literacy or the art and technologies of writing and reading. Orality signifies the capacity to create sound through the voice, in speech genres which include statements and queries, riddles and proverbs, declarations of intent, abuse and teasing, speechifying, and prayers. The use of the voice is also integral to spoken or sung jokes and stories, lyric expression, meditation and praise. Since speech is a natural attribute of human beings, orality predates the skill of literacy, which is a human invention, an artificial extension of orality. Literacy enables ideas or the content of sound to reach further in space and in time than the human voice can carry. Technological leaps in the twentieth century have, in addition, enabled sound itself to be amplified, reaching beyond earshot of the physically prox-imate audience; more than that, sound has been captured, stored and relayed, so that audiences in spaces and in times distant from the emanation locus can hear the original utterance. But the scribal does not replace the oral in absolute terms; and even so the scribal is given live expression by its vocaliza-tion. Oral and scribal modes therefore coexist in an ongoing, close and sym-biotic nexus.[1]

Orature or oral literature is the artistic expression of orality.[2] That literature may have been orally created in the first place; conversely, it may first have taken shape as a written composition and subsequently verbalized. Some examples in the latter category may exhibit a closer relationship with scribal techniques than oral ones, in the same way that discourse intended to be silently read can employ more involuted syntax, more sophisticated lexicons, and more complex sequencing than discourse intended to be read aloud. Most of the poems we consider in academia begin as written documents, but their potential energizing into sounded texts has been a central impetus of Kamau Brathwaite's literary trajectory since the 1960s.

At least two factors may account for Kamau Brathwaite's preoccupation with capturing West Indian sounds, voices and speech acts in his own poetic production. One factor may lie within the evolution of English poetry itself, that is, the struggle by some English poets to capture and reproduce the sounds and rhythms of various English regional and occupational dialects and period styles.[3] We may recall the rhythmic dislocations in the iambic pen-tameter wrought by John Donne and William Shakespeare in the seventeenth century, and the abandonment of traditional English metres by Gerard Manley Hopkins and the American Walt Whitman in the nineteenth century. These were all attempts to approximate an authentic "speaking voice".

Another influence on Brathwaite must surely have been the orality of African poetic performance, its rhythms, word morphology and ideophonic features, to which he was exposed during his employment in Ghana from 1955 to 1963. Such poetry was chanted and declaimed on state and religious occasions, during festival processions and rituals, at funerals, weddings and naming ceremonies. The applicability of this model to West Indian poetic concepts and practice must have suggested itself to Brathwaite, since anyone sensitive to language and familiar with the two geographical locations cannot fail to have had the experience of hearing West Africans speak and thinking for a sudden, startled moment that one was listening to West Indians, because the rhythm or intonation or volume or emphasis was the same – or by the reverse, overhearing West Indians hailing each other or conversing, and checking oneself with the thought: was that a snippet of an African language I was hearing? The intuition of the artist sensitive to words and to sounds led Brathwaite to pay particular attention to the vocal aspects of poetic expression in his post-Ghana phase of poetic production.

Creole Language Syntax, Idiom and Vocabulary

By the time Brathwaite verbalized in *History of the Voice* his theories on the symbiosis between sound and poetry, he had coined the term "nation language" to apply to the vehicle used by those types of West Indian poetry which exhibit marked levels of orality.[4] Such poetry tends to use the creole languages of the Caribbean as its vehicle. Creole languages are largely stocked by the vocabulary of a European language, even though a noticeable segment of their lexicon derives from Native American, African and Asian sources.[5] Meanwhile, their syntax or grammar – that is, the sequencing of words in sentences and idiomatic formulations – is as strongly influenced by the syntactic practices of western and west-central African languages as by the grammatical conventions of western European languages.[6] Creole languages then, embody features which attest to their origin in the economic and cultural contacts among Africa, Europe and the Americas. This hybridization results in grammar and word choice such as we find in Jamaican Louise Bennett's "Dutty Tough":

> Sun´ a shine´ but tings´ no bright;´
> Doah pot´ a bwile,´ bick´le no nuff;´
> Riv´er flood´ but wat´er scarce,´ yaw;
> Rain´ a fall´ but dutt´y tough!´[7]

In Standard English this says, "The sun shines, but things are difficult; / although I have things to cook, there is insufficient food; / the river overflows, but water is scarce, you hear; / rain falls, but the ground is dry."

But language involves more components than lexicon and grammar, both of which have successfully been reproduced by writing, for integral to speech are suprasegmental or paralinguistic features which have been difficult to transfer to written or print formats. Punctuation marks such as question or exclamation signs attempt to indicate intonation contours, and syllabic pitch is signalled in some scripts by diacritics. Apart from voice pitch and intonation contours and glides, paralinguistic properties include word- and phrase-rhythm, as in Spanish, for instance, where word-rhythm is conditioned by stress and indicated by superscript diacritics called accents. Then there is volume, only occasionally indicated by bold print or capital letters; there is pause, but length of pause is difficult to reproduce on paper, as are timing, speed of delivery and voice quality. The significance of these paralinguistic elements to nation language is apparent in the instance of Linton Kwesi Johnson's "Five Nights of Bleedin' ", cited by Brathwaite in his presentation on the topic.[8] Despite its largely English vocabulary and syntax, its Caribbean orality lies in the phonological treatment of its consonants and vowels in recording, the rhythmic patterns of its author's phrasing, its choice of idiomatic expression. Here, Johnson apparently employs capital letters to suggest importance and to signal volume; forward slashes suggest pause to exploit the meaning of morphological segments of words; and alterations to normative English spelling point to divergent (that is, Caribbean) pronunciation.

> night number one was in BRIX/TON:
> SOFRANO B sounn sys/tem
>
> was a-beatin out a riddim/ wid a fyah,
> commin doun his reggae-reggae wyah

Indeed, a complex mix of phonological, idiomatic and grammatical features has now come to characterize our best verbal productions. Apart from theme and treatment of theme, metaphorical brilliance and distinctiveness, our artists' harnessing of mechanisms to recreate the spoken word may indeed be one of the major factors for the genius and memorability of their work. Careful analysis of prose by Samuel Selvon, Earl Lovelace, Olive Senior, Erna Brodber and Curdella Forbes, among others, and of poems by Kamau Brathwaite, Derek Walcott, Lorna Goodison and Merle Collins reveals a deceptive disjuncture between the surface English words and syntax which predominate and the received Caribbeanness of the piece. This, for instance, is evidenced in the following extract from Earl Lovelace's *Salt*, with its subtle modulations in and out of third-person narrative voices and interior monologue, gliding between English and Creole idioms and syntax (the latter distinguished below by italics), and through formal and colloquial modalities. In his or her inner ear, the Trinidad and Tobago reader hears this selection in any number of versions of a Trinidadian idiolect:

> One day she listened to the harshness of her voice, talking with Valerie and she realized, No, this is not me. No. *I not going* to let these people sour and harden me. No, sir; not me. That was now the battle, the fight with her own toughness: between her toughness and her vulnerability. She tried to soften and to still hold on to herself. She would go on the beach with suntan lotion and stretch out on a towel in the sun. Who *ever hear* of Blackpeople tanning? *Blackpeople place* is in the shade, but she lay there till her skin glowed purple, people watching her with amazement. She must be a foreigner, she must be a madwoman. Beachbums would come over to chat her up and she would want to talk to them, but would remain silent until they had finished their spiel before she spoke and then when they heard her accent they would *catch themselves,* scratch their heads and drift away.[9]

Rhythm

In addition to the vocal inflections and syntactic code switching which produce nation language, there seem to exist rhythmic mechanisms which exist in our folk musics and which transfer themselves into poetry when our poets extricate themselves from what Brathwaite considers "the tyranny of the pentametre".[10] English prosody is based on stress quantity per line, a system which is becoming increasingly difficult for younger generations of West Indians to "hear" in their inner ear since, with virtually no Britons in classrooms, in the clergy, or even in the financial sector in the post-independence era, West Indians rarely hear British Received English, or Standard English, for that matter.[11] Yet children are introduced by way of nursery rhymes to the trimeter (triple time), and the dimeter (duple time) and hence the tetrameter (twice the dimeter), but their attention is not drawn to rhythmic analysis and labels for their body swaying and hand clapping during the primary school years, and so the concepts appear foreign by the time academic literary study begins.

Jack´ and Jill´
Ran up´ the hill´   (duple)

Row,´ row,´ row´ your boat´   (quadruple)
Merr´ily down´ the stream´   (triple)

Dick´ory, dick´ory, dock´
The mouse´ ran up´ the clock´   (triple)

In contrast to the stress-timed metre of English, some other speech cultures measure poetic lines or breath groups by their syllabic quantity. Latin, French, Spanish and African languages do so. Even in English, there can be synchrony between stress-timed rhythm and syllable quantity. A few examples will demonstrate this: Thomas Gray's

The cur´few tolls´ the knell´ of part´ing day´

or William Shakespeare's

The qual´ity of mer´cy is not strain´d´

contain ten syllables to five stresses, that is, two syllables per foot. Slight variations occur from time to time, such as Shakespeare's eleven syllables to five stresses in

To be´ or not´ to be,´ that is´ the ques´tion,

but more appropriately matching rhythm to sense,

To be´ or not´ to be,´ that´ is the ques´tion.

Thus English breath phrasing is dominated by stress, with emphasized syllables achieving sharper vocal prominence than medium-stressed and unstressed syllables, in descending order of pulmonic force. By contrast, anglophone Caribbean Creoles distribute pulmonic force more evenly to syllables, thereby modifying the significance of stress for comprehension. For instance, Caribbean anglophone Creoles often lengthen and therefore accent syllables which are unaccented in British English. So we hear and say: "yu look´in´ fu troub´le´", where in addition to the English emphasis given to "look" and "troub", West Indian pronunciation lends pitch and stress prominence to "in" and "ble", so that the phrase carries a very different rhythmic pulse from its English equivalent. This difference is obvious in an advertisement on Jamaican television (from the year 2000) for "Lovable" disposable nappies, where the female voice reprimands the male: "Dat's because you didn't buy Lovabuls", where the English unstressed "bles" is accented and lengthened. Again, a television spot for Carvan cellular phone service is an exaggerated exploitation of sequential stress prominence in Jamaican speech,

particularly when the actress boasts of being able to do "tex'' mess'age'-in'''"
even punctuating each syllable with rhythmic jerks of alternate shoulders.

Increasingly, too, Caribbean Creoles negate the English grammatical difference signalled by stress-shifting on analogous syllable sequences:
"com'pound", "prog'ress", "con'test", "con'flict'" as nouns, as against "compound'", "progress'", "contest'", "conflict'" as verbs. Several polysyllablic
words which carry stress on the initial syllable in Standard English tend to
have stress shifted to the second syllable in Creole: "hosp'ital" to "hospi'tal",
"comm'unal" to "commun'al", "reg'ister" to "regis'ter". And where the prominence of stress in English pronunciation causes syllable syncopation in words
like "police" [plis], "towel" [taal], "collapse" [klaps], "Korea" [kria], "interesting" [IntristIŋ], and "ordinary" [ɔdInrI], Caribbean Creole speakers render
these words with greater syllable quantity, thus making the first three words
carry two syllables each, "Korea" three, "ordinary" four, and "interesting"
either three or four.

Syllable Quantity as a Basis of Poetic Form

The salience of stressed syllables in Creoles is one of those features which
cause West Indian Creoles to give the momentary illusion of being West
African speech. And, as we observed with lengthening and stress in speech,
sequential syllable prominence means also that in Caribbean music, English
unstressed syllables can occupy higher melodic registers than their preceding
syllable and can also be held on sustained notes. These correspondences suggested the possible applicability of syllable-quantified analyses to Caribbean
oral and scribal poetry. The relevance of syllable quantification to identify
rhythmic patterns in song and poetry was brought to my attention by the
comment of the veteran Ghanaian musicologist, Kwabena Nketia, regarding
the "tendency in many African societies to . . . make the musical phrase coterminous with a syntactic unit or breath group".[12]

Prosodic Methodology

I began my investigation by applying a *syllable-based scansion* to the lines of
two Trinidad calypsos, "Ten to One is Murder" by The Mighty Sparrow
(Slinger Francisco, 1960), and "Dus' [Dust] in Dey Face" by David Rudder
(1992).[13] Remarkable consistencies in the number of syllables per line

emerged. This accorded with Nketia's observation that "[o]ne of the controlling principles [of African poetry, sung or spoken] is symmetry".[14] However, to integrate the factor of stress integral to English language and poetic traditions, I incorporated a *stress-based scansion* based on rhythmic analysis of the actual musical renditions. This two-dimensional framework then revealed evenness and unevenness of *intervalic stress,* which helped account for tempo changes, and illustrated rigidity of form as against fluidity of rhythmic movement. These structures could then be matched with meaning, intention and mood.

The symmetry in the structure of "Ten to One Is Murder" lies not only in its obvious sequencing of rhyming couplets, but also in the consistency of its syllable quantity. Syllable quantification revealed that it carried a steady thirteen syllables per line, varying occasionally with one less or one more syllable, and dropping in one case to ten, signifying a longer duration on one of the syllables: in this event, the word "say". By contrast, the longest line, of seventeen syllables, required a rushed delivery of "Well you could" and "not a":

Well, they play´in bad´	6 }	
They have me feel´in sad´	7 }	13
Well, they play´in' beas´	6 }	
Why they run´ for police?´	7 }	13
Ten crim´inals attack´ me outside´ a' Mir´amar		13
Ten´ to one´ is murd´er!´		6
About ten´ in the night´ on the fift´ of Octo´ber		13
Ten´ to one´ is murd´er!´		
Way down Hen´ry Street,´ up by H ´GM Walk´er		12
Ten´ to one´ is murd´er!´		
Well, the lead´er of the gang´ was hot´ like a pepp´er		13
Ten´ to one´ is murd´er!´		
And ev´'ry man´ in the gang´ had a white´-handle raz´or		14
Ten´ to one´ is murd´er!´		
They say´ ah push´ they gyal´ from Grena´da,		10
Ten´ to one´ is murd´er!´		
Well, ah back´-back until´ ah nearly fall´ in the gutt´er		14
Ten´ to one´ is murd´ er!		
Well you could imag´ine my posi´tion, not a pol´ice in the ar´ea!		17
Ten´ to one´ is murd´ er!´		

This rather even syllabic structure is all the while contained within four strong rhythmic beats (4/4) to the line, that is, the sense-group. This structure assists the maintenance of a high emotional charge throughout.

The correlation between phrase length and stress suggests that the lyricist composes with his verbal formulations anchored by a sense of rhythm, that words are not chosen and strung together separately from the timing desired. The timing may be established either by the creator tapping a hand on a table, tapping a foot on the ground, or strumming on a guitar. The rhythmic dictates of musical phrasing, therefore, appear to engineer consistency in syllable quantity per line or breath group.[15]

In "Ten to One" Sparrow narrated a personal confrontation. On the other hand, David Rudder's "Dus' in Dey Face" captures the intensity of the annual competition among steelband orchestras on the two islands, Trinidad and Tobago, which culminates at the start of Carnival week with a show named "Panorama".

	Stresses	Syllables
O´ gorm!´	2	2
A fell´a bawl´ out like Sprang´alang´[16]	4	9
O´ gorm!´	2	2
Was a man´ from a big´ steel´ban	3	8
Shot´ call´	2	2
A fell´a stan´ up and start´ to cuss´	4	9
How´ come´	2	2
Dey gi´ di firs´ prize to Ex´odus?´[17]	4	9
Well, dey come´ from de eas´	2	6
An dey play´ like dey mad´	2	6
An dey wheel´ and dey tumb´le	2	7
An when di dus´ done clear´	2	6
An de mas´ declare´	2	5
Big men´ start to grumb´le	2	6
Even´ Lord Kitch´ener´	3	6
Start´ to make´ he man´ima´	3	7
Say, "Dey cyar´ ketch me´ for nex´ year Pan´orama;´	5	12
Tell´ dem boys´ dey have to beg´ for dey supp´er	4	11
We com´in an is yoi,´ yoi´, yoi,´ yoi,´ yoi,´ yoi,´ yoi´"	8	12

	Stresses	Syllables
Refrain		
Ei!´ When´ you see we´ come dong´	4	7
Tell us war´ declar´in in tong´	3	8
Dus´ in dey face,´ dus´ in dey face´	4	8
Guns´ will´ be blast´in for sure´	4	7
In´ dis mus´i´cal war´	4	6
Tell yu, dus´ in dey face,´ dus´ in dey face´	4	10
I tell´in yu, we loo´k in for fight´	3	9
Is troub´le tonight´	2	5
We feel´in alright´	2	5
Is a pan´man war´	2	5
Yes,´ mi brudd´er	2	4
We come´ out for war´	2	5
Buya´ga	1	3
To sett´le a score´	2	5
Buya´ga	1	3
Wid ten´or saw dong´[18]	2	5
Bu´yaga, bu´yaga	2	6
Ei´ ma´ma!	2	3
Is dus´ in´ dey face´	3	5
dus´ in´ dey face´	3	4
dus´ in´ dey face´	3	4
Is dus´ dus´ dus,´ ei!´	3	5

The calypso exploits emotional urgency by fixing the contest in the metaphor of a gun battle on the dusty grounds of the Queen's Park Savannah where "Panorama" is held. But another metaphoric allusion is to the indigenous stickfight, traditionally a feature of the Carnival, by invoking words like *manima*,[19] and the athleticism of "wheel" and "tumble", and by alluding to Lord Kitchener, whose classic 1950s calypso, "Trouble in Arima", was a paean to the stickfight and its virtuosos. The kalinda/stickfight reference is also very much present in the rhythm of both these Kitchener and Rudder songs. The kalinda rhythm is allied to the driving 2/2 stamping processional of the *jab-jab* masquerade,[20] and its short call-and-response phrases.

These musical traditions are established in the introit to "Dus' in Dey

Face", which starts with a *lavway* or exclamatory cry of two long syllables:[21] "O gorm", which converts in subsequent lines to "Shot call" and "How come", all of the same vowel, melodic contour, and note length. The virtual responses to these lavways ("virtual" because they are still sung by the same lead voice) are varied, but all of them contain nine syllables. Those responses are: "was a man from a big steelban"; "a fella stan up an start to cuss"; "dey gi di firs prize to Exodus". Another of the responses contains only eight syllables, but the extra syllable required to make up the established nine is gained by prolongation of the vowel in "steel". This quick-tempoed rhythm of quavers and semiquavers is sustained in another sequence of six- and seven-syllabled lines: "Well dey come from de eas / An dey play like dey mad . . ." The lines lengthen to register Lord Kitchener's boast as the premier composer of calypso melodies for the steelband.

The first part of the refrain averages about seven syllables to four stresses per line, before advancing to a sequence of two stressed lines averaging four to five syllables, and ends with four lines which prolong the time spent on "dus" to produce three stresses per line. This overweighting of stresses within the four or five syllables of the last four lines suggests a slowing of pace and a longer, smoother texture to the melody. But where syllables lengthen lines in the refrain it is due to the addition of interjections, conjunctives and direct audience address. These devices are in keeping with the narrative embedding of the theme and the dramatic performative tags used in African and Caribbean storytelling accounts. So "Tell yuh" and "I tell yuh" iterate direct address; "An is" constitutes an emphatic device that focuses or points to the following noun; while "Yoi" and "Ei" replicate the violence of gunshots and jabjab whips. All of these interpolations and introductory tags punctuate and syncopate the rhythms, lending variety and excitement to the delivery. But syllable quantification allows us to excavate the underlying rhythmic coherence of line sequences, that is, to establish stanzas; to discover the structural segmentalization of the whole; and to more accurately convert the lyrics to poetic scribal form.

Meanwhile, the demands of the musical rhythm require changes in stress placement in several instances: "Exo'dus", rather than normative "Ex'odus", and "buya'ga" replacing the mimetic gunshot "bu'yaga". The back-up singers accent "buya'ga" on the second syllable, while Rudder himself places the emphasis on the first. Similarly, the words "Sprang'alang'" and "pan'ora'ma" receive stress and pitch prominence on both first and third syllables, just as they do in Trinidadian speech. Both stress shifting and vowel lengthening render the normative "mus'ical" as "mus'i'cal", since the medial vowel is prolonged and receives higher pitch prominence than either of its adjacent syllables.

Differential Stress Intervals

The inverse of abnormal syllable lengthening to accommodate fewer syllables in the rhythmic unit occurs when Caribbean folk music exhibits lines which virtually double the established syllable quantity. This creates the illusion of accelerated tempo, an acceleration not induced, as in Greek and Eastern European folk music, by speeding up the tempo, but instead by crowding more syllables into the rhythmic pulse already established in the song. This is an aesthetic coloration reintroduced into Jamaican music since the late 1980s by dancehall singers such as Admiral Bailey, Papa San and Shabba Ranks. It is a device used in Central African music and is found, for example, in Kongo songs performed in Trinidad, Martinique and Jamaica. Take the acceleration of delivery demanded in the third line of this Trinidad song about the Boer War:[22]

	Stresses	Syllables
E' Mboz'	2	3
Mbong'a Maju'ba	2	6
Ta n'tele nle'zi na bo'di ye'kiti	4	11
Men'ga ma'	2	3

The same effect occurs in the penultimate line of a chant by Imogene "Queenie" Kennedy of Jamaica.[23] Each verse of her melody exhibits remarkable internal symmetry of stresses per breath phrase, with the rapidly delivered line of eleven or twelve syllables (and even the final line of the first stanza with its nine syllables) contrasting with the more measured pace of the lines with four to eight syllables:

	Stresses	Syllables
Mm		
Cha'geni mba'la	2	5
Ya'bala ndum'be	2	5
Ko'ya ko me'ka ndom'be	3	7

	Stresses	Syllables
Aya ko´ meka ngo´lo	2	7
Ko´ya na ngen´ga	2	5
Ko´ya ko me´ka ngo´lo	3	7
Ya ko meka kwen´da ya´bala ndom´be	3	11
Ma´la ya mala kwen´da yan´de	3	9
O ye e e		
Nim´ba wen´da	2	4
Ko´ya ko mie´ka	2	5
Nzon´ge nzon´ge mba´la	3	5
Ya´bala ndum´be	2	5
Ko´ya ko me´ka nzan´ge	3	7
Ya´ko meka ko´no yande ya wa ndom´be	3	12
Ko´no ko me´ka nkwen´da	3	7

The rhythmic contrast between the Sparrow and Rudder calypsos above, and between the shorter and longer lines of the Kongo songs just discussed, allows us to observe a further element of prosody, which is the regularity or irregularity of stress intervals in the breath group or semantic phrase. As seen particularly in Rudder's calypso, a number of words receive stress shifts in order to conform to the musical beat; also, syllables have to be hastened, that is, unstressed, in order to accent the required number of stresses per breath group. This precipitates an uneven pattern of stress intervals, and accounts for what Brathwaite observed as the tendency of the calypso to employ dactyls, a pattern of unstressed + unstressed + stressed syllable sequences: in notation mode, ˘˘ ´.[24]

Transference of Song Rhythms to Poetry

The prosodic system based on syllable quantity contained within a given number of heavy stresses carries over from song into West Indian poetry, particularly where the artist deliberately evokes the rhythms of a specific musical genre or song.

The evenness of stress-to-syllable distribution characterizes much of Louise Bennett's poetry, since her rhythms are dominated by nursery rhyme, hymn and ballad sequences of alternating four- and three-stressed lines containing eight or seven, and seven or six syllables; in other words, one strong stress is accompanied by one light stress, on the average:

> From´ de grass´ root to´ de hill´-top,
> In profess´ion, skill´ an trade,´
> Jamai´ca o´man teck´ her time´
> Dah mount´ an meck´ de grade.´

But intervalic stress can be varied to achieve semantic and dramatic emphases: the next stanza allows the performer several alternative stress options, in particular in the first, third and fourth lines:

> Some(´) back a man´ a push,´ some(´) side´ a
> Man´ a hole´ him han,´
> Some(´) a lick´ sense´ ee(´)na man´ head,´
> Some(´) a guide´ him pon´ him plan!´[25]

In fact, Mervyn Morris has perceptively observed the unhelpfulness of relating Bennett's "prosody to an iambic stress pattern". Rather, he detects "a quatrain in which eight syllables are followed by six, then eight, then six, with the rhyme scheme *abcb*. An extra syllable here, a syllable short there" produces a system in which "even more reliably, each pair of lines tends to have fourteen syllables (or their equivalent in time)".[26]

Brathwaite reproduces the duple insistence of the bass line in Rastafari drumming in "Wings of a Dove", written in evenly stress-spaced four-syllable lines, with the sentence subject "dem" sonically and even visually serving as an off-beat at the end of the line rather than preceding its verb on the following line.

> Watch´ dem ship´ dem
> come´ to town´ dem
>
> full´ o' silk´ dem
> full´ o' food´ dem[27]

In another poem, "The Stone Sermon" in *Islands,* Brathwaite echoes the duple-beat folksong "Sammy Dead", with the minimally longer last line of its refrain replacing "dem" for "o" in the original. So

> Samm´y dead´
> Samm´y dead´
> Samm´y dead´ o

becomes

> Keep′ ya Cross′
> Keep′ ya Christ′
> Keep′ ya nun′ dem. . . .[28]

In "Limbo", the poet recreates the rhythms of a folksong while substituting new words, as in the third line here:

> lim′bo′
> lim′ bo like me′
> long′ dark′ night′ is the si′lence in front′ of me(′). . . .

Among the long lines of the folksong are: "I want′ a woman′ to lim′bo like me′'" and "The girl′ must be good′ to lim′bo like this boy(′)", of ten and eleven syllables respectively.[29] Brathwaite's eleven- and ten-syllabled phrases replicate this length: "long dark night is the silence in front of me"; "long dark deck and the water surrounding me"; "stick hit sound / and the ship like it ready".[30]

Brathwaite's "Calypso" carries a first line of twelve syllables, which could easily be dismantled into two parts of six syllables each, given that in near parallel fashion the following two lines contain six and seven syllables, with three strong beats.

> The stone′ had skidd′ed arc′d′ and bloomed′ into is′lands:
> Cu′ba and San′ Domin′go
> Jamai′ca and Puer′to Ri′co
> Grena′da Guade′loupe Bonaire′[31]

The mimicking and creative reproduction of folksong rhythms by some of our poets invites us to examine instances where the poet takes another approach to these traditions. Derek Walcott's approach shows less concern with harmonizing his prosodic form with the oral prosodies of folk arts, but by intertextual allusions, evocation of place and folk custom, the incorporation of idioms, proverbs and Creole grammatical expressions, he accomplishes the Caribbean resonances that he desires. So rhythmically, poems like "Mass Man" and "The Spoiler's Return" are firmly anchored in the iambic pentameter, and in "The Spoiler's Return" the regularity of stress every second syllable (the iambic foot), together with the poem's consistent rhyming couplets, place the poem in the tradition of English eighteenth-century satiric verse best exemplified by Dryden and Pope.[32]

I have´ a room´ there where´ I keep´ a crown,´
and Sa´tan send´ me to´ check out´ this town.´
Down there,´ that Hot´ Boy have´ a ste´reo´
where, whole´ day, he´ does blast´ my ca´iso´

In rhythmic contrast because of the uneven number of syllables between each stress, the refrain from Spoiler's "Bedbug" calypso acts as a foil:

I goin´[33] to bite´ them young´ ladies, part´ner,
like a hot´dog or´ a hamburg´er
and if you thin,´ don´t´ be in´ a fright´
is only big´ fat wo´men I´ goin to bite.´[34]

Walcott himself comes nearest irregularity of stress intervals when he wishes to create song, as in *Ti Jean and His Brothers*. Below he signals a calypso not only by sardonic humour and the rhyming couplet, but by reproducing through the tetrameter the 4/4 beat of many calypsos, and by the irregular stress intervals of the lines:

Down´ deep in hell´, where it black´ like ink,´
Where de oil´ does boil´ and the sulph´ur stink´
It ain't have´ no ice,´ no refrig´erator´
If´ you want wat´er, and you ask´ the wait´er,
He go bring´ brim´stone with a salt´petre chas´er,
While´ de dev´ils bawl´ing.[35]

Syntactic Parallelism as a Rhythmic Device

Another structural factor related to rhythm is the use of syntactic parallelism. Syntactic parallelism involves lexical and phrasal repetition with variation, and is universally a signifier of poetic expression. The very fact of repetition introduces rhythmic patterning in the sense of rhythmic stability, though not necessarily sameness. But it is clear that lexical and syntactic parallelisms involve parallelism of syllable quantity as well. Here is an instance from Walcott's "Mass Man", where the parallel sequences carry syllable quantities of eleven, ten and eleven, while the concluding line half-measures these to six:

some skull must rub its memory with ashes,
some mind must squat down howling in your dust,
some hand must crawl and recollect your rubbish,
someone must write your poems.[36]

Brathwaite utilizes the device more extensively, since it concurs with his oral imperatives. Two random examples will suffice:

. . . no ill.´ ill wind.´ no ill´
in. tent.´ no dis´

. respect.´ no dis´
-content.´[37]

This is a sequence of jagged single-stress phrases within two-syllable combinations, or, were one to analyse on the basis of the semantic units, a syllable-sequence of 22444. "Wake" in *Islands* initially presents a gentle sound-image, with its incremental syllable sequences of 7363.

there are sha´dows about´ me
eyes´ like mine´
pores´ sweating fears´ like mine´
sour´ing wine´

But expansiveness followed by abrupt contraction is conveyed by the go/stop rhythm of 7272.

There is no grey´ on the sea´
with wind´
there is no grey´ in the sky´
with rain´[38]

Conclusion

Investigating the syllable quantities of indigenous lyrics provides a platform from which to appreciate the technical characteristics of art forms we hardly think of in terms of shape and structural coherence. This process unmasks the symmetry of the poem's rhythmic structure, same-rhythm aggregations, and the correspondence between tempo and syllable quantity per line. Combining such quantification with the rhythmic dictates of the music which is the vehicle of the verbal flow elucidates tempo shadings and enhances our understanding of mood and meaning. Hopefully, this article has demonstrated the relationship, sustained or occasional, between folk-music prosody and some of the anglophone Caribbean's twentieth-century poetic styles.

But of course, syllable quantification cannot account for all the rhythmic features of West Indian verse. This is so because most twentieth-century West Indian scribal poets work in free verse, a European system devised to break with the regularity and predictability of its earlier prosodies. Such poetry does not tend to yield syllable-length coherence of its segments. Line and stanza length are deliberately made irregular, so that a poem such as D.H. Lawrence's "Snake" has consecutive lines of eight, fourteen, three syllables, and in the following stanza, thirteen, nine, seventeen.[39]

It is art meant for melodic or rhythmic vocalization which demands symmetry of its verbal element. This symmetry is therefore a hallmark of traditional lyric and narrative form, whereas irregularity of structure is a signifier of prose. In the evolution of West Indian poetry, from the late 1930s Louise Bennett made vocalization an intrinsic part of her presentation of poetry as dramatic performance,[40] an outgrowth of her nurturance within the lively inventiveness of folk speech, the expressiveness of street calls, "tracing matches", folktales and folksongs, and her own attraction towards the theatre. She did not, however, articulate a conceptual framework, and her methodology found no sustained creative imitators until the 1960s, after Mervyn Morris critically acclaimed the virtue of her poetry in the immediate wake of political independence,[41] and after Brathwaite advocated resurrection of the ancient connection between verbal art and music, first theorizing it in his essay "Jazz and the West Indian Novel" (1967–68), and exemplifying it in the methodologies and reading performances of his poetic *oeuvre* from the 1960s onwards. In his further testament to this connectedness, *History of the Voice* ventilates his theory of nation language, illustrating how anglophone Caribbean orality impinges on poetic expression. While the intertextuality and interrelationship between his poetry and jazz have been well documented,[42] the nexus between syllable quantity and rhythm in indigenous musical forms has not been considered. Such an examination, however, indicates the existence of a subterranean prosodic system employed by our folk vocalists, perhaps unconsciously, but following in long-established traditions of verbal-musical composition.

Meanwhile, Brathwaite's ongoing fascination with the syllable as component of the word, his extraction of polyvalent semantics from the word's deconstructed elements, and his dalliance with homophony propel him towards startling neologisms and sound parallels. The word is for Kamau Brathwaite a site for explosion and revisioning of our collective and personal experiences, in physical, phonological and semantic senses. While this may appear to be an idiosyncratic tendency, this too falls within the ambit of nation language, since it is a parallel exploitation of the African verbal traditions which have been revived in Rastafari's verbal remodelling of concepts and experience.[43] This creativity is among the reasons Brathwaite defines the poet as a craftsperson of "wordsongs, wordsounds, wordwounds & meanings" who gives figuration to "a certain [certain] code" that is at once both "order" and "dis/order" [this order].[44]

Notes

1. See Walter Ong, *Orality and Literacy: The Technologizing of the Word* (London and New York: Methuen, 1982).
2. On the basis of the etymological connection between the Latin *liter,* "letter of the alphabet", and "literature", Ong considers literature as referring only to that which is written (ibid., 13–14). This dichotomy makes sense in a highly literate society, but is inadequate for societies like the Caribbean which, while generally literate, rely very heavily on oral communication and oral art forms.
3. I use "dialect" in a linguistically neutral sense, not pejoratively.
4. The coinage is based on the use of the term "nation dance" in Carriacou and Grenada, especially, to refer to open-air dance occasions in which descendants of various African ethnic groups, such as Igbo and Kramanti, unify to perform the dances typical of their group. Maroon dance occasions also follow this format. See Kenneth Bilby, *Music of the Maroons of Jamaica,* Ethnic Folkways Records, FE 4027; Bilby, "The Kromanti Dance of the Windward Maroons of Jamaica", *New West Indian Guide* 55, nos. 1–2 (1981): 52–101; Lorna McDaniel, *The Big Drum Ritual of Carriacou: Praisesongs in Rememory of Flight* (Gainesville: University Press of Florida, 1998).
5. See Frederic Cassidy and Robert Le Page, *Dictionary of Jamaican English* (1967; reprint, Kingston, Jamaica: University of the West Indies Press, 2002); Rawwida Baksh-Soodeen, "A Historical Perspective on the Lexicon of Trinidad English"

(PhD diss., University of the West Indies, 1994); Richard Allsopp, *Dictionary of Caribbean English Usage* (New York: Oxford University Press, 1996).

6. For some of the controversies over the degree of influence from various sources, see Salikoko Mufwene, ed., *Africanisms in Afro-American Language Varieties* (Athens and London: University of Georgia Press, 1993); Mikael Parkvall, *Out of Africa: African Influences in Atlantic Creoles* (London: Battlebridge, 2000).

7. Louise Bennett, *Selected Poems*, ed. Mervyn Morris (Kingston, Jamaica: Sangster's Book Stores, 1983), 25. In this chapter stress in quoted text is indicated where this factor is being highlighted, and stressed syllables carry the sign ´ *after* them. "Dutty" is a Twi word from the Gold Coast meaning "ground".

8. Edward Kamau Brathwaite, *History of the Voice: The Development of Nation Language in Anglophone Caribbean Poetry* (London and Port of Spain: New Beacon Books, 1984), 35. "History of the Voice" also forms one of the essays in Brathwaite, *Roots* (Havana: Casa de las Américas, 1986), 259–304.

9. Earl Lovelace, *Salt* (New York: Faber and Faber, 1996), 98–99; emphasis added.

10. Brathwaite, *History of the Voice*, 30n40.

11. British Received Pronunciation is a class dialect of English characterized by a particular enunciation. Standard English refers more specifically to observation of the rules of English grammar, and incorporates several dialect pronunciations of the language.

12. J.H. Kwabena Nketia, "The Linguistic and Literary Aspects of Style in African Music" (typescript).

13. First done for the Colloquium on Music and Linguistics sponsored by Columbia College (Chicago), Centre for Black Music Research, Hilton Hotel, Port of Spain, 23 May 2001.

14. Nketia, "The Linguistic Aspect of Style in African Languages", *Current Trends in Linguistics* 1 (1971): 744. This feature of African prosody was expounded by H.F. Morrris, *The Heroic Recitations of the Bahima of Ankole* (Oxford: Clarendon Press, 1964).

15. The creative process is probably complicated by an initial and perhaps subsequent interplay with melodic snatches as well.

16. The pseudonym of a local comedian.

17. The name of a major steelband.

18. One of the tonal sections of a steelband orchestra comprises the tenor pan, which carries the treble notes on a steeldrum cut to about a sixth of its height. The analogy here is to a sawn-off shotgun.

19. A word occurring in stickfight songs, and perhaps derived from Kongo *manama*, "standing over, hung/positioned over", referring to a threatening, dominant posture over the opponent.

20. "Jab" derives from the French *diable*, "devil". These masqueraders paint them-

selves black or blue, and originally represented ancestral spirits. See Maureen Warner-Lewis, *Guinea's Other Suns: The African Dynamic in Trinidad Culture* (Dover: Majority Press, 1991), 182–83.

21. *Lavway,* French Creole (perhaps from the French *la virée,* "the return"), is a refrain sung on high notes, to which response is made on lower notes. The high-pitched call serves to excite listeners into an ecstatic mood, especially since the pitches tend to be either level or in ascending scale.

22. See Maureen Warner-Lewis, *Central Africa in the Caribbean: Transcending Time, Transforming Cultures* (Kingston, Jamaica: University of the West Indies Press, 2003), 54.

23. Performed during an interview with Maureen Warner and Monica Schuler, Trench Town, Kingston, Jamaica, June 1971.

24. See Brathwaite, *History,* 17.

25. This stanza and the preceding are from Bennett, "Jamaica Oman", in *Selected Poems,* 22.

26. Mervyn Morris, introduction to *Selected Poems,* by Louise Bennett, xiv.

27. Brathwaite, *The Arrivants: A New World Trilogy* (Oxford: Oxford University Press, 1973), 45.

28. Ibid., 256.

29. Quoted from Edric Connor, *Songs from Trinidad* (London: Oxford University Press, 1958), 57–58.

30. Brathwaite, *The Arrivants,* 194.

31. Ibid., 48. As performed by Brathwaite on *Rights of Passage,* vol. 2 (Argo, DA 102), Brathwaite does not establish a credible calypso melody in the first line, though he maintains the requisite rhythm. Rhythmic and melodic factors, however, synchronize in the second and third lines, but the rhythmic consistency breaks down by the fourth line, which is pulsed as follows: "Grena´da Guad´elou´pe Bonaire´". It is instructive that this line is spoken, the poet himself perhaps sensing his inability to coordinate a calypso-like melody and rhythm.

32. For Walcott's and Thieme's comments on the prosody of "Spoiler's Return", see John Thieme, *Derek Walcott* (Manchester and New York: Manchester University Press, 1999), 22–23.

33. Treated as one syllable by the calypsonian.

34. Derek Walcott, *The Fortunate Traveller* (London: Faber, 1982), 53.

35. In Walcott, *Dream on Monkey Mountain and Other Plays* (New York: Farrar, Straus and Giroux, 1970), 150.

36. Walcott, *The Gulf* (London: Jonathan Cape, 1969), 19.

37. Brathwaite, "Esplanade Poem", in *Words Need Love Too* (Philipsburg, St Martin: House of Nehesi, 2000), 43.

38. Brathwaite, *The Arrivants,* 208.

39. In Wilfred Guerin et al., *Literature and Interpretive Techniques* (New York: Harper and Row, 1986), 487–89.

40. The arts of poetry recitation and public oratory were much in vogue at that time, and good performers were required to display appropriate gesture and verbal articulation. It should also be mentioned that Claude McKay had produced verse in Jamaican Creole during the 1900s, at the instigation of an expatriate mentor. After leaving Jamaica for the United States, McKay discontinued this poetic route.

41. Mervyn Morris, "On Reading Louise Bennett, Seriously", *Jamaica Journal* 1, no. 1 (December 1967): 69–74. The piece had won the Jamaica Festival essay competition in 1963.

42. See Gordon Rohlehr, *Pathfinder: Black Awakening in* The Arrivants *of Edward Kamau Brathwaite* (Tunapuna, Trinidad: G. Rohlehr, 1981), 71–98; Louis James, "Brathwaite and Jazz", in *The Art of Kamau Brathwaite,* ed. Stewart Brown (Bridgend, Mid Glamorgan, Wales: Seren, 1995), 62–74.

43. See Mervyn Alleyne, *Roots of Jamaican Culture* (London: Pluto Press, 1988), 146–48; Maureen Warner-Lewis, "African Continuities in the Rastafari Belief System", *Caribbean Quarterly* 39, no. 3 (1993): 108–23; Velma Pollard, *Dread Talk: The Language of Rastafari* (Kingston, Jamaica: University of the West Indies Press, 2000).

44. Brathwaite, *Barabajan Poems* (Kingston, Jamaica, and New York: Savacou North, 1994), 21.

3

Keeping Your Word
Contracts, Covenants and Canticles

J. Edward **Chamberlin** |

I was born close by the rainforest, and for a while we lived in a little cottage owned by one of the woodsmen, right under the bridge that spanned the entrance to the harbour we called Lion's Gate. Later, I went to the interior where my relatives lived and got to know the desert lands between the mountains, and the savannahs beyond. Great rivers ran through this country, one of them over twelve hundred miles long, its watershed covering more than a quarter of a million square miles with rapids and waterfalls rivalling any in the world, and the flow of water twice that of the Nile. When my grandfather first went there, very few travellers had been through before, though Amerindian peoples had lived there for millennia.

There had been slavery in the place where I grew up, and there were people who remembered that grim story, familiar to many here: how the slaves and indentured labourers harvested the rich resources of the land, while its wealth was accumulated by a small elite. But for all its wretchedness, the society was rich in artistic creativity, with dancing and drumming and carving and painting and beadwork and basketry of exquisite craft and design. So important was dancing, in fact, that when the colonial government passed a law banning it, the people responded with stubborn independence. A strict law bids *us dance,* they said, in words that became an anthem of resistance for many of my generation.

There was a lot of trade in the region, both along the coast and into the interior; and many of the stories and songs I first learned were about either fascinating old trade routes or the mysterious bonds of kinship. Politics played its part in all this, further fractured by class and ideology: basically, those working the land formed one group, and their managers and overseers another. Every time one group would come into power, some of the others would end up in jail. Criminalizing the opposition was a local custom.

There were places of refuge, maroon fastnesses where runaways nurtured their distrust of their enemies and worked on their dislike of each other. Some came from far away across the waters to hide out in the mountains and valleys, shaping societies that were locked in time as much as they were held in place.

The languages people spoke varied widely, with English taking on a homemade inflection that was routinely mocked by our colonial schoolmasters. There was a pidgin language that had developed out of the coastal trade, and some of its words found their way into the lexicon of Standard English and onto the map as place names. And there was another language, which we would probably now call a creole. I used to hear it occasionally around the house, for the spiritual guide assigned to me when I was born spoke it. And there were still other languages brought there by people who came looking for gold, or sent by God. I recall listening to one community singing psalms in a language I had never heard before, and seldom since. Because they had been persecuted throughout much of their history, and for over three centuries had been on the run across continents and oceans, they had coded their own experiences and beliefs into these psalms and sang them not only in their – to me – strange language but in a style designed to make them unintelligible to almost anybody else, the words being drawn out over a succession of musical phrases that were further extended by the staggered breathing of the chorus to produce a continuous sound and little interpretable sense. "The singing of psalms is like honey", began one of them. It took over five minutes to sing those seven words, syllable by syllable.

In secular as well as sacred ceremonies, oral traditions were a central part of my world. Teaching was mostly memorization; political gatherings were arenas of dramatic oral performance; and laws had to be read out before they came into effect. Most religious practices were syncretic, with a mix of spoken and written texts and of new and old rituals, though many maintained that their particular practices were drawn from a pure source, of distant but (at least in the minds of the custodians) distinct memory. And everyone prayed in several places and forms, inhaling everything from exotic incense to local opiates, and from the finely pulverized wood of the rainforest to the salt sea air. We were hedging our bets, to be sure; but this was also part of our search for a ceremony of belief that could give meaning and value to our lives, and to the land.

It was not Guyana, though it shared many things with that country, which is perhaps why Wilson Harris has always seemed such a congenial spirit to me – as he has been to Kamau Brathwaite, who uses as the epigraph to his book *Mother Poem* a passage from Harris's *The Whole Armour:* "We're the first potential parents who can contain the ancestral house." Nor was it any part of Surinam, or Belize or anywhere else in the Caribbean. It was the northwest coast and mountainous interior of Canada. Looking at a map of the Americas in 1858, Queen Victoria had added the word "British" to distinguish it from the Caribbean Colombia, with which it shared much both geographically and demographically. So British Columbia it was called (though its founding father, James Douglas, was of African as well as Scottish heritage).

The rainforest was temperate, but it was an overwhelming presence in our lives; the Amerindians were Kwakwaka'waku and Kootenai and Tlingit and Gitksan and Nisga'a and Nuuh-chah-nulth, all of whom had slaves well into the nineteenth century. The pidgin language was Chinook, in which I learned my first greeting, *kla-how-ya, tillicum. Tamahnous* were duppies; *skookum* meant strong; and *chuck* referred to river or sea water: the ocean was the salt chuck, and skookum chuck was a dangerous bit of rapids or a rip tide. *Kloosh* meant good; so a translation of the Bible published by the London British and Foreign Bible Society in 1912 referred to the Gospels as "Kloosh Yiems". Good Stories.

Michif was the creole language, born two hundred years earlier of contact between French, Cree and Ojibway traders, and further enriched by other encounters. It was spoken only on the edge of my country, but it represented something important about our hybrid culture. Linguists continue to argue about Michif, calling it variously a pidgin, a creole or a dialect of Cree. My godmother – the spiritual guide I mentioned earlier, who also taught me card tricks – spoke Michif; but she was of the generation, once again familiar to many here, who thought it nothing more than a slang, spoken by half-breeds like herself.

The psalm singers were Doukhoubors; their name, originally derogatory, means spirit wrestlers. They were refugees from religious persecution in Russia who had come to British Columbia around the turn of century and retreated into the mountains, the most radical of them calling themselves Freedomites and reading the Bible as an exile's covenant. Even more sternly than Rastafarians, they rejected any compromise with Babylon, burning houses and possessions (including occasionally all of their clothes) in acts of ritual purification. They also refused to send their children to school, believing like Rasta that it was head-decay-shun; and so the authorities sent in the police to take the children away. And then they built a special jail, hundreds of miles away beyond the mountains, for some of their more belligerent parents who had turned to occasional acts of violence against Babylonian institutions. *Terror in the Name of God* was the title of an unfriendly book written about them in the early 1960s . . . just about the time, come to think of it, that Rastafarians were being demonized in the Caribbean. Soon the rest of the community, many of them very old and most of them women, walked all the way down to the coast to sing their psalms outside the walls of the prison where their fathers and husbands and sons were being held. They used to say that when they stopped singing psalms in that way, they would stop being a people. Hearing them sing, listening to my godmother speak Michif, learning Chinook words from my mother – these are among my most precious memories, and shaped my sense of the power of words and music, and of the forms of resistance they can represent.

There is much more that I could say to create what might be common ground among us all, but that is not my purpose. I have indulged in this long catalogue – which is almost identical to some that I have heard from the Caribbean – in order to make a more contentious point. Over the years, many of us who grew up in British Columbia have tried to find ways of celebrating the complex realities, including the relentless antagonisms, of the place, and of accommodating the diversity and the division, the remembering and the forgetting, that are its uneasy heritage. We wanted to believe in ourselves as a community, even though many of us didn't much like one another. The mountains and the sea offered us a convenient isolation, so we could find some solidarity in feeling variously lucky and left out; and with a kind of collective bravado we made constant threats to separate from the federation we had fallen into years before . . . not as loudly as Quebec perhaps, on the other side of the continent and with its own distinct linguistic and cultural history, but with even greater local support (which always surprises outsiders). But at the end of the day we didn't do anything. We didn't *really* believe in ourselves; or at least we couldn't find anything to believe in other than our differences, and our difference. Our contracts with each other, our covenants with the land, and the canticles we sang to celebrate our livelihoods as hunters, trappers, loggers, miners, fishermen, farmers and factory workers were wracked with old anxieties about native and newcomer, the metropolis and the hinterland, tradition and progress, and riddled with the deceptions and deceits by means of which we managed these conflicts. As for an imaginative vision, we didn't have one out there in the parishes of the northwest. We still don't. Tourists come to marvel and spend money, while we continue to hew wood, draw water and hustle cash in any number of ways, and to complain about folks from foreign who don't understand us, or just plain don't like us. "Who *are* we?" we ask ourselves; and when we can't come to any consensus, we ask "Where is here?" This, of course is also the question Brathwaite asks in arguably his finest book, *X/Self,* which is a spiritual biography of Kamau and of the Caribbean. The experiences it chronicles and the uncertainties it commemorates are familiar to me, and widely shared in the Americas.

I *come* from the Americas. Not from Europe or Africa or Asia. None of my family's stories, going back generations, have to do with anywhere else. In a contradictory way, that is what I bring here today. Nothing but what is already here, and a sense that the Caribbean represents the dynamics, if not the details, of my heritage as much as anybody else's, or anywhere else. The fact is that many of the contradictions and contentions that define Caribbean society also shape other communities throughout the hemisphere, and I don't mean only those of African or Asian heritage. A number of Caribbean writers and artists and dancers and drummers have recognized this, and a few of its historians and social scientists, foremost among them Rex Nettleford and Barry Chevannes. But Kamau Brathwaite belongs in a special class. He has given all of us in the Americas, of which the Caribbean is like a tuning fork, a sense of what an imaginative vision of the past and of the place might be like, of the deep contradictions that will inevitably be at its heart, and of the dangerous confusions that it will foster. Like all good historians he looks to the future as much as to the past; and so he has demanded that Caribbean people believe in themselves . . . and then insisted that such belief must always be surrounded by doubt. There is nothing particularly postmodern or postcolonial about this, which may be why he has not been taken up by many of its patrons. There is simply an ancient dedication to ceremonies of the word.

Doubt is where they all begin. It is where language begins, first of all with the wonder of how a word can be both something – the thing it refers to or represents – and nothing but a word; and secondly, with the uncertainty about whether someone really means what they say, and whether metaphor is to be believed or not. Religious creeds continually put this to the test, providing testimony of communal consent to what sometimes seem very doubtful ceremonies of belief; but let me give another kind of example, one that turns us towards the idea of a more deliberate social contract. In 1890 the people of the state of Montana came into the American federation with some words that affirmed who they were and why they belonged right there. They called it a constitution; and it is interesting to compare the constitutions of Montana and of the United States to illustrate how different kinds of communities imagine themselves. Both begin with the words "we the people". The United States Constitution then identifies the specific purposes of government, immediately reducing the contract to its instrumental dimension. Montana's constitution, on the other hand, begins this way: "We the people of Montana, grateful to God for the quiet beauty of our state, the grandeur of its mountains, the vastness of its rolling plain . . ."

Why did they go on like this? "It would be possible to argue that they were simply being long-winded in a document which should be lean and concise," says the philosopher and politician Daniel Kemmis, who lives there now. "But it could also be argued that they said not a word more than they had to say; and that what they had to say was that the way they felt about the place they inhabited was an important part of what they meant when they said 'we the people'."[1] Indeed, the United States soon caught up with Montana, not only in its national anthem but also in its unofficial praise songs like "America the Beautiful". And when Woody Guthrie got tired of hearing Kate Smith sing it, what did he write? "This Land Is Your Land, This Land Is My Land". Native Americans found that a particularly fascinating contradiction.

We don't need to be poets or psalm writers to know that words of praise and thanksgiving, especially those in elegant or unordinary language, should always be taken seriously. We all know that the reality of a people's circumstances is inseparable from the way in which they imagine their community. What is not so often acknowledged is that the embarrassing enthusiasm, the exaggerated artifice, the strange unreality of many expressions of community are an important part of their appeal. At the same time, communities are as simple, as natural, as familiar as the sunrise and the sunset. They wake us in the morning, and allow us to sleep at night.

But wait a minute. There is nothing at all natural about the sunrise or the sunset. The sun does not rise and set; in fact, relative to the earth, it doesn't do anything at all. But we find it convenient to imagine that it does . . . even though we have known for centuries that it does not. A few years ago, I helped in a small way to bring together a large gathering of Rastafarian elders on the Mona campus of the University of the West Indies. Mortimo Planno took the lead in organizing it, with Barry Chevannes and Jalani and many others, and the result was a lively reasoning of secular and sacred issues – and of their inseparability – by scholars and teachers of the Rastafarian community. Just before it all began, Ras Kumi said to me, "There will be people at our gathering who think the world is round. And people who think the world is flat. Same people."

The wisdom here is at the heart of Rastafari, and I will return to it in a moment. But for now I want to keep with its contradiction, for it is crucial to the way in which we imagine our communities. At the end of *Portrait of the Artist as a Young Man,* James Joyce has his character vow "to forge the uncreated conscience of his race". The word "forge" is carefully chosen to catch the contradiction: it is both a forging and a forgery, both a natural process and the most obvious artifice. We balance these every day in our complementary – and contradictory – notions of human society. On the one hand, we accept that communities – from families to neighbourhoods – are the first and natural form of human organization. On the other, we say that they are humanity's most ingenious inventions. There are two radically different theories of human society at work here, as distinct as a flat earth and a round earth: societies are natural and organic; or they are artificial and organized. From each comes a distinctly different theory of human identity: either we exist prior to the tribe or state, and give it whatever significance it has; or we receive life and meaning *from* the state, much as a branch does from the tree. But at the end of the day we embrace them both, even though they contradict each other; and the two theories become like warp and woof, weaving the fabric of all human communities. Surely one is true and the other false? Yes, and no. The same way that the word C-A-T is a cat, and is not a cat.

We grow up with these kinds of contradictions. I believe we need to recover some of the wisdom – and some of the wonder – of those early years of listening to stories and songs. "It was, and it was not" is how storytellers of Majorca begin their stories. Among the herders and hunters of southern Namibia and the Kalahari, the word /garube is used; it means "the happening that is not happening". "Once upon a time" is the phrase I was brought up on, and when I heard it I moved into a place where, as one youngster put it, things happen that don't. The novelist E.L. Doctorow was once criticized for bringing characters together in his historical novel *Ragtime* who could not possibly have met in real life. "They have now," he replied. This is why the central figures in so many storytelling traditions of the world are tricksters, from the classical god Hermes and the West African (and now West Indian) spider Anancy to the crafty Coyote and unreliable Raven of native America. *All* stories and song – including all contracts and constitutions and covenants and canticles – are tricks. What greater trick could there be – and I say this with respect – than making a song about the *impossibility* of singing the Lord's song in a strange land into the most powerful inspiration for doing just that. Now *that's* a trick.

The original Greek word for a trick was *dolos,* and the first trick in Greek mythology was baiting a hook for a fish. Hermes, the messenger of the gods, began his career when he was one day old by stealing cattle from Apollo, which he then barbecued – he seems to have been an Arawak at heart – but did not eat, thereby making the point that some things are valuable not because they are useful but because they are special. Or, if you are a thief, because they belong to someone else. Lewis Hyde, in *Trickster Makes this World,* catches the character of this kind of imaginative sleight-of-hand when he says that "Hermes is neither the god of the door leading out nor the god of the door leading in – he is the god of the hinge".[2] Just as others have argued that the crossroads is a more convincing image for the Caribbean than the crossing, I suggest the hinge is more compelling than the door, even the door of no return. The Caribbean *is* the hinge of the Americas, at once the purest and the most polluted product of Carib and Arawak and Taino generosity – the sacred gift of their lives and of their land – and of European thievery. Or let me put it differently: The Caribbean is the trick; and if a trick is any good – this is where our stories about tricksters mislead us – it is always more important than the trickster. Just as a poem is more important than the poet.

"By the meaningless sign linked to the meaningless sound we have built the shape and meaning" of society, said Marshall McLuhan.[3] He was talking about words and images, and how we recognize them as representations; but he could have been talking about all the ceremonies of belief that make up our imaginative (and spiritual) lives. It is the embrace of arbitrariness and the assigning of significance to various forms of representation that constitute our communities.

Which is where Kamau comes in, with his call to embrace nation language. Here I need to move carefully, because I do not want to be misunderstood. Nation language does not exist, any more than beauty and grandeur and vastness do. Let me put this another way, as Kamau himself did when he posed the question that has haunted the Caribbean for generations, the question about something else that does not exist . . . and is the only thing that matters. "Where then is the nigger's home," he asked, "in Paris, Brixton, Kingston, Rome? Here, or in heaven?"

Home. It may be the place we came from, five or fifty or five hundred years ago; or the place we are going to when our time is done. It may be where we hang our hat, or where our heart is . . . which in turn may be the same place, or maybe not. It is all of these things, and none of them. It is nowhere – that's what "utopia" means; and it is here and now – that's also what utopia means, in a pun that Thomas More made famous in his great vision of community. In Herman Melville's novel *Moby Dick*, Ishmael tells us that the strange harpooner Queequeg with whom he is sharing a bed at the Spouter Inn was born on the island of Kokovoko. Then he adds, "it is not down in any map; true places never are". Nation language is like that. It is not down in any map. True languages never are, as Maureen Warner-Lewis has demonstrated so convincingly. I have been working in the Kalahari region of southern Africa for the past five years with a San (Bushmen) community whose language has five clicks and eight tones, along with a remarkable range of other sounds. Its written form is just being developed, following the model of Khoikhoi, a related language spoken in southern Namibia for which there is an orthography. You can imagine its complexity, and its artifice. Nobody pretends that the written form is the *same* as the spoken form, whatever that might mean; and if speech is said to be the "true" form of language – which many of us might want to dispute on other grounds – then the written form can *never* be. It is not because nation language is a real language spoken by everyone that it has its hold, but because – in its *written* form – it is an imagined language spoken by no one. *That* is its hold. In all his writings on language, Kamau has presented us with this riddle of language, analogous to his riddle of home.

Kamau did something else. He brought dread back into poetry, as the Rastafarians brought it back for awhile into politics. And he did so, I believe, in order not to lose that sense of wonder without which the imagination cannot function. It is only through the pressure of our imagination that we can resist the overwhelming pressure of reality. In this sense, all stories are resistance stories, and all songs are songs of resistance, pushing back against the tyrannies of the everyday as well as the terrors of the unknown. When Kamau called for a poetry to accomodate the force of the hurricane he was proposing that the artifice of form – the meaningless sign linked to the meaningless sound – shapes, and thereby controls, the power of nature. He was also calling for a surrender to the natural, and to its power.

Our first instinct, of course, *is* to try to take control, especially if we have been living lives in which everything seems out of control. But we know this is a mistake; we know it in our bodies and our souls. We know that we cannot control most of the things that happen to us, which is why surrender to a greater power – to Jah, or Jehovah, or Allah, or God – has a perennial hold on our imaginations. But that's not the end of the story. If you do try to take control of the hurricane, or the desert, or the sea, you go mad. And if you don't, you also go mad. That is the conundrum, the contradiction, the riddle of community.

The same contradiction is true of the past. We need to both remember it and forget it. This is especially the case with the various horrors that haunt us, which may be why we are so addicted to celebrating achievements, successes, moments when a human stamp is put on an inhuman world. But failure has its place too, and may also bear the mark of a dignified humanity; which is why it needs to be celebrated as well. History is mostly built not around achievement – as that old trickster Vidia Naipaul put it, baiting the hook – but around failure. Most of us are, at one time or another, abject failures. Many of our families are failures, at least from time to time. Our nations are almost always grotesque failures, at least according to the ideals we have of them and parade out every time we wave the flag or sing the national anthem. So, I might add, are Rastafarianism, Anglicanism, Seventh Day Adventism, Socialism, Capitalism, Democracy and Oxfam . . . I am trying to make sure I spread my insults around. Failure, like doubt, is the food of faith and hope and charity. And we must not abandon our imaginative enterprise just because we encounter failure or have doubts. Indeed, without them, there can be no trick . . . and no Caribbean.

> I say we had best look our times and lands searchingly in the face, like a physician diagnosing some deep disease. Never was there, perhaps, more hollowness at heart

than at present. . . . The underlying principles of the state are not honestly believed in (for all this hectic glow, and these melodramatic screamings), nor is humanity itself believed in. What penetrating eye does not everywhere see through the mask? The spectacle is appalling. We live in an atmosphere of hypocrisy through-out. The men believe not in the women, nor the women in the men. A scornful superciliousness rules in literature. The aim of all critics is to find something to make fun of. A lot of churches and sects usurp the name of religion. . . . From deceit in the spirit, the mother of all false deeds, the offspring is already incalculable. The depravity of our business classes is not less than has been supposed, but infinitely greater. The cities reek with respectable as much as non-respectable robbery. . . . True, indeed, behind this fantastic farce enacted on the visible stage of society, solid things and stupendous labours are to be discovered, existing crudely and going on in the background, to advance and tell themselves in time. Yet the truths are none the less terrible. I say that our New World democracy, however great a suc-cess . . . in materialistic development, products and in a certain highly deceptive superficial popular intellectuality, is, so far, an almost complete failure in its social aspects, and in really grand religious, moral, literary and aesthetic results.[4]

This is not the Caribbean in 2002, but Walt Whitman in 1870, speaking of the United States. But then – and this is where Kamau comes in again – Whitman sings one of his great praise songs.

With strong music I come, with my cornets and my drums
I play not marches for accepted victors only, I play marches for conquer'd and slain persons.

Have you heard that it was good to gain the day?
I also say it is good to fall, battles are lost in the same spirit in which they are won . . .

Vivas to those who have fail'd![5]

This is the music of failure. It is all of our music. It is the music that Kamau has made into the chorus of the Caribbean, first with Count Ossie and the Mystic Revelation of Rastafari and in many other forms since. It is the music of Psalm 137, of the sufferers, of the half that has never been told, of Buju Banton's "Untold Story" and Lorna Goodison's "Mother, the Great Stone's Got to Move". It does not constitute a recipe for acquiescence – try suggesting that to Lorna Goodison or Buju Banton or Kamau or Ras Kumi. On the contrary, it is the only real programme of imaginative resistance, for it is the only one that holds us close to the centre of contradiction, the centre of both our failure to catch speech in writing – an inevitable shortcoming, and also the site of new freedom – and our failure, or at least the failure of our great singers and storytellers, to turn the representation of suffering into an experience of anguish. They do the opposite. "By the Rivers of Babylon" is sung with heartfelt dread and holy joy, which the sweet sound of the Melodians – who gave it a contemporary harmony – intensifies. U2's great hymn, "I Still Haven't Found What I'm Looking For", surely the signature statement of human failure, brings not only tears to the fifty thousand fans singing it at the rock concert but also the purest pleasure. How can it "feel so good to hurt so bad?" asks Elton John in "Sad Songs". This paradox is the basis of our most powerful forms of art. Loss of a loved one, longing for home, looking for something and failing to find it – these don't make us feel very good. But stories and songs about them do. Listening to Linton Kwesi Johnson read "Reggae fi Dada", I am both broken into pieces and made whole. And I am not alone.

We have all but forgotten about this contradiction; or at least critics seem to have, for no good writer or artist can. It is closely related to the contradiction at the heart of all representation. "It was, and it was not." "The happening that is not happening". If we try to choose between them, we lose both. Fortunately, we know much more about this than we sometimes admit. There are nursery rhymes and national anthems. And riddles, to which we are introduced very early in our lives, have the same character. For a riddle to work, we must both believe its nonsense – a cherry without any stone, a chicken without any bone – and disbelieve it; otherwise, when told about the cherry blossom and the egg, we will just shrug our shoulders.

Some riddles – as it were on behalf of metaphors and myths – are harder to shrug off because their answer presents another riddle, like a set of Chinese boxes or Russian dolls nested inside each other, except in this case they get larger and larger rather than smaller and smaller.

> Tyger, Tyger, burning bright
> In the forests of the night,
> What immortal hand or eye
> Could frame thy fearful symmetry?

And some riddles push us to the brink of incomprehension and panic . . . or maybe it is the peace that passeth understanding. "This is my body," says the priest at a Christian communion, holding a wafer and quoting Jesus at the Last Supper. Then he eats it, and asks us to do the same. Does he think we're crazy; or worse still, that we're cannibals? Is he?

Well, not exactly; and yet anyone who takes the Christian communion seriously believes that the wafer and the wine at the very least "stand for" the body and the blood of Christ. Some even accept that the wafer and the wine, at least for the moment of communion, *are* the body and the blood. Theologians call it transubstantiation. Literary critics call it metaphor. We might as well call it a contradiction. And a pretty unnerving one at that.

Yet we are remarkably comfortable with it. Not necessarily with the communion service, of course, though lots of people the world over believe in something like this within their various religions. But even those who do not, those who are unlikely to believe in things such as transubstantiation, routinely repeat the creed of their faith in defiance of the very dubious things that it contains and the doubt that is in their hearts. I mean no disrespect by this; for at the moment of saying so they *do* believe.

There's something else that's odd here. These moments of confessional contradiction, singing psalms or hymns or along with Buju Banton and U2, are usually communal – with witnesses, that is. Why would we want to say such questionable things where others can hear us? We do so quite often. When we sing our national anthems we use words and phrases about people and places that we would almost certainly question in any other context. We say we believe when maybe we really don't . . . except right at that moment, the ceremonial moment when the border is crossed and the covenant is renewed. Religious creeds are believed, Oscar Wilde used to say, not because they are true but because they are repeated. This was not a way of dismissing them; it was a way of acknowledging them. In Caribbean political and cultural studies, we need to bring this understanding of metaphor and ritual to bear on all aspects of social expression *not* as cultural documents but as arenas of contradiction, the kind of contradiction that literature and liturgy represent all the time.

In the early 1980s Mortimo Planno wrote down his history of Rastafari – which he gave to Lambros Comitas, who returned it to him, bound in glory, on the occasion of the first Caribbean Culture conference at the University of the West Indies in honour of Rex Nettleford in 1996. Ras Kumi called it "The Earth Most Strangest Man", and it tells how Rastafarians overstand the world and their place in it. It is both an elegy and a redemption song. Most of all, it is a riddle about home and a testimonial to the imaginative contradiction at the heart of the Rastafarian community.

"Believe it or not" seems to be its challenge, as it seems to be the challenge of every riddle. But in fact this should be rephrased. Believe it *and* not is the fundamental challenge of every riddle, of every metaphor, of every myth, of every religion, of every community. They come to life in contradiction, not uncertainty. Kamau Brathwaite, Ras Kumi and Rastafari are determined to keep the challenge and the contradiction alive, as Michael Smith did so memorably in his great poem, "Mi Say Mi Cyaan Believe It". When we lose a sense of this, myth degenerates into ideology, religion into dogma, and communities into totalitarian chaos or civil war. *Did the Greeks Believe Their Myths?* asks the French classicist Paul Veyne in the title of his wonderful book. Yes and no, he answers.

"As it is written in the Psalms of David," says Ras Kumi, " 'To Every Song is a Sign' and I an I always Sing the Songs of the Signs of the Time . . . get[ting] solace from the words of the Bible."[6] The contradictions in which he engages us go very deep into how we understand who we are and where we belong. They are also deeply troubling to many people. And so they must be, if they are to nourish our imaginations and – we don't want to forget this – sustain our realities. In a long tradition of visionary thinking, Ras Kumi insists that the past *is* present, and that Africans in the Americas *are* the Israelites in Babylon. This kind of radical imagining – in which the contradiction is as clear as it must be in any metaphor – is for Ras Kumi the only kind that can resist the grotesque pressure of historical reality. Literary critic Hugh Hodges reminds us that for Rastafari, Babylon is not a metaphor for the world; the world is a metaphor for Babylon. Africa is not a metaphor for home; home is a metaphor for Africa. The world is a metaphor for the Word. To become preoccupied with the literal and the figurative is to miss the point entirely, muffling the dread that accompanies all true acts of the imagination.

These radical reimaginings of reality, these reversals of the direction of metaphor, are vintage Rastafari. And they recall those of that other visionary, William Blake, whom I just quoted – an Englishman, which I realize requires a radical reimagining of another sort for many in the Caribbean! Babylon was a place of the diminished imagination for Blake, as it is for Ras Kumi; and the only freedom worthy of the name is to be found in the liberated and inspired imagination. The turn to the Bible – for Blake as for Rastafari – is not an escape from the world but an acceptance of it, creating what Blake's contemporary Samuel Taylor Coleridge called "a science of realities".

This is a compelling notion, and it is absolutely central to metaphor and indeed to all imaginative revelations of the word. But it is not comfortable, for it informs both the fundamental imaginings of Blake and Ras Kumi and Kamau Brathwaite and the fundamentalism of those who would interpret the Bible literally in ways they might not accept. It comes down to a question of whose science, and whose realities. As historian Donald Akenson has pointed out, for those who see themselves as chosen people – he talks specifically about Afrikaaners, Israelis and Ulster Scots, but he could be talking about Africans in exile – the Bible is not a code to be deciphered but a code that determines their destiny, the way their genetic code does. Chosen to suffer. Bound to return. Both in a binding covenant.

The most urgent challenge facing all of us who believe in the power of the word lies right here: to negotiate between the word as a determining force and the word as a form of freedom. This is an ancient challenge, and an urgently contemporary one. It is bound up in contradictory ideas about language itself: determining thoughts and feelings on the one hand; and empowering them on the other. In the first mode, language is a prison-house; in the second, it is a liberating agent. But the first also gives us a sense of community – there's no community quite like a prison community – in which every language, every dialect, is (in Frantz Fanon's words) a way of thinking. Once again, this is where the idea of nation language can be so unsettling – and *must* be, if it is to have any force other than as a postcolonial fetish. For like all things national, nation language generates categories of both loyalty *and* betrayal, and creates the illusion – or is it the reality? – of both a binding covenant and the birth of a new day. As Akenson suggests in the last lines of his book *God's Peoples,*

> the Hebrew covenantal structure has lasted from the middle bronze age to the pres-
> ent. It is one of the few things in human society that we can take for granted in the
> sense that it will be here longer than we will. Indeed, much longer. Modern-day
> Israel is only the most recent society to conform to the covenantal blueprint, but
> it will not be the last. Others will follow, for the covenant, as found in the books
> of Moses, is particularly suited to the sorts of smaller societies that are inevitably
> produced as great empires come apart and as small ethnic groups become inde-
> pendent of their former masters. Far from disappearing . . . the covenantal cosmol-
> ogy, based on the ancient Hebrew template, will be one of the most effective ways
> for a myriad of small nations to fortify themselves in a world that will increasingly
> be confusion and whirl.[7]

Whether this is a genial prospect I leave it for you to decide.

. . . • . . .

Let me close with a final story, turning back to where I began on a note of hope. Two stories in fact, based on quite different understandings of the world, and of the word. The Gitksan people of the northwest of British Columbia have lived in the mountains fishing and hunting and farming and trading for thousands of years. They have a story that tells of changes to one of the river valleys, near the mountain called Stekyooden, across from the village of Temlaxam. It was once the centre of their world, one of those places that bring peace and prosperity to the people who live there.

This valley nourished the Gitksan people so well that they became unmindful of their good fortune and forgot the ways that the mountains and the rivers and the plants and the animals had taught them. The spirit of the valley, a grizzly bear called Mediik who lived by Stekyooden, warned them and gave them many signs of his anger; but they ignored these warnings, until finally he got so angry that he came roaring down from the top of the mountain. Grizzlies running uphill are breathtakingly fast; I've been chased by one, and he looked like a freight train impersonating a gazelle. But because their front legs are short, grizzlies sometimes tumble coming downhill . . . and Mediik brought half the mountain with him, covering the valley floor and the village of Temlaxam and all the people there. Only a few survived, those who were out hunting in the high country or berry picking on the opposite slopes or doing the hard work that makes for an easy life.

This was just about thirty-five hundred years ago. Over time, the people returned to the valley, and although never the rich and fertile home it once had been, it always held its place in their history; and they remember the great grizzly and the lesson he taught them. Today the stories of the Gitksan move out from that valley like spokes from the centre of a wheel or children from their parents. It is the centre of their lives, the place they came from, and the place to which they return their thoughts and their thanks. Their present-day claims to the territory arise from the claims which the valley has on them, and the story of the grizzly and the slide confirms both claims.

Several years ago, when the Gitksan were forced to assert their claims in the courts of the new people in the valley, my people, they told this story. They told it with all the ritual that it required, for the stories and songs that represent their past are about belief, and therefore need ceremony.

So do all stories, they realized. They also realized that the story of the grizzly and the sacred mountain called Stekyooden and the village of Temlaxam,
which in their minds confirmed the presence of their people in that place for
millennia, might not be believed by the judge, schooled as he was in stories
of a different sort. So one of their leaders, Neil Sterritt, suggested they draw on
another story line to complement their own. They had geologists drill under
the lake (now called Seely Lake) that fills the valley and take a core sample and
analyse it. A scientific ceremony. They discovered soil and plant material
which matched the clay high up on the mountain slope, exposed where the
grizzly had taken down the hillside – or where the earthquake had produced
the slide that brought down half the mountain. And the sample was dated
exactly when their story said the grizzly grew angry with the people in the valley, thirty-five hindred years ago.

The court was inclined to see the scientific story as confirming the leg-
endary one. However the elders of the Gitksan were at pains to persuade the
judge that each story was validated by the other: that neither had a monop-
oly on understanding what happened; that the story line of geology was
framed by a narrative just as much the product of invention as the story told
by their people; and that each storyteller's imagination – whether telling of
tectonic plates or of grizzly outrage – was engaged with a reality that included
much more than the merely human. That was the trick.

The story of the grizzly is a very old one, hardened on an anvil of ancient
tellings and tested by memories that disputed it for much longer than our
seismic and sedimentary theories. The Gitksan believe both of them. Both, for
them, are true. Both are necessary for their people to live their lives. And both
are revealed in stories. The Mediik story is familiar, of course, because it is the
story of a flood: *the* flood, for the Gitksan. But its power comes not from that
connection alone, nor from the fact that flood stories are very common across
cultures, but from the way it complements other historical and scientific
accounts, and insists on its own authority. By putting such stories side by side
we can see how, in their different ways, they display both the ordinariness of
human existence and the extraordinary powers that surround and affect us.
This is the best words can do. And it is a great deal.

Notes

1. Daniel Kemmis, *Community and the Politics of Place* (Norman, Okla.: University of Oklahoma Press, 1990), 3–4.
2. Lewis Hyde, *Trickster Makes this World: Mischief, Myth and Art* (New York: Farrar, Straus and Giroux, 1998), 209.
3. Marshall McLuhan, *The Gutenberg Galaxy: The Making of Typographic Man* (Toronto: University of Toronto Press, 1962), 50.
4. Walt Whitman, "Democratic Vistas", in his *Complete Poetry and Selected Prose*, ed. James E. Miller, Jr. (Boston: Houghton Mifflin, 1959), 461.
5. Whitman, "Song of Myself", in *Complete Poetry and Selected Prose*, 37.
6. From "The Earth Most Strangest Man", transcribed from the handwritten original by Lambros Comitas and given back to Ras Kumi in a ceremony at the University of the West Indies in Jamaica in 1997. I published excerpts (with Ras Kumi's permission) in an issue of *Index on Censorship* on "Tribes: Battle for Land and Language" that I co-edited in 1996; the full text has circulated in the Rastafarian community, but not far beyond.
7. Donald H. Akenson, *God's Peoples: Covenant and Land in South Africa, Israel and Ulster* (Montreal: McGill–Queen's University Press, 1991), 356–57.

4

When Form Becomes Substance
Discourse on Discourse in Two Calypsos

Hubert **Devonish** |

Theoretical Background: The Performance Speech Event

Language distinguishes itself from other communication systems in a variety
of ways. One such is its ability to communicate messages about any topic its
users may wish, including messages about language itself. The entire discipline of linguistics, for example, uses language to communicate about language, its forms, its structures and its meanings.

When language is used in social contexts, there exists a range of rules and
conventions about who speaks, when, how, about what and to whom. Thus,
in some cultures, a social visit might involve an exchange of greetings
between the visitor and the visited, an invitation to enter and be seated from
the host, and an exchange of inquiries about the health and welfare of the
interlocutors and of members of their respective families. This could be followed up by an offer of refreshments and an exchange over what refreshments the visitor would prefer. After this, there might occur a less predictable
body of conversation and then, after a remark by the visitor that it was already
late and that the host had been inconvenienced sufficiently, a leave-taking
exchange, inclusive of goodbyes, door opening and waving. These verbal rit-

uals are rule governed. This can be seen by considering how the meanings of the verbal exchange would be affected if communication sequences were altered. What if, on the approach of the visitor, the host said "Goodbye" instead of "Hello"? Or if there had been a switch in who said what, so that, towards the end of the conversation, it was the host rather than the guest who indicated that it was already late and that she or he had been inconvenienced enough already!

Language communication always involves a social context and a series of rules governing the internal structure of the discourse. The term used in linguistics to cover an entire body of discourse such as that of a social visit would be a speech event. The specific phases such as the greeting exchange, the dialogue surrounding the offer of refreshments, the leave-taking sequence and so forth are referred to as speech acts.[1]

It is significant that not only can language be used to discuss itself, but bodies of discourse such as speech events and their component speech acts can also be used to communicate messages about themselves. Formal negotiation between a trade union and an employer constitutes a speech event. A frequent feature of such negotiations is negotiations about negotiation: that is, negotiation between the two parties about the form negotiations should take, the order in which matters would be discussed, who would speak first, and so on. These are talks about talks. Put another way, discourse is being used to discuss the structure of discourse.

In normal or what I shall call nonperformance speech events, the forms of communication are subordinate to meanings they communicate. The structure of the speech events and the speech acts that constitute them are primarily means to an end; the end is to communicate a set of messages or information aimed at successfully pursuing a transaction. Thus, political oratory, bargaining over the price of produce in the market, or the negotiation of a salary agreement between employer and trade union may all be pursued in ways that are admired by observers or other participants. However, inducing pleasure in observers or other interlocutors is merely a means to some other end.

Contrast this with the subtype of speech event I shall refer to as the performance speech event. Performance speech events tend to be governed by discourse rules far more complex and constraining than those of normal speech events. There is another feature that distinguishes performance speech events: their primary objective is to evoke admiration and pleasure. The object of this admiration and pleasure is the verbal skill involved in executing a creative speech act within the extremely tight formal constraints imposed on it by the requirements of the performance speech event. These constraints may, depending on the traditions of the speech community, involve poetic metre, rhyme, alliteration, versification and musical form. By way of contrast with nonperformance speech events, here the communication of informational content, though necessary, is merely a means to an end, the end of producing speech acts possessing an aesthetically pleasing form.

Performance speech acts, like nonperformance ones, can have as their information content their own structure and that of the speech events of which they are a part. Here too, discourse can be the subject of discourse, with discourse being used to reflect upon and discuss itself. As already pointed out, however, the form of performance speech events is primary. Any content is merely a device for enhancing the appreciation of the form of the performance discourse. This is equally true when the topic is some aspect of the discourse itself. However, things can and do get a bit more complicated. This is certainly the case when performance speech acts have as their topic their own form or that of the speech event to which they belong. In such a case, the actual form that that speech act eventually takes can convey messages that either reinforce or undermine the content. It is this relationship between form and content that this chapter will examine, using two calypsos sung by the 2001 Pic-O-De-Crop Calypso Monarch for Barbados, Adrian Clarke, to win the calypso competition. The songs are "This Melody" and "Judgement".

The Pic-O-De-Crop Calypso Competition

The model for calypso competitions around the Caribbean is that of Trinidad. The variant adopted in Barbados is fairly typical; it involves a contest between singers, not songs. To qualify to be part of the competition process, a performer must have a minimum of two songs, each of which must be new and, in the competition, sung by only one competitor. Songs used at any level of the competition – that is, in the tents, in the semifinal or the final – must conform to this requirement. The requirement that the songs be new and exclusive to individual competitors is important: it helps to maintain the fiction that performers have written and composed the songs they sing and have done so specially for the current year's competition. This, in turn, adds to the spirit of competition amongst the performers and to the heightened public interest and partisanship the competition produces.

The place where an individual competitor performs these songs for the competitive process is the calypso tent. These tents open at the start of the Crop Over season of which the competition is a part, and play to paying audiences in halls, with the support of a backing band, back-up singers and an emcee. Tent performances typically are divided into two sessions, separated by an intermission. In the first session, the performers belonging to the tent perform one song and in the second session, another. A judging panel appointed by the National Cultural Foundation, the organization running the competition, will, in the course of the season, visit each of the tents. Using a set of judging criteria and a system of points, they judge each performer based on the presentation of his or her two songs. They choose the best sixteen performers to be entered into the Pic-O-De-Crop semifinals.

In the semifinal, performing before a much larger audience than in the tents, the selected semifinalists perform two songs. The order of performances is determined by the drawing of lots. The songs are usually but not necessarily the same two that were performed in the tent. A panel of judges selects seven of the competitors for the Pic-O-De-Crop final. The reigning monarch, the winner from the previous year, is an automatic entrant in the final, bringing the total number of competitors in the final to eight.

For the final, the audience before whom the performances take place is larger than at any other stage of the competition. The final consists of two sessions; each of the eight competitors performs two songs, one song per session. The order of performance is again determined by drawing lots. As for the songs performed, these are most often but not necessarily the songs performed at other stages of the competition. A panel of judges hears and witnesses the performances and, based on a set of scoring criteria, assigns points for the various performances and uses their scores to identify the Pic-O-De-Crop Calypso Monarch for the year. On the announcement of the winner, the band strikes up and the winner does a verse or two of one of his or her songs, the musical equivalent of a lap of honour.

The Calypso Competition as Speech Event

The calypso competition is a single, albeit complex, speech event. It lasts over several weeks. It proceeds firstly by way of speech acts performed by the calypsonians in the calypso tents, and then by speech acts performed by smaller and smaller subgroups of singers as the competition moves through the semi-final and final stages. However, there are shared features which hold all of these speech acts together as part of a single speech event. Each speech act "belongs" to a specific interlocutor, a calypsonian-cum-competitor, and is directed at one set of hearers, the judges. Each speech act has a single commu-nicative purpose: to so distinguish itself in its form by comparison with speech acts performed by other competitors that its performer is adjudged winner of the Pic-O-De-Crop Calypso Monarch competition.

Specifically, the features of form that were part of the 2001 judging criteria were: lyrics – 30 per cent, melody – 30 per cent, rendition – 20 per cent, orig-inality – 15 per cent, presentation – 5 per cent.[2] Given that this is a competi-tion involving songs with lyrics, it is understandable that an equal number of points are available for lyrics and for melody. With reference to the points for rendition and originality, these presumably are divided equally between lyrics and melody.

There is absolutely no restriction placed on the possible topics or combina-tion of topics which can be covered by songs. Topics cover an enormous range: history, political and social commentary, sex, tragedy, and comedy. However, the Pic-O-De-Crop competition has produced, over the years, a set of closely related topics specific to itself as a speech event. These involve: (1) the lyrical or musical form of the genre of calypso, including if and how a particular song that has been or is being used in competition fits into this genre; (2) the quality of singers and/or songs in the current or previous com-petitions; (3) the judges' decisions in previous competitions and the likely decisions in the current one. We have here discourse, in the form of a speech act, having discourse as its subject. This can be the speech act itself or the speech event of which the speech act is a part.

This discourse about the discourse is the product of the competitive nature of the speech event. The musical, lyrical and performance standards for the speech acts – that is, the songs – which make up the speech event are not gov-erned by any explicit formal code. Rather, these standards exist in collectively held notions that are constantly the subject of communal negotiation. This negotiation involves, among others, the lyrics writers and music composers, the performers, the judges, and members of the public. There is a continuing pressure to stay within what are considered to be the rules for the genre; com-peting performers in a calypso competition need to be considered to be singing calypso rather than some other type of song. On the other hand, there is the requirement that songs and performances be original, with judges awarding points for originality. This produces pressure in the opposite direction: to extend each speech act or song beyond established limits, thus potentially compromising the identity of the genre.

Evidence of this constant negotiation can be found in the *Dictionary of Caribbean English Usage* with regard to the entry "soca". Currently, soca is accepted as a subgenre of calypso; however, at the time of its rise to popularity in 1978, its identity as calypso was heatedly contested by many. To assist with the definition of the term "soca", the dictionary provides us with a passage in which the word is used in context. The passage turns out to be a classic example of the public controversy involved in identifying musical norms within the context of calypso competitions as speech events. It is a telling extract from a 1978 report in the Trinidad press on what appears to be a statement by the Calypsonians' Association about the position of the Carnival Development Committee, the body then in charge of Trinidad and Tobago Carnival, with regard to soca songs in the calypso competition of that year: "The association is refusing to accept the CDC's statement that they leave it all up to the judges to decide what is soca and what is calypso and to draw the line between them."[3]

The Data

This chapter carries out an analysis of the two songs sung by the winning performer, Adrian Clarke, "AC", during the Pic-O-De-Crop Calypso Monarch Competition of Barbados 2001. "This Melody" was sung during the first session of the final, and "Judgement" during the second. In subtly different ways, both these calypsos are examples of artistic speech acts that involve discourse about discourse.

"This Melody" – Praise Song to a Praise Song to Soca: Form Reinforcing Content

The topic of "This Melody" is soca, itself a disputed synonym for modern calypso in its more upbeat and danceable form. An innovation in Trinidad during the 1970s, soca forced its way, in the face of fierce opposition, into some level of acceptability as a type of calypso; it has since then become the most popular form of calypso. "This Melody", from the perspective of the first-person speaker ("I"), presents a dream in which soca, represented by the third-person singular feminine ("she, her"), is dying. The lyrics encapsulate criticisms of soca in its current form:

> She needed transfusions of melody
>
> . . .
>
> Lyrically soca was sufferin'
> Repeatin' topics endangerin'
> Her life hanging on a string
>
> . . .
>
> She ha' de syndrome of jump and wave
>
> . . .
>
> No fresh topics, lyrics or melody

For the transfusions that she needed "[t]here were hardly donors in sight", even though, as

> Soca's children gather roun' she
>
> . . .
>
> They were powerful performers
> Sweet singing and lyrical masters
> Trying to orchestrate a plan. . . .

Obviously alluding to the Mighty Shadow, a veteran innovator within calypso and the winner of the 2001 Calypso Monarch Competition in Trinidad and Tobago, Clarke sings,

> Suddenly hope was found
> Dressed in black from head to toe
> Wearing a grey beard he casted a shadow
>
> . . .
>
> Sweet melodies flowed from his veins
> To give soca fresh lease on life again.

The performance of the song seeks to derive authority from the Mighty Shadow, the then current winner of the premier calypso competition, through the following lines:

As soca rose to her feet
He said it was up to you and me
To keep her out of the casualty
So you see why I'm singing
This melody. . . [chorus continues].

The "you" in the reporting of Shadow's statement refers to Clarke and the "me" to Shadow. Clarke, the aspiring monarch, is associating himself with Shadow, the reigning monarch in Trinidad, the home of calypso. The song delineates what the singer's ideal soca is, involving original lyrics, fresh topics and sweet melodies. The performance speech act that is "This Melody" has the form of soca as its topic, a case of discourse on discourse. Clarke's ideal of soca is revived in the song by the man dressed in black, wearing a beard and casting a shadow – that is, the Mighty Shadow.

This is, in the first instance, a praise song to Clarke's own ideal form of soca. However, through obedience to the pretended injunction from Shadow, the song he is singing is able to save this ideal soca form. We are dealing with a praise song to a praise song.

This melody
I'll give to she
Powerful and strong
To help soca push on.
Each note I sing
I hope will bring
Soca aroun'
To a healthier position.

It is by means of this praise song to the praise song that the singer, Clarke, seeks to beg the question which the judges are supposed to be determining: whether "This Melody" is indeed a quality calypso. The clear aim is to convince the judges that the song represents a fine example of the model of calypso being praised. This is reinforced by the fact that "This Melody" seeks to be, at the level of music, lyrics and topic, that very ideal of soca. There is a clear attempt at achieving congruence between the formal ideals expressed in the content of the lyrics and the actual form of the calypso in which these ideals are expressed.

"Judgement": The Anti-Praise Song to "Authentic" Calypso

Speech Act on Speech Act: Form Versus Content

The content of this performance speech act involves much more than comments on the musical form and verse structure of calypso as a speech act. The scope of the song covers, in the extracts below, respectively, issues of (1) the presentation of the calypso, inclusive of props; (2) the topics covered by the songs; (3) the quality of his own singing; (3) the style of the song, that is, the slow "ballad" as distinct from jump-up calypso; (5) the beat and chord structure of the calypso; (6a) the lyrical content of the calypso, inclusive of the use of the word "wukkie-wukkie", a reference to a song which the Mighty Gabby had won the competition with the previous year; and (6b) stage costume, a reference to the song performed by Gabby in the second session, prior to Clarke's performance of "Judgement", as well as to Clarke's own costume.

Kaisonians spend thousands on presentation
Only gettin' five points and losin' de crown
. . .
Do de judges mean social commentary
Calypso topics on de top, see!
. . .
Half a dem can't sing like me
Dey singin' out a key and come before AC [*line sung out of key*]
. . .
An' tell Elombe dat Adrian holdin' on
To de calypso ballad crown like Rudder, Aloes an Baron
. . .
What kaisonians call a beat roun'
Play de drum [. . . *inaudible*] and let me expoun'
De one four five chord structure
Characteristic of de kaiso genre
. . .
Look, to win a kaiso competition at the stadium
Yu mus' say wukkie-wukkie inside of my song
Do a wedding dance wid a veil 'pon me [*at this point he dons a veil and discards his stage costume to reveal a wedding dress*]
Who de hell does be judgin' we?

Focusing on the last extract above, including the word "wukkie-wukkie" in the song and wearing veil and wedding dress were intended to pillory the reigning monarch, the Mighty Gabby. Singing earlier in the second session, the latter had, as had been expected, appeared on stage in a wedding dress and performed a song about a wedding between two men. Clarke is claiming to sing "authentic" calypso, within which "wukkie-wukkie" and gimmicks such as a wedding veil have no place. However, to make this point he actually uses "wukkie-wukkie" in the song, and chooses as well not just to sing about the wedding veil but to don one on stage. Adopting forms of lyrics and presentation of which he is critical, he deliberately subverts the ostensible substance of the song – that is, that judges who would favourably evaluate songs presented in such a form are unfit to be judges. The singer, knowing the judges to be using criteria with which he does not agree, sings a calypso claiming to be "authentic". The song is critical of the judges but includes the very features which, according to the singer's own criteria, make the calypso inauthentic. However, these features, according to the view presented by the singer, make the song acceptable to the judges, the persons to whom the entire speech act is being directed.

The most interesting interaction between content and form takes place in the first two lines of the song:

> In authentic calypso, dey use to sing the firs' line, boy, did you know
> Dat in authentic calypso, dey use to sing the firs' line, boy, did you know

Not only does the content state that the first line is repeated in authentic calypso, but the first line is actually repeated in the making of this assertion. The notional form of an "authentic" calypso, requiring the repetition of the first line, has been converted into content, by way of an assertion to this effect. In turn, this content has been converted into form, by way of the actual repetition of the first line. Together, these lines seek to establish that the song belongs in the competition as an authentic calypso. On the face of it, it is a classic case of form supporting content. Significantly, however, we get no repeat of the first line in the other two verses of the song. One is left to wonder whether contained in this deviation from the stated ideal form of "authentic calypso" is a suggestion that this song is really itself an imitation rather than the real thing, a hint that the listener should not take the singer or the song too seriously. Form may again not be reinforcing content but rather subverting it.

Other statements are made in the calypso about form. These tend not, however, to reduce the significance of the inconsistency that exists between the formal ideals presented in the content and the actual form of the calypso. This is demonstrated by the following example:

> Well in dat case den, brother man
> For years we haven't had a kaiso competition
> Explain to me how Gabby won wid de tune he sang
> Win a kaiso crown singin' a ringbang.

The issue of form here involves the suggestion that the reigning monarch, against whom the singer is competing, won the crown fraudulently the previous year by singing a ringbang – this is a hybrid musical form involving calypso influenced by rhythms of the Barbadian tuk band. The singer's commitment to "authentic" calypso, it seems, may be merely a tactical convenience in the context of a competitive speech event, the calypso competition.

Speech Act on Speech Event: Speech Event Versus Content

In a speech event particular roles are assigned to specific interlocutors who, in the course of the speech acts that make up the event, perform the role of either speaker or listener, addresser or addressee. In "Judgement" the issues of who the interlocutors are and whether they have a right to be performing their roles are explicitly addressed.

In a calypso competition the crowd before whom the performance takes place is merely a secondary audience: the real or primary addressees are the judges. The purpose of participating in such a competition is to win. The people who determine the winner are the panel of judges. The entire performance of a speech act – a song – is, therefore, targeted at primary addressees. "Judgement", as a calypso, does not simply look inwards at itself and its form; it also concerns itself openly with the response it is likely to get from those to whom it is addressed, the judges.

In parts of the song the judges are addressed directly in their role as primary addressees, referred to in the second person ("you", "your"):

> What's your credential?
> Do you have a right to judge me at all?
> Do you know a major from minor key?

Are you de [. . . *inaudible*] musically?

You go to de tents, you love kaiso

Dat gives you de right to judge, I want to know

Crowd response and favouritism

And politics does judge de calypsonian

You do de wrong ting to get dis kaisonian upset

Crowd response you want, is crowd response you gon get [*accompanied by a gesture inviting the crowd to cheer*].

The norm in a calypso competition would be to pretend that the judges do not exist, and directly address the audience; this was the approach adopted in Clarke's first song, "This Melody". Here, however, the topic of the song is the judges' right and competence to judge. The existence of the judges as the primary addressees is, therefore, openly acknowledged, and the judges are addressed directly with the pronouns "you" and "your". It is significant, in the above lines, exactly when the secondary addressees, the live audience, come to be acknowledged by the singer: it is at the point where the singer claims to disagree with the judges for taking into account extraneous factors, such as crowd response, in making their decisions. Implicitly accepting that this is part of how the judges actually do make up their minds, the singer asks the crowd to give him the response he needs in order to win. The singer, in the course of challenging what he claims are implicit rules governing the speech event, panders to them in pursuit of victory. The substance of the position he is criticizing is turned into a form and formula calculated to bring victory.

The alternative and more usual way to present a calypso is to pretend that the secondary addressees, the crowd, are the primary audience, and, where an address form is required, to address them as "you". This is the approach adopted for most of "Judgement". The judges become inadvertent third-person eavesdroppers, referred to as "they" and "them" as they are attacked for, among other things, not knowing what "authentic" calypso is. The use of this strategy is seen in the following examples:

An' dem kaiso judges, please doan blame dem for me

Is not dey fault dat dey cannot judge properly

. . .

Who de hell does be judgin' we?

. . .

> When dey announce Gabby win de crown
> Cameras zoom in on RPB and King John
> Maybe de Bag look like a Johnny
> So who de hell does be judgin' we?
>
> . . .
>
> An' de Party Monarch was like Nixon's Watergate
> De extra time he took can't be found on any tape
> Dey unfair Rupee but he jump everybody
> Win road march from Bridgetown to Miami
> So who de hell does be judgin' we?

This pattern continues into the pseudo-extemporaneous portion of the song towards the end of the presentation. This section involves new lyrics which are prepared for the occasion of the final and delivered as if they were improvised on the spot. The lines in this portion of the song often deviate from the core subject of the song and tend to mock other contestants, the critics and the judges.

> Do you remember 1988 Crop Over
> Who de hell does be judgin' we?
> When dey gi' de King Crown to Queen Rita
> Who de hell does be judgin' we?
> Put a light on dem judges quick leh me see [*exactly on cue, a bright white spotlight shines on the judges' enclosure*]
> Who de hell does be judgin' we?

Of course, in spite of the rhetorical question, "Who de hell does be judging we?", Clarke would have known the names of the judges; he did not need the aid of the spotlight to be able to discover their identities. Neither did he really question the right of the judges to select a calypso monarch; his very participation in the competition contradicted a literal interpretation of the lyrics of "Judgement". The only possible primary addressees in the speech act that is a calypso competition are the judges. If he did not want to be assessed by this panel of judges, what was he doing on stage as a contestant in the Pic-O-De-Crop final?

Conclusion

In performance speech acts such as the ones analysed in this chapter, form often becomes the subject of the content. However, in performance speech acts content is secondary; form is primary. The most effective way to communicate about form in such a speech act is to use it. Thus, in a performance speech act that has lyrical content proposing some ideal form of the speech act genre, one would expect that ideal form to be used in the actual performance of the speech act. In such circumstances the form of the speech act ends up reinforcing the content. In "This Melody", Adrian Clarke sings praises to what he proposes to be soca in its finest form, and uses as his medium a soca song which corresponds to the ideals he presents. In "Judgement", by contrast, he sings praises to authentic calypso by way of a calypso which is designed to be inauthentic according to the very standards laid down in the song. The decision about which option to select is made strategically in light of the goal of all competitors: to win the competition.

A dilemma was created for the singer, Adrian Clarke, when he was declared winner of the Pic-O-De-Crop Calypso Monarch Competition for 2001. It is traditional for the winner to sing, in celebration of victory, a couple of verses from the more popular or competitive of the two competition songs. "Judgement" was clearly the more popular of his two songs; it was also the one he considered more competitive, since he chose to sing it in the second session rather than in the first. Clarke's dilemma was that to sing "Judgement" would have confirmed that incompetent judges, swayed by "wukkie-wukkie" lyrics, gimmicks and crowd response, had named him, the singer of an "inauthentic" calypso, winner. He would also have been rejecting their decision by asking the question, "Who de hell are you to judge me?"

His choice of "This Melody" as the "victory lap" song made a clear statement about the real intent behind the lyrics of "Judgement". It was not to call the competence of the judges into question but to pander, albeit mockingly, to the whims of the judges in order to achieve victory. The goal of participation in a calypso competition is, in spite of occasional protestations to the contrary, to win, and by any means necessary.

Appendix 1

This Melody

1

Last night as I lay sleeping
I had a dream and I woke up crying
Cause it frighten me
I dreamt soca was dying
Vital signs need stabilising
Lord [. . . *inaudible*] beat
Her BPM was 150
She needed transfusions of melody
There were hardly donors in sight
Could she make it through the night
Her pulse was not of a consistent beat
And her heart was getting weak
Must do something quick
Before to the great beyond she slip
So that is why I am singing

Chorus
This melody
I'll give to she
Powerful and strong
To help soca push on.
Each note I sing
I hope will bring
(My) Soca around
To a healthier position.
Oh, la, la, I say oh
We carry Miss Soca home.

2

Soca's children gather roun' she
With solemn faces and eyes all teary
Wanting to lend a hand
They were powerful performers
Sweet singing and lyrical masters

Trying to orchestrate a plan
Lyrically soca was sufferin'
Repeatin' topics endangerin'
Her life hanging on a string
Need an antidote, the right medicine
She ha' de syndrome of jump and wave
Destined to take her to her grave
Fever rose another degree
Soca demise seem likely
So you see why I'm singing

(*Chorus*)

3

Then now she's lost and lonely
No fresh topics, lyrics and melody
Suddenly hope was found
Dressed in black from head to toe
Wearing a grey beard he casted a shadow
On all gathered around
People [. . . *inaudible*] a topic
Or to fight for good [. . . *inaudible*] lyrics
Sweet melodies flowed from his veins
To give soca fresh lease on life again
Check dem, her pulse and her heart beat
As soca rose to her feet
He said it was up to you and me
To keep her out of the casualty
So you see why I'm singing

(*Chorus*)

Adrian Clarke (2001)

Appendix 2

Judgement

1

In authentic calypso, dey use to sing the firs' line, boy, did you know
Dat in authentic calypso, dey use to sing the firs' line, boy, did you know
Well in dat case den, brother man
For years we haven't had a kaiso competition
Explain to me how Gabby won wid de tune he sang
Win a kaiso crown singin' a ringbang.
An' dem kaiso judges, please doan blame dem for me
Is not dey fault dat dey cannot judge properly
Kaisonians spend thousands on presentation
Only gettin' five points and losin' de crown
We put on a show fuh Minister Maguffy
So who de hell does be judgin' we?
In de lyrics category
Do de judges mean social commentary
Calypso topics on de top, see!
So who de hell does be judgin' we?
Half a dem can't sing like me
Dey singin' out a key and come before AC
Kid Site, could you explain dat to me quickly
Who de hell does be judgin' we?
An' tell Elombe dat Adrian holdin' on
To de calypso ballad crown like Rudder, Aloes and Baron
You want a man who does sing ballad sweeter than Birdie
If Sparrow was me, he would say, Mottley,
Who de hell are you to judge me.
Aha, kaiso . . .

2

Calypso is Calypso
I wonderin' if dem so-called judges know
What kaisonians call a beat roun'
Play de drum [. . . *inaudible*] and let me expoun'
De one four five chord structure

Characteristic of de kaiso genre
So don't be ashamed cause you didn't know
What constitute authentic calypso
And de other judges, self-appointed, is true
Dey flappin' dey mouth and dem just don't have a clue
Look, he play kaiso, so suddenly
He feel he ha' de right to say "Lef me at de semi"
I don't admire you givin' you mouth liberty
Who de hell are you to judge me?
You serenade we jokers in de pack
But dis joker heah still got [. . . *inaudible*] back
I really tink you should be up heah wid me
But who de hell are you to judge me?
When dey announce Gabby win de crown
Cameras zoom in on RPB and King John
Maybe de Bag look like a Johnny
So who de hell does be judgin' we?
Maybe was money talkin' through he big mouth
It was beyond de imagination how dem two get beat out
John wasn't so bad but sixth place for RPB
Make de five time monarch ask me,
Who de hell does be judgin' we?
Aha, kaiso . . .

3

What's your credential?
Do you have a right to judge me at all?
Do you know a major from minor key?
Are you de [. . . *inaudible*] musically?
You go to de tents, you love kaiso
Dat gives you de right to judge, I want to know
Crowd response and favouritism
And politics does judge de calypsonian
You do de wrong ting to get dis kaisonian upset
Crowd response you want, is crowd response you gon get
Look, to win a kaiso competition at de stadium
You mus' say wukkie-wukkie inside of my song
Do a wedding dance wid a veil 'pon me

Who de hell does be judgin' we?

Seven crowns and three motor car

An' still he got to drive roun' wid a chauffeur

An' got de guts to come to carry way my Mitsubishi

Who de hell does be judgin' we?

As fuh de one dat dey call Fingall

He doan give a damn bout de judges at all

Rat in de prelim, ride out di semi

For who de hell does be judgin' we?

An' de Party Monarch was like Nixon's Watergate

De extra time he took can't be found on any tape

Dey unfair Rupee but he jump everybody

Win road march from Bridgetown to Miami

So who de hell does be judgin' we?

Would you sing with me, sing it out, sing it out, I beggin' you

Who de hell does be judgin' we?

Do you remember 1988 Crop Over

Who de hell does be judgin' we?

When dey gi' de King Crown to Queen Rita

Who de hell does be judgin' we?

Put a light pon dem judges quick, leh mi see

Who de hell does be judgin' we?

Dey fire one last year, she sue me an' TC

Who de hell does be judgin' we?

Now you tink I got better legs than Gabby?

Who de hell does be judgin' we?

                              Adrian Clarke (2001)

Notes

1. D. Hymes, "The Ethnography of Speaking", in *Readings in the Sociology of Language*, ed. J. Fishman (The Hague: Mouton, 1962), 99–138.

2. *Weekend Nation* (Barbados), 3 August 2001, 35.

3. R. Allsopp, *Dictionary of Caribbean English Usage* (Oxford: Oxford University Press, 1996), 517. The extract is taken from the *Trinidad Express*, 10 January 1978, 1.

5

A Language of Myth

Jeanne **Christensen** |

In his 1967–68 article "Jazz and the West Indian Novel", Kamau Brathwaite writes:

> It should be clear by now that what I am attempting in this study is the delineation of a possible alternative to the European cultural tradition which has been imposed upon us and which we have more or less accepted and absorbed, for obvious historical reasons, as the only way of going about our business.[1]

Paget Henry also calls for an alternative to the "Western project" in the passionate closing remarks of his landmark study, *Caliban's Reason:* "What is the anthropological significance of the Western project?" he asks.

> What is the meaning of its complete rejection of the need for mythic compromises? Is it, as Foucault asks, that man's destiny includes "positing himself also as he who has killed God and whose existence includes the freedom and the decision of that murder?" Is this *Yuruguan* hubris or is it the grandest vision of the human so far imagined? If we think that it is the former, then it is important that we disengage more radically from the momentum and rhythms of the Western project, while allowing the projects that have been taking shape in Caliban's reason to come to fruition.[2]

Brathwaite focuses on folk culture and Henry emphasizes the importance of integrating the poeticist wing of Caribbean philosophy. In both cases, these alternatives fall within a larger category which I am here calling a language of myth.

In this chapter I would like to examine a discourse – to which Brathwaite, Henry, Wilson Harris, the Rastafari and many others in the Caribbean are making important contributions – that challenges the dominant orientation of Western intellectual thought. Two broad tendencies within this thought are: an assumption that the development of reason, objectivity and science render a language of myth superfluous – that a language of logic outgrows a language of myth as an adult outgrows a child – and a related assumption that this so-called evolution from myth to logic is universal and in the nature of things, and cultures in which a language of myth continues to be operative are simply childlike, backward or primitive. The discourse I wish to examine here struggles against these assumptions.

These two assumptions of Western intellectual thought have a long history, going back perhaps to Plato's banning of poetry from his utopian society, the Republic. According to Eric Havelock,

> [Plato] seems to want to destroy poetry as poetry, to exclude her as a vehicle of communication . . . [He] attacks the very form and substance of the poetised statement, its images, its rhythm, its choice of poetic language. Nor is he any less hostile to the range of experience which the poet thus makes available to us. [The poet] can admittedly represent a thousand situations and portray a thousand emotions. This variety is just the trouble. . . . All of this is dangerous, none of it acceptable.[3]

Why would poetry be seen to be dangerous? Poetry for Plato was synonymous with an oral state of mind which he saw as the main obstacle to the development of rationalism. For Plato poetry locked the individual in unanalysed tradition. The listener was caught in the experience of a recitation of mere words. Plato was pushing his students to "separate themselves from it instead of identifying with it; they themselves should become the 'subject' who stands apart from the 'object', reconsiders it and analyses it and evaluates it".[4] In advocating a different way of knowing, Plato insisted that the oral tradition be left behind, moved beyond. Poetry was rejected as imprecise and incapable of carrying calculation, measurement, ordering and classification. Poetry (oral tradition) was presented by Plato as ultimately simply a shadow-show. "If in every European language the word 'myth' is defined as a 'fiction'," Mircea Eliade writes, "it is because the Greeks proclaimed it to be such twenty-five centuries ago."[5]

This tendency continued with the advent of science and the intellectual tradition of the Enlightenment. Accompanying each step towards greater rationality was the sense that something must be shed in the process. The moorings that had anchored the human soul must be cut; that which had been must be sloughed off in order to move forward towards that which could be. Francis Bacon described himself as "a pioneer, following in no man's track, nor sharing these counsels with anyone". Karl Marx lamented that "the tradition of all dead generations weighs like a nightmare on the brain of the living", and Friedrich Nietzsche wrote, "It comes to a conflict between our innate inherited nature and our knowledge, between a stern new discipline and an ancient tradition, and we plant a new way of life, a new instinct, a second nature, which *withers the first*".[6]

Forward linear progress that rejected cyclical return and renewal, and reliance on self that required no counsel from the ancestors were tenets of this new enterprise. Goethe's rendition of the Faust myth captured "this new sense of power, control, omnipotence, the very rival of divinity, this vast power to change the boundaries of the world".[7] Other voices have been concerned not with the power Faust gained through his pact with the devil, but rather with what he was being asked to surrender in exchange for this power: a sense of sacredness, connection and continuity, being part of something larger than self. A language of myth encourages community that has the potential to curb the unbridled individualism of the Faustian project, and a sense of the sacred that has the potential to temper its hubris.

"If we contrast [the] form of logical conception . . . with the mythic and linguistic conception," Ernst Cassirer writes, "we find immediately that the two represent entirely different *tendencies* of thought."[8] In other words, one does not grow out of the other, but rather they exist as parallel ways of knowing. A.H. Almaas calls these two ways of knowing ordinary knowledge and direct knowledge.[9] Ordinary knowledge (a language of logic) is the attempt to use the mind to define, classify, order and control. This way of knowing is not enhanced by metaphor, which opens out, allowing a word to mean all that it can mean. Plato bans poetry because it interferes with the precision necessary for the tasks of defining, classifying and ordering. Likewise, direct knowing (a language of myth) can never be accessed through logic: "[W]herever the poetry of myth is interpreted as a biography, history, or science, it is killed."[10] The former is the language of the human mind working to control and manipulate the environment. The latter opens to the mystery of a life not entirely under our control, not subject to human manipulation.

Ordinary knowledge employs words to describe an objective world. Direct knowledge is constituted by the word: "My confession to myself," Paul Ricoeur writes, "is that man is instituted by the word, that is, by a language which is less spoken *by* man than spoken *to* man."[11] Direct knowledge "regards all spontaneous action as *receptive,* and all human achievement as something merely bestowed".[12] Ordinary knowledge breaks down, takes apart, tries to understand the pieces and how they fit together. Direct knowledge is holistic, each piece precisely the same as the whole:

> Every part of the whole is the whole itself; every specimen is equivalent to the entire species . . . they are identical with the totality to which they belong; not merely as mediating aids to reflective thought but as genuine presences which actually contain the power, significance and efficacy of the whole.[13]

Objective knowledge, the language of logic, and direct knowledge, the language of myth, are two ways of knowing – each having value, each serving a function.

The discourse under examination here does not challenge the development of a language of logic. Rather, it challenges the ideology that maintains that a language of logic can exist only at the expense of a language of myth. This ideology came to regard a language of myth as mere decoration or diversion compared to the important work of science. Eventually myth became simply innocent fiction. Our other voices have maintained, however, that myth is essential to human societies, and that all societies have myths or stories they tell themselves about who they are. Rather than being fiction, myth is a way of making "sense in a senseless world . . . a narrative pattern that gives significance to our existence".[14] In this sense the rationale of rationalism is itself a story or myth. The myth to which Western culture primarily adheres is the conviction that absolute truth exists in the external world, and the goal is to find and understand it. Yet, according to Cassirer,

> All schemata which science evolves in order to classify, organize, and summarize the phenomena of the real world, turn out to be nothing but arbitrary schemas – airy fabrics of mind, which express not the nature of things, but the nature of mind. So knowledge, as well as myth, language, art, has been reduced to a kind of fiction – to a fiction that recommends itself by its usefulness but must not be measured by any strict standard of truth, if it is not to melt away into nothingness.[15]

The scientific project is one culture's attempt to make sense in a senseless world. What makes this myth "particularly insidious", to use the words of Lakoff and Johnson, is that "it purports not to be a myth, and makes myths and metaphor objects of scorn".[16]

A key to sorting out the difference between these two ways of knowing is the way one understands words – the word. A language of logic assumes that "reality", or "things", exist prior to language; language manufactures words to *represent* that reality, those things. A language of myth, however, sees language not as a dead tool, as the above implies, but rather as living process. Language does not objectively *describe* a static external reality; rather it *creates* a dynamic subjective reality. "Reality" or "things" *come into being* as a result of being named. Cassirer points out that religious traditions throughout the world have in common a deep spiritual veneration for the Word. The Word carries power, the ability to generate life, and in many traditions is even used interchangeably with the ultimate creator: " 'In the beginning the word gave the Father his origin'. . . . Words have a generative quality . . . a sort of primal force, in which all being and doing originate."[17]

This is the understanding of a language of myth, and while it has been pushed into the shadows by the myth of rationalism, it is no stranger to the African nor to his or her descendents in the Caribbean. *Nommo* is an African (Bantu) concept which, according to Janheinz Jahn, proposes that words are "the life force . . . giving life to everything, penetrating everything, causing everything".[18] Because the word creates, it has the power to *be* that which it names; it *is* the force rather than merely representing the force. The word becomes flesh. Brathwaite identifies the Afro-Caribbean sensitivity to the word with this African concept of *nommo,* but concludes that "an attitude to the *word,* the atomic core of language . . . is something that is very much present in all folk cultures, all pre-literate, pre-industrial societies".[19] The concept of *nommo* was carried to the Caribbean (Carry-Beyond) where it was preserved in story and myth. Anancy, the central trickster figure brought from Africa,

> was always in the habit of "mouthing", that is, working with his mouth, shifting his mouth and tongue, of circumlocutive speeches, of changing accents and pronunciations, of distorting old forms or deriving new forms from old, of "riddling" and "guessing" and exaggerating, of deliberately creating ambivalent expressions and double meanings. Ananci uses words as weapons or instruments in the contest for survival.[20]

This understanding – that words have power to generate and not simply to designate reality – is a powerful refutation of the second assumption of the dominant Western intellectual tradition. This assumption proposes that since the objectivity of a language of logic overrides the subjectivity of a language of myth, all societies everywhere at all times will be the same. A language of logic is universal. Once again, the issue in question is not the potential to create a set of precepts and terms which can be taught and understood on some level by all human beings, but the assumption that this man-made system of understanding replaces and overrides the diversity, uniqueness and spontaneity of cultural myths created through the words of the many languages of the world. Such an assumption of universality was contested almost immediately after it was proposed. Johann Gottfried Herder wrote in 1793, "Only a real misanthrope could regard European culture as the universal condition of our species. The culture of man is not the culture of the European, it manifests itself according to place and time in every people."[21] Kamau Brathwaite makes a similar point about this universalizing tendency of European culture:

> There is an argument, of course, that holds that our experience is in fact the world's; by which I think, is meant Western Europe's, certainly Britain and North America's. I would dispute this and I would also add that those people who delight to share our experience as international, as cosmopolitan, tend to see it *only* as these things. When pressed, they are able to provide little *basis* for their wide horizons. It is my contention that *before it is too late* we try to find the high ground from which we ourselves will see the world and towards which the world will look to find us.[22]

A language of myth based on the power of the word to create poses this challenge to the idea that man-made, rational, scientific understandings are universal: a subjective language had to already have existed *before* these rational understandings could be posited. "All theoretical cognition takes its departure from a world already performed by language," Cassirer points out. "Language never denotes simply objects, things as such but always conceptions arising from the autonomous activity of mind. The nature of concepts, therefore, depends on the way this active viewing is directed."[23] What one names, gives a sound to, marks by a word is singled out from an infinity of possible experiences because it has significance inwardly for the viewer. This implies that some experiences do not get stamped with meaning, and therefore remain in the shadows. Another person, another culture might give meaning to what we leave in the shadows, and leave in the shadows that to which we have given meaning. "The grandeur and depth of human life is too great to be captured in one culture,"[24] Bhikhu Parekh writes. Words do not *have* a universally prescribed meaning. The imposition of European culture on other cultures under the assumption that it is somehow universal is simply asking that these cultures

> worship someone's else's ancestors, [asking them] to imagine the past as a succession of military, political, and economic struggles beginning in antiquity and culminating in the "progress" manifested by the nation state in our own day. . . . The idea of history as synonymous with European "progress" has elevated a minute part of global experience to the center stage of history, while lumping all the rest into a kind of contextless "other" worthy of mention only when it impinges on the European consciousness.[25]

This distortion is also an act of power, as Brathwaite clearly recognizes when he writes, "[I]t was in language that the slave was perhaps most successfully imprisoned by his master, and it was in his (mis)use of it that he perhaps most effectively rebelled."[26] In a brief but marvelous piece he contributed to a discussion of the Maroons of Jamaica, Brathwaite captures the multilayered consequences of the imposition of the English language on the African descendants of the Caribbean. Nanny, a central figure in the African tradition preserved by the Maroon communities around Moore Town, becomes invisible within a culture whose historical language stamps meaning only on the British side of this fascinating encounter between an African spiritual leader and a British military force. Brathwaite does more than simply uncover that which was hidden – in this case the heroic figure of Nanny. In the content and the style of this piece he expresses his passionate commitment – both sane and good-natured – to resisting the leveling forces that would reduce the magical tale of Nanny of the Maroons (a language of myth) to a footnote of British colonial history (a language of logic). "Nanny," Brathwaite writes,

> was *buttockicized* (& that the word is awkWEIRD & ungainly is no accident) because she was black & therefore a slave no matter what & therefore how could she possibly be a leader, far less a *black* leader – far less a black *woman* leader – and physically & metaphysically so successful that by 1720 the Br (certainly some key planters in the Port Antonio area – on the Grandee Nanny firing line, as it were) were contemplating abandoning their Plantation Xperiment in Jamaica. . . .[27]

The recovery of a language of myth brings with it the recovery of the diversity of culture, and it is therefore no surprise that those contributing to this recovery are those engaged in finding their own unique cultural voice. Kamau Brathwaite has contributed importantly to that endeavour in the Caribbean.

In closing I would like to explore for a moment the significance of the project of recovering a language of myth or direct knowing. What does a language of myth provide? *How* does direct knowledge help to make sense of a senseless world? What does the nation language Brathwaite champions contribute to human understanding? What is it that is lost when the language of logic rids itself of the language of myth? "The very disconcerting paradox of this great conquest of rationality," writes Paul Ricoeur,

> is that it commands simultaneously the *forgetting* of the question of the origin and the meaning of our life. A forgetting which we all feel and whose symptoms overrun us. . . . It is the struggle against this central nuclear forgetting which gives me the task of preserving beside scientific language, which objectifies, the language which understands; beside technological language, which disposes, the language which awakens possibilities.[28]

A language of myth, Ricoeur implies, struggles against forgetting. In the modern world struggling against forgetting has been seen as the project of history, not poetry. Upon closer examination, however, history does not really lead us to (in Brathwaite's terms) re-member. It is precise and useful at recapturing facts about the past, at recapturing already created human forms which make up the substance of earlier human events. It fails, however, to capture the *essence* of the past, "its sacredness, its mystique, and its unchallengeable authority. In this respect, history as information *about* tradition seem[s] to eviscerate the very thing it attempt[s] to preserve."[29]

The relationship between history and poetry is at the centre of much recent Caribbean discourse. Brathwaite, a poet and literary critic, proposes that folk culture is the avenue through which the Caribbean is going to "remember" its own unique being. The insight at the core of Paget Henry's exploration of Caribbean philosophy proposes that the historicist tradition by itself has not been capable of "radically disengaging" from the Western project; it must be balanced by the poeticist tradition. History limits the potentialities of the self due to the "closed posture the self assumes in historical action". History as such does not possess "*original meanings*".[30] According to Mircea Eliade, what we call history – that period between the beginning and the present – is insignificant in assisting initiates during rites of passage in understanding the significance of their lives. This understanding comes about through return to the beginning, where one enters "a sacred time at once primordial and *indefinitely recoverable*".[31] Henry's discussion of West African religion makes this same point. Narratives about origin, not secular history, allow us to tap into the "creative agency of the unmanifested spiritual world". The purpose of education in West African traditional societies is not to know the events of the past, but to achieve "a reversing of the forgetful turn of the ego".[32]

What is being recovered in recovering a language of myth is this ability to begin to re-member, to be able to create anew, to begin afresh, to move beyond regeneration to transformation *before* historical time. Herein lies the real power and importance of the recovery of a language of myth. In the closing paragraph of his little essay, *Language and Myth,* Cassirer writes:

> But there is one intellectual realm in which the word not only preserves its original creative power, but is ever renewing it; in which it undergoes a sort of constant palingenesis, at once a sensuous and a spiritual reincarnation. The regeneration is achieved as language becomes an avenue of artistic expression. Here it recovers the fullness of life.[33]

Metaphor and symbolic language – the Word – has the power to reinvent reality so that something new, unexpected, can be allowed to arise. Metaphorical language, Ricoeur points out, shatters our old reality and in so doing "releases signification".[34] Wilson Harris refers to this shattering as an eruption of the unconscious through the conscious, which can "address one in a startling way that strikes at one's presuppositions. So that one's presuppositions, which are so dear to one, are dislodged."[35] Brathwaite refers to this power of a language of myth as transformation, "a shift from rhetoric to involvement", and proposes "a connection with the hounfort: the heart and signal of the African experience in the Caribbean / New World".[36] A language of myth has the potential to return us to a time and place *before* the split, before there was time or place, before there was the duality of a language of logic and a language of myth. From this place we have the potential to "re-member" ourselves.

Notes

1. In Edward Kamau Brathwaite, *Roots* (1986; reprint, Ann Arbor: University of Michigan Press, 1993), 17.
2. Paget Henry, *Caliban's Reason: Introducing Afro-Caribbean Philosophy* (New York: Routledge, 2000), 278.
3. Eric A. Havelock, *Preface to Plato* (Cambridge, Mass.: The Belknap Press of Harvard University, 1963), 5.
4. Havelock, *Preface*, 47.
5. Mircea Eliade, *Myth and Reality* (New York: Harper Torchbooks, 1963), 148.
6. Charles Whitney, *Francis Bacon and Modernity* (New Haven: Yale University Press, 1986), 83; Bruce Jennings, "Tradition and the Politics of Remembering", *Georgia Review* 31, no. 1 (Spring 1982): 177; Whitney, *Francis Bacon*, 103 (italics mine).
7. Rollo May, *A Cry for Myth* (New York: W.W. Norton and Company, 1991), 224.
8. Ernst Cassirer, *Language and Myth*, trans. Susan K. Langer (New York: Dover Publications, 1946), 90.
9. A.H. Almaas, "The Nature of the Soul" (lecture given at the Ridhwan School, Boulder, Colorado, February 1998).
10. Joseph Campbell, *The Hero with a Thousand Faces* (1949; reprint, Princeton, N.J.: Princeton University Press, 1968), 217.
11. Paul Ricoeur, *The Philosophy of Paul Ricoeur: An Anthology of His Work,* ed. Charles E. Reagan and David Stewart (Boston: Beacon Press, 1978), 237.
12. Cassirer, *Language and Myth,* 60.
13. Ibid., 91–92.
14. May, *Cry for Myth*, 15.
15. Cassirer, *Language and Myth,* 28.
16. George Lakoff and Mark Johnson, *Metaphors We Live By* (Chicago: University of Chicago Press, 1980), 186.
17. Cassirer, *Language and Myth,* 45. This is an understanding of the Uitoto people of Colombia.
18. Janheinz Jahn, *Muntu: An Outline of the New African Culture* (New York: Grove Press, 1961), 124.
19. Brathwaite, "The African Presence in Caribbean Literature", in *Roots,* 236.
20. Dennis Forsythe, *West Indian Culture through the Prism of Rastafarianism, Caribbean Quarterly* monograph (Kingston, Jamaica: University of the West Indies Press, 1985), 76.
21. Johann Gottfried Herder, *Briefe zu Beförderung der Humanität,* translated in footnote in F. M. Barnard, *Herder on Social and Political Culture* (Cambridge: Cambridge University Press, 1969), 24.

22. Brathwaite, "Jazz and the West Indian Novel", in *Roots,* 108.

23. Cassirer, *Language and Myth,* 31.

24. Quoted in Madeleine Bunting, "The West's Arrogant Assumption of Its Superiority Is as Dangerous as Any Other Form of Fundamentalism", 8 October 2001, www.commondreams.org/views01.1008-01.htm.

25. George Lipsitz, *Time Passages: Collective Memory and American Popular Culture* (Minneapolis: University of Minnesota Press, 1990), 27.

26. Brathwaite, *The Development of Creole Society in Jamaica, 1770–1820* (Oxford: Clarendon Press, 1971), 237.

27. Brathwaite, "Nanny, Palmares and the Caribbean Maroon Connexion", in *Maroon Heritage: Archaeological, Ethnographic, and Historic Perspectives,* ed. Kofi Agorsah (Kingston, Jamaica: Canoe Press, 1994), 122.

28. Ricoeur, *Philosophy,* 226, 231.

29. David Gross, *The Past in Ruins* (Amherst: University of Massachusetts Press, 1992), 81.

30. Henry, "African and Afro-Caribbean Existential Philosophies", in *Existence in Black,* ed. Lewis Gordon (New York: Routledge, 1997), 31–32.

31. Eliade, *Myth and Reality,* 18.

32. Henry, *Caliban's Reason,* 25, 41.

33. Cassirer, *Language and Myth,* 98.

34. Ricoeur, *Philosophy,* 132.

35. Wilson Harris, "The Composition of Reality", *Callaloo* 18, no. 1 (Winter 1995): 20.

36. Brathwaite, "The African Presence", 234.

PART TWO

Jah Music and Dub Elegy
Soundings on Kamau Brathwaite and Mikey Smith

6

The Music of Kamau Brathwaite

Lilieth **Nelson** |

Kamau Brathwaite's work has always claimed the authority of the spoken and heard tongue of "nation language", his term "for the languages West Indian peoples actually speak". The audiophonic nature of his writings has much to do with the "shape and surge of his poetry off the page" as they embody "his fundamental concerns as a poet" and historian.[1] For even as he is concerned with "the retracing of our people's movement through space and time, and the resurrection of their cultural materials",[2] the medium which he uses to communicate his concerns is truly polyphonic and reflects a profound sensitivity to the elements of music. "Africa, jazz and the issues around a West Indian poet's use of language" have been the "three inter-connected concerns that have most particularly shaped his consciousness".[3]

In his introduction to *The Art of Kamau Brathwaite*, Stewart Brown quotes Brathwaite as having spoken of the "tyranny of the pentameter" and speaks of his finding "ways to accommodate rhythms and voices that had hardly been heard before in 'English' poetry". Brown calls Brathwaite's interest in jazz and the music of the Caribbean "one of the lasting and most significant influences on the shape, sound and content of [his] poetry".[4] Mervyn Morris has explored this extensively in his essay "Overlapping Journeys: *The Arrivants*", which appears in the same volume.[5]

Brathwaite has grappled over the years with the "confrontation between the languages which enforced slavery and those which endured and overcame it".[6] As he experiments with crafting the right words to express "the common experience of a community", with overtones and undertones of the "strength of the origins from which the disconnections were imposed", he has evolved his own style of composition of opus-after-opus, which reflects his profound sense of form, melody, tempo, dynamics, harmony, tonality, rhythm, timing, texture and flow, which are recognized elements of music. It must be clear at the outset, though, that some of the similarities to musical forms are to be interpreted in a literal sense, such as the references to rhythm, tempo and tonality, while others, such as melody and harmony, are to be understood in a metaphorical sense. Much has been written which reflects Brathwaite's level of comfort with music, ranging from the percussive drums of Africa to jazz to the popular music of the Caribbean.

Brathwaite perfected the art of the trilogic form, which, to use his own words from an interview with Nathaniel Mackey, is "based upon the question, an answer and resolution of that answer". I take the liberty to liken this to three of the four movements in the format of the symphony. Brathwaite says he feels free to abandon "the notion of three", and make it four – more like the symphony I dare to add – because he has "no fixed, no real, overall, absolute, fixed idea about things".[7] I interpret this to be another step in response to the guiding of his creative spirit to fashion a new musical form. So he does not see "three as a closed set", but is prepared to experiment with a nine-movement "symphony" (in my terms), juggling the order as the spirit leads, overthrowing the Hegelian notion of "one-two-three", and creating with his own tidalectic notion, drawn from "the movement of the water backwards and forwards as a kind of [cycle]". The continuities remain, however, with the symphonic movements which explore the tonality of the "psycho-natural elements of wind, water, metal, fire and green history".[8]

As Brathwaite's words, seen on paper or heard, take us through the disequilibria and equilibria dynamics of our history, the music of our nation language, as he calls it, is woven with those words "not only to revolt against" the imposition of the colonizers, "but to discover [our] own coral, [our] own roots".[9] He speaks of experiencing movement from fragmentation to coherence, as he works through the various "shafts of sunlight, the little intuitions",[10] the "auto-anthropology" of the self. This is exactly akin to the framework within which the musician composes. So history throws up periodically a Mighty Sparrow, a Don Drummond, a Miles Davis, a Bob Marley, a Peter Tosh, a Jimmy Cliff, a David Rudder and a Kamau Brathwaite.

Brathwaite's search, reflected in *Rights of Passage, Masks* and *Islands,* is lead-ing to a "special kind of aesthetic" emerging "out of fragmentation". Brathwaite himself makes the point that coherence comes "in the effect of the poem" that "to be able to write a poem which is built up on fragmented sliv-ers, but still has an overall archetype of coherence" is akin to the "form within music, that you might break it down into movements within the overall form but that the overall form is very confident and certain".[11]

I take my cue from this to find parallels in Kamau Brathwaite's work with certain elements of music. In discussing the music of Kamau Brathwaite I am forging parallels between musical scores and compositions set out on pages using deliberate forms and styles; between stanzas and groupings of words and phrases horizontally or vertically, left, right or centre; between bars and his unique grouping of syllables, words or phrases with actual or implied bar lines; between notes of varying values, depending on rhythms and accentuation, and his syllables and words; between rests and his spacing and pauses. As men-tioned before, some of this may be taken literally and some, metaphorically.

I use the word "opus", a musical term which indicates the chronological place of a particular composition within a composer's entire output (thus Opus 1, Opus 2 . . .); the numbers are usually applied in the order of publica-tion rather than composition. The works to which I will refer in this chapter are found in *The Arrivants* (1973), *Middle Passages* (1992), *Words Need Love Too* (2000), and *Ancestors: A Reinvention of Mother Poem, Sun Poem and X/Self* (2001), as well as some published in *Caribbean Quarterly* (September–December 2000) and *Monograph* (January 2002).

Kamau Brathwaite's music (work) is structurally unique. He uses the African-derived call and response, which was used in the work songs of the Caribbean to relieve the monotony of labour. As in these songs, the same refrain is not used every time:

stick is the whip
and the dark deck is slavery

limbo
limbo like me

drum stick knock
and the darkness is over me

knees spread wide
and the water is hiding me

limbo
limbo like me

knees spread wide
and the dark ground is under me

down
down
down

and the drummer is calling me
limbo
limbo like me

sun coming up
and the drummers are praising me

out of the dark
and the dumb gods are raising me

up
up
up

and the music is saving me
hot
slow
step

on the burning ground.[12]

He mastered the doubling up of syllables or words for emphasis or to communicate the superlative, another retention in the Caribbean which is distinctively, although not exclusively, African. In Jamaica we say "*saka saka*"
(cutting in a jagged way), "*meke meke*" (messing up), "*nice nice*" (very nice),
"*big big*" (huge), "*chaka chaka*" (very untidy). Brathwaite writes:

Come
come bugle
train
come quick
bugle
train, quick
quick bugle
train, . . .

. . .

long long
boogie woogie
long long
hooey long
journey to town.[13]

At the same time he uses repetition and incremental increase of syllables and words to build tension, in the same manner as the drummer builds to a climax. See, hear and feel this in these two extracts.

like she lik mih
like she lik mih
like she lik mi wid grease like she grease mih[14]

and

If this is all
I have
if this is all
I have
I can travel no farther

you must pour
you must pour
you must pour me out
so the god can enter the silver
so the god can enter the river[15]

In addition to mastering rhythms of Africa or sounds of jazz, Brathwaite uses rhythms found in Caribbean folk music which are not your "common or garden" iambic pentameter, but which are unique in internal structure and form. Teachers in the Jamaican school system use words or syllables to more effectively communicate rhythms being introduced to children, for example: "*Come here and get mi cawfe*", "*Go deh, go pick it up*", and "*Mosquito one, mosquito two, mosquito jump in a hot callaloo*". Rex Nettleford, in conveying rhythms to members of the National Dance Theatre Company of Jamaica, masters this communication by using syllables such as "*ka-tung, ka-tung, ka-tung, tung, tung*", or "*koong koo-ka-tung, koong koo-ka-tung, koong koo-ka, koong koo-ka, koong koo-ka-tung*". So, in Brathwaite's work, we find the following:

Kon kon kon kon
kun kun kun kun
Funtumi Akore
Tweneboa Akore
Tweneboa Kodia
Kodia Tweneduru[16]

and

Bambalula bambulai
Bambalula bambulai

stretch the drum
tight hips will sway

stretch the back
tight whips will flay

bambalula bambulai
bambalula bambulai[17]

and

So sistren & breddren
we is all gather here
tonight to praise

the lord an raise
a anthem to his holy name
amen

we is goin to leave
this vale a shame
an narrow mind-

edness an breathe agen
the vivid hair a god's
blue feels an mountain

tops. . . .[18]

The elements of music which are reflected in Brathwaite's poetry are exemplified as follows:

Form – the structure which distinguishes one kind of music from another. Thus a madrigal has a different form from an oratorio, and though *London Bridge Is Falling Down* and *Dis Long Time Gal Me Nevah See Yuh* have the same one-two-three-four beat, the syncopation of the Jamaican folksong reflects a different form. Thus, to illustrate the difference musically, note that the strong beats fall on the first syllable of the first word – *Lon-* – then on alternating syllables – *bridge, fall-* and *down* – in the English song, while in the Jamaican song the first beat is an upward, light one followed by strong beats on *long, gal* and *see,* with the triplet *me nevah* preceding the strong *see* to enrich the syncopation. Similarity to the folk form is seen in Brathwaite's

> brown is good
> white as sin?
> An' doan forget Jimmy Baldwin
> an' Martin Luther King. . . .[19]

Here the strong beats may be placed on *brown, white, doan, Bald-, Mar-* and *King,* with a light upward beat on *An'* and half beats on *Jimmy.*

Melody is "the musical line . . . or curve . . . that guides our ear through a composition. The melody is the plot, the theme of a musical work, the thread upon which hangs the tale. As Aaron Copland aptly puts it, 'The melody is generally what the piece is about.' "[20] In the melodic lines of his poetry Brathwaite often uses a succession of single tones which the mind of the reader may perceive as a unity by finding significant relationships among the consistent tones. We thus derive an impression of a conscious arrangement – a beginning, a middle and an end. We hear his words as they progress, not singly, but in relation to his thoughts as a whole. In his work we perceive tones, not separately, but in relation to each other within a pattern. So the melodic lines of the poetry move up and down, with individual tones being higher or lower than each other, while at the same time moving forward in time, one tone claiming our attention for a longer or shorter duration than another. From the interaction of the two dimensions emerges the total unit which is the melody.

> Always when hungry
> The lamb will bleat
> The lion will roar
> The dog will fawn
> On his master
> But to whom does the stranger
> Return when touched by disaster?[21]

In addition, his melodies move stepwise (as along a scale) or at times leap to a tone several degrees away. The leap may be narrow or wide, as may the range of the melody. Some of his works then may be classified as atonal and modern in construction, in terms of the distance from the highest to lowest tones. Thus compare the narrow range and the stepwise movements of "Yao", above, and "Vulture", below –

> She's black but prefers to be brown
> it's as simple as that
>
> just like you
>
> turning old would prefer to be young
> her eyes are dark but he dreams them blue
>
> lovers love golden curls he believes
> rather like you
>
> and why is my voice so husky she grieves
> I would rather trill like a bird. true-
>
> pitch. slanting the heavens. than mourning
> in leaves the passing and pain of this soft passive
>
> love. What new
> worlds to conquer. Columbus not down-
>
> hearted Caliban is who she is after
> rather like you[22]

– with the bold leaps and far-flung activities of the more vigorous melody of "Rasta" or "Agoue":

> brothers flying from branches to irie
>
> and as they fly
>
> . not flying . not falling .
> but like flow
> -ing
> flow
> -ing
>
> .
>
> here is the king . king of kings
>
> .
>
> iya[23]

Brathwaite's melodies, like those of musical compositions, may be fast or slow, loud or soft. The fast, loud melody with its built-in accelerando and crescendo exemplified in

it

it

it

it is not

it is not

it is not

it is not enough[24]

creates an atmosphere of self-assurance, braggadocious and jaunty, while the slow, soft melody of "Praise Poem 2000" suggests a human-like serenity and peace:

It's so difficult to start like all over & over again. the
egg dead in its locked cell. the heart so full of moon
it will soon burst

from my stretched bed my eyes open again & for the last
time on the marine blue. the Caribbean colours
of our royal sea. the waves breaking white outside the

window

i have tried so long to properly describe these things
the sea's ceaseless sound & colour. how its waters
snake these coral beaches & how the sunlight lights

them . . .[25]

Brathwaite's poetry (music) defies the constraints of symmetry which results in predictable phrases. In music, as in language, a phrase denotes a unit of meaning within a larger structure. Two phrases together form a musical period. Each phrase ends in a kind of resting place, known as a cadence, that punctuates the flow of the music. When a phrase ends in an upward inflection like a question, the cadence type is inconclusive – indicating, like a comma in punctuation, that more is to come. When a phrase ends in a full cadence this creates a sense of conclusion and decisive ending. Some believe that the progress of Brathwaite's work from the early years to the present parallels the development of some forms of music such as jazz, becoming more and more difficult to follow, less and less predictable, with more examples of

the inconclusive cadence. This tendency is illustrated in the following
extracts.

&

mumma!

uh fine

a cyaan get nutten

write

a cyaan get nutten really

rite

while a stannin up hey in me years & like I inside a me shadow
like de mahn still mekkin mwe walk up de slope dat e slide
in black down de whole long curve a de

arch

i

pell

a

go[26]

and

This **echo** hear i call see i face lift up from the salt

waters

aguoe

agoue

agoue

agoue

catch

i hand to the rope
hanging from i hear all afternoon
the music in fragile hull of bone & new & blossom
gleam & kingdom come
& push off through splinters & sparks of yr poem
towards the distance island of sound[27]

Brathwaite, like many composers, often unifies his structure by repeating
some of his musical ideas. Thus phrases may begin in identical fashion, then
the contrast is supplied by fresh material (as in "Caliban"). Through repetition

and contrast he achieves both unity and variety. This combination of traits is basic to musical architecture, resulting in unity rather than chaos, and variety rather than boredom. So Brathwaite's melodic lines do not always leave off haphazardly, as if they suddenly found something better to do, but often they end on a tone that produces the effect of having reached a goal. For centuries this has been a basic principle in music. Brathwaite's poems reflect a melody that moves forward in time, now faster, now slower, in a rhythmic pattern that holds our attention, even as does its up and down movement:

> Without the rhythm the melody loses its aliveness. . . . [and] could not be organized into clear-cut phrases and cadences. . . . What makes a striking effect on the listener is the climax, the high point in the melody line that usually represents the peak of intensity. The climax gives purpose and direction to the melody line. It creates the impression of crisis met and overcome.[28]

Rhythm – Much has been written about the rhythmic patterns which pervade Brathwaite's work, especially about the percussive sounds deeply rooted in his grasp of his Africanness, coupled with this inescapable Caribbeanness. It probably remains necessary to make a few more observations within the framework of the definition of rhythm as musical time or

> the controlled movement of music in time. The duration of the tones, the frequency, and the regularity or irregularity with which they are sounded determine the rhythm of a musical passage. Rhythm is the element of music most closely allied to body movement. . . . Its simpler patterns when repeated over and over can have a hypnotic effect on us.[29]

To say that Brathwaite's poetry (music) has rhythm is to say that it has a lively quality, almost independent of the syllables and words.

> Dumb
> dumb
> dumb
> the drum trembles
> the knocking wakes its sound
> the tambourine tinkles
> and my feet have found
> the calling clear
> the bubble eyes
> the river.[30]

Just as we organize our perception of time and the universe by means of rhythm, such as the ticking of the clock, the ebb and flow of night and day, desire and appeasement, life and death, or Brathwaite's "question, answer and resolution", so we automatically impose our response to patterns in the written word. Thus while Brathwaite deliberately defies the metrical patterns of duple, triple, quadruple or compound metres, we feel or hear and respond to the percussive sounds in his work – be they high or low pitched, rattling, tapping on hollow tubes or solid lengths, scraping or clicking – as well as to the pulsations or beats – be they accented (strong) or weak, syncopated or smooth. See "Noom": "*Like a rata like a rat like a rat-a-tap tappin*". See also "In a little shanty town. . . .", "Kaiso", "Shandy", "Shango/train", "Shango/stone sermon", "Mento", "Rasta", "Cakewalk" and "Pan".[31]

Tempo or musical pace (how slow or how fast) and dynamics or musical volume (degree of loudness or softness), both of which are reflected in Brathwaite's work, elicit certain responses from his readers/listeners. Thus the largo (broad, very slow) or the allegro (fast, cheerful) stands out in many of his poems, as do the pianissimo (very soft) and the fortissimo (very loud).

Harmony – The last element of the music reflected in Brathwaite's work, which I wish to explore briefly, is harmony. In the musical world this means musical space. Plutarch wrote that "music, to create harmony, must investigate discord".[32] Much has been said about the polyphonic nature of Brathwaite's poetry. As the word suggests, this is "many sounds" coming together at the same time, often in unexpected ways, as against a central melody with predictable chord progressions (homophonic). I wish here to comment on the notions of *dissonance* and *consonance* in Brathwaite's music (work). Harmonic movement "is generated by the tendency of active chords to be resolved in chords of rest".[33] This movement receives its maximum impetus from dissonance. While consonance is interpreted as denoting relaxation, fulfilment (and resolution), dissonance is associated with restlessness, activity and the creation of tension. It must be noted, however, that without dissonance "a work would be intolerably dull and insipid". Machlis comments, "What suspense and conflicts are to the drama, dissonance is to music", for it

creates the areas of tension without which the areas of relaxation would have no meaning. Each complements the other; both are a necessary part of the artistic whole. . . . [Music] has grown more dissonant through the ages. . . . A combination of tones that sounded extremely harsh when first introduced began to seem less so as the sound became increasingly familiar.[34]

Indeed we come to recognize it as consonance, pleasing to the ear. I venture to say that this has been the experience of Brathwaite's poetry (music) – to use a personification – over time. The harmony in the work, which is uniquely his own, has grown more and more sophisticated throughout the years, so that we hear it in depth as he defies "man's age-old attempt to impose law and order upon the raw material of sound".[35] If dissonance is interpreted as the juxtaposition of unexpected meanings that startle the reader, then one can experience in a metaphysical sense the dissonance in the following:

Nam(e)tracks

•

But

muh

muh

muh

me mudda

mud

black fat

-soft fat man-

ure

kukoo

-cook-

in pot herb

wollaboa wood-eve-

nin time smoke

sleep

sleep

rest

• 36

Notes

1. Stewart Brown, introduction to *The Art of Kamau Brathwaite,* ed. Stewart Brown (Bridgend, Wales: Seren, 1995), 8.
2.   *Edward Kamau Brathwaite: An Interview with Yolande Cantu* (London: British Council, 1980), sound cassette, quoted in ibid., 7.
3. Brown, introduction, 9.
4. Ibid.
5. Mervyn Morris, "Overlapping Journeys: *The Arrivants*", in *The Art of Kamau Brathwaite,*122–29.
6. Ibid., 10.
7. Nathaniel Mackey, "An Interview with Kamau Brathwaite", in *The Art of Kamau Brathwaite,* 13, 14.
8. Ibid., 14, 15.
9. Ibid., 17.
10. Ibid., 18; Brathwaite attributes the phrase to (presumably T.S.) Eliot.
11. Ibid., 19.
12. Edward Kamau Brathwaite, *Islands,* in *The Arrivants: A New World Trilogy* (Oxford: Oxford University Press, 1973), 194–95.
13. Brathwaite, *Rights of Passage,* in *The Arrivants,* 33.
14. Brathwaite, "Speaking the Slave", in *Caribbean Quarterly: Kamau Monograph,* ed. Rex Nettleford (Kingston, Jamaica: University of the West Indies, 2002), 162.
15. Brathwaite, *Islands,* 186.
16. Brathwaite, *Masks,* in *The Arrivants,* 98.
17. Brathwaite, "Pan", in *Caribbean Quarterly: Kamau Monograph,* 153.
18. Brathwaite, "Shango/stone sermon", in *Caribbean Quarterly: Kamau Monograph,* 148–49.
19. Brathwaite, *Rights of Passage,* 56.
20. Joseph Machlis, *The Enjoyment of Music: An Introduction to Perceptive Listening,* 3rd ed. (New York: W.W. Norton, 1970), 12.
21. Brathwaite, *Words Need Love Too* (Philipsburg, St Martin: House of Nehesi, 2000), 35.
22. Ibid., 10.
23. Ibid., 65.
24.   Brathwaite, "Rasta", in *Caribbean Quarterly: Kamau Monograph,* 150.
25. Brathwaite, *Words Need Love Too,* 48.
26. Brathwaite, "X/self xth letter from the thirteenth provinces", in *Ancestors: A Reinvention of Mother Poem, Sun Poem and X/Self* (New York: New Directions, 2001), 450.
27. Brathwaite, *Words Need Love Too,* 70.

28. Machlis, *Enjoyment of Music*, 13–14.

29. Ibid., 19.

30. Brathwaite, *Islands*, 186.

31. From *Caribbean Quarterly: Kamau Monograph*, 146–53.

32. *Demetrius*, section 1.

33. Machlis, *Enjoyment of Music*, 18.

34. Ibid.

35. Ibid., 19.

36. Brathwaite, "Nam(e)tracks", in *Ancestors*, 95.

7

"Travelling Miles"
Jazz in the Making of a West Indian Intellectual

Donette A. **Francis** ▌

Examining the place of music in the black Atlantic world means surveying the
. . . symbolic use to which [this] music is put by other black artists and writers.

– Paul Gilroy, *The Black Atlantic*

One can see in [Brathwaite's] poems the restless movement from place to place.

– Gordon Rohlehr, *Pathfinder*

Jazz is not only America's music. Crisscrossing the black Atlantic, it has produced palpable transnational reverberations. Jazz, I argue, laid the foundation
for Kamau Brathwaite's work on Caribbean culture, since it was through jazz
that he first discovered an aesthetics of dissonance that enabled him to conceive of an alternative to Eurocentric culture and aesthetics. While critics have
discussed the jazz sounds emanating from his critical and creative writings,[1] I
focus on how central jazz was to Brathwaite's intellectual formation. Such a
mapping underscores the transatlantic routes implicit in the making of West
Indian intellectuals. If "roots" has become the core metaphor that both
Brathwaite and his critics use to characterize his work, then I foreground the

importance of "routes".[2] That is, even at home in the Barbados of the 1940s, he had already travelled miles, musically and culturally. This travel altered his cultural orientation, which he incorporated into his way of seeing not only Caribbean culture and identity but also African diasporic cultural identity.

Brathwaite's involvement with jazz in many ways brings into tension the dominant narrative about the radicalization of West Indian intellectuals. This account often places their awakening in metropolitan locations abroad rather than at home.[3] And, here the experience of racism is often the catalyst for radicalization. Brathwaite's story tells a slightly different tale about place and radicalization. Winning the island scholarship to Cambridge, he departed for England in 1950 at twenty years old. He spent four years in England and another seven in Ghana before returning to the West Indies.[4] While his radicalization bloomed in England and Ghana, the seeds of his cultural reorientation were firmly planted in Barbados – where his exposure to jazz served as a major catalyst. Here I am using James Clifford's definition of travel, that foregrounds "exploration, research, escape and transforming encounter",[5] rather than the more conventional sense of travel as the physical movement from geographic place to place. I do not want to exaggerate the importance of such "conceptual journeying", but I do want to propose that an entire black world, counter to Brathwaite's colonial context, opened up for him through jazz. Therefore the search for an African world view, which is characteristic of Brathwaite's work, began at home in Barbados in the 1940s, rather than in Ghana in the 1950s.

"Jazz and the West Indian Novel" is perhaps the capstone of Brathwaite's jazz-inflected writings. Published in 1967–68, but written during the 1950s in Africa, this essay is one of Brathwaite's first attempts to create a critical theory for Caribbean literature.[6] In the essay Brathwaite outlines three features, in addition to the primacy of sound, that a novel should possess in order to be considered a "properly" jazz novel: first, it had to be rooted in an African presence; second, it had to express protest; third, it had to communicate the "communality of [West Indian] societies".[7] Altogether, these elements should express the individual's relationship to the group, with the group's folkways providing the basic syntax for the novel's composition. If a West Indian novel failed to convey a communal sensibility, then it did not perform the right function of the jazz novel. Based on such prescriptions, Brathwaite identifies Roger Mais's *Brother Man* as an exemplary West Indian jazz novel, since it captures the quotidian group life experiences of tenement-yard dwellers in the slums of Kingston in the 1930s and 1940s. In the novel Mais experiments with form, so that the people who live in the tenement yard appear as one choral voice.[8] Also, because these yard dwellers band together as a group, they emerge victorious in spite of their dire economic circumstances. It is not surprising that Brathwaite found this novel successful in terms of his definition of a West Indian jazz novel, given its emphasis on the communality of West Indian societies and its deployment of a group voice as an organizing syntax.

Leaving aside the problematic that only one novel fits the criteria, in an earlier version of this chapter that focused on Brathwaite's poetics, I asked why, in the immediate post-independence period of nation building, when nationalists were seeking to identify the distinctiveness of the region's literature, would Brathwaite choose jazz – an African-American idiom? And secondly, did privileging jazz as an aesthetic model distract him from seeing the radicalism in early forms of ska and calypso? Did choosing jazz reflect a diasporic imagination centred in the United States? Or was jazz able to transcend its locality and enable him to theorize an African diasporic aesthetic?

Because the essay was written in Africa, we are also left to wonder why he did not choose an African musical form. Brathwaite provides an answer to these questions when he states that in jazz he was searching for a "a possible alternative to the European cultural tradition which has been imposed upon [West Indian writers] and which we have more or less accepted and absorbed, for obvious historical reasons, as the only way of going about our business". According to Brathwaite, he chooses jazz because it is

> an urban folk form that has wider and more overt connections and correspondences with the increasingly cosmopolitan world in which we live, than the purely West Indian folk forms. . . . Most importantly, jazz, in several quarters, is already *seen* to be, or to represent, an alternative to the "European" tradition.[9]

Here he makes four important claims for jazz: that it is urban; that it is a folk form; that it is cosmopolitan; and that it is already visible as an alternative metacritical language. That Brathwaite could see the music as simultaneously urban, folk and cosmopolitan indicates that he was already collapsing the divide between high art and popular culture. In addition, since jazz is perhaps the first African-diasporic music to achieve appeal beyond its local context, he wants to free the music from being landlocked as an African-American idiom, solely. Instead, he uses it to examine the interlocking dimensions of the black diasporic experience. In choosing jazz, Brathwaite chooses a cultural expression that captures the sound of the modern black experience in the movement from slavery to freedom, from countryside to urban metropolis. Jazz offers a language to articulate the modernist impulse – of alienation, chaos, disillusionment and yet hope – which is the signature not only of African American or West Indian literatures, but of black cultural expressions in the New World. Hence the essay is most productively read as one of the earliest attempts to theorize an African-diasporic cultural aesthetic transcending national borders and disciplinary boundaries, linking the United States to the Caribbean, African-American music and literature to West Indian literature and music. This invocation of diaspora is not simply about sameness, but rather how one form gets routed out of its cultural context to take on new meaning elsewhere.

Not incidentally, choosing jazz was also an acknowledgement of the power relations of critical theory, and of which paradigms travel best. Recognizing the relative global visibility of jazz, a black American form, compared to the virtual invisibility of Caribbean forms like calypso and reggae – at that historical moment – Brathwaite cast his critical lot with jazz. In so doing, he appropriated an idiom that enabled him to establish and circulate a vernacular criticism relevant to his West Indian context. In this way, deploying jazz was not mere mimicry, but an attempt to create new cultural and political possibilities, and a cross-cultural dialogue.

But there is another, perhaps even more *original* reason why Brathwaite chooses jazz, which goes back to his days as a student at Harrison College in the 1940s. Discovering and understanding jazz then was, as Brathwaite puts it, "quite outside our curriculum", and "it just struck me that [jazz] was my sense of dissonance".[10] That is, being rooted in a Eurocentric educational system where he would have been schooled in the British literary canon in addition to studying Latin and Greek, one can imagine that the music of Sarah Vaughan, John Coltrane and Louis Armstrong struck an altogether different chord. Through jazz, Brathwaite realized that he could be trained in the classics and yet not produce Shakespearean poetry.

But how did a Harrison College boy become exposed to jazz in Barbados in the 1940s when, prior to 1962, Barbados had no radio station of its own and what they had, Radio Rediffusion wire service, was primarily interested in spreading English culture? Two important events occurred in Barbados in late 1947 that provided routes to new kinds of music for Brathwaite and his schoolmates. First, a record shop opened in Bridgetown where they could purchase modern records to play on their gramophones. Second, the "pickup" – a crude, electrically driven turntable connected to the radio, from which the sound came – became available. These new outlets allowed them to travel miles culturally through listening to this new black music. Excited by these new sound possibilities, Brathwaite and fellow Harrison College schoolmates formed a music group that included Cedric Phillips, Patrick Haynes, Ben Dash, Keith King, Archie Harper, Austin Husbands, Edson Roach, Clyde Turney, Briggs Archer, Bentley Storey and Charles Pilgrim, among others.

Within this group Cedric Phillips, who was also a pianist and had connections to black America, played an important role because, according to Brathwaite, "as a musican listening to Nat King Cole, Phillips understood what [the music] meant . . . not simply what Nat was playing".[11] Because of Phillips's American connection, they would get the American jazz magazines *Downbeat* and *Metronome,* which they read voraciously, subsequently ordering records by artists like Charlie Parker and Miles Davis to be played at their music group's listening sessions. Listening to and understanding jazz, therefore, enabled Brathwaite and his small group to break away from the trappings of their "colonial deadication".

Immersed in jazz and the emergent bebop music, Brathwaite and his cohorts attempted to create a public audience for jazz. First, since there were no reviews of jazz music in the local papers, Brathwaite started writing a jazz column in the school paper, the *Collegian*.[12] Second, they hosted two jazz programmes on Harrison College's radio station, playing the iconoclastic sounds of the avant-gardists. "We didn't get beyond two programmes, though. The first one I did; and even as I was on the air people were phoning in, asking what was going on."[13] Shortly after their programme was pulled off the air, the young Brathwaite attended a gathering of social elites at Frank Collymore's, where he received a firm class critique: "fancy a Harrison College boy at that playing that kind of music".[14] His critic suggests that he is both a "cultural and class traitor", discarding the kind of respectability his very affiliation with Harrison College should have inculcated in him. In the 1940s jazz was certainly not respectable people's music – anywhere, but especially not in Barbados. If the Barbadian cultural elite did listen to jazz, Brathwaite maintains that it was the very melodic sounds of white swing band leaders like Jack Teagarden and Paul Whiteman, whereas he liked the " 'new' very Africanized sounds of Albert Ayler, Archie Shepp and John Coltrane".[15]

More pointedly, just coming out of World War II in 1945, the majority of

Barbadians were fervently loyal to England and things English. Jazz was not perceived as a musical form that emulated the British crown, nor could it draw Barbadians together in creating a national culture. Brathwaite's attraction to this foreign – African-American – music served in many ways to further alienate him from his people. As his fellow classmate Charles Pilgrim recalls, "consensus was that we had gone mad to like the noise of these new fangled impostors".[16] But in jazz they found a form that was "out of tune" with orthodox habits of behaviour. In other words, jazz becomes a counter-hegemonic discourse not only to Eurocentricity, but to a localized black Barbadian cult of respectability.

One might ask how it is that Brathwaite hears dissonance in the work of Armstrong, Nat King Cole and Sarah Vaughan on the one hand and Coltrane, Ayler and Shepp on the other, especially as some of their tunes are decidedly melodic. I would argue that there are two types of dissonance at work: what I am calling here a *dissonance of form,* characterized by an absence of harmony and playing the wrong note; and a *dissonance of content,* characterized by a story that is "out of tune" with the normative, mainstream representation. The latter kind of dissonance is even more poignant when the story is being told while executing the perfect voice, timbre and pitch. For example, to tell a story about lynching in a melodic rather than moaning blues, or a field holler, is in and of itself disjunctive, and creates a surprise dissonance for an audience expecting to hear swing music. Armstrong, who had a profound impact on Brathwaite, embodies this latter form. By all accounts, Armstrong sings and plays melodic tonal music, yet I would argue that there is a dissonance of content made all the more profound by the façade of harmony in his vocal stylings.

For a young Brathwaite, steeped in the British canon, Armstrong's manipulation of classical form and instrument would have had a profound impact. That is, Armstrong has the physical skill and technical prowess of a classically trained musician, but does not apply it in a traditional Western mode; instead he reapplies it in a distinctly black fashion. Through jazz and Armstrong, Brathwaite discovers that "the establishment is not the only thing that there is",[17] which leads him to pen his own poetry, writing blue notes – deploying dissonance of both form and content. In other words, since his own folk roots are unavailable to him, he detours to a universal black folk idiom in jazz.[18]

Armstrong – the musician and the man – had a particularly formative impact on Brathwaite's consciousness. Today Brathwaite remembers "a surrealist poem on Louis Armstrong" in Nancy Cunard's voluminous 1934 publication, *Negro: An Anthology,* that had a profound impact.[19] Simply entitled "Louis Armstrong", that poem by the Belgian lawyer, playwright and poet Ernst Moerman uses Armstrong and his music to portray grim images of physical and sexual violations committed against black bodies on American soil. This poem, while awakening Brathwaite to the horrors of American racial conditions, introduced him to protest poetry as well. According to Brathwaite, reading this poem introduced him to a new notion of poetry, where one could, as he puts it, "take an icon and make something of his presence".[20] In other words, he learns that cultural icons could be used as vehicles to discuss the social worlds they inhabit. This awareness is visible in his subsequent poems about musical figures like Don Drummond, Miles Davis and John Coltrane, in which one sees that Brathwaite dislocates cultural icons from their local contexts to resituate them transculturally.

Armstrong's impact is clearly evident in Brathwaite's 1976 collection of poetry, *Black and Blues.* The collection, an ode to Armstrong, takes its title from Armstrong's 1929 remake of Fats Waller's "Black and Blue".[21] The lyrics profoundly describe the ache of double consciousness in the African-American context.

> I'm white . . . inside . . . but, that don't help my case That's life . . . can't hide . . . what is in my face . . . My only sin . . . is in my skin What did I do . . . to be so black and blue

The melodic timbre and toothy grin characteristic of Armstrong's performance could not mask the pathos being communicated in this and his other songs. This styling is representative of dissonance of content. Pointedly, the lyrics of "Black and Blues" express Armstrong's own struggle and ambivalence as a cultural mulatto or, in Caribbean terms, an "Afro-Saxon". This experience would have struck a chord with Brathwaite, since he describes feeling neglected and misunderstood in Cambridge. In Barbados his colonial education taught him that he was a man of "Kulture", yet the experience of racism in Europe shattered the illusion created by his colonial education that he could be a fully accepted Afro-Saxon. Not surprisingly, it is after his stay in England that Brathwaite pens *Black and Blues,* since in England he personally experienced "race as dissonance". Therefore, from Armstrong, I believe Brathwaite learns new ways to address how it felt to be black and blue, which he adapts to describe his colonial context.

Of equal importance is that in this 1976 publication, Brathwaite translates the poetic rhythm from jazz to reggae.[22] This collection of poetry crystallizes his shift to local Caribbean rhythms, which Brathwaite himself acknowledges: "[W]hat you see in my early work is an alternative music giving me an alternative riddim, as it were, but as I get to know more about the Caribbean the emphasis shifts from jazz to the Caribbean to calypso, to reggae, to our folk music, to the religious music."[23]

Salient here is that although jazz was Brathwaite's first language of dissonance, it does not inhibit him from acquiring other idioms. He perfected his craft on jazz sounds, sharpening his ears, his voice, his sense of time, rhythm, pacing and abstraction. In his creative and critical prose, jazz becomes a vehicle for him to discuss language, identity and representation. Yet the improvisation characteristic of the medium itself enables him to discover other chords of dissonance. These new chords lead him back home to calypso, reggae and Caribbean folk music.

If we consider seriously the Harrison College years, then Brathwaite's story suggests that even though bodies might actually remain static, music and books travel, and with them ideas inviting new ways of seeing the world. Through jazz Brathwaite had already gotten the sense of "a flattened fifth – . . . that aesthetics of dissonance" from as early as 1948.[24] Hence, his physical travels – to England and to Ghana – meet him in the middle, not at the beginning, of his journey towards cultural reorientation. Ultimately, then, Brathwaite's multiple uses of jazz illustrate how Caribbean intellectuals have adopted and re-tuned seemingly imperial cultural currents, reforming how we think about cultural exchanges in the black Atlantic world.

Notes

1. Several critics have talked about jazz and Brathwaite's work. See Louis James, "Brathwaite and Jazz", in *The Art of Kamau Brathwaite,* ed. Stewart Brown (Bridgend, Wales: Seren, 1995); Gordon Rohlehr, *Pathfinder: Black Awakening in* The Arrivants *of Edward Kamau Brathwaite* (Tunapuna, Trinidad: G. Rohlehr, 1981); Glyne A. Griffith, "Kamau Brathwaite as Cultural Critic", in *The Art of Kamau Brathwaite,* 75–85; and Michael Dash, *The Other America: Caribbean Literature in a New World Context* (Charlottesville: University Press of Virginia, 1998). James suggests that we see Brathwaite's use of jazz as cultural history, where he explores the history of the African diaspora through forms of black music from work songs and blues through jazz and calypso. This is most evident in Brathwaite's *Arrivants.*

2. See, for example, Brathwaite's 1963 essay, "Roots: A Commentary on West Indian Writers", *Bim* 10, no. 37 (July–December 1963): 10–21. Of critical importance is that when Brathwaite chooses to have the essays from the 1950s through 1960 republished, he titles the collection *Roots.* I would argue that even the focus on rootlessness does not get at the importance of routes.

3. Here I have in mind Harold Cruse's *Crisis of the Negro Intellectual* (New York: Quill, 1984); George Lamming's *The Pleasures of Exile* (Ann Arbor: University of Michigan Press, 1992); and Winston James's *Holding Aloft the Banner of Ethiopia* (London and New York: Verso, 1998).

4. Brathwaite stayed in Ghana, West Africa from 1955 to 1962 working as an education officer for the Ministry of Education. In 1962 Brathwaite returned to the West Indies, first to St Lucia and then to Mona, Jamaica in 1963. From 1965 to 1967, he went back to England to conduct research for his PhD dissertation at the University of Sussex. He returned in 1967 to Jamaica, where he stayed until his departure for New York in 1991.

5. James Clifford, *Routes: Travel and Translation in the Late Twentieth Century* (Cambridge, Mass.: Harvard University Press, 1997).

6. The essay was first presented in 1967 at a meeting of the Caribbean Artists Movement in London.

7. Brathwaite, "Jazz and the West Indian Novel", in *Roots* (1986; reprint, Ann Arbor: University of Michigan Press, 1993), 107.

8. Louis James attributes Mais's use of the choral form to his "love of European music and Greek classical drama"; see his essay "Brathwaite and Jazz", 65.

9. Brathwaite, "Jazz", 72, 77.

10. Brathwaite, interview by author, New York, NY, 20 September 2001.

11. Ibid.

12. He borrowed a format from *Metronome* magazine that asked a person to listen to a particular record and note what they had to say about it. According to Brathwaite, he founded *The Collegian* with Fabian Holder.
13. Brathwaite, interview.
14. Quoted in Rohlehr, *Pathfinder*, 5.
15. Brathwaite, "Jazz", 78.
16. Charles Pilgrim, correspondence with author, 5 December 2001.
17. Brathwaite, interview.
18. As Gordon Rohlehr points out, between 1950 (when Brathwaite published his first poem, "Shadow Suite", in *Bim*) and 1962, much of his poetry was "organized along the lines of musical suites", comprising four to eight movments (*Pathfinder*, 4).
19. Brathwaite, interview. If the music itself linked Brathwaite to black Harlem, through his classmate Cedric Phillips he would encounter Nancy Cunard's voluminous 1934 publication, *Negro: An Anthology*. The anthology, covering both Africa and the diaspora, brought together more than two hundred contributors to expose black oppression, to plead for racial justice, and ultimately to celebrate black achievement and endurance. The anthology stands as a virtual ethnography of 1930s racial, historical, artistic, political and economic culture, despite its problematic aspects (Cunard – great-granddaughter of the founder of the Cunard shipping lines, modernist poet, editor, publisher and bohemian – published the anthology after her voyeuristic travels through Harlem and the Caribbean). That this anthology provided Brathwaite's first textual vision of the Harlem Renaissance and the New Negro indicates a renaissance not simply rooted in New York, but with broader transatlantic routes which included the Caribbean and Africa.
20. Brathwaite, interview.
21. Armstrong's recording of this song was for the hit Harlem musical production "Hot Chocolates".
22. Brathwaite himself points out that "a lot of the poems in black and blues were influenced by reggae and have been read to reggae" (Brathwaite, interview).
23. Quoted in James, "Brathwaite and Jazz", 71.
24. Brathwaite, interview.

8

Remembering Michael Smith
(Mikey, Dub and Me)

Linton Kwesi **Johnson** |

The late Jamaican poet Michael Smith was, to my mind, one of the most interesting and original poetic voices to emerge from the English-speaking
Caribbean during the last quarter of the twentieth century. He was the quintessential performance poet, gifted with an unrivalled talent for mesmerizing
his audience. With an actor's sense of the dramatic and a musician's acute
sense of rhythm, Mikey enthralled audiences from the Caribbean to Europe
with his electrifying performances.

He was a gifted wordsmith who could deftly negotiate the verbal contours
of Jamaican speech, creating memorable poetic discourse that spoke to the
conditions of existence for the "oppressed" and "dispossessed" in their everyday language. He drew from a wide range of oral sources, always on the look-
·out for the ironic and the paradoxical. Mikey was essentially a political poet,
a people's poet, who wrote about the dehumanization of the poor and their
struggle against poverty and injustice. He wrote with conviction and performed with passion.

Contemptuous of the main political parties in Jamaica, Mikey was identified with the radical left. He was not averse to engaging people in high places
in heated verbal combat. He once told his editor, Mervyn Morris, that he had
an "anarchist tendency" and that he was "close to rasta". For Mikey writing

poetry was, to quote him, "a vehicle of giving hope . . . building awareness
. . . [as] a part of the whole process of . . . liberation".[1]

Michael Smith was born in 1954. He came from a working-class background; his father was a mason and his mother a factory worker. He attended
various schools and graduated from the Jamaica School of Drama in 1980
with a diploma in theatre arts. He began writing poems at the age of fourteen,
when he was hospitalized with a broken leg which left him with a permanent
limp. Soon he began reciting his verse at various youth clubs in Kingston and,
by the end of the 1970s, he had earned a reputation as one of the most
dynamic performers on the Jamaican poetry scene.

In 1978 Michael Smith represented Jamaica at the eleventh World Festival
of Youth and Students in Cuba. That year saw the release of his first recording,
a twelve-inch forty-five titled *Word*, followed by another, *Mi Cyaan Believe
It/Roots* (on which he was accompanied by Count Ossie's Rastafarian drummers), both on the Light of Saba label in Jamaica. In 1981 Mikey performed in
Barbados during Carifesta (a Caribbean regional cultural festival), and was
filmed by British Broadcasting Corporation (BBC) Television performing "Mi
Cyaan Believe It" for the documentary *From Brixton to Barbados*. In 1982
Mikey took London by storm with performances at the Camden Centre for
the International Book Fair of Radical, Black and Third World Books and also
at the Lambeth Town Hall in Brixton for Creation for Liberation.[2] Whilst in
Britain, together with Oku Onuora, Mikey also did a successful poetry tour
and recorded a reggae album which Island Records released under the title *Mi
Cyaan Believe It*. And the story did not end there: the BBC's Anthony Wall
made a television programme about Mikey for the flagship arts series *Arena*.
Entitled "Upon Westminster Bridge", the programme was broadcast on BBC2
that year and again after Mikey's death in 1983. In November 1982 Mikey performed in Paris for UNESCO and went on to do a reading in Milan. He
returned to Jamaica briefly and then came back to London for another tour,
this time as an opening act for the reggae band Black Uhuru, to promote his
recently released album. He returned to Jamaica soon after.

What Michael Smith had achieved in such a short period was nothing if
not remarkable. His untimely death on 17 August 1983 brought to an abrupt
end the promise that had so excited those of us who had witnessed his mete-
oric rise to fame. The circumstances of his death have been shrouded in controversy. As far as I understand the facts, Mikey had attended a meeting in
Stony Hill where the ruling Jamaica Labour Party (JLP)'s minister of educa-

tion, Mavis Gilmour, was speaking, and had heckled her. The following day he was confronted by three party activists. An argument ensued. Stones were thrown and Mikey died from a blow to his head. It was I who, upon hearing of Mikey's death and getting an account on the telephone from journalist John Maxwell, mobilized the international poetry community to send telegrams and letters of protest demanding that Mikey's killer or killers be brought to justice. I was also instrumental in the organization of a demonstration outside the Jamaican high commission in London, supported by Creation for Liberation and the alliance of the Black Parents Movement, the Black Youth Movement and the Race Today Collective. I handed a letter to Herbert Walker, Jamaica's high commissioner at the time, demanding justice. There was also a demonstration in Jamaica, organized by Mikey's friend Dr Freddie Hickling. Two people were eventually arrested, but nothing came of the case for lack of independent witnesses.

A couple of years later I was verbally chastised for my response by Olivia "Babsy" Grange, from the then JLP prime minister's office, when I met her in Jamaica. She said that I had been used by the JLP's enemies for political purposes. More significantly, I discovered from friends that Mikey's mental health had deteriorated not long after his return to Jamaica. Looking back, I remember that from his first visit to London, Mikey's behaviour at times had seemed strange. He would be suspicious of people for no good reason, would be almost paralysed with fear before a performance, and was aggressive towards me on a couple of occasions. After his death I learned that he had assaulted Honor Ford-Smith, his former drama tutor and intimate friend.

Between 1984 and 1986 a number of poetic tributes to Michael Smith were published in *Race Today* magazine and in *Race Today Review* in London. These were: "For Michael Smith" by Bob Stewart and "Godfather's Sermon and Mikey Smith" by Archie Markham in *Race Today Review* 1984; and, in the December 1986 issue of *Race Today*, "I and I (For Michael Smith)" by Jayne Cortez and "Stone for Mikey Smith" by Kamau Brathwaite. Abdul Malik recorded a reggae rendition of "Instant Ting", written in 1985 and published in his collection, *The Whirlwind*, in 1988.[3] There was also a tribute in prose by John La Rose, entitled "Fallen Comet", published in *The Guardian* (UK) newspaper on 2 September 1983 and also in *Race Today Review* in 1984. *It A Come*, Michael Smith's only collection of poems, was edited by Mervyn Morris and published in 1986 by Race Today Publications and in 1989 by City Lights in the United States. A memorial tribute for Mikey was held on 3 November 1983 at Lambeth Town Hall in Brixton, at which African-American poet Amiri Baraka, Mutabaruka and Oku Onuora from Jamaica and I read. There were a number of tributes to Mikey from novelist and writer Farrukh Dhondy, William Tanifeani, a cultural activist from Benin, and Kenyan novelist Ngugi wa Thiong'o, among others.

The Trinidadian poet and publisher John La Rose locates Michael Smith's poetry in the postcolonial revival and renewal of orality in Caribbean poetry.[4] Mikey belonged to a school of Jamaican oral poetry called "dub poetry", which came into currency towards the end of the 1970s. Dub poetry was largely associated with a group of poets at the Jamaica School of Drama and, apart from Mikey, included Noel Walcot, M'bala, Jean Binta Breeze and Oku Onuora, dub poetry's main exponent and explainer. Other dub poets in Jamaica at the time included Malachi Smith, Mutabaruka – who had not attached that label to himself then – and a group of poets called Poets-In-Unity. My own work has also been dubbed "dub poetry", in spite of my attempts to distance myself from the term. It was actually I who coined the term. As a student of reggae music I was trying to analyse its lyricism in a sociological context. In an essay of mine entitled "Jamaican Rebel Music", published in *Race and Class* in 1976, and another entitled "The Politics of the Lyrics of Reggae Music", published in the *Black Liberator* in 1977, I used the terms "dub lyricism" and "dub poetry" to describe the art of the reggae deejay. Recently I reread what I had written in the *Black Liberator* essay and discovered that I had written, and I quote, "dub poetry that 'scatter matter shatter shock' ". The "scatter matter shatter shock" is a line from my poem "Bass Culture", about reggae music. What I was doing there, whether consciously or not, was identifying my own verse with the art of the reggae deejay. And yet by then I had defined my verse as reggae poetry.

What is this dub poetry at which Michael Smith so excelled? A survey of some of what has been written on the subject turns up some interesting, if at times unhelpful, answers. In his essay "Dub Poetry?", Mervyn Morris offers, perhaps, the most clinical definition:

> The word "dub" in "dub poetry" is borrowed from recording technology, where it refers to the activity of adding or removing sounds. "Dub poetry" which is written to be performed, incorporates a music beat, often a reggae beat. Often, but not always, the performance is done to the accompaniment of music, recorded or live. Dub poetry is usually, but not always, written in Jamaican language; in Jamaican

Creole/ dialect/ vernacular/ nation language. By extension, it may be written in the informal language of people from anywhere. Most often it is politically focussed, attacking oppression and injustice. Though the ideal context of dub poetry is the live performance, it also makes itself available in various other ways: on the radio, on television, in audio recordings, video recordings and on film. Many dub poets also publish books.[5]

There is an echo of Mervyn Morris's definition in the observation by J. Edward Chamberlin that "dubbing words over a musical background became common enough that dub poetry came to include any rendition incorporating reggae musical rhythms, and any verse combining reggae rhythms with local speech. . . . But musical accompaniment is not as important to dub poetry as hearing the reggae rhythm in the poem." Pamela Mordecai tells us that the voice of the dub poet is "a voice meant to be propelled from the page onto the stage and into the sound studio where reverb, sound separation, amplification etc. would enhance its statement".[6]

Gordon Rohlehr, who has written extensively on popular culture and the literary arts in the English-speaking Caribbean, has outlined four categories of dub poetry: "Dread Talk, Dub Sermon, Prophet Sight and Prophesy, which have grown out of the speech and music rhythms of reggae and rastafari". Rohlehr asserts that "dub poetry is, at its worst, a kind of tedious jabber to a monotonous rhythm. At its best it is the intelligent appropriation of the manipulatory techniques of the DJ."[7]

Although Kwame Dawes sees some merit in some dub poetry, he says that "in its dogged adherence to the reggae backbeat, quite often phrasing in ways which are counter to the natural rhythms of speech, [it] can sound as if it has been stretched awkwardly to find a way into the grooves of the music". For Dawes dub poetry is only interesting when it points to the possibilities for a reggae aesthetic. He writes, "Perhaps it has taken the exploration of a reggae sensibility in other forms (in fiction, in poetry which is concerned with the written as well as the performance, dance, drama and painting and sculpting) to enable us to recognise that there is an aesthetic which crosses forms."[8]

The Oxford Companion to Twentieth Century Poetry quotes London-based Jamaican poet James Berry, OBE, describing "dub poetry" as "over-compensation for deprivation". The definition goes on to tell us that "rage and belligerent overstatement are its keynotes, but also optimistic vitality, energy and exuberance". I will end my literature review with this quote from Pamela

Mordecai in which she captures the real significance of dub poetry: "If nothing else does, 'dub' [poetry] lays to rest the notion that Jamaican poetry is still 'copying' the forms and devices of any other literature."[9]

What my brief survey of commentators on dub poetry suggests is that there is mostly unanimity about its content and form. There is also agreement among the most informed critics about the structural integrity of Michael Smith's poetry. Chamberlin points to Mikey's use of language to create "a poetic style that sustains the plain-as-life qualities of speech and the heightened sense of and highly structured intensity of personal revelation that is the business of certain kinds of poetry, especially lyric poetry, to achieve". Kamau Brathwaite, who was a seminal influence for most of the prominent dub poets, rightly asserts that they are inheritors of the revolution (that he led) against the dominating influences of the English poetic canon on Caribbean poetry. He states that, in Mikey's case, "a quite remarkable voice and breath control, accompanied by a decorative S90 noise . . . becomes part of the sound structure and meaning of the poem" – the S90 noise being that of a motorcycle. Morris, too, asserts that in Mikey's poetry

> one can hardly fail to notice his firm sense of structure and of rhythmic patterning. The rhetoric of preachers and politicians, the cries of pedlars; allusions to proverbs, nursery rhymes, children's games . . . and to flashpoints in Jamaican and international news – they are pulled together or set against each other in what are usually well articulated rhythmic structures.[10]

Michael Smith was clearly a serious poet whose work has been taken seriously.

What was the relationship between Michael Smith and myself? I did not know Mikey well enough for long enough to say that we were close, but I think I can get away with saying we were friends. Thanks to Mervyn Morris, we had knowledge of and admiration for each other's work by the time we first met in Kingston in 1980. I had been in correspondence with Mikey since 1979. Mikey was very striking in appearance. Tallish, dark, with nascent locks, beard, protruding front teeth and a winning smile, he impressed me with his sincerity and I concluded after our first meeting that we were kindred spirits. We saw each other on a number of occasions during my stay in Jamaica. I remember accompanying him to the Gun Court, where I sat in on one of his regular workshops which he held with a group of prisoners. (The Gun Court had been instituted in the 1970s by Michael Manley's People's National Party [PNP] government to deal with rising gun crime, fuelled by political warfare.

Possession of guns or ammunition meant indefinite incarceration in the specially built jail.)

As far as Mikey was concerned, I was this big-time poet and reggae artist
from London who was involved in the struggle and therefore had an obligation to lend a helping hand to a struggling poet from yard committed to the
same ideals. The moral blackmail was not necessary, because I admired his
poems and had already decided that I would try to do whatever I could to promote his work. In those days I was a member of the Race Today Collective and
our magazine, *Race Today,* had an international circulation. I was the poetry
editor, and as soon as I returned to London I arranged for the publication of
Mikey's celebrated poem "Mi Cyaan Believe It" in the December 1980 issue of
Race Today Review, our annual publication devoted to arts and culture.

In 1980 I established LKJ Records, and the label's first release was Mikey's
recording of "Mi Cyaan Believe It" and "Roots". As luck would have it, the following year I received a telephone call from Alan Yentob, who was then editor of the BBC Television arts programme *Arena.* Yentob asked me if I knew
anything about Carifesta, and I said yes. The next thing I knew, I was off to
Barbados with director Anthony Wall and an American film crew, as
researcher, interviewer and presenter of a documentary about the festival
which was broadcast that year under the title *From Brixton to Barbados.* I was
surprised to meet Mikey there, and suggested to Anthony Wall that Mikey was
someone who had to be included in the programme.

The next time I met Mikey was in London in the following year, 1982. As
a member of *Race Today's* editorial board, I was also a member of the organizing committee of the first International Book Fair of Radical, Black and Third
World Books, organized jointly by New Beacon Books, Race Today
Publications and Bogle-L'Overture Books. It was I who suggested that Mikey
and Oku Onuora be invited to participate in the book fair festival. Creation for
Liberation had already arranged for Oku Onuora and Mikey to come to Britain
for a poetry tour. I was also involved in the making of "Upon Westminster
Bridge", which Anthony Wall made for BBC Television.

Mikey was keen to record a reggae album and had brought with him a
demo tape of three or four of his poems, which was made with the assistance
of Ibo Cooper, then a member of the reggae band Third World. I agreed to
co-produce the album with Dennis Bovell, and persuaded Chris Blackwell of
Island Records to sign Mikey to his label. Later that year I received an invitation from Edouard Glissant, the Martiniquan poet and novelist who was then

editor of UNESCO's *Courier*, to take part in poetry events in Paris and Milan. The events were to be held in November. I knew I would be in Jamaica then, researching *From Mento to Lovers' Rock*, my BBC radio series on the history of reggae, so I suggested Mikey as an alternative and Edouard agreed.

The Michael Smith Memorial Committee that was formed in Jamaica by Freddie Hickling and others has ceased to function. Len Dyke, of Dyke and Dryden in London, and myself wanted to donate some money for a plaque or something permanent in memory of Mikey. Mervyn Morris suggested that the money be donated to some kind of student fund at the Jamaica School of Drama. Between us we donated a thousand pounds sterling to this end, and agreed to top up the fund from time to time. This was only a couple of years after Mikey's death; I do not know what became of the fund. The person who was then principal of the School of Drama hadn't even heard of Michael Smith, the college's most famous past student at the time. It is unfortunate that Michael Smith's only collection of poems, *It A Come*, is no longer available in Britain with the demise of Race Today Publications. Neither is his only reggae album, *Mi Cyaan Believe It*. His poetry continues to be taught in schools in Jamaica and at the University of the West Indies. The people's poet has left a lasting legacy to Caribbean literature.

Appendix

Michael Smith Bibliography

Poems by Michael Smith published by *Race Today* (London)
"Mi Cyaan Believe It", *Race Today Review* (December 1980–January 1981)
"Say Natty Natty", *Race Today* (February–March 1982)
"Mi Feel It Yuh Si", *Race Today Review* (1983)
Books by Michael Smith
It A Come: Poems by Michael Smith, ed. Mervyn Morris (London: Race Today Publications: 1986). Reissued in 1989 by City Lights in San Francisco.

Michael Smith Discography

Word (Light of Saba: 1978)
Mi Cyaan Believe It/Roots (Light of Saba: 1978)
Mi Cyaan Believe It/Roots (LKJ Records: 1981)
Mi Cyaan Believe It (Island Records: 1982)

Notes

1. Mervyn Morris, "Building Awareness: Mikey Smith Interviewed", in *Making West Indian Literature* (Kingston, Jamaica: Ian Randle, 2005), 100, 105, 99. First published in *Jamaica Journal* 18, no. 2 (May–July 1985).
2. Creation for Liberation, of which I was a founding member, was started in the late 1970s in London, and was linked to the Race Today Collective (publishers of *Race Today* magazine). It was engaged in promoting cultural activities.
3. Delano Abdul Malik De Coteau, *The Whirlwind* (London: Panrun Collective, 1988).
4. John La Rose, "Fallen Comet", in *Race Today Review* (1984), 4–5.
5. Mervyn Morris, "Dub Poetry?", in *Is English We Speaking and Other Essays* (Kingston, Jamaica: Ian Randle, 1999), 36.
6. J. Edward Chamberlin, *Come Back to Me My Language* (Urbana and Chicago: University of Illinois Press, 1993), 235; Pamela Mordecai, introduction to *From Our Yard: Jamaican Poetry Since Independence,* ed. Pamela Mordecai (Kingston, Jamaica: Institute of Jamaica Publications, 1987), xxiii.
7. Gordon Rohlehr, introduction to *Voiceprint: An Anthology of Oral and Related Poetry from the Caribbean,* ed. Stewart Brown, Mervyn Morris and Gordon Rohlehr (Harlow: Longman, 1989), 18.
8. Kwame Dawes, *Natural Mysticism: Towards a New Reggae Aesthetic in Caribbean Writing* (Leeds: Peepal Tree Press, 1999), 82–83.
9. James Berry, "Dub Poetry", in *Oxford Companion to Twentieth Century Poetry,* ed. Ian Hamilton (Oxford: Oxford University Press, 1994); Mordecai, introduction to *From Our Yard,* xxiii.
10. Chamberlin, *Come Back to Me My Language,* 238; Kamau Brathwaite, *History of the Voice: The Development of Nation Language in Anglophone Caribbean Poetry* (London and Port of Spain: New Beacon Books, 1984), 46; Morris, "Editor's Notes", in *It A Come: Poems by Michael Smith,* ed. Mervyn Morris (London: Race Today Publications, 1986), 10.

PART THREE

The Sea Is History
Tidalectics, Middle Passages and Migrant Crossings

9

Routes and Roots
Tidalectics in Caribbean Literature

Elizabeth **DeLoughrey** |

move with me across the weeping atlantic
through the blood tears death pain and hurt
through the thundering angry sighing sobbing fury
of the startled atlantic
throbbing with the pulsating pages of a story
written as footnotes to an eager quest for land.

  – Merle Collins, "Chant Me a Tune"

History can be found underwater.
Yes – some history is only underwater

  – Michelle Cliff, *No Telephone to Heaven*

Caribbean cultural production has long been concerned with establishing a methodology for decolonizing history that is appropriate and attentive to local complexity. By excavating what Kamau Brathwaite refers to as those "alter/native" signifiers of history that are not overdetermined by the Euclidean grids of the plantocracy, we open up the possibility of rediscovering the past in the continual "tidalectic" between the Caribbean land and sea. In

Brathwaite's definition, this "tidal dialectic" draws upon "the movement of the water backwards and forwards as a kind of cyclic . . . motion, rather than linear". As a methodology, this foregrounds historical trajectories of migrancy and dispersal, and highlights the waves of various emigrant landfalls to the Caribbean and the process of settlement and sedimentation.[1] This approach is vital to complicating colonial myths of island isolation because it engages local space in relation to temporal duration. To engage island tidalectics is to historicize the process by which discourses of rootedness are naturalized in national soil, and to establish a series of external relationships through transoceanic routes and flows.

The ocean has long been imagined as a space of evolutionary and cultural origins. Since the peopling of any island demands the crossing of water, Caribbean literary theorists across the region have been concerned with plumbing the fluid spaces of the Caribbean and Atlantic as a source of cultural, ethnic and regional origins. Like Brathwaite, Derek Walcott, Edouard Glissant and Antonio Benítez-Rojo have employed what I call a "transoceanic imaginary" as a trope for Caribbean history, migration and regionalism. This can.be characterized as a type of cultural oceanography that maps a transatlantic and regional identity, engaging Walcott's suggestion that the "sea is history" alongside Brathwaite's declaration that Caribbean "unity is submarine".[2] The concern with re-mapping Caribbean seascapes differs from other theories of re-territorialization because tidalectics are concerned with the fluidity of water as a shifting site of history, and document the peoples who navigated or were coerced into transoceanic migrations. The first part of this chapter addresses the routes of the Middle Passage and the ways in which the ocean functions as a metonymic history for the millions of Africans that were transported across the Atlantic. The "sea is history" is demonstrated in a story of Edwidge Danticat's which compresses space/time by suggesting that contemporary Haitian refugees are afloat in a black diasporic tautology. The second part examines regional tidalectics through Ana Lydia Vega's depiction of refugees afloat in the Caribbean Sea. In an important counter to scholarly celebrations of diaspora and cosmopolitanism, Vega reveals the limitations of aquatic metaphors when "roots", or national sovereignties, are unattainable for refugee subjects. Both stories are vital reminders that while water may ebb and flow, or connote borderlessness, it is still patrolled by economic and military powers that claim their own type of territorialization. The tidalectics discussed here suggest that there is an imperative to inscribe a nativizing

Caribbean seascape, yet I argue that one cannot do so without addressing neoimperialist projects in the Caribbean and the need for what Marlene NourbeSe Philip refers to as "I-lander" sovereignty.[3] Thus I read tidalectics as an important imagining of both the Caribbean Sea *and* landscape – the "movement of the water backwards and forwards as a kind of cyclic . . . motion" which incorporates both routes and roots.

The Sea Is History

> History is built around achievement and creation; and nothing was created in the West Indies.
>
> – V.S. Naipaul, *The Middle Passage*

> Where are your monuments, your battles, your martyrs?
> Where is your tribal memory? Sirs,
> In that grey vault. The sea. The sea
> Has locked them up. The sea is history.
>
> – Derek Walcott, "The Sea Is History"

Edouard Glissant begins *Poetics of Relation* with a chapter entitled "The Open Boat" in which he theorizes watery origins for the peoples of Africa relocated to the Caribbean. The image of an oceanic grave for the lost souls of the Middle Passage is central to his effort to emphasize the diverse and transnational histories of the Caribbean. His emphasis on what Grace Nichols calls the "middle passage womb" displaces the continental/colonizing frames that surround the Caribbean basin.[4] In an attempt to destabilize a filial relationship to monolithic origins (which he sees as the precursor to colonial invasion), Glissant explains: "the abyss is a tautology: the entire ocean, the entire sea gently collapsing in the end into the pleasures of sand, make one vast beginning, but a beginning whose time is marked by these balls and chains gone green".[5]

The Middle Passage becomes a site of cultural oceanography, a historically complex space in which fluidity becomes the privileged sign over the linearity of colonial history. Monolithic (upper-case) History only recognizes the colonial monuments invoked in Walcott's poem, or Naipaul's Eurocentric definition of achievement. In contrast, Glissant's tidalectics are concerned with aquatic spaces that are materially unmarked by monuments or gravestones. To foreground Middle Passage history and the other transoceanic trajectories that brought African, Asian and European settlers to the region destabilizes genealogical or filial roots and offers an aquatic re-territorialization in opposition to the colonial architecture which literally attempted to construct the region as European. The element of water appeals because of its lack of fixity and rootedness. As Gaston Bachelard explains, "water is truly the transitory element. It is the essential ontological metamorphosis between heaven and earth. A being dedicated to water is a being in flux."[6] Since migration and creolization are so characteristic of Caribbean cultural formations, watery trajectories provide an apt metaphor for ethnicities "in flux".

The tautology of the Middle Passage is perhaps best exemplified by Edwidge Danticat's short story, "Children of the Sea".[7] In keeping with Glissant and Brathwaite's efforts to complicate linear historiography, this work compresses time/space so that contemporary Haitian refugees find themselves in the Middle Passage. The narrative takes place during the violently repressive reign in Haiti that followed President Aristide's first expulsion. Danticat inscribes the separation of families, friends and lovers in their flight from physical and political oppression inflicted by the *tonton macoutes* of Haiti. The story is told in epistolary form, where two young lovers write to each other after forced separation. The male narrator is one of the few to avoid violent execution by escaping with other Haitians in a small boat headed for Miami. He writes to his lover back home in his journal, which is eventually thrown into the sea when the boat starts leaking. The epistolary narrative form reflects the orality of call and response and incorporates the tidalectic between land and sea, with the notable irony that the letters never reach their intended objects, and that we, as readers, become their audience and intermediaries.

Although the unnamed male narrator initially observes that "there are no borderlines on the sea", in a way that resonates with Bachelard and Glissant, the story clearly shows that the trauma of the Middle Passage determines their contemporary exodus. The process of traversing space makes the passing of time visible, so the protagonist first turns to geography, adopting the tools of the colonial project. He is positioned as a New World cartographer, remarking, "maybe the world is flat and we are going to find out, like the navigators of old". But these "boat people" don't have the luxury of an exploratory seascape or voyage, and the fact that they are unsure as to whether they are one or a hundred miles off the coast of Haiti underlines their inability to chart their (national) journey.[8]

Danticat's "children of the sea" articulate their voyage as a microcosm of the global history of diaspora and displacement. The passengers on the boat "see themselves as Job or the Children of Israel", adopting an ethnic framework from the Jewish diaspora and then reconfiguring it as state dispersal when the passengers sing their national anthem: "Beloved Haiti, there is no place like you. I had to leave you before I could understand you."[9] The anthem suggests that historically, Haitian nationalism has been and continues to be created by territorial displacement, or "being(s) in flux". The placement of the refugees in the Caribbean Sea encodes a transoceanic imaginary that is deeply tied to nation building. The destabilizing routes of the sea are tidalectically complemented by the female narrator's reports of the violence of the *tonton macoutes* that results in her own flight into the Haitian countryside. For her the "blood drenched earth" still provides some escape; for the oceanic refugees, their attempts at national belonging are overwritten by the terror of the Middle Passage. They become "children of the sea" because its "abyss is a tautology".

In Danticat's work, the voyage of the Haitian refugees across space reflects a return to the Middle Passage, upholding the cyclical motion of "the sea [a]s history". In fact, the narrator's exposure to the sun ensures that he is "finally an African", and he remarks that they are "sailing for Africa . . . to Guinin, to live with the spirits, to be with everyone who has come and has died before us".[10] As the journey to Miami progresses and the passengers run out of food and water, the narrator increasingly references slave ships, Agwè (the Dahomeyan vodoun of fishing), and the Middle Passage. A pregnant character on the boat, Célianne, has been a victim of rape in a reinscription of many women's experiences of the African diaspora. Her child is stillborn and she eventually follows the child into its watery grave, suggesting the other "empty faces" of children who remind the narrator "of the hopelessness of the future in [his] country".[11] He begins to believe that

> it was always meant to be, as though the very day that my mother birthed me, she has chosen me to live life eternal, among the children of the deep blue sea, those who have escaped the chains of slavery to form a world beneath the heavens and the blood-drenched earth where you live.[12]

Here the tautology of oppression, forced migration, and cultural displacement are inescapable. The passage above reiterates Glissant's evocation of the space "whose time is marked by these balls and chains gone green". Later the narrator comments, "there are special spots in the sea where lost Africans who jumped off the slave ships still rest, that those who have died at sea have been chosen to make that journey in order to be reunited with their long-lost relations".[13] Although one might assume that water cannot be territorialized in the way of land occupation, Danticat's story reveals that the sea is marked by cultural and economic histories and is literally occupied by past and present bodies of refugees and slaves. Thus the Caribbean Sea is territorialized by particular histories that affect all migrants who cross its expanse. Here the sea is not a void, *aqua nullius* to be filled with the expectations or national identifications of the migrant, but has its own compression of diasporic history into which the Caribbean subject is incorporated. Danticat suggests that the Middle Passage must be cognitively mapped, but without recognition of the ways in which state-sanctioned violence (either in European slaving or Haitian autocracy) is repeated, Caribbean peoples become caught in the same violent cycles of diaspora. What Walcott refers to as the "grey vault" has not been opened, therefore Danticat's characters are caught in the tautological process of having to rediscover and be reclaimed by the cycles of transoceanic history.

Since the constant movement of the ocean means that the Middle Passage cannot be materially fixed and marked as a site of history, it is literally charted in Glissant and Danticat's texts through the transoceanic imagination. By populating the ocean (with peoples and associated Afro-Caribbean deities) and documenting the site of historical and present violence, these authors make the sea into a space of recognizable history. This imaginative return to the abyss engages an aquatic symbology that brings together transoceanic routes alongside terrestrial national roots, destabilizing the colonial *telos* of history through a continual tidalectic between land and sea.

The Sea as a Regionalist Metaphor: Peoples of the Sea

The sea is not only a space for diasporic historiography, but is also employed as a trope for Caribbean regionalism. In fact, the transoceanic imagination often utilizes the Middle Passage as a unifying site of history for the Afro-Caribbean region. Because this is a region that is one of the most diverse in the world, the strongest justification for addressing the Caribbean as an entity lies in its geography and the oceanic currents that surround the region and facilitate its complexity. Similar to the efforts of Caribbeanists to turn away from colonial monuments towards the "unmarked" and unifying Atlantic ocean, the watery surroundings of the Caribbean islands function as a space of uncharted historiography which is not overdetermined by colonial territorialization. In other words, the Caribbean Sea is an element "in flux" which highlights migrancy, but it is also a space which seems unoccupied by colonial presence and could unite the region in ways that offer an alternative to colonial fragmentation.

If Caribbean "unity is submarine", as Brathwaite writes (and Glissant is fond of quoting), then the islands can be seen as autonomous and geopelagically, politically and culturally connected to their island neighbours. To Glissant this aquatic interconnectedness represents a nativizing return to cultural interrelation. "Before the arrival of Columbus the Caribbean archipelago was constantly linked by a system of communication, from the continent to the islands of the north" and vice versa. Yet "colonization has balkanized the Caribbean, that is the colonizer who exterminated the Carib people in the islands, and disturbed this relationship".[14] Despite the continued balkanization of the Caribbean along colonial/linguistic categorizations and the pressures of neocolonial US presence, the reconstruction of this "system of communication", a view of the Caribbean as an aquatic rhizome, is shared between these theorists whose works permeate linguistic borders.

For example, Antonio Benítez-Rojo's *Repeating Island* bears remarkable similarities to Glissant's tidalectics, employing aquatic metaphors to focus more specifically on the waters that encompass the Caribbean, asserting that the Caribbean is a "meta-archipelago" which has the "virtue of having neither a boundary nor a centre".[15] He highlights the dispersal of Caribbean peoples in an effort to destabilize ethnic essentialism, and configures the region as being as much "in flux" as the waters that surround it. By visualizing the archipelago as an island that repeats itself into varying fractal spaces, Benítez-Rojo concludes,

> The culture of the Caribbean . . . is not terrestrial but aquatic, a sinuous culture where time folds irregularly and resists being captured by the cycles of clock and calendar. The Caribbean is the natural and indispensable realm of marine currents, of waves, of folds and double folds, of fluidity and sinuosity.[16]

The geography and climate of the Caribbean, especially its fluid borders, provide Benítez-Rojo with an alternative to colonial linear temporality and territorialism. Like Glissant, Benítez-Rojo utilizes Deleuze and Guattari's theory of rhizomes to destabilize the filial roots of empire. Yet unlike Glissant's tidalectics, Benítez-Rojo draws upon a gendered essentialism that is overlaid upon the supposedly unmarked and sinuous sea. While Glissant manages to avoid the conflation of watery borders with feminized fluidity, Benítez-Rojo's imagery of the Caribbean region reiterates the gendered dualisms that can be traced back to Spanish imperialism when the region was known, as Alfred Crosby points out, as the "Golfo de Damas, the Ladies' Gulf".[17]

While *The Repeating Island* does much to politicize ahistorical uses of poststructural theory (particularly those forms that avoid the mutually constitutive histories of colonialism), the text's celebration of Caribbean fluidity deflects the larger question of history and how, as Danticat has shown, migratory routes are constituted by terrestrial roots. In Glissant's terms, "the Caribbean Sea does not enclose; it is an open sea. It does not impose one culture, it radiates diversity." Benítez-Rojo builds upon Glissant's theory of tidalectics in which "each island embodies openness. The dialectic between inside and outside is reflected in the relationship of land and sea."[18] Yet Glissant warns about the dangers of reifying geography when he describes the Caribbean as "a sea that explodes the scattered lands into an arc. A sea that diffracts. *Without necessarily inferring any advantage whatsoever to their situation,* the reality of archipelagoes in the Caribbean or the Pacific provides a natural illustration of the thought of Relation."[19] Their theoretical divergence lies in Glissant's refusal to idealize the trajectories of Caribbean migration.

Benítez-Rojo suggests that the Caribbean Sea unites island peoples and breaks down the artificial, ideological boundaries of nation states. Water is employed to consolidate aquatic regionalism, as its limitless flows *seem* to work against national territorialism. Yet Ana Lydia Vega's short story "Cloud Cover Caribbean" is a good example of some of the more troubling aspects of patrolled aquatic borders, and the way in which women's bodies function as regional or aquatic metaphors while women subjects are excluded from regional participation. It is important to juxtapose Benítez-Rojo's theory of Caribbean fluidity with Vega's story because the latter highlights the ways in which a masculinist Caribbean regionalism is sustained by marine currents, and how the process of US imperialism racializes these male Caribbean subjects. Like Danticat's work, Vega's story calls attention to the Caribbean imperative for sovereign national space; it poses questions about the possibilities for regional agency when national sovereignty cannot be attained and trade and economic parameters are externally determined.

The story begins with Antenor, a Haitian floating on a raft amidst the "muscled arm of the sea", who first pulls in the shipwrecked Diogenes from the Dominican Republic and then the Cuban Carmelo. The sea's description as "muscled" is not accidental, as the story's conclusion will reveal. Although they can't linguistically understand each other, they establish "an international brotherhood of hunger, a solidarity of dreams". The men complain of "the endless pain of being black, Caribbean and poor; of deaths by the score; they cursed clergy, the military and civilians" for forcing their emigration.[20] As for the future, one character wonders if he might fall off the edge of the world,[21] which, as in Danticat's story, underlines the impossibility of a national (or territorialized) future for the rootless Caribbean subject.

While Benítez-Rojo asserts that "the Peoples of the Sea [are] traveling together toward the infinite",[22] one has to question whether their journeys unite the region and if their destinations are not overdetermined by imperial forces. In Vega's text, the three men on the boat soon start fighting, underlining the lack of regional identification despite dire circumstances. The only moment where they find common ground is when they speak of the "internationally famous backsides of the island's famous beauties".[23] Their disparaging comparisons between Dominican Republic "whores" and Cuban feminists indicate that the objectification of women solidifies this "international brotherhood". It is in this sense that Vega's story offers an important critique of masculinist regionalist paradigms. Like Benítez-Rojo's theory of regionalism, which is based on women's symbolic "otherness", the men of Vega's story eschew ethnic and cultural solidarities in favour of establishing a regional identity based on the conflation of women with the land. While Vega critiques the feminization of Caribbean sea/landscapes, Benítez-Rojo establishes his regionalism through women's "heteroclitic" otherness.[24]

While the men find temporary solidarity through their shared masculinity, power is *not* synonymous with the men afloat in their regional sea. Their claims to sovereignty are subverted by neocolonialism, symbolized by the American ship that rescues them. Run by an "Aryan, Apollo-like seadog", the captain has the men pulled on board and exclaims, "get those niggers down there and let the spiks take care of them".[25] Below the deck, the registers of identification change: the men can no longer rely on their masculinity to solidify their "brotherhood"; under the Aryan master they become interpellated as "niggers" and "spiks". Moments later the Dominican and Cuban men have the initial "pleasure of hearing their mother tongue spoken". But Vega quickly dismantles the linguistic identification when a "Puerto Rican voice growled through the gloom: 'if you want to feed your bellies here you're going to have to work, and I mean work. A gringo don't give nothing away. Not to his own mother' ".[26] Like the colonial myth of benevolence towards its dependencies, the US ship of state "rescues" a floundering Caribbean regionalism in order to racialize and exploit their labour in the "muscled arm of the sea". The earlier regional connections that were established through gender, ethnicity, language, history and a shared sea are discarded when the men become interpellated under the objectifying rubric of migrant labour. In this story the only possible regional identity is imposed through the masculinist, "Aryan" nation state which disrupts Caribbean familial and national identification. The logic of imperialist capital denies a relationship to the worker's mother/family and the potential for alternative ethnic and national origins. The story builds upon what C.L.R. James had declared two decades before: "the Caribbean is now an American sea. Puerto Rico is its show piece".[27] Although Glissant has defined the Caribbean as "the estuary of the Americas",[28] Vega's short story suggests that without national sovereignty, this sea is *already* territorialized as an American lake.

Vega's short story brilliantly adopts and then discards all the possible sites of identification for Caribbean "people of the sea": from geopolitical status to masculinity, from linguistic affiliation to the coerced indoctrination into global capitalist production. The story closes with their literal containment in the patrolled marine space of the larger US ship, where they work for the Aryan state and its unequally affiliated citizens, the Puerto Ricans. Vega highlights some of the more pressing material concerns that need to be accounted for when assessing the unifying metaphor of oceanic fluidity. While the waters that link the Caribbean are central to the vision of Caribbean regionalism, this unified vision should not ignore neocolonial presence in sovereign territories. In an effort to counter postcoloniality's "belatedness", more scholarship needs to be conducted on the current US presence in the Caribbean alongside the more distant history of European colonization. For it is the *lack* of national sovereignty which contributes to the human flotsam depicted in Vega and Danticat's short stories.

These works suggest that it is not enough to reclaim marine currents as an "alter/native" space of regional history in an attempt to reposition the agency of the Caribbean "I-lander". As in Brathwaite's work, it is the nonlinear tidalectic between land and sea, an engagement between routes and roots, which is of crucial significance. Black diaspora studies has turned to the ocean as a site of history, most notably in Paul Gilroy's book *The Black Atlantic*. The focus on marine currents is a conceptual break from the homogenizing discourses of the nation state, where historical, cultural and economic events are traditionally viewed within national parameters. But the focus on marine routes cannot be divorced from associated national territory. The aquatic space of Haitian nation building in Danticat's story and Vega's characters who build an aborted regional identity in the Caribbean Sea are all informed by diasporic histories and national sovereignties. ✓

The Caribbean islands can be defined through "submarine roots: that is floating free, not fixed in one position in some primordial spot, but extending in all directions in our world through its networks and branches",[29] but that should not ignore the ways in which other national branches reach *towards* the Caribbean and displace regionalism through the "muscled arm of the sea". An engagement with the roots of routes, a "tidal dialectic", is necessary in order to understand the process by which "peoples of the sea" navigate cultural and national sovereignty.

Acknowledgements

This chapter is a revision of two articles: "Some Pitfalls of Caribbean Regionalism: Colonial Roots and Migratory Routes", *Journal of Caribbean Literatures* 3, no. 1 (Summer 2001): 35–56, and "Tidalectics: Charting Caribbean 'Peoples of the Sea' ", *SPAN: Journal of the South Pacific Association for Commonwealth Literature and Language Studies* 47 (October 1998): 18–38.

Notes

1. Kamau Brathwaite, interview by Nathaniel Mackey, *Hambone* 9 (Winter 1991): 44. See also Brathwaite's "Caribbean Culture: Two Paradigms", in *Missile and Capsule,* ed. Jurgen Martini (Bremen: distributed by Universität Bremen, 1983).

2. See Walcott, *Collected Poems: 1948–84* (New York: Farrar, Straus and Giroux, 1986) and Brathwaite, "Caribbean Man in Space and Time", *Savacou* 11/12 (September 1975): 1–11.

3. In the longer version of this piece, I draw from Marlene NourbeSe Philip's theories of "I-land" sovereignty. See her "A Piece of Land Surrounded", *Orion* 14, no. 2 (Spring 1995): 41–47.

4. See Nichols, *I Is a Long Memoried Woman* (London: Karnak House, 1983).

5. Glissant, *Poetics of Relation,* trans. Betsy Wing (Ann Arbor: University of Michigan Press, 1997), 6.

6. Bachelard, *Water and Dreams: An Essay on the Imagination of Matter,* trans. Edith R. Farrell (Dallas: Pegasus Foundation, 1983), 6.

7. Danticat, "Children of the Sea", in *Krik? Krak!* (New York: Random House, 1996).

8. Ibid., 6.

9. Ibid., 7, 9.

10. Ibid., 11, 14.

11. Ibid., 5.

12. Ibid., 27.

13. Ibid., 28.

14. Glissant, *Caribbean Discourse: Selected Essays,* trans. J. Michael Dash (Charlottesville: University Press of Virginia, 1989), 248.

15. Benítez-Rojo, *The Repeating Island,* trans. James Maraniss (Durham: Duke University Press, 1992), 4.

16. Ibid., 11.

17. Alfred W. Crosby, *Ecological Imperialism: The Biological Expansion of Europe, 900–1900* (Cambridge: Cambridge University Press, 1986), 117. Benítez-Rojo feminizes aquatic space so that women can only participate metonymically in Caribbean regionalism. His description of "the painfully delivered child of the Caribbean, whose vagina was stretched between continental clamps" (*Repeating Island,* 5) employs the usual feminized colonial landscape, reminiscent of early colonial narratives.

18. Glissant, *Caribbean Discourse,* 261, 139.

19. Glissant, *Poetics of Relation,* 33–34; emphasis added. "Poetics of Relation" are defined as "the dialectics between the oral and the written, the thought of multilingualism, the balance between the present moment and duration, the ques-

tioning of literary genres, the power of the baroque, the nonprojectile imaginary construct" (p. 35).

20. Ana Lydia Vega, "Cloud Cover Caribbean" ("Encancaranublado"), in *Her
    True-True Name,* ed. Pamela Mordecai and Betty Wilson (Portsmouth, N.H.:
    Heinemann, 1989), 107.

21. Ibid., 106.

22. Benítez-Rojo, *Repeating Island,* 16.

23. Vega, "Cloud Cover Caribbean", 109.

24. Benítez-Rojo, *Repeating Island,* 25.

25. Vega, "Cloud Cover Caribbean", 110.

26. Ibid., 110, 111.

27. James, *The C.L.R. James Reader,* ed. Anna Grimshaw (Oxford: Blackwell, 1993),
    308.

28. Glissant, *Caribbean Discourse,* 139.

29. Ibid., 67.

10

Kamau Brathwaite and the Haitian Boat People

Dream Haiti or the Nightmare of the Caribbean Intellectual

Marie-José **Nzengou-Tayo** ▌

In *The Other America,* Trinidadian critic J. Michael Dash states, "it was in Haiti that Caribbean thought first emerged as a contestation of the reductive mystification of colonialism", and he stresses the importance of the Haitian experience, "since the Haitian Revolution signaled a new way of fashioning identity in the new World".[1] Indeed, the revolution fed the imagination of many writers of the neighbouring countries. Bridget Jones has documented Brathwaite's interest in Haiti and the French-speaking Caribbean in her seminal essay, " 'The Unity Is Submarine': Aspects of a Pan-Caribbean Consciousness in the Work of Kamau Brathwaite". Her analysis shows that Haiti attracted Brathwaite's attention for both historical and cultural reasons, as the Caribbean country which witnessed the first successful slave revolution and in which remnants of African culture were evident. Jones recounts Brathwaite's visit to Haiti in 1968–69, and she notes that "[t]he living presence of Africa in the Haitian people, especially their vodoun religion, seems to have inspired a privileged sense of recognition not dissimilar though less intense than that experienced in Ghana".[2]

Jones also quotes from *Contradictory Omens,* in which Brathwaite expresses his surprise at the resemblance between the Haitian countryside and West Africa.[3] Analysing recurrences in Brathwaite's poetry of allusions to vodoun divinities (with a strong preference for Legba, the *lwa* of crossroads), and rituals with the drawing of *vèvès,*[4] Jones finds that "[t]he impact of Haiti seems strongly visual, Brathwaite captivated to perceive so much of Africa in the markets, in the style of movement and daily behaviour, admiring also the brilliance of the painters and muralists".[5] According to her, Brathwaite was also impressed by "the glory of the Haitian Revolution", and "he can be seen ordering what he sees in and reads about Haiti into the patterns of region-wide resistance . . . recompos[ing] a synthesis of psychical and actual 'maroonage' which further post-colonial research in slave revolts has confirmed".[6]

Based on Jones's analysis of Brathwaite's response to Haitian culture and history, we see that it falls in line with pre-1980 images of Haiti in Caribbean literature.[7] Brathwaite, like his fellow Caribbean writers, found in Haitian history "the symbol of something important for the entire Caribbean and America: the country itself and its past give the primary signs of the American potential in terms of literary imagination".[8] In addition, Haitian history and culture reinforced the development of black consciousness, and constituted a unifying factor in the Caribbean at a moment when a process of reconquering the control of one's environment was taking place.

However, the deterioration of living conditions in Haiti, the brutality of the Duvaliers' dictatorship (1957–86), and the massive illegal migration which took place in the late 1970s and early 1980s have shaken the literary stereotypes associated with Haiti. Caribbean writers could not ignore the plight of Haitian people, and this has appeared in many works of fiction as early as 1981 (for example, Ana Lydia Vega from Puerto Rico in several stories of *Encancaranublado*).[9] In Brathwaite's case, we must note that his interest in the Haitian "boat people" develops in the 1990s, at the most tragic period of Haitian illegal migration to Florida (1991–92), that is, after the *coup d'état* against President Jean-Bertrand Aristide. In addition, the fact that Brathwaite's personal experience mingled with that of the Haitian illegal migrants gives a particular resonance to the poem *Dream Haiti.* It is clear that the 1992 Savacou publication of *Dream Haiti* breaks away from a tradition of writing about Haiti.[10] Taking into account the fact that both Jones and Gordon Rohlehr put this poem in a sombre period of Brathwaite's inspiration during which he wrote the *Dreamstories* poems (published in 1994), one is struck by the triple conjunction among the poet's personal traumas,[11] his interest in the contemporary tragedy of the Haitian people (especially the "boat people"), and the "dream" framework chosen for the poem. This chapter will take a closer look at the poem along these three axes, trying to see how the poet's experience could draw from the Haitian one or shed new light on it, and how the Freudian principle of dream was used to shape the symbolic representation of both experiences.

In his introduction to the Longman edition of *Dreamstories*, Gordon Rohlehr tells of the change in Brathwaite's inspiration, a change triggered by three dramatic experiences that shattered his life. One was the loss of his wife (in 1986), the second was Hurricane Gilbert (in 1988) and the third was a robbery that made him fear for his life (in 1990). Rohlehr links these three traumas with the sombre mood of the *Dreamstories* poems, and reads them as an attempt at exorcizing painful memories.[12] He considers them as "closely associated with the poet's personal quest or ordeal", which would justify the dream form of the poem. Following the psychoanalytical principle of the dream, the poems of the collection allow for introspection: "[They] all are corridors through which the archetypes are revisited and experienced anew, modes of descents into self and into the formative historical experience of a civilisation."[13]

Freud taught us that in dreams real experience is reorganized symbolically during our sleep, a state of unconsciousness during which the ego's defences are lowered, allowing the metaphorical expression of thoughts, feelings and that which would otherwise be silenced or repressed by our consciousness.[14] These characteristics of dream have been taken on by the surrealist writers and transposed in literature through the technique of the awakened dream and automatic writing. These practices tell us what to expect from Brathwaite's dream poems: chains of associations not necessarily coherent yet developing themselves within a symbolic framework. As stated by Rohlehr in his introduction, the title of the collection indicates that the poems

> are about the relationship between the definite and indefinite; the world of reasonable everyday expectations and that of surprising sequences, abrupt transitions, sheer irrationality of associations. . . . Since these dream stories are mode [*sic*] of coping with trauma through imposing on it the shape of fiction, they challenge the reader to interpret them as allegories of the author's situation.[15]

In *Dream Haiti* we hear three voices: the Haitian refugee, the poet, and a distant voice which seems to be a second and omniscient manifestation of the poet, looking at himself from outside (or above). However, there is no "dialogue" between the personae of the poem, they simply alternate, sometimes unexpectedly, as allowed by the "dream" nature of the poem. As Rohlehr notes, the poems of *Dreamstories* "lack the polyphony of *The Arrivants* or *Mother Poem*. . . . The natural medium of the dream is monologue and most of these stories employ a first person narrator."[16]

A closer examination of the shifts in the narrative voice shows an intricate pattern due to the presence of a "we", an inclusive figure linking the persona to the larger group of refugees or Caribbean intellectuals.[17] The hypothetical reader is also inscribed in the text with "you", even if it is through the rhetorical expressions "if you see what i mean" and "if you know what i mean" (*Dreamstories,* 14). More complex is the "you" referring to the persona, since the dream condition allows for a distancing of the "I" with itself. A critical eye/I is able to observe itself from above, commenting on the actions of a "you":

> . . . & you swimmin there in the dark of the water
> & throwin them scream –
> in to some –
> body else out there . . .
> & they was suppose to be some kind of rope . . .
> that you grip in yr hann when you toss its white little
> sweetie over the side . . .
>
> (p. 17)

The distinction between the voice of the poet and that of the Haitian refugee is sometimes blurred since we are in a dream, as we are reminded:

> And it was not that *we* was goin anywhere if *you* see
> what *i* mean
>
> –
>
> . . .
>
> *i* mean *we* was not goin anywhere although the ship was
> movin *i* suppose . . .
> & yet in *my dream* it was juss like on board anyship . . .
>
> (p. 14, emphasis added)

The disoriented persona in the dream seems to be the poet himself and, at times, the refugee taken on board by the American coast guard. However, the imaginary world of the dream allows for a switching of personalities and indefinite identities:

> *i do not know why i am here - how i come to be on board*
> this ship - this navel of my ark –
> w/ my nerves as I say comin & goin & my head spinnin soff
> ly & beginnin to wet & giddy & my heart pushin hard > the daylight of my body
>   & swishin for the peace & darkness &
> the spice of gumbo Sundaes
> since *i am suppose to be a poet* not a coast guard cutter
> or fireman or one or two others on this deck . . .
>
>   (*Dreamstories*, 16, emphasis added)

Similarly, the personae switch when Brathwaite evokes the drowning/ drowned Haitians:

> &
> i remember that it was like some dark gaoler of convex of glass
> was like lockin us up agains // & against // & i cd hear the long
> echo
> ing noise of the metal doors of my lungs . . .
> & we were trying to reach the lifelines that were made of the same material as
>   the thongs of our fingers . . . although we cd hardly see that nobody had
>   started throwin any of them overboard to help us . . .
>
>   (p. 39)

A guilty conscience lays the base for Brathwaite's poem *Dream Haiti*. Under the dedication to David Rudder, we find these lines in bold capitals in epigraph:

> **HAITI I'M SORRY**
> **WE MISUNDERSTOOD YOU**
> **ONE DAY WE TURN OUR HEAD**
> **AND LOOK INSIDE YOU**
>
> **HAITI I'M SORRY**
> **HAITI I'M SORRY**
> **ONE DAY WILL TURN OUR HEAD**
> **AND RESTORE YOUR GLORY**[18]

The poet reappropriates Rudder's apologies, which are offered in the name of a collective "we". We could assume that he is speaking in the name of the region. The date mentioned on this front page (18 May 1992) reminds us that the poem was created during the period of the 1991–94 *coup* against President Aristide, one of the most tragic periods of the boat people's migration. *Dream Haiti* can be read as a call for regional solidarity, as the Haitian boat people's experience is exemplary of "the seemingly endless / purgatorial x / perience of black people" (p. 4). May 18 is also full of meaning for a Haitian reader, because it curiously coincides with the anniversary of the creation of the Haitian flag by Dessalines.

Brathwaite recalls the part played by the Americans in the Haitian tragedy. They appear as unlikely "saviours", since for most of the refugees these rescuers are reluctantly throwing the "lifelines" which would take them out of the water (*Dream Haiti*, 36, 39). The coast guard cutter becomes a "gutter" (pp. 18, 20–21, 30) with all the negative connotations of the word. One persona of the poem, the Haitian refugee maybe, reads the inscription "US / COAST / GUARD / GUTTER" (p. 18) both in the right way and reversed (p. 20). He interprets his reading as signs to be posted on one's coffin (p. 21). Though the reverse spelling is meaningless as such, it stands, threatening, as a cryptic bad omen:

RETTUG DRAUG TSAOC SU[19]

This because the French and Creole (maybe illiterate) speakers cannot interpret or decipher it.

The plight of the Haitian people appears to be foretelling the future of the Caribbean people (we are all in this together / we are not in this together). The poet indicates the dubious/ambiguous position of Caribbean intellectuals/ artists confronted with the Haitian tragedy. Witnesses in spite of themselves, they seem indifferent.

> we was all standin they in that kind of windy silence of this dream – not close
>> together of course since we was all artists and strangers to each other & not
>> soldiers or sailors or dwarfs as i have to go on insistin even though
> we was on the same trip as
> Black Stalin
> had said so many years ago
>> *(Dream Haiti, 26)*

The persona/poet stresses the stunned silence of the artists, expressing their deep shock at the situation. However, they do not relate to each other ("strangers"), conveying lack of solidarity and absence of a community. The "dream" situation contributes to the uncanny dimension of the scene ("evvating was like movin so strangely" [*Dream Haiti*, 27]). The artists seem to disown their embarrassing Caribbean neighbour. The overcrowding of the boat – twenty-five people in a space designed to accommodate between thirteen and fifteen (p. 29) – and the fact that one gets the impression that the refugees and the artists-cruisers / coast guards are on the same boat ("just like us on ?Salvages?" [p. 29]). Yet, the poet makes it clear ("as i have to go on insistin even though" [p. 25]) that the intellectuals/artists should not be assimilated with the US sailors or firemen or "dwarf[s]" (p. 25).

The Haitian experience evoked by Brathwaite in *Dream Haiti* is that of a peasant forced to abandon his land because of the (Duvalier) dictatorship (suggested by the reference to the "macoute" on page 31), though the context of the Haitian boat people's migration is that of the 1991 *coup*. The anachronism comes from time contraction and collision due to the dream. Macoutes are evoked because the poet is brought back to the time of his 1968–69 visit to Haiti, under the Duvalier regime. At the same time, he associates them with the recent events of the post-1991 *coup* (the Titanyen common grave [p. 38], and the US coast guard blockade along Florida to prevent the Haitians from landing in the United States [pp. 46–47]). Similarly, the image of the "lambi" brings back memories of childhood (the child bleeding on the beach [p. 31]). By association of ideas, thinking of the macoutes suggests the iron fist of the Duvalier regime, which in turn conjures up the images of two governing "iron ladies" (Margaret Thatcher and Eugenia Charles [p. 33]), under the cover of the name of a business woman in Port-au-Prince: Margaret Eugenia Azuchar (p. 30). The surname "Azuchar", phonetically close to the Spanish *azucar* (sugar), reminds the Caribbean reader of the reason for colonizing the region: the colonial exploitation of sugar cane and the plantation system.

The glorious images of the Haitian past are still present (Christophe, Toussaint [*Dream Haiti*, 39]) but they have lost their mobilizing power. More present and more demoralizing is the vision of drowning refugees (pp. 39–45, 47). In the most tragic section of the poem, the persona shifts back and forth from the onlooking intellectual/writer/poet to the drowning Haitian, represented by a young child (seen on television [p. 43]). In his nightmare, the poet sees himself catching the drowned little boy and then dropping him back into the water (p. 43). The imagination of the poet is incensed by the innocence of the victim, and his emotion and horror are heightened (pp. 42–43).[20] The plight of the Haitians is also associated with his own period of personal trauma (the death of his wife, "Mexican", and Hurricane Gilbert, the "Gilbattery" [p. 25]) and "non-creativity", not only his own, but also others': "nobody had written anything serious since Mexican die & the Gilbattery of 1988" [p. 25]). Evoking the dying Haitians allows the poet to evoke his own dying wife, his feeling of loss heightened by the destruction caused by the hurricane. The technique of the dream allows for the mixing of images, in order to translate the inner turmoil of the traumatized consciousness.

Brathwaite associates the journey of the boat people with the memory of the Middle Passage, but a passage done "in reverse": "as if i was already turning the leaves of the waves for a long long history of time" (*Dream Haiti*, 24), and also "the green tide ruining us all the way back to distant Dakar to the dungeons of the cyclops' Gorée, Gorée, Gorée, Gorée" (p. 42). In this respect, he highlights one of the most significant symbolic aspects of the Haitian boat people's migration and, as such, connects with some Haitian writings. For instance, Anthony Phelps's "Même le soleil est nu"/"Even the Sun Is Naked" (1992) echoes Brathwaite's nightmare.

> O nights dreaming of the day's bread
> Cruelness long madness on the waters
> noon mutilated like windburned statements
> tongue of salt and mapmakers' skins
> Grammatical men articles of my delivery at *four centuries away*
> the frightening dream of the sea on the salt road
> Death watches over them A few get by
> essence of sugar and coffee[21]

Similarly, in Edwidge Danticat's "Children of the Sea" (1992), the young narrator on the boat makes the analogy of his experience with that of his forefathers crossing the Atlantic.[22] There is even a *clin d'oeil* to Brathwaite's writing ("the unity is submarine")[23] when the young traveller imagines a long chain of drowned bodies linking Africa to the Caribbean, the old bodies of the Middle Passage and the new ones of the Haitian boat people.

The dream situation allows also for a questioning of Caribbean solidarity, and a subtle critique of the willingness of Caribbean leaders to bow to US hegemony in the region. It also raises a doubt about the power of intellectuals to influence political choice in the region, as they kept their mouth shut in a "windy silence" (*Dream Haiti*, 25). Haunted by the horror of the Haitian boat people's experience, *Dream Haiti* does not offer the optimistic epic view of the early 1960s; instead we see unfolding the nightmare of the powerless intellectual (bought and bound by the comfort of US money?).

> That we are they brothers and fellow writers bound to them by all kinds of travellers cheques and the content of our character as if did not memember how they have put on they shoes that afternoon . . . before takin us up to Jacmel to Marigot to Pétionville . . . to see wher
> Hector
> Hyppolyte live
>
> (pp. 46–47)

Unable to effect change, Caribbean writers have become silent accomplices to what is done to Haitians. We cannot help but read the final line of the poem as an ironical Freudian slip. While the reader logically expects "watchin them *drownin*", the poet surprises, by substituting instead the word "poem":

> we stann on the soff hard deck of the
> Coast Guard
> Impeccable[24]
> watchin them poem
>
> (p. 49)

Isn't it a way to tell us that no matter how unbearable or shocking the horror he witnesses is, the writer/artist will only visualize it as a potential work of art, in this instance a piece of poetry?

In conclusion, Brathwaite's evocation of the Haitian boat people in *Dream Haiti* reveals the ambiguity of artistic creation. While as a critic he has always valued "the writer's relationship with the people, the society, the cultural habitat informing the creation of his or her text",[25] as a poet he sees himself confronted with the "unspeakable" / "non-communicable" nature of the Haitian boat people's experience. Therefore, what better way than the dream form for him to express the confusing and revolting nature of the experience? Through free association of ideas/images, Freudian slips, repetition and stuttering, the poet has tried to overcome his personal grief in order to empathize with the Haitian boat people. The shocking experience of the Haitians has lead him to question the evolution of the Caribbean region and to redefine the function of its poets and artists, hence his indignant protest against attempts to

> chide [him] . . . for lament
> =ing this seem
> =ing perpetu
> =al progrom and pro
> gram lik this?
> this
> season on season
> persist
> =uant anomie?
> for trying to *ghost*
> *words to*
> *holler* this tale

(*Dream Haiti*, 46–47, emphasis added)[26]

Notes

1.   J. Michael Dash, *The Other America: Caribbean Literature in the New World*, New World Studies, ed. A. James Arnold (Charlottesville: University Press of Virginia, 1998), 42, 44.
2.   Bridget Jones, " 'The Unity Is Submarine': Aspects of a Pan-Caribbean Consciousness in the Work of Kamau Brathwaite", in *The Art of Kamau Brathwaite*, ed. Stewart Brown (Bridgend, Wales: Seren, 1995), 91.
3.   Edward Kamau Brathwaite, *Contradictory Omens: Cultural Diversity and Integration in the Caribbean* (1974; reprint, Kingston, Jamaica: Savacou Publications, 1979), 43.
4.   *Vêvê* or *vèvè* is the name of the drawing made with flour by the vodoun priest on the floor of the temple in order to summon the vodoun spirits or *lwa*.
5.   Jones, "Unity", 92. The Brathwaite texts to which Jones refers are *Islands* (1969), *The Arrivants* (1973), and *X/self* (1987).
6.   Ibid., 93.
7.   See M.J. Nzengou-Tayo: "Re-Imagining History: The Caribbean Vision of the Haitian Revolution and of the Early Independence Days", *Espace Caraïbe*, no. 3 (1995): 105–20.
8.   Ibid., 116.

9. See Elizabeth DeLoughrey's analysis of Vega's short story "Encancaranublado" in the preceding chapter.

10. Brathwaite, *Dream Haiti* (New York: Savacou North, 1992). See Nzengou-Tayo, "Re-Imagining History", on this point.

11. See Gordon Rohlehr, "Dream Journeys", introduction to *Dreamstories*, by Edward Kamau Brathwaite (Harlow: Longman, 1994), iii–xvi.

12. Ibid., iii.

13. Ibid., vi, vii.

14. Sigmund Freud, *Introduction à la psychanalyse* (1916; reprint, Paris: Petite Bibliothèque Payot, 1978), 195–97.

15. Rohlehr, "Dream Journeys", ix.

16. Ibid., x–xi.

17. Brathwaite, *Dreamstories*, 14, 46. Hereafter cited in the text.

18. I am quoting from the Savacou edition of *Dream Haiti* (New York: Savacou North, 1995); hereafter cited in the text. The epigraph appeared also in the 1994 collection *Dreamstories* (London: Longman).

19. This could be read as "re(-)tug dra(-)g (i)t's (a) oc su", and, among various other possibilities, interpreted as "pull again, drag, it's o.k, sir".

20. This section is omitted in the Longman version of *Dream Haiti*.

21. Anthony Phelps, "Même le soleil est nu" ("Even the Sun Is Naked"), in *Haiti: The Literature and Culture*, ed. Charles Rowell, special issue of *Callaloo* 15, no. 2 (Spring 1992): 358.

22. Edwidge Danticat, "Children of the Sea". The story was first published in 1992, then appeared in *Krik? Krak!* (1995; reprint, New York: Random House, 1996).

23. Statement at Carifesta Forum, 1976; quoted in Edouard Glissant, *Caribbean Discourse: Selected Essays*, trans. J. Michael Dash (Charlottesville: University Press of Virginia, 1989), 66.

24. How not to read "impeccable" here as its etymology suggests: "without any sin"? About multiple meanings in Brathwaite's choice and mix of words, see Pamela Mordecai, "Prismatic Vision: Aspects of Imagery, Language and Structure in the Poetry of Kamau Brathwaite and Derek Walcott" (PhD diss., University of the West Indies, 1997), 297–99.

25. Silvio Torres-Saillant, *Caribbean Poetics: Towards an Aesthetic of West Indian Literature* (Cambridge: Cambridge University Press, 1997), 96.

26. The use of bold and very large fonts in the Savacou edition marks the poet's indignation at the idea of being silenced or scorned ("you chide me") for writing about the Haitian boat people. The use of "progrom" and "program" hints at an organized scheme to exclude, with an allusion to Wole Soyinka's *Season of Anomie*.

PART FOUR

Creolization, Historiography and Subalternity

11

Whose World View Rules?
Sublated Contradictions of African and Creole in the Caribbean Historiography of Kamau Brathwaite

Cecil **Gutzmore** |

[T]he submerged mother of the creole system, Africa.

– Edward Kamau Brathwaite, *Contradictory Omens*

The Arrivants is a poem of remarkable complexity, depth and dimension, and one which opens myriad windows into the possibility of an indigenous and rooted craft growing out of Caribbean soil.

– Gordon Rohlehr, *Pathfinder*

This is one reason why history proves to be so perplexing an experience for the colonial; the victim and the murderer were both ancestors. Tradition for him becomes . . . irony, paradox, perplexity and at times crucifixion.

– Rohlehr, *Pathfinder*

The cultural model [the East Indian] was asked to copy in the Caribbean was clearly non-Indian. . . . There developed among the Indian immigrants a tendency to resist creolization . . . and hark back to India.

– Brathwaite, *Contradictory Omens*

Introduction

Even after Paget Henry's study, *Caliban's Reason: Introducing Afro-Caribbean Philosophy*,[1] there remains an intellectual lacuna to be filled by an epistemological, ontological and cultural project that interrogates the concepts and imagery through which Caribbean scholars and creative writers seek to establish critical knowledge of Caribbean society. Such ostensibly first-order concepts as "plantation society",[2] "plural society"[3] and "creole society"[4] are meant to be applicable both at the regional level and to particular Caribbean social formations. There are claims, also, for their applicability beyond the Caribbean area.[5] Other concepts and images such as "limbo society",[6] "Callalou society",[7] societies of "mimic men",[8] "societies outside history",[9] "repeating islands",[10] the home of "Caliban's reasoners",[11] and so forth, have all been variously deployed in Caribbean intellectual and artistic discourses.

This essay is a partial critique of one of the above concepts, namely "creole", and the conceptual cluster constituted by such terms as *creolization, creole society, creole culture, creole complex*, "marginal"/"non-sugaring creole societies",[12] *creole continuum,* and *créolité*. More specifically, the essay focuses on the problem of creole-related discourse in Caribbean historiography, through a close reading of the output of certain major figures in this field, particularly Edward Kamau Brathwaite, historian, social and literary critic, poet and "proet" – to use one of his neologisms. In epistemological, ontological and even cultural terms, this cluster of creole ideas and images represents a more complex problem than previous critiques have recognized.

The case explicitly advanced here against creole-based academic discourse and usage[13] makes the following claims: (1) creole discourse in Caribbean studies – especially historiography – is very problematically theorized; and (2) most of its empirical results could have been obtained without using creolist concepts and discourse. Invariably, the achieved results derive their power not from the operation of creolist tropes but from concepts such as *acculturation, interculturation, transculturation, indigenization, socialization* and *secularization,* taken fully formed from such disciplines as anthropology and sociology. Crucially, however, none of these concepts has been substantively developed by their specific utilization in creolist discourse, hence the concurrent problems of a certain theoretical vacuity and redundancy. (3) Academic creolist discourse and everyday usage have tended "objectively" to exclude several Caribbean communities, especially Asians but also Amerindians, Maroons,

Jews, Portuguese and others. In addition, "subjectively", the term *creole* has tended to be rejected by Indians/South Asians and Chinese, and perhaps by others also, as a tool of both self-designation and self-definition. The light generated from academic attempts to fit South and East Asians into creolist discourse has not generally been worth the candle. (4) Academic creole discourse joins everyday usage in a tendency to de-Africanize and inferiorize Caribbean and continental Africans. Indeed, some practitioners of creole discourse appear quite uncomfortable with the well-attested fact of African folk/popular cultural centrality within the expressive arts of the Caribbean region. They have also sometimes appeared strongly opposed to Caribbean African assertions of pan-Africanism.

The above claims signal an important contradiction within Caribbean historiography which is strikingly evident in the work of Kamau Brathwaite, where he contrives a unique resolution. Richard Allsopp, the Guyanese linguist whose work Brathwaite calls "mind-blowing",[14] offers the following summary of the history of the word *creole*:

> The term, in all its senses; connotes New World, esp[ecially] Car[ibbean area], family stock, breed, and thence quality. Originally (17C) it was used with pride by European colonists (esp[ecially] the Fr[ench]) to refer to themselves as born in the New World and spelt with a capital C. . . . It was then extended to distinguish "local" from imported breeds, esp[ecially] horses and livestock, then slaves locally born as different from African importees. With *this sense the status of the word dropped (18–19C) amongst whites but rose among blacks and COLOURED locally born, and freedmen. In many post-emancipation Caribbean Area societies (19–20C) the term became generally a label either of a class embracing non-white persons of "breeding" or an excluded class of "ill-bred" blacks.*[15]

Historian Barry Higman supplies the following authoritative insight into Caribbean historiography's appropriation of creolization discourse:

> [T]he region's historians have made their histories "creole" in a fundamental sense. . . . [F]rom the 1940s anthropologists began to call many of the societies of tropical America "creole cultures" and to identify a process of creolization extending far beyond the linguistic sphere. In the late 1960s Brathwaite advanced the "creole society" concept *as a means of comprehending the creativity of the West Indian people* and in opposition to the competing plural society/tower of Babel models. The creole idea also came to be used to distinguish history written from a Caribbean rather than imperial perspective, leading critics . . . to talk of "the creolization of

Caribbean history". These concepts have spread far and wide, along with the diaspora of the Caribbean people in the Atlantic world and beyond . . . through music,
language and life-style, giving creolization a significance comparable to the globalization model.[16]

The question that arises directly for Caribbean historiography is this: How
can it be valuing creolist discourse in the manner authoritatively indicated by
Higman, if Allsopp is even largely correct about the historical evolution of the
word *creole* in the Caribbean? The question in approaching Brathwaite's work
then becomes the following: Why has Brathwaite – implicitly identified by
Gordon Rohlehr as the major pan-Africanist voice in modernist Caribbean letters[17] – sought to combine his Africanist perspective with creolization discourse, when the latter is inescapably compromised by a deep-seated
anti-Africanism, amongst other major defects? These questions, like their
answers, are initially connected to the differing weights professional historians attach to methodological as opposed to theoretical/epistemological concerns. To historians historical methodology is *de rigueur,* while historical
theory is a kind of optional extra.

Towards an Epistemological Critique of Creole Discourse in Caribbean Historiography

Kamau Brathwaite is indisputably the leading theorist of creolization in the
post-1945 anglophone Caribbean,[18] and his work resonates with similar discourses in the wider Caribbean/New World terrain.[19] Kamau Brathwaite published his acclaimed monograph, *The Development of Creole Society in Jamaica,
1770–1820,* three decades ago in 1971.[20] Both Rohlehr and Maureen Warner-
Lewis have demonstrated that by then Brathwaite had long found his continental African roots and his Afro-Caribbean cultural identity was fully
developed, as evinced in his marvelous poetry and brilliantly insightful literary and social criticism. His 1974 essay, *Contradictory Omens,*[21] heralded a
more expansive creolist mode, evident in three later texts that consolidate his
creole-society project: "Caribbean Man in Space and Time", "Kumina: The
Spirit of African Survival in Jamaica", and "Caliban, Ariel and Unprospero in
the Conflict of Creolization: A Study of the Slave Revolt in Jamaica in
1831–32".[22]

According to Verene Shepherd and Glen Richards, when *The Development of Creole Society in Jamaica, 1770–1820* first appeared, "the term 'creole', as an alleged description of specific New World cultures and societies, was already in widespread . . . use". They also point out that Richard Adams had earlier described creole culture as "the ways of life that have emerged in the New World specifically in those societies where plantations have served as a dominant element of the social structure".[23] To interpret Adams as saying that Caribbean/New World social formations which are tropical lowland "plantation societies" are also creole societies is to begin to glimpse the degree of overlap that exists between some of the concepts of Caribbean sociohistorical and critical analysis mentioned at the start of this article.[24] It is in this vein that Howard Johnson rightly lauds Kamau Brathwaite's contribution to the historiography of Jamaica. He calls *The Development of Creole Society in Jamaica, 1770–1820* "a work clearly *in the tradition of 'creole' scholarship*".[25]

Brathwaite's historical opus, *The Development of Creole Society in Jamaica*, passed with flying colours the tests of historical methodology set by historiography (sound archival research, the production of well-written articles or monographs demonstrating also an unimpeachable knowledge of the secondary literature). But Brathwaite had accomplished much more in two significant respects. First, by adding, at the highest theoretical level of his monograph, creole society/creolization discourse, he had clearly come to be seen by historians as providing an alternative to M.G. Smith's plural-society theory. Second, he included, and published separately at a popular price, his very Africanist chapter on the "folk culture" of the enslaved Africans in Jamaica. Thus, rather than a simple monograph reporting the fruits of empirical historical research, the book established Brathwaite's popular African, creolist, historical, methodological and theoretical credentials.

Johnson and Higman comment on the creolist facet of Brathwaite's historiography in order to designate an indigenous tradition of Caribbean historical scholarship that is locally focused and uses local sources, including the oral.[26] They contrast this with an earlier "imperial" history-writing that relied on colonial archives and texts. Interestingly, Philip Curtin, whom Johnson credits for initiating this trend in Caribbean historiography, gave no great salience to terms from the creole ideas cluster. I could find "creole" used only once in Curtin's 1955 book, *Two Jamaicas*, with reference to French immigrants to Jamaica from revolutionary Haiti.[27] The trend noted by Johnson and Higman could thus be termed the partial "localization" or indigenization of Caribbean history writing. There is no disputing Higman's recognition of the need for a critical and conceptual language in which to "comprehend the creativity of the Caribbean people".[28] But there is good reason to doubt that ideas like creolization, creole society and creole culture can or should provide the basis of such a language.

There has been very little discussion of the fact that Kamau Brathwaite's essential contribution to creole discourse in Caribbean historiography is his elevation of several of the terms of the creole ideas cluster to the level of first-order analytical concepts in his historiography and cultural criticism. This contrasts with the previously prevailing situation in the early decades of the second half of the twentieth century, when these ideas functioned fairly widely within this broad terrain, but as second- or middle-order analytical ideas. Following their elevation by Brathwaite, they have been unable to bear the intellectual weight assigned them. Further empirical and theoretical inquiry is called for to verify the precise analytical level at which these ideas have functioned both before and after Brathwaite's complex intervention in the field. However, my own perusal of the literature confirms that, after *The Development of Creole Society in Jamaica,* creole discourse has tended to be built on somewhat contrary, if not contradictory, assumptions: first, that these ideas belong at the highest level of historical, social and literary analysis; and second, the unvoiced assumption that the conceptual apparatus of creolization discourse is a bit wobbly. Hence, the theoretical underpinning takes the form of conceptual borrowing. I now explore this state of affairs, beginning with M.G. Smith and Elsa Goveia, two key producers of creole-related intellectual works pre-dating Brathwaite's. I then turn to H. Orlando Patterson, Kamau Brathwaite himself, and Walter Rodney. Some other contributors to the debate are more briefly addressed. The methodological significance of these authors' work within this article is that each represents an important site of creole discourse in the evolving area of broadly historical Caribbean writing (history itself, historical sociology, historical anthropology, diachronic cultural criticism).

Historical anthropologist, poet and social analyst, M.G. Smith, the chief founder of Caribbean plural-society discourse, used creole terms precisely as second-order ideas. Writing in the 1950s and early 1960s, he gave the notions *creole, creole culture* and *creole complex* a place of considerable significance within and alongside his emerging plural-society theorization of Caribbean society. He divided these societies into a "creole complex" and a "mestizo complex".[29] His "creole complex" purportedly described only some Caribbean societies and, indeed, applied only to some facets of the societies so described. Others – and Caribbean societies more comprehensively – would, of course, have been covered by his plural-society concept. Smith preceded many in arriving at a fully developed conception of the phenomena connoted by the expression "Caribbean creole culture". He also recognized the relevance of Melville and Frances Herskovits's output (especially on Africa, Surinam, Haiti and Trinidad) to the debate. The following passage from a 1961 essay, republished in Smith's *The Plural Society in the British West Indies,* demonstrates that by 1961 the creole theory of Caribbean society had been taken to the outer boundaries of its limited possibility:

> British Caribbean culture is one form of Creole culture; the French or Dutch West Indian cultures are other forms. *Creoles are natives of the Caribbean;* formerly, people born in Louisiana were Creoles also. Creole cultures vary a good deal, but *are sharply distinct from the mestizo cultures of Spanish-American derivation which dominate Middle America.* The Creole complex *has its historical base in slavery, plantation systems and colonialism.* Its cultural composition mirrors its *racial mixture.* European and African elements predominate in fairly standard combinations and relationships. The ideal forms of *institutional life, such as government, religion, family and kinship, law, property, education, economy and language are of European derivation;* in consequence, differing metropolitan affiliations produce differing versions of creole culture. But in their Creole contexts, these institutional forms *diverge from their metropolitan models in greater or less degree to fit local conditions. . . . The* Creole culture, however, also contains many elements of African and slave derivation which are absent from metropolitan models. Perhaps *this combination of European and African traditions is the most important feature of Creole life. . . . The Creole culture area remained defined by the formative situation of African plantation slavery.* Within this New World context, Old World cultural forms assumed new features and functions. . . . Professor and Mrs *Herskovits have shown the importance of African contributions to the Creole cultural complex. "African" elements are observable in language, diet, folklore, family and kinship, property, marketing, medicine, magic and religion, exchange – labour,* economic organisation such as the susu or partner. In music, dress, dancing, and domestic life the African contribution is unmistakable. Only rarely, however, do we find African traits persisting in pure form; more generally they are overlaid with Creole influences . . . or they are associated with elements of European origin.[30]

Comparable remarks by Kamau Brathwaite a decade later and on essentially the same subject matter, in *The Development of Creole Society in Jamaica,* raise the following key question: to what extent did the latter genuinely advance creole discourse beyond the point arrived at in Smith's work? M.G. Smith, of course, had an unrivalled grasp of precisely those concepts arrogated by later creolists and stored, as it were, "against their ruin". Other anglophone Caribbean studies that share similar approaches to Smith's are Elsa Goveia's *Slave Society in the British Leeward Islands at the End of the Eighteenth Century,* and H. Orlando Patterson's *The Sociology of Slavery: An Analysis of the Origins, Development and Structure of Negro Slave Society in Jamaica.*[31] Both employed *slave society* as the central or first-order concept of their analysis, placing this squarely in their titles/subtitles and, of course, retaining its leading place throughout the texts. Each, like *The Development of Creole Society in Jamaica* later, was concerned to provide a primarily empirical, sociohistorical analysis of specific Caribbean slave societies, essentially in the later eighteenth and early nineteenth centuries.

Goveia and Patterson both employed *creole, creole society* and *creole culture* as middle-level analytical concepts. Goveia differs from Patterson and concurs with Brathwaite in her acceptance of the idea that Caribbean slave social formations *were* societies/communities and not the *non-societies/communities* of Patterson's allegedly bleaker vision. Goveia announced no less in the very first sentences of her preface:

> The term *"slave society"* in the title of this book refers to the *whole community based on slavery, including masters and freedmen as well as slaves.* My object has been to study the political, economic, and social organisation of this society and the interrelationship of its component groups and to investigate how it was affected by its dependence on the institution of slavery. *I have tried to identify the basic principles which held the white masters, coloured freedmen, and Negro slaves together as a community, and to trace the influence of these principles on the relations between the Negro slave and his white master, which largely determined the form and content of the society.* The British Leeward Islands were chosen because I wanted to analyse a West Indian community where slavery had been long established and because a group of islands promised a more representative picture of slave society than any one island by itself.[32]

Conversely, Patterson argues thus:

> In contrast to Latin America and North America, Jamaican *slave society* was loosely integrated; so much so that *one hesitates to call it a society since all it amounted to was an ill-organised system of exploitation.* . . . There was . . . no collectively held system of values, no religion, no educational system to reinforce the laws. Even more sig-

nificant was the nature of the political system. Jamaica was the plantocratic society par excellence.[33]

Patterson's claim differs from Brathwaite's creolization thesis. The question
is: how *well* or *ill organized* was that system and how, if at all, was it internally
integrated? It was at the level of *system* – the economic and institutional and
the plantation slave-labour process – that integration principally existed and
was secured in Jamaica. Community was only very dubiously present in
Jamaica, a slave society characterized by estates exceptionally large by all New
World standards.[34] Incidentally, this problem of theorizing community is
encountered elsewhere in the disciplines of history, anthropology and sociology.[35] Here originated the kind of consideration that drove Orlando Patterson
to his conclusion regarding the absence of community from Jamaican slave
society. Kamau Brathwaite's commitment to a "creole" perspective, like
Goveia's before him, drove him to speak of society/community where these
appear to have been only minimally present. When Brathwaite responded
directly to Patterson on these matters, he sought resolution not by bringing
forward evidence of the existence of a real community constituted by
social/human relations that embraced slave, master and coloureds; instead, he
stressed evidence of the quality of the communal life of the Jamaican whites
in the last few decades of the period of chattel slavery.[36]

Goveia, as previously observed, had no recourse to any idea from the creole cluster as her principal concept. None enters her analysis before page 111,
where, in a footnote, John Piney – speaking of fellow whites – is quoted thus:
"The Creoles in general are a set of lazy indolent people."[37] For Goveia – as a
matter at once of historical usage and largely unquestioned theoretical practice – the main social groups in her slave societies all included increasing
numbers of "creoles", meaning no more, in the first instance, than those born
in the Indies. It is as if the presence of creoles, so defined, in and of itself jus-
tified speaking of the existence of *creole society*. Goveia's view was that the
combination of system and social integration produced particular varieties of
Caribbean culture, manifested amongst each of her identified social groups.
While the notion "creole" remained in her analysis, she appears to have seen
no reason to theorize it either rigorously or elaborately. For example, it suf-
ficed Goveia to be able to say about the enslaved that

> the pressures of slavery and the emergence of a Creole population had largely
> effaced the original differences amongst [the imported enslaved Africans] and had

produced instead a certain homogeneity of culture, common to the majority of slaves and shared by the long-resident Africans as well as by *slaves born in the islands*.[38]

It seems clear that Goveia's final phrase could easily have been used elsewhere in the quoted passage and throughout her analysis to speak of the relevant members of the social "ranks"/populations, without any significant theoretical or empirical loss to her project. In the pages of her analysis immediately following these remarks, she addresses the "common culture of the slave population [that] was shaped primarily by their conditions of enslavement". Like Smith and Brathwaite, she saw this common culture as new and also as retaining a very considerable African element, based chiefly on those features of the African cultural heritage which were able to survive, not only because they were often common to the different "tribes" of the slaves, but because they did not conflict with the requirements of the slave system. The common culture was based, in fact, on a combination of those surviving African customs with patterns of behaviour derived from slavery; the resulting mixture was not African but "creole".[39]

Only that final clause is objectionable, and I believe it appears solely because Goveia was writing before the formal academic emergence of the concept "diasporan African".[40] What would now be said is that the resulting culture was "no longer continental but now diasporan African culture". There are also "creoles" in Patterson's *Sociology of Slavery*; according to him, these are "creole slaves" and "creole whites". The coloured would, by definition, be "creoles", although there is a possibility that some mixed African and European people arrived from West Africa. It was never quite true, as Brathwaite was to claim in his famously sharp review in the journal *Race* of Patterson's *The Sociology of Slavery*, that Patterson "largely ignored the group of white masters".[41] For, of Patterson's pages 15 through 50, seven pages deal directly with the whites, while his pages on slave laws are objectively as much about the slave-master class and its state as they are about the enslaved. It may even be that Patterson's brief description of the white creoles somewhat disappointed Brathwaite. Certainly, Patterson touched upon this group's "early local patriotism" that at times took the form of the "strong republican sentiments . . . in evidence among the early [white] residents of the island". According to Patterson,

by 1700 local patriotism was so pronounced among the early settlers, and their children who became known as the "creole party", that on several occasions they attempted to exclude English-born persons from filling posts in the island and even went so far as declaring that they "[would] not allow themselves to be called Englishmen".[42]

He asks, almost wistfully, why this early local patriotism failed to develop appreciably, and the answer he supplies is only weakly disputed by Brathwaite. Indeed, as I suggest below, the failure of creole whites to develop in the manner suggested by Patterson and Brathwaite was later to present an almost insurmountable problem for the latter's own creolization-focused analysis.

In light of Brathwaite's antecedents, I now interrogate Brathwaite's theoretical project in *The Development of Creole Society in Jamaica, Contradictory Omens,* and the other three essays that advance his "creole society" project. Here, for the first time in Caribbean historiography, "creole culture", "creole society" and "creolization" are made to function as first-order concepts, providing the analytic structure of the works. "Creolization" functions in the first of these texts as the central concept, but it would have been perfectly feasible to conduct precisely the empirical analysis Brathwaite does on Jamaican society in that period without using any of the terms of the creole conceptual cluster.

The theoretical import of *The Development of Creole Society in Jamaica* lies in the title's foregrounding of "creole", a first in any major text in Caribbean historiography. The imperative of originality provides historiography with its first indigenous general theory of Caribbean culture. Brathwaite's explanation for placing "creole" in his title is that "Jamaica" was little more than a geographical description – an extension of Europe's colonial mercantilist complex.[43] Unfortunately, he immediately undermines this justification, because the Jamaica that he declares to be no more than a "geographical description" is the very society whose British and West African people, within the terms of his study, "contributed to the formation of a society which developed, or was developing, *its own distinctive character or culture*".[44] This offers a powerful rationale to call the society being thus created "Jamaican". Brathwaite avers that his study evolved from

> a conviction that a study of the forms, institutions, and attitudes of West Indian society during the period of slavery is essential to an understanding of [the] present. . . . Our present condition and cultural orientation . . . are as much the result of the process of *creolization* as of the slavery which provided the framework for it.

. . . One of the arguments of this book is . . . that an understanding of the nature and development of *inter-culturation* in West Indian slave society must precede, since it determines, the question of national identity. *The entire structure of European-derived institutional life in the Caribbean was determined by its "creole" development.*[45]

No one can miss the boldness of these claims, which build on his challenging epigraph, drawn from Elsa Goveia's *Historiography*.[46] Several major concepts and propositions jostle each other, awaiting explanation and substantiation. Of these, "West Indian society" is, apparently, expected to be self-explanatory. What is it? And why is "West Indies" not, like "Jamaica", a mere geographical expression? Further, the proposition that slavery represents *a framework* for the process of creolization poses a considerable problem. The reader may be expected to understand intuitively that it must apply to slavery in the Caribbean island of Jamaica as an instance of the macro structure of Atlantic chattel slavery. But Brathwaite makes little effort in the text to show exactly how, in Jamaica's case, slavery, *as opposed to colonialism, say,* provided the specified framework. Arguably, he demonstrates the contrary. He focuses on *institutions* such as the church, the vestries, the militia and above all the House of Assembly,[47] but slavery *per se* is not an object of analysis.

The proposition that the life of these institutions was "European-derived" and determined by Jamaican "creole development" poses a difficulty of a different kind, for its principal function is precisely to allow the historian to treat his empirical account of these "institutional" developments as prima facie evidence for the theoretical claim that such developments were instances of or driven by creolization. Then there is the problem of the concurrent and interchangeable usage of "interculturation" and "creolization". If, as we are later to be told by Kamau Brathwaite in *Contradictory Omens,* "interculturation" is one of the two major facets of "creolization" (the other being "acculturation"), how and why exactly are either or both of these terms deployed concurrently with "creolization"? Either the term representing the whole or that denoting the constituent facets is redundant. This is a crucial epistemological issue to which I return below, but it is apparent that creolization represents by far the more vacuous term.

From the outset, Brathwaite discusses the problematic ideas of "creole culture" and "creolization" not as outcome but as process. This approach enables a certain flexibility, but it begs the question of the theoretical substance of these concepts. In fact, Brathwaite's definitions of creole and creole society share substantive similarities with those proffered by M.G. Smith. The authors define institutions in broadly similar ways, and agree that these differed from their metropolitan prototypes as a result of processes that took place locally in the Caribbean, sometimes under powerful external pressures. But Smith sees Spanish Middle American societies as not "creole", whereas they are, for Brathwaite, simply variants of creole-type societies. Brathwaite discovers the relevance of Melville and Frances Herskovits's work to the debate, a full decade after Smith.[48] I would argue that M.G. Smith, like Goveia and Patterson, had come up against the limits of theory based on the creole conceptual schema. The fact that Brathwaite's predecessors in the so-called creole tradition of West Indian historiography did not attempt to theoretically elevate creole concepts represented not a failure on their part, but a deliberate refusal.

What exactly are the substantive new theoretical elements added to so-called "creole" historiography by Kamau Brathwaite? There is the clearly innovative titling of *The Development of Creole Society in Jamaica*. But if, as I have already suggested, there are no innovations in its preface and introduction, how sound is the theoretical practice of the body of the text? There Brathwaite has to advance his claim to be building creole theory, redeeming the promise of his title. He seeks to do this via his overwhelmingly empirical accounts, largely of Jamaican *institutional* life, accompanied by some brief, formally theoretical argumentation. To suggest that such descriptive analysis of changing institutions represents the primary content of *The Development of Creole Society in Jamaica* is to deny neither the reality of the processes Brathwaite addresses nor the high quality of his monograph at the strictly empirical level. It points instead to the vacuity of the creolist theorization at the heart of the major creolist text in anglophone Caribbean historiography.

The brief theoretical argumentation just alluded to appears mainly in three relatively short chapters that include creole terms in their title, and they deserve, for this reason, particular attention. The first, chapter 7, is entitled "A Creole Economy". Its clear object is the effect upon the Jamaican economy of the American Revolution – taking place in the thirteen colonies of British North America with which British West Indian economies had previously been highly articulated. That effect should have been to drive the late-eighteenth-century Jamaican economy in the direction of a sort of autarchy. But even had the impact of the American Revolution been such, the Jamaican economy would no more have been made into an economy properly describable as *creole,* than was Southern Rhodesia (now Zimbabwe) a *creole* economy after that country's Unilateral Declaration of Independence (UDI) in the 1960s.

Brathwaite's own conclusion appears devastating to his overall case. His allegedly *creole* Jamaican whites were not creole enough, and therefore failed abysmally: "The opportunity offered . . . by the American Revolution, in its dislocation of traditional American/Caribbean economic connections, was not taken full advantage of by Jamaica. The island's sugar planters remained conservative."[49] Brathwaite then explains this as a matter of necessity, given the prevailing *colonial* power relations. The text of this chapter, therefore, cannot be said to fulfil the promise of its title in terms of shedding theoretical nor even confirmatory empirical light on the process of creolization within Jamaica's economy, under the severe pressures of the impact of the American Revolution.[50] In other words, a chapter ostensibly written to demonstrate "creolization" does no such thing. Nor does it illustrate Brathwaite's fall-back process, "incomplete creolization", since the evidence and arguments confirm the pervasive power of *colonial* forces in Jamaica during the period of the study.

The second chapter with a creole term in its title is chapter 8; its title asks the question, "Jamaica: Colonial or Creole?" The author's initial answer is that Jamaica was both, although considerably more colonial than creole. This has negative implications for the titling stratagem discussed above: why not, therefore, entitle the book *The Development of Colonial Society in Jamaica*? Brathwaite picks up on his explanation from the previous chapter of why the so-called creolizing opportunity offered by the American Revolution was not exploited by Jamaica's conservative plantocracy. His substantive explanation points clearly to Britain's power, as the colonial master, to intervene in the island's institutional and economic life. Brathwaite concludes as follows:

> What this study is concerned with, therefore, is determining how far colonial status (and the mentality that went with it) affected the process of creolization. Was the failure of political action, the failure to make the economy viable, in locally autonomous terms, a result of colonialism, a failure of the creole society, or (as was more likely) a combination of the two? If the latter, how much of one and how much of the other? After all, Jamaican creoles were colonials but it does not follow that all colonials in Jamaica were creolized. The assumption is, of course, that the process of creolization, since it created, by its very nature . . . a way of life essentially different from the metropolitan model, would tend to make for the creation

of attitudes which in their evolution would alter the very nature of colonial dependence. This was certainly the case in the Americas. But why was it not so also with the Jamaicans?[51]

The author of this passage could be said to be in as much theoretical trouble as were the Jamaican creole whites he depicts in practical difficulty as a result of their attitudinal and structural colonial dependency. Brathwaite's empirical analysis is inexorably undermining the theoretical claims purportedly being established by it. At the beginning of this chapter his readers are one hundred pages into the text and, by Brathwaite's own account, "creolization" is still manifestly subordinate to colonialism in the making of the institutions of white Jamaican society. Nor is any substantive evidence put forward in subsequent pages that this relationship came to be reversed before the end of Brathwaite's period of study.

Revealingly, the chapter of Brathwaite's study that deals with slave culture does not contain "creole" in its title; it is chapter 15, entitled "The 'Folk' Culture of the Slaves". Why not *creole* slave culture? This seems a reasonable question. Clearly the culture involved does not fall under the designation "European-derived", as is the case with institutional Jamaica. For Brathwaite the culture of diasporic Africans was no more than European influenced. It was subject to strong Jamaican slavery–dictated acculturation, and to a much weaker interculturation. No serious argument is sustained in *The Development of Creole Society in Jamaica* that "creolization" represents an adequate or accurate term for theorizing the Jamaican remaking of continental African culture that is richly manifest in Brathwaite's account of the "folk culture" of enslaved African-Jamaicans. That the whites, like those they enslaved, were culturally modified by real sociocultural processes in Jamaica – a key point of the book – is not in any fundamental sense evidence of creolization, but of their partial indigenization under the uneven impact of acculturation and interculturation processes. Whites born in the region were, as is well known, brought up by black women, and thus strongly influenced by them. Brathwaite observes, "In the case of Jamaica's slaves, the 'great tradition' was clearly in Africa, in the same way that the white Jamaican's was in Europe – both, in other words, external to the society."[52]

It has not often been remarked that there are, in fact, two versions of this chapter: the one in *The Development of Creole Society in Jamaica,* and the other pre-dating it as Brathwaite's 1970 booklet, *Folk Culture of the Slaves in*

Jamaica.[53] Under the heading, "The African Orientation of Jamaican Folk Culture", shared by chapter and booklet, Brathwaite inserted two extra paragraphs into the booklet. These are entirely in keeping with that heading, and strikingly non-confirmatory of the presence of any powerfully operative "creolization" process on the majority of enslaved Africans. Of course, their culture was developing, as it would have been had they remained in Africa and as was occurring in Maroon communities.[54] Of the white creoles in the English-speaking islands, Brathwaite states that "for most of the period of their presence in the Caribbean they continued to refer almost exclusively to their 'great tradition' and so contributed very little to the texture of local customary and spiritual life beyond the framework of the Great House and the plantation". He contrasts the whites with those he refers to, somewhat strangely to my mind, as "the *ex-African* slaves and creole blacks", who

> began from their first landings to adapt their African heritage to the new and changed conditions. As time went on, certain European customs and forms, inevitably, were incorporated into their evolving "little" or "folk"; but it is an inaccurate and unwarranted assumption to claim, as is popularly and academically done in the West Indies, that this was a European-oriented adaptation . . . there was very little "European" to adapt to. The European-orientation of the black West Indian does not derive from this pristine period; but from the post-emancipation and colonial periods [*sic*], when the blacks, "getting education", found themselves open to the influence of their white literate teachers.[55]

Nuanced as this is, it is fundamentally an Africanist and not a creolist rendering of the position. And it is very much in the former manner that Kamau Brathwaite continues,

> It was during this period [of slavery] that we can see how the African, imported from the area of his "great tradition", went about establishing himself in a new environment, using the available tools and memories of his traditional heritage to set going something new, something Caribbean, but *something nevertheless recognisably African.* . . . It is the thesis of this paper . . . that it is in the nature of the folk culture of the ex-African slave, still persisting today in the life of the contemporary "folk", that, we can discern that the "middle passage" was not, as is popularly assumed, a traumatic, destructive experience, separating the blacks from Africa, disconnecting their sense of history and tradition, but a pathway or channel between this tradition and what is being evolved on new soil, in the Caribbean.[56]

This strongly African-Caribbeanist thesis represents one cornerstone of the position underpinning the present chapter. It also represents the basis of my own deep respect for Kamau Brathwaite's academic and creative contribution. Unfortunately, however, Brathwaite's creolization discourse hampers analysis of the specificities of the multiracial, multiethnic, multicultural and, for me, primarily African process of cultural Caribbeanization in the region. Yet this is precisely what Brathwaite repeatedly calls for in his work – including in his later creolist publications.

Chapter 19 of *The Development of Creole Society in Jamaica,* entitled "Creolization", is the third in the monograph that uses a term from the creole ideas cluster. Its opening claim is that

> [t]he most important factor in the development of *Jamaican* society was not the imported influence of the mother country or the local administrative activity of the white elite, but the cultural action – material, psychological and spiritual – based upon the stimulus/response of individuals within the society to their environment and – as white/black cultural groups – to each other.[57]

Brathwaite draws upon the unpublished work of Duncker[58] and the not unfamiliar contemporary output of planter historians and their friends to try to establish that the process of creolization was a society-wide reality. But the reader already knows from the Africanist fifteenth chapter – especially from its pamphlet version – that most slaves experienced no such process. What the enslaved actually experienced were the brutalities of "seasoning", a process involving a number of distinct facets and described by Brathwaite thus: "a period of one to three years, when slaves were branded, given new names and put under the apprenticeship of creolized slaves. During this period the slave would learn the rudiments of his new language and be initiated into the work routines that awaited him." Brathwaite here reserves the notion "socialization" for "participation with others through the gang system, and through communal recreational activities such as drumming and dancing and festivals. From this would follow identification with the group."[59] He then categorizes the enslaved as the "conservative", the "docile", the "venial", the "curious and the self-seeking", though not the rebellious. It is to the "curious and the self-seeking" that the practice of "imitating the master" is initially credited, though house slaves, urban slaves and slaves involved in certain cultural performances also indulge in it. To make sense of this, it is necessary to return to the notions of social and system integration. Thus, the enslaved who were in day-to-day contact with whites in the great house or in the towns had the possibility of social (sociocultural/sexual) integration with them, and there was acculturation and interculturation as a result.

The generality of the enslaved were subject primarily to the system integration of the plantation labour regime, driven by coercion in the first and last instances. Day-to-day resistance-in-accommodation was their principal option, rebellion their option of last resort. The continental African culture of the enslaved in this new space was self-modified into its new diasporan African form. For the vast majority of the enslaved, nothing that can be validly termed cultural creolization could arise. As for the minority of the enslaved, there is in fact no theoretically sound reason for trying to make creolization do the work performed by a set of much more appropriate and content-infused social science concepts, which historians may borrow more or less effectively.

Brathwaite's final chapter opens with what must be recognized as a tautology: "Creolization, then, was a cultural process that took place within a creole society that is, within a tropical plantation polity based on slavery."[60] There is no theoretical basis for the large claim this entails: that the purportedly high-level concepts "creolization", "creole culture" and "creole society" have been validated by the preceding chapters of overwhelmingly empirical analysis. The conclusion seems inescapable that these putative concepts have not even been well illustrated. The broad processes involved could and should, with considerably less theoretical vacuity, be termed Caribbeanization, Jamaicanization, or indigenization – enabled by some amount of acculturation and minimal interculturation, and by other equally specific processes like socialization.

It is to Brathwaite's considerable credit that, appearing to realize the glaring absence of theoretical – as opposed to empirical – substance to the architecture of *The Development of Creole Society in Jamaica,* he set about the theoretical substantiation of its key concept, "creolization". This takes place mainly in *Contradictory Omens* and the three other essays cited above. In ordinary epistemological terms this is an impossible task, commendably undertaken. In *Contradictory Omens* the effective concepts that set intellectual production in motion are not just the near-vacuous terms of the creole ideas cluster but others, not freshly minted but boldly borrowed, to do the work that creole terms simply cannot perform. This is disclosed in the definition of "creolization" in the introduction:

[T]he term creolization as used in this paper and in my work refers to a cultural process perceived as taking place within a continuum of space and time, but which, for purposes of clarification may be divided into two aspects of itself: *acculturation*, which is the yoking (by forces and example deriving from power and prestige) of one culture to another (in this case the slave/African to the European); and *inter-culturation*, which is an unplanned, unstructured but osmotic relationship proceeding from this yoke. The creolization which results (and it is a process not a product) becomes the tentative norm of the society.[61]

Here is another major move by Brathwaite in his creolization chess game, like that bold opening gambit in *The Development of Creole Society in Jamaica*. There is, after all, little basis for simply borrowing these and the other mentioned, well-established terms from the social sciences in this manner. In their original disciplinary homes they denote processes likely to be found occurring in all social formations where different groups meet in conditions of dominance and subordination – where, despite disparities of power, the sub- and superordinate alike radically impact on each other's cultures, possibly resulting in the appearance of new cultural formations. This broad process is easily detectable in operation in the Caribbean throughout the entire modern era. Accordingly, there are no theoretical effects derivable from the simple act of declaring these concepts and processes two – or more – aspects of creolization, in order to make them specifically Caribbean. Nor is there anything in their operation to prevent them making the vacuous terms of the creole cluster redundant. The borrowed concepts occupy the space supplied by creolist theoretical vacuity.

I would argue, further, that despite Kamau Brathwaite's double intervention in creole discourse (that is to say, the elevation of certain creole terms and the borrowings to shore them up), what has tended to occur in history has been for historians to return to the pre-Brathwaite approach in their own use of creole ideas. That is to say, several scholars have used these ideas, but few have deployed them as the central conceptual operators in their work on Caribbean history. The scope of the present text does not allow for a lengthy exploration of this claim. Rather, I will merely illustrate the argument with reference to one other major Caribbean theorist: Walter Rodney. In his posthumously published *History of the Guyanese Working People, 1881–1905*, he uses the notion "creole(s)" on numerous occasions. His approach is more inclusive of Caribbean Asians, and he defines "creole" and "creolization" as follows: " 'Creole' describes 'anyone of immigrant ancestry who is locally born'. Used without qualification, the word 'Creoles' refers to persons of African or part-African descent; but 'Creolization' refers to an indigenizing experience, and it encompasses all racial groups."[62] Rodney continues:

> One of the most evocative uses of the word "Creole" in the Guyanese context is its association with the "Creole gang" – that gang comprising children who did manuring and other light field tasks as soon as they were physically able so to do. Each *Indian* born on the estate or growing up as a child there would inevitably have passed through the Creole gang. *It was the earliest socializing work experience,* and work experience was one of the imperatives of *indigenization. Africans* and *Indians* marked out the same "tasks" between the dams and the drains, and they faced the same vexations from overseers "aback" and at the pay table. Besides, residential separation must not obscure the fact that each group at different times came to understand what it meant to be at the total mercy of the planters in the plantation logies of the "Niggeryard" and "boundyard".[63]

It is true that Rodney always refers positively to nineteenth-century African-Guyanese when he uses the expression "Creoles".[64] Even so, this passage adds to a certain confusion. Rodney knew better than most that Guyana's population largely consisted of several diasporas, especially Africans, Indians/South Asians, Chinese and Portuguese. *His* sociohistorical analysis gained nothing from frequently joining in the academic and popular practice of misnaming one of these as "creoles". That Rodney, the scholar, was also a pan-Africanist in no way diminishes my point that to refer to such persons as "creoles" dislocates focus from their diasporan African culture, a practice not redeemed by prefixing with "Afro-". It is worth remembering that Rodney, as politician, himself made a famous speech deploring the fact that Africans, alone amongst the major racial groupings of humankind, lost original racial designation upon departure from the ancestral continental homeland. That some of the persons Rodney was referring to may have called themselves "creoles" and had newspapers which incorporated that name represents weak evidence in favour of its theoretical usage. In all probability, those who did so tended to regard themselves as superior to most of their fellow African-Guyanese. That crucial instrument of early socialization in the workplace, of which Rodney speaks, *was* called the "Creole gang". This is what some would term a *brute fact* of Guyanese history that cannot be ignored. But one real effect of Rodney's text is immediately to relocate discussion of the impact of the "Creole gang" away from the vacuous discourse of "creolization" to the theoretically more specific one of the existence of some common structures of early socialization and indigenization in post-emancipation Guyana. Rodney, incidentally, goes on immediately to mention some later ones. This is but another instance of the theoretical rescue operation involving the importation of strong, relatively well-founded, working concepts from elsewhere in sociohistory at any and every crucial point in creolization discourse where its own conceptual thinness is revealed.

Conclusion

It is possible, necessary even, to see creole society/creolization theory as Caribbean historiography's gain from Kamau Brathwaite's major intellectual effort at creolist-theory building since the late 1960s. History, thereafter, could square up to the social sciences with their "plural society" and "plantation society" theories. Since his creolization theory was delivered on the back of a methodologically sound monograph, even serious epistemological problems could be largely ignored by fellow historians. Brathwaite, for his part, was from 1970 committed to the terms of his own creolist revolution in Caribbean historiography. What he thereafter saw as needed was not any fundamental re-examination of his concepts – entailing the possibility of their rejection – but rather procedures to do with shoring up their foundations. Readers of Thomas Kuhn's *The Structure of Scientific Revolutions* will immediately understand Brathwaite's and the historians' attachment to their new paradigm.[65] Followers of Sir Karl Popper may have some difficulty with it. But the epistemological discourse of these philosophers of science is neither Brathwaite's point of departure nor his terminus. So, I re-ask the question: What explains the pan-Africanist Brathwaite's apparent unconcern about the negative effects of the history of creole day-to-day usage and formal discourse on the ontology of his fellow Caribbean Africans?

Part of the answer, I suggest, lies in Brathwaite's strong tendency towards sociocultural totalization and the cultural resolution of issues. This is a feature of even his most sharply observed macrohistorical *proems,* such as "Metaphors of Underdevelopment: A Proem for Hernan Cortez".[66] Another major part of the answer lies in the fact that Brathwaite, consciously or not, is reaching out to ancestral philosophies and world views other than the European. South Asian philosophy is able to transcend the so-called logical law of noncontradiction: there "A" can be both "A" and "Not-A" simultaneously. The vodoun priest "knows things" not written in Hamlet's philosophy. Walter Rodney, for his part, remarked on the extent to which Rastafari reasoners possess knowledge that high-flying academics were struggling to grasp.

Yet another, related, part of the answer can be found in the body of Brathwaite's work, as this evidences the mind of a Caribbean-African creative intellectual in genuine struggle with one of the most intractable facets of Caribbean history, that "the victim and the murderer were both ancestors".[67] Historian's, social critic's, proet's and seer's visions have been fused in the management of this task. A higher proetic, creative, even cosmic episteme is brought into play. This gives everything a place in the re/creative mix that is Brathwaite's vision of Caribbean creolization. "Missile" and "capsule" belong. Creolization thus becomes, as he notes in "Caribbean Man in Space and Time",

> a process, resulting in subtle and multiform orientations from or *towards* ancestral originals. In this way, Caribbean culture can be seen in terms of a dialectic of development taking place within a seamless guise or continuum of space and time; a model which allows for blood flow, fluctuations, the half look,[68] or the look both/several ways; which allows for and contains the ambiguous, and rounds the sharp edges of the dichotomy.[69]

This creolization incorporates both "plural society" and "plantation society" perspectives and, drawing on the latter, proposes to give full recognition to the dynamics of the "inner plantation".[70] This makes a kind of non-sense of the question of whether Kamau Brathwaite ever takes on board the specifics of the negative history of the usage of the word "creole" brought out in the Allsopp epigraph. Why, indeed, should he? For, in dread talk: "Di I did ovastan dat lang time." The meaning of the underlying historical experience has become, in his work, a tool with which to think creatively the totality of Caribbean cultural experience and meaning. For him everything (almost?) belongs within the remix, even if this produces apparent self-/contradiction. Accordingly, "creole institutions" can be very clearly declared "African" in the Africanist chapter on the "folk culture" of the enslaved African (and as modified in the pamphlet) in the book that inaugurates his creolist project. But, when they are perceived to belong within the province of that "inner plantation", their Africanity is at once concealed and highlighted. And so – "consciously" or not, and whatever the consequent problems of European

epistemology posed – Brathwaite fills the ontological problem spaces identified early in the present text with his own message. It is a message sourced out
of the philosophically richer African-Asian ancestral thought-world, and not
the one-dimensional logic of that which calls itself "modem European mind"
even if it creeps and crawls all the way back to those classical intellectual and
artistic "borrowers", the Greeks.

Brathwaite thus tends to make the intercultural almost all in Caribbean
experience. Hence, in his article, "Kumina: The Spirit of African Survival in
Jamaica", the twentieth-century Kongo envisionings and continental-African
language performance of the Kumina priestess Miss Queenie are taken as evidence of Caribbean creolization. This totalizing vision also guides Brathwaite
in his handling of the evidence from that major moment in African-
Caribbean resistance, the British Caribbean's last servile "war of respect", Sam
Sharpe's emancipation revolt. That event is his object of analysis in "Caliban,
Ariel and Unprospero in the Conflict of Creolization: A Study of the Slave
Revolt in Jamaica in 1831–32". Thus, Nanny's,[71] Sam Sharpe's, Paul Bogle's,
and Marcus Garvey's ancestral homeland – the motherland, too, of all those
unnamed millions of departed Africans, of us Africans alive today and of
Africans coming up behind – in Brathwaite's philosophy of Caribbean totalization, creation and reconciliation amazingly becomes "the submerged
mother of the creole system, Africa".[72] The overarching, inclusivist
Brathwaitian vision has dissolved, or better, sublated, one more conflict – that
between African and creole.

Notes

1. Paget Henry, *Caliban's Reason: Introducing Afro-Caribbean Philosophy* (New York: Routledge, 2000).
2. This idea was first developed by non-Caribbean theorists. In the late 1960s and 1970s Caribbean thinkers Lloyd Best and George Beckford, with Canadian Kari Levitt, applied it in a new way to Caribbean society. See Dennis Pantin and Dhanayshar Mahabir, eds., *Plantation Economy Revisited*, special inaugural issue of *Marronage: Journal of the Association of Caribbean Economics* 1, no. 1 (September 1998).
3. M.G. Smith was foremost in developing this concept for the Caribbean, having borrowed and reformulated it from work by J.S. Furnivall on the Dutch East Indies, first published in the 1940s. Smith published a number of books reporting empirical work on Grenada, Cariacou, Jamaica and Nigeria, as well as his collections of essays *The Plural Society in the British West Indies* (Berkeley and Los Angeles: University of California Press, 1965) and *Corporations and Society* (London: Duckworth, 1975).
4. Creole society is the object of the present article and is extensively referenced below.
5. The wider applicability of the "plural society" idea is illustrated by Leo Kuper and M.G. Smith, eds., *Pluralism in Africa* (Berkeley, Los Angeles and London: University of California Press, 1969). The extent of the applications of the "plantation society" idea may be seen in George L. Beckford's *Persistent Poverty: Underdevelopment in Plantation Economies in the Third World* (New York and London: Oxford University Press, 1972). That creole societies/cultures are said to exist beyond the Caribbean is mentioned and referenced on a number of occasions below.
6. This is an idea to be found in the work of Wilson Harris. It was first drawn to my attention by then graduate student Sonia Stanley-Niaah, now a lecturer at the University of the West Indies, during a cultural studies seminar I was leading at the University of the West Indies, Mona, Jamaica. The idea is formally discussed by Barbara J. Webb in *Myth and History in Caribbean Fiction: Alejo Carpentier, Wilson Harris and Edouard Glissant* (Amhurst: University of Massachusetts Press, 1992).
7. See Judith Bettelheim, John Nunley, and Barbara Bridges, introduction to *Caribbean Festival Arts: Each and Every Bit of Difference*, ed. Bettelheim and Nunley (Seattle and London: The Saint Louis Art Museum and University of Washington Press, 1988), 31–37.
8. V.S. Naipaul has made much of this idea. See, for example, his novel *The Mimic Men* (London: Andre Deutsch, 1967).

9.   H. Orlando Patterson put forward this idea in a short article entitled "Jamaica: Society outside History", which appeared in *New Left Review* in 1965.

10. This is Antonio Benítez-Rojo's notion; see *The Repeating Island: The Caribbean and the Postmodern Perspective* (Durham and London: Duke University Press, 1992).

11. See Henry, *Caliban's Reason*.

12. These ideas (that is, "marginal"/"non-sugaring creole societies") occur in Benítez-Rojo, *The Repeating Island*.

13. *The* massive exception here is Caribbean creativity that deploys creole languages as its main instrument. This is the object of language and linguistic studies in the Caribbean.

14. See Edward Kamau Brathwaite, *History of the Voice: The Development of Nation Language in Anglophone Caribbean Poetry* (London and Port of Spain: New Beacon Books, 1984), 14.

15. Richard Allsopp, entry on "Creole" in *Dictionary of Caribbean English Usage* (Oxford and New York: Oxford University Press, 1998), 176–78; emphasis added.

16. B.W. Higman, *Writing West Indian Histories* (London: Warwick University Macmillan Education, 1999), 5–6; emphasis added.

17. See Gordon Rohlehr, "Articulating a Caribbean Aesthetic: The Revolution of Self-Perception", in *My Strangled City and Other Essays* (Port of Spain: Longman Trinidad, 1992), 8–16.

18. I believe, with some others, that the use of terms like "anglophone" misrepresents the linguistic situation in the Caribbean, since this has the effect of concealing the fact that the various so-called creoles are the first languages of the majority of the peoples of the societies concerned.

19. In the francophone Caribbean the intellectual charge for the idea of *créolité* has had Edouard Glissant as its leader. The Spanish equivalent of the concept "creole culture/society" has a substantive history. It makes a recent and relatively complex appearance in the work of Benítez-Rojo, who differentiates between a creole culture characterized by its "local customs" and another that is "national" in character. He also identifies creole culture in "marginal" or "non-sugaring creole" enclaves located not just in Cuba but in a number of other parts of the early Spanish Caribbean. These he contrasts with a "colonial" and "plantation" reality, the "creole" content of which he specifies with far less precision than he does in instances he terms "marginal". Benítez-Rojo deploys the concepts of both "creole" and "pluralism", while dealing extensively with the "*Africanization* of [Caribbean] culture" in both the "marginal" and the "plantation" creole sectors of the Spanish Caribbean. I surmise that his disposition to do so may very well be not unrelated to his own Cuban background. I have in

mind the cultural situation that prevails in socialist Cuba, where it is a remarkable and somewhat neglected fact that postrevolutionary Cuban national cultural policy frequently and fundamentally asserts precisely the centrality of the African cultural contribution in Cuban culture-history. A recent commentator may not be quite correct about the comparative proportions, as opposed to the numbers, of diasporan Africans in Cuba and Jamaica, but she is accurate in holding that "[i]n Cuba . . . those involved in the arts seem to have decided long ago that what was unique about their country was its African connection" (Annie Paul, "Pirates or Parrots? A Critical Perspective on the Visual Arts in Jamaica", *Small Axe*, no. 1 [1997]: 49–64). I accept her view despite the writings of Carlos Moore, who generally argues for a contrary position. But the focus of this critique is the anglophone Caribbean, and only the briefest further remarks will be offered on variants of creole discourse being articulated elsewhere in the region. I should confess to my own neglect to mention here the Danish and Dutch Caribbean. This for no other or better reason than that I am sadly unfamiliar with their creolization discourses.

20.   Brathwaite, *The Development of Creole Society in Jamaica, 1770–1820* (Oxford: Clarendon Press, 1971).

21.   Brathwaite, *Contradictory Omens: Cultural Diversity and Integration in the Caribbean* (1974; reprint, Kingston, Jamaica: Savacou Publications, 1979).

22.   Brathwaite, "Caribbean Man in Space and Time", *Savacou* 11/12 (*c*.1975): 1–11; "Kumina: The Spirit of African Survival in Jamaica", *Jamaica Journal*, no. 44 (September 1978); 45–63; "Caliban, Ariel and Unprospero in the Conflict of Creolization: A Study of the Slave Revolt in Jamaica in 1831–32", in *Comparative Perspectives on Slavery in the New World Plantation Societies,* ed. Vera Rubin and A. Tuden (New York: New York Academy of Sciences, 1977), 41–62.

23.   *Konversations in Kreole: Essays in Honour of Kamau Brathwaite,* ed. Verene Shepherd and Glen Richards, special issue of *Caribbean Quarterly* 44, nos. 1–2 (March–June 1998): vi.

24.   Brathwaite's own work also gives every appearance of taking such overlap and interlinkages as a given: this is most evident in his essay "Caribbean Man in Space and Time".

25.   See Howard Johnson, "Historiography in Jamaica", in *General History of the Caribbean,* vol. 6, *Methodology and Historiography of the Caribbean,* ed. B.W. Higman (London and Oxford: UNESCO/Macmillan, 1999), 508.

26.   See Erna Brodber, "Oral Sources and the Creation of a Social History of the Caribbean", *Jamaica Journal* 16, no. 4 (November 1983): 2–11.

27.   Philip D. Curtin, *Two Jamaicas: The Role of Ideas in a Tropical Colony, 1830–1865* (Cambridge, Mass.: Harvard University Press, 1955).

28. Higman, *Writing West Indian Histories*.

29. Evidence of this is scattered throughout Smith's work. See, for example, Smith
     Plural Society, 5–9, 307–10. Much of this material was researched, written and
     often originally published well before its appearance in these texts.

30. Ibid., 5–6; emphasis added.

31. Elsa V. Goveia, *Slave Society in the British Leeward Islands at the End of the
     Eighteenth Century* (New Haven and London: Yale University Press, 1965); H.
     Orlando Patterson, *The Sociology of Slavery: An Analysis of the Origins,
     Development and Structure of Negro Slave Society in Jamaica* (London: Macgibbon
     and Key, 1967).

32. Goveia, *Slave Society*, vii; emphasis added.

33. Patterson, *Sociology of Slavery*, 70; emphasis added.

34. See B.W. Higman, *Jamaica Surveyed: Plantation Maps and Plans of the Eighteenth
     Century* (Kingston, Jamaica: Institute of Jamaica, 1988), 5.

35. A classic instance is the debate that was generated around Max Gluckman's "An
     Analysis of a Social Situation in Modern Zululand" (*Bantu Studies* 14 [March and
     June 1940], and later, if I rightly recall, issued as an occasional paper of the
     Rhodes-Livingston Institute). It is the old historians' question: "What made the
     'starving peasants' of the Vendee support the social forces of the Ancient
     Regime?"

36. Brathwaite, "Jamaican Slave Society: A Review", in *Race* 9 (1968): 331–42.

37. Goveia, *Slave Society*, 111. Piney is the major character in Richard Pares's *A West
     Indian Fortune* (London: Longmans, Green and Co., 1950).

38. Goveia, *Slave Society*, 244–45: emphasis added.

39. Ibid., 245.

40. Arguably, however, this idea had been always there. In the work of writers like
     Sydney Olivier the equivalent term, "transplanted African", appears frequently.
     And, of course, Marcus Garvey's "Africans abroad" connoted no less.

41. Brathwaite, "Jamaican Slave Society: A Review". The myth of Patterson's partial-
     ity dies hard. Thus Howard Johnson asserts that "[Brathwaite] unlike Patterson,
     based his analysis on an examination of the 'whole community based on slav-
     ery, including masters and freedmen as well as slaves' " ("Historiography in
     Jamaica", 508). This is unsustainable. The difference between Patterson and
     Brathwaite was in their interpretation of the extent to which the social forma-
     tion could be represented a community. Both recognized the classes extant in
     the social formation, and treated each in accordance with the reasonable dic-
     tates of his particular methodological focus.

42. Patterson, *Sociology of Slavery*, 34.

43. Brathwaite, *Creole Society*, vii.

44. Ibid., xiii; emphasis added.

45. Ibid., vii; emphasis added.

46. Elsa V. Goveia, *A Study of the Historiography of the British West Indies to the end of the Nineteenth Century* (1956; reprint, Washington, D.C.: Howard University Press, 1980).

47. Brathwaite, *Creole Society,* xiii.

48. Brathwaite comes to expound the importance of the Herskovits's work in his introduction to the reprint of Melville Herskovits's *Life in a Haitian Valley* (1937; reprint, Garden City, N.Y.: Doubleday Anchor Books, 1971). Their work is not in the index of *The Development of Creole Society in Jamaica,* but it is in the bibliography, as well as appearing on some four occasions in footnotes to chapter 15, "The 'Folk' Culture of the Slaves".

49. Brathwaite, *Creole Society,* 80–95, especially 92.

50. This is a matter addressed by several major Caribbeanists both before and after Brathwaite. See, *inter alia,* Reginald Coupland in *The American Revolution and the British Empire* (London and New York: Longmans, Green and Co., 1930); Lowell Ragatz, *The Fall of the Planter Class in the British Caribbean, 1763–1833* (New York and London: The Century Co., 1928); Eric Williams, *Capitalism and Slavery* (Chapel Hill: University of North Carolina Press, 1944); Selwyn H.H. Carrington, *The British West Indies during the American Revolution* (Dordrecht and Providence: Foris, 1988).

51. Brathwaite, *Creole Society,* 101.

52. Ibid., 213.

53. Brathwaite, *Folk Culture of the Slaves in Jamaica* (London: New Beacon, 1970). There is, strictly speaking, a third physical manifestation of this work: in Brathwaite's doctoral thesis. Kamau Brathwaite himself told me that thesis and book are "identical". This was said in answer to a question that I asked him in the social gathering after his moving and insightful 2000 Elsa Goveia Memorial Lecture which has Professor Goveia, herself, as its topic.

54. See the case of Bush Negro wood carving as set out by Richard Price in "Saramaka Woodcarving: The Development of an Afroamerican Art", *Man* 5, no. 3 (September 1970): 363–78.

55. Brathwaite, *Folk Culture,* 4.

56. Ibid., 4–5; emphasis added.

57. Brathwaite, *Creole Society,* 296.

58. Sheila Duncker, "The Free Coloured and the Fight for Civil Rights in Jamaica, 1800–1830" (MA thesis, University of London, 1960); pages 231–32 are cited by Brathwaite.

59. Brathwaite, *Creole Society,* 298.

60. Ibid., 306.

61. Brathwaite, *Contradictory Omens*, 56.

62. Walter Rodney, *A History of the Guyanese Working People, 1881–1905* (London: Heinemann Educational Books, 1981), 178.

63. Ibid.; emphasis added.

64. Ibid., *inter alia*, 72, 140, 178, 204, 215, 216.

65. See Thomas Kuhn, *The Structure of Scientific Revolutions* (London: Phoenix Books; Chicago: University of Chicago Press, 1962).

66. In *The Art of Kamau Brathwaite*, ed. Stewart Brown (Bridgend, Wales: Seren, 1995), 231–53.

67. Gordon Rohlehr, *Pathfinder: Black Awakening in* The Arrivants *of Edward Kamau Brathwaite* (Tunapuna, Trinidad: G. Rohlehr, 1981), 9.

68. And the half-exposure, or what looked to one foreign commentator as "the ole fashioned fan-dance rather than full-frontal nudity". See Brathwaite, *Contradictory Omens*, 5.

69. Brathwaite, "Caribbean Man in Space and Time", 7.

70. Ibid, 6.

71. See Brathwaite's booklet, *Wars of Respect: Nanny, Sam Sharpe and the Struggle for People's Liberation* (Kingston, Jamaica: Agency for Public Information, 1977).

72. Brathwaite, *Contradictory Omens*, 6.

12

Kamau Brathwaite and the Creolization of History in the Anglophone Caribbean

Glen **Richards** |

Kamau Brathwaite is one of the central historians and one of the most significant theoretical analysts of his generation of professional academics in the anglophone Caribbean. His historical and literary work has been instrumental in shaping the contours of postcolonial theory in the Caribbean. Indeed, the extent of his intellectual influence on the evolution of historical writing in the English-speaking territories of the Caribbean places him alongside such Caribbean historians as C.L.R. James, Eric Williams, Elsa Goveia, Douglas Hall, Walter Rodney, and other Commonwealth Caribbean theorists from outside the discipline of history whose influence has been similarly extensive, including W.A. Lewis, Lloyd Braithwaite, M.G. Smith, Orlando Patterson, Lloyd Best, George Beckford and Vidia Naipaul.

Historical writing on the Caribbean began as a story of European imperial expansion, focusing on the military, administrative and mercantile activities of the European imperial conquerors in a New World setting.[1] In this era Caribbean history became a praise song for European valour and intelligence and a justification for European conquest. As slavery became an intrinsic part of the Caribbean economy, the discussion of the enslaved people also became a major concern of Caribbean history, particularly in the case of the French and English colonies where the sugar plantation had become predominant. In *A Study of the Historiography of the British West Indies to the End of the Nineteenth Cenrtury,* Elsa Goveia points to the primacy of discussions of race and "Negro" slavery in seventeenth- and eighteenth-century histories of the region, and the great lengths to which historians of this period went to justify the institution. The rationalization for black enslavement provided in eighteenth-century histories of the anglophone Caribbean rested largely upon European claims about the intellectual and cultural inferiority of African peoples. The racist justifications advanced by early amateur historians of the anglophone Caribbean, such as Edward Long and Bryan Edwards, are far too well known to require elaboration here, but these historical interpretations continued to exercise wide influence with the emergence of professional history writing in the nineteenth century.

Professional History and the British Empire

The growth of history as a professional academic discipline in nineteenth-century Britain coincided with the global expansion of the British Empire. As British (and American) professional historians turned their attention to Britain's oldest colonies in the Caribbean, the broad historiographical tendencies established in the seventeenth and eighteenth centuries were further reinforced. Nineteenth- and early twentieth-century professional historians maintained the focus on the activities of European nations and European peoples in the region, as a look at the titles and subject matter of many of the historical works written by professional historians during this period will reveal.[2] Historical discourse during this period also continued the anti-African bias established by the histories of the seventeenth and eighteenth centuries. However, the association of professional historians with the standards of academic study and research, and their consequent claim to scientific objectivity, gave their historical findings the aura of academic truth. The negrophobic prejudices exhibited by an Edward Long in the eighteenth century were now protected by the intellectual mantle of the academic gown. Thus, for the doyen of British academic historians in the late nineteenth century, Lord Acton of Cambridge University, "it did not seem an intolerable wrong to rescue men from the devil-worshippers who mangled their victims on the Niger or the Congo".[3] James Froude, Regius Professor of History at Oxford

University, in his West Indian travel journal entitled *The English in the West Indies or the Bow of Ulysses* (1888), advanced the call for the strengthening of British colonial rule in the region with the argument that the African-Caribbean population was "of an inferior race" and had displayed "no capacity to rise above the condition of their ancestors except under European laws, European education and European authority, to keep them from making war on one another". He added, "Give them independence and in a few generations they will peel off such civilisation as they have learnt as easily and as willingly as their coats and trousers."[4] Indeed, he warned that the granting of self-government to such a people would be to "wilfully drive them back into the condition of their ancestors, from which the slave trade was the beginning of their emancipation".[5]

Another highly influential argument later advanced by the world-famous British historian Arnold Toynbee, in his acclaimed *Study of History* (1934), declared, "The Negro had not indeed brought any ancestral religion of his own from Africa. . . . His primitive social heritage was of so frail a texture that every shred of it was scattered to the winds at the first impact of Western Civilization."[6] Nor were these negrophobic prejudices limited to British professional historians. Lowell Ragatz, the American historian whom Eric Williams so admired, proclaimed in *The Fall of the Planter Class in the British Caribbean, 1763–1833* (1928) that "[t]he West Indian negro had all the characteristics of his race. He stole, he lied, he was simple, suspicious, inefficient, irresponsible, lazy, superstitious, and loose in his sexual relations."[7]

The Evolution of a Nationalist School of Historical Writing in the Anglophone Caribbean

By the time Brathwaite published his first major historical work in 1971, the racist views of British and American professional historians writing on the anglophone Caribbean had already been effectively answered by Caribbean scholars, some of whom were themselves descendants of African slaves. J.J. Thomas, the creole linguist from Trinidad, and N.D. Davis of Grenada, an amateur historian, had both provided scathing rebuttals to J.A. Froude's travel journal.[8] But the publication of *The Black Jacobins: Toussaint L'Ouverture and the San Domingo Revolution* by C.L.R. James in 1938 marked a seismic shift in historical writing on the region. James, "tired of reading and hearing about

Africans being persecuted and oppressed in Africa, the Middle Passage, in the USA and all over the Caribbean", set out to "write a book in which Africans or people of African descent instead of constantly being the object of other people's exploitation and ferocity would themselves be taking action on a grand scale".[9]

Rejecting the claims of those who argued that the slaves who crossed the Middle Passage brought nothing with them, James observes, "The Negroes who came from Africa brought themselves. . . . The report says that they left everything behind. But the Africans themselves are the most important and most valuable representatives of their civilisation."[10] However, James still sees Caribbean history as progressing in parallel with that of Europe, part of the great global march forward to world communism as laid out in his Marxist paradigm. Thus the Saint Domingue Revolution is treated as an extension of the French Revolution, Toussaint and the revolutionaries of Saint Domingue are portrayed as "Black Jacobins", and Toussaint himself becomes the "Black Consul". Indeed, the achievements and historic value of African-Caribbean peoples are assessed in terms of their contribution to Western civilization for, as James argues, it was "[p]eople of African descent, the African from Africa, [who] made the perpetuation of western civilisation possible in the West Indies".[11]

James's fellow Trinidadian and former pupil, Eric Williams, also set out in his historical writings to reject the racial explanations and justifications for slavery that had been advanced by British and American historians of the region. In *Capitalism and Slavery,* first published in 1944, Williams writes, "Here, then, is the origin of Negro slavery. The reason was economic, not racial; it had to do not with the color of the laborer, but the cheapness of the labor. As compared with Indian and white labor, Negro slavery was eminently superior."[12] Later in his work Williams continues, "Negro slavery therefore was only a solution, in certain historical circumstances, of the Caribbean labor problem. . . . Slavery in no way implied, in any scientific sense, the inferiority of the Negro."[13]

But the focus of Williams's historical writing remains largely the impact of Europe and America on the Caribbean, and the rise and decline of the sugar plantation. His main topics are European trade and mercantilism, the sugar plantation and the emergence of industrial capitalism in Britain, and the process of abolition and the part played by various British interests.[14] Williams's central difference from imperial historians such as Froude is that he situates the Caribbean colonies not in the tail of empire but in the cockpit. His history of the Caribbean, however, remains closely entwined with the history of empire, be it European or American.[15]

The establishment of a department of history and the appointment of the first professor of history at the University College of the West Indies, Mona, in 1949 further accelerated the process which Barry Higman has described as the "West Indianization of professional history-writing".[16] As Higman points out: "The professionalization of history-writing in the English-speaking Caribbean was firmly rooted in the metropolitan models of Great Britain and the United States."[17] Although the newly created history department of the University College of the West Indies (later University of the West Indies) facilitated the emergence of a nationalist school of historical writing in the anglophone Caribbean, the early historians associated with the university, while seeking to answer comprehensively the racist allegations of the imperial historians, continued to focus on the institutional aspects of slavery, sugar planting and colonial rule. John Parry, the first professor of history in the history department, and Philip Sherlock note in the preface to their joint work, *A Short History of the West Indies* (1956), that "West Indian history appears disjointed and unreal to West Indians today". Pointing to the source of the problem, they observe,

> It is a story told from someone else's point of view. The political history of the islands has been written in terms of the struggle of Europeans (or North Americans) for possession or control; their economic history in terms of crops for export – of sugar and tobacco, not of yams or cassava or saltfish; their constitutional history in terms of greater or lesser degrees of imperial supervision.[18]

Yet the chapter headings of their text and the main subjects of study retain the same focus on the activities of the colonizing powers in the region and on the colonial economy and institutions. Similarly, Douglas Hall, the fourth historian to join the staff of the history department, in his *Free Jamaica* (1959), focuses on the economics of sugar production in post-emancipation Jamaica and the role of the imperial and colonial government. Even his chapter on "peasants and rural labourers" devotes as much attention to the relation between the estates and the peasant labourer, and the agricultural and taxation policies of the local legislature, as to the economic activities of peasant producers.[19]

The historical approach of Elsa Goveia, the second historian appointed to the staff of the history department, exhibited notable differences. Although her *Slave Society in the British Leeward Islands at the End of the Eighteenth Century* (1965) examines the colonial political system, sugar planting and the slave laws of the Leeward Islands colonies, her approach provides a much stronger focus on local history and a detailed account of both the activities of the free coloureds and the working lives of the slaves. But the almost inevitable focus on the institutions of slavery, particularly the slave laws and the plantation labour regime, yields a picture of the slaves more as they were acted upon than as actors. Yet Goveia's work stands as one of the most detailed depictions of the daily lives of the slaves and of their social interactions with the other sectors of plantation society provided, to that point, by a modern historian. It supplies a detailed illustration of the sense of "property" ownership among slaves and their engagement in negotiations for additional benefits from their masters, as well as the utilization of slave labour by privileged slaves. Goveia also notes the survival of African traits and practices among the slave population of the Leeward Islands, but cautions that these persisted because they "did not conflict with the requirements of the slave system" and should therefore be seen not as "African" but as "Creole".[20]

Intellectual Influences on Brathwaite's Theory of Creolization

Brathwaite's theory of creolization was developed partly in response to the legacy of racist thought that had helped to shape the written history of the region. It rejected the view that Africans, and their descendants in the Americas, had been clean slates to be written on by Western civilization, and valorized the cultural assets of Africans and their descendants. It advanced the view that African cultural norms had played a decisive role in the formation of the culture of the local population in the anglophone Caribbean, and that this culture was not merely a poor imitation of Europe's but a new "creole" culture.

Some of the foundations for Brathwaite's work had been laid by several intellectual precursors, working largely outside of the field of history, the most important of whom was the American anthropologist, Melville Herskovits, who had written two significant anthropological studies on the Caribbean – *Life in a Haitian Village* (1937) and, with his wife Frances, *Trinidad Village* (1947) – demonstrating the survival of African elements in the daily lives of the local populations of these two Caribbean territories. His most influential work was *The Myth of the Negro Past* (1941), which scientifically set out to debunk several key myths about African descendants in the Americas. One of these myths was the charge that African culture was "so savage and relatively so low in the scale of human civilizations" that it could not withstand the "superiority of European customs", and so the African slaves and their descendants abandoned "such aboriginal traditions as they may otherwise have desired to preserve".[21] Through a systematic comparison of African-derived culture in the Americas and African culture in Africa, he demonstrated that the captive African populations had come from "relatively complex and sophisticated cultures" and, in the "acculturative situation" of the New World, Africans from different areas in Africa had enough common cultural factors to permit "a consensus of experiences to be drawn on in fashioning new, though still African-like, customs".[22]

In the 1960s, when Brathwaite commenced his academic career in the history department of the University of the West Indies, academic scholarship in the region was caught up in an intense and far-reaching debate on the nature of Caribbean society. Several contending interpretative models of Caribbean society were being advanced by certain Commonwealth Caribbean scholars attached to the university, including the anthropologist M.G. Smith, the sociologist Lloyd Braithwaite, the historian Orlando Patterson, and the economists Lloyd Best and George Beckford. M.G. Smith, while acknowledging the process of creolization, advanced the plural society model which held that creole society in the Caribbean was segmented into three distinct cultural divisions or pluralities: the whites, the browns and the blacks. Lloyd Brathwaite, on the other hand, while recognizing elements of pluralism in Caribbean society, emphasized the "universalistic [creole] values" which served to unite the population. Orlando Patterson, in his study of the slavery period, utilized historical data to demonstrate the evolution of the process of segmentary creolization advanced in the plural society model. Meanwhile, the plantation society model put forward by Lloyd Best and George Beckford largely recast the plural society model in starker economic class or caste terms.[23]

Brathwaite on Creolization

The description of Caribbean culture as creole preceded Brathwaite's entry into the academy. His principal contribution was the theoretical development of the concept of creolization, and his advancement of the creole society model as a positive counter to the negative implications for Caribbean social development inherent in the plural society model. In *The Development of Creole Society in Jamaica, 1770–1820* (1971), Brathwaite notes that the social dichotomy which was the legacy of a racialized slavery in the Caribbean "has led to the agnostic pessimism of writers like Derek Walcott, Orlando Patterson and Vidia Naipaul. It has also led to the intellectual pessimism of the sociologist's formulation of the concept of 'the plural society' with its prognosis (Despres) of tension and violent conflict, or negation (Smith)".[24] Brathwaite advances a very different picture of the Caribbean, which sees

> the society, not in terms of white and black, master and slave, in separate nuclear units, but as contributory parts of a whole. . . . Here . . . were two cultures of people, having to adapt themselves to a new environment and to each other. . . . The white plantations and social institutions described in this study reflect one aspect of this. The slaves' adaptation of their African culture to a new world reflect another.[25]

The creolization process as represented by Brathwaite is not a one-way transference of social values and norms, the Westernization of the black slave population, as traditionally depicted, but a dynamic process in which the white Jamaican elite could also be seen adopting the patterns of speech, headdress and culinary tastes of their black slaves. Brathwaite, however, does not portray creolization as a blending process in which the European and African communities were fused together in a cultural melting pot. He recognizes, in agreement with Orlando Patterson and the exponents of the plural society model, the continuation of cultural distinctions along ethnic lines, with the development of a "European-oriented creole form (Euro-creole) and an African-influenced creole form (Afro-creole)", but notes that "they existed together within, often, the same framework". Brathwaite sees the "African-influenced creole form" as the creative and dynamic centre of the creolization process in the Caribbean, for it was this Afro-creole "little tradition" among the black slave population which provided the possibility for cultural autonomy, and ultimately political independence, in the region. It was the failure of both the white masters and the elite blacks and free coloureds, particularly in the case of the former, to recognize the humanity of the black slaves and to "make conscious use" of their "rich folk culture" which helped to perpetuate first slavery and then colonial dependency.[26]

In his second major publication on the subject of creolization, *Contradict-ory Omens: Cultural Diversity and Integration in the Caribbean* (1974), Brathwaite further refines the theoretical outline of the creole society model, identifying two main and parallel processes: acculturation and interculturation. The for-mer he describes as "the process of absorption of one culture into another", and the latter as "a more reciprocal activity, a process of intermixture and enrichment".[27]

Brathwaite also expands on the dominant cultural patterns in creole soci-ety, identifying "four inter-related and sometimes overlapping orientations . . . European, Euro-creole, Afro-creole (or folk) and creo-creole or West Indian".[28] But perhaps the most significant feature of this later work is Brathwaite's application of the creole society model to the post-emancipa-tion period. The creolization process, Brathwaite argues, was slowed and ren-dered even more incomplete by the large-scale importation of Portuguese and Asian labourers to meet the labour needs of the post-slavery plantation. Indeed, this process had led to a "plural society, in which the new East Indian and other elements had to adjust themselves to the existing creole synthe-sis".[29] The new East Indian populations of the region, Brathwaite observes, tended to resist creolization "in very much the way that African slaves did", engaging, on the one hand, in a process of "selective creolization" – a con-scious adaptation to the cultural norms of the "master-culture of Euro-America" and selective participation in those creole social institutions which facilitated social advancement – and, on the other, in the promotion, partic-ularly by both the traditional and a newly emerging Indian middle class, of an exclusively Indian culture which was not "the authentic culture of their 'little' tradition, but an imported and 'processed' 'great' tradition" from the Indian subcontinent itself. At the same time that the educated black middle class in the anglophone Caribbean was turning to the European "great tradi-tion" and "acquiring pseudo-European norms", an East Indian middle class was turning to India and "acquiring pseudo-Indian ones".[30] The cultural dynamic of creolization, however, still continued to assert itself in the largely unconscious process of "lateral creolization", as cultural interaction between the two numerically dominant ethnic groups, Africans and Indians, particu-larly at the lower levels of the social scale, promoted a cultural exchange – notably in the areas of food, speech, music and even religion. Brathwaite observes, they [East Indians] have contributed to new configurations of creole. Indian pukko in Jamaica is only one manifestation of this. In some Jamaican cults, worshippers are possesed by 'Indian' gods. In Trinidad, East Indian festivals like Hosein have been integrated into the creole imagination; while some Indians consult obeah-men or are themselves such.[31]

This process of lateral creolization would progressively roll back the tendencies to pluralism.

Subsequent writings by Kamau Brathwaite on the subject of creole society, however, have displayed a strikingly different orientation, demonstrating an ever-increasing and, indeed, almost exclusive focus on the African elements of creolization. In his 1977 article, "Caliban, Ariel and Unprospero in the Conflict of Creolization: A Study of the Slave Revolt in Jamaica in 1831–32", Brathwaite portrays creolization as a process of dynamic opposition between an exploitative European "missile" culture and a liberating African "capsule" culture. While still rejecting the "pessimistic notion of a plural society", he assigns a greater level of independence and cultural integrity to the two primary cultural orientations, advancing a "prismatic conception" which

conceives of all resident cultures as equal and contiguous, despite the accidents of political history, each developing its own life-style from the spirits of its ancestors – but modified – and increasingly so – through interaction with the environment and the other cultures of the environment, until residence within the environment – nativization – becomes the process (creolization) through which all begin to share a style, even though that style will retain vestiges (with occasional national/cultural revivals back towards particular ancestors) of their original ancestral heritage.[32]

Brathwaite's increasing focus on the African element in creolization has been accompanied by an apparently reduced concern with the question of "completing" the creolization process, as well as the increasing marginalization of the Asian population of the Caribbean in his discourse on creole society. This development is perhaps most clearly seen in Brathwaite's *History of the Voice: The Development of Nation Language in Anglophone Caribbean Poetry* (1984). In discussing language use in the region, Brathwaite divides the dominant language patterns into imperial, creole (an adaptation of the imperial language), nation language (the imperial language as understood or misunderstood and improvised and developed on by "slaves and labourers, the servants who were brought in by the conquistadores") and "the remnants of ancestral languages".[33] In a further definition of nation language, Brathwaite writes, "Nation-Language is the language which is influenced very strongly by the African model, the African aspect of our New World/Caribbean heritage . . . . Nation language . . . is the submerged area of that dialect which is much more closely allied to the African aspect of experience in the Caribbean."[34] Brathwaite thereby helps to marginalize the significant influence of the Asian population, particularly East Indians, on the language and, even more generally, the culture of the region.

The Intellectual Response to Brathwaite's Creolization Theory

Barry Higman, in acknowledging the intellectual significance of Kamau Brathwaite's " 'creole society' concept", has noted that the concept has "spread far and wide, along with the diaspora of West Indian people in the Atlantic World, travelling even further than the people themselves through music, language, and life-style, giving creolization a significance comparable to the globalization model".[35] Brathwaite's work has proved widely influential among leading Caribbean scholars of his and succeeding generations, including, most notably, Gordon Rohlehr, Maureen Warner-Lewis and Erna Brodber, whose doctoral thesis he supervised. But Brathwaite's work has received a far more welcome response in the academic fields of literature and linguistics than in his chosen professional discipline, history. This could partly be explained by what Higman describes as Brathwaite's attempt "to subvert the boundary installed by the academy, the division of knowledge into disciplines and the distancing of higher learning from the wisdom of the folk".[36] Some historians, perhaps questioning Brathwaite's historical objectivity, have responded to his attempt to integrate his several disciplinary streams of interest into a theoretical whole by silence. This is clearly seen in volume 2 of the UNESCO *General History of the Caribbean,* edited by Barry Higman and dedicated to the "Methodology and Historiography of the Caribbean". For instance, Bridget Brereton, while discussing the "shift from Eurocentrism since 1956" in her article "Regional Histories", describes Franklin Knight's work, *The Caribbean,* as exemplifying the "Creolized stage of Caribbean history", but never mentions Brathwaite's regional contributions.[37] Indeed, of the twenty-two historiographical articles in this volume, Brathwaite's work receives significant acknowledgement in only two: Howard Johnson's

"Historiography of Jamaica" and Francisco Scarano's "Slavery and Emancipation in Caribbean History".

In his 1976 publication, *British Slave Emancipation: The Sugar Colonies and the Great Experiment, 1830–1865,* William Green utilizes the idea of creolization, but largely as a descriptive tool. In his opening chapter, "West Indian Society", he notes that the "creole culture which gradually arose among West Indian slaves was neither European nor African. It comprised an eclectic blending of various African customs, pragmatic adjustments to harsh Caribbean circumstances, and selective borrowings from the dominant European culture."[38] Green does not acknowledge Brathwaite's contribution to the concept of creole culture, and the three references in his opening chapter to Brathwaite's *Development of Creole Society in Jamaica* (published five years earlier) are to factual historical details taken from Brathwaite's work. Brathwaite's work necessarily receives greater acknowledgement in Green's later article, entitled "The Creolization of Caribbean History".[39] However, the focus of the article is not the concept of creolization, as the title would lead the reader to expect, and the article could have been more accurately titled "The Caribbeanization of Caribbean History". Green's main field of engagement is with the danger posed by the growing association between creolization and what he describes as dialectical analysis. After giving a very brief account of the idea of creolization and Brathwaite's role in its development, Green focuses his attention on attacking the purveyors of dialectical analysis, notably Peter Wilson and Monica Schuler, and on issuing his advice that "[c]reolization has . . . extended the scope of West Indian history. But creolization is in danger of going awry. It is time we considered the wisdom of disengaging it from the dialectic."[40] The advances in creolization theory made by Brathwaite between the publication of *The Development of Creole Society in Jamaica* in 1971 and the publication of Green's article in 1986 are totally ignored by Green, who sees creolization as a descriptive term rather than a distinct and evolving theoretical concept capable of further intellectual development.[41]

Perhaps the most extreme form of the invisibility of Brathwaite's historical work in the writing of other scholars can be seen in the case of R.D.E. Burton, a French linguist whose foray into the field of Anglo-Caribbean history, entitled *Afro-Creole: Power, Opposition and Play in the Caribbean,* seeks to revive Patterson's concept of "segmentary creolization", and thereby the plural society model, by identifying three separate creole zones: the Euro-creole, the

Meso-creole and the Afro-creole.[42] While obviously engaged with Brathwaite's ideas, Burton mentions Brathwaite directly only in two of his footnote references. In one, he maintains that despite Brathwaite's "ingenious attempt to show otherwise . . . the 1831–32 Baptist War in Jamaica was clearly Afro-Christian rather than "African" in inspiration".[43] In the other reference, in support of his argument that Jonkonnu represented the appropriation of European elements of power – "the wooden sword . . . fragments of military uniform . . . effigies of the ultimate expression of power in plantation society, the Great House itself" – by the slaves, he sarcastically refers to Brathwaite's alternate view "that all the apparently secular objects worn or carried in Jonkonnu have a ritual significance as 'fragments of God' ".[44]

Yet, invisible or not, Kamau Brathwaite's historical vision continues to exercise a significant influence on historical writing in the anglophone Caribbean. The growing focus on cultural and ethnographic history in the region has been inspired by the changes in direction and subject matter of academic study which his historical writings have helped to initiate.

"Missiles and Capsules": The Poetic Vision in History

The extensive influence which Brathwaite exercises in the field of Caribbean studies raises certain serious concerns about the intellectual direction of his work, particularly for the historian. His historical representation of European and African cultures as conflicting and spiritually opposed "missiles" and "capsules" raises the real risk of stereotyping and ideological subjectivity in the academic discipline of history. The contrasting portrayal of an exploitative and expansive European "missile" culture and a sympathetic and conserving African "capsule" culture threatens to distort and render monochromatic not only the history of Europe but, even more so, the history of Africa. For were the sacrifices of captive slaves or the king's wives at the Annual or Grand Customs of the Alladoxnu kings of Dahomey examples of an expansive missile culture or merely the conserving religious practices of a capsular culture engaged in " 'watering the graves' of [their] forebears with the blood of the victims and recommitting the nation to the care of the ancestral spirits"?[45] The "missile" and "capsule" or "circle" patterns are neither culturally nor genetically specific, but fixed categories which may illustrate some patterns of behaviour but are dangerous if used too rigidly to describe whole cultures.

Equally of concern is Brathwaite's increasingly Afrocentric focus and his identification of creole formations such as "nation language" with "the African aspect of experience in the Caribbean". Such an approach marginalizes the significant contribution of Asian, particularly East Indian, culture and language to the new creole linguistic formation, particularly in central words and the concepts springing from and activities associated with them – such as curry, chutney, collie, chillum and ganja. The increasingly narrow and almost exclusive focus on Africa among some Afro-Caribbean academics, while understandable, serves also to retard the concept and process of creolization, leaving it incomplete. For those who seek to study and advance creolization in the Caribbean today, it will be important to look not only to Africa, but also to the Indian subcontinent, China, Java, the Middle East and indigenous America, for the "existing submerged mother[s] of the creole system".[46]

Notes

1. This trend was reflected in the titles of the earliest Caribbean histories, including Richard Hakluyt's *The Principal Navigations, Voiages, and Discoveries of the English Nation, made by Sea or overland to the most remote and farthest distant Quarters of the earth at any time within the compasse of these 1500 years* (1589); A. de Herrera y Tordesillas' *Historia general de los hechos de los Castellanos en las Islas y Tierra Firma de mar oceano* (4 volumes, 1601–13); and Jean Baptiste Du Tertre's *Histoire Generale des Antille Habitees par les Francois* (1667). See Elsa Goveia, *Historiography of the British West Indies to the End of the Nineteenth Century* (Washington, D.C.: Howard University Press, 1980), 12–19.
2. Some of the principal works on the Caribbean by professional historians during the late nineteenth and early twentieth century include: James Froude, *The English in the West Indies or the Bow of Ulysses* (London, 1888); Lilian Penson, *The Colonial Agents of the British West Indies: A Study in Colonial Administration Mainly in the Eighteenth Century* (London, 1924); Lowell Ragatz, *The Fall of the Planter Class in the British Caribbean* (New York and London, 1928), Arthur Newton, *The European Nations in the West Indies* (London, 1933); William Mathieson, *The Sugar Colonies and Governor Eyre, 1849–1866* (1936). For a further examination of these works see Goveia, *Historiography*; Eric Williams, *British Historians and the*

West Indies (Port of Spain: PNM Publishing 1964); and B.W. Higman, *Writing West Indian Histories* (London and Basingstoke: Macmillan, 1999).

3. Williams, *British Historians*, 55.

4. Quoted in ibid., 140.

5. Quoted in Denis Benn, *The Growth and Development of Political Ideas in the Caribbean, 1774–1983* (Kingston, Jamaica: ISER Publications), 59.

6. Quoted in ibid., 153.

7. Quoted in Higman, *Writing West Indian Histories*, 176.

8. N.D. Davis, *Mr Froude's Negrophobia or Don Quixote as a Cook's Tourist* (Demarara, 1888); J.J. Thomas, *Froudacity* (London, 1889). For more on these works see Goveia, *Historiography*, 154–55; Higman, *Writing West Indian Histories*, 52–58.

9. Quoted in Higman, *Writing West Indian Histories*, 94.

10. James, "The Making of the Caribbean People", 174.

11. Ibid.

12. Eric Williams, *Capitalism and Slavery* (London: Andre Deutsch, 1964), 19.

13. Ibid., 29.

14. Chapter 12 of *Capitalism and Slavery*, entitled "The Slaves and Slavery", has as much to do with British abolition policy and the responses and attitudes of white planters in the British colonies as with the ideas and responses of the slaves themselves. Indeed, the slaves described in this chapter remain an undifferentiated mass.

15. See, for example, Eric Williams, *From Columbus to Castro: The History of the Caribbean, 1492–1969* (London: Andre Deutsch, 1970).

16. Higman, *Writing West Indian Histories*, 128.

17. Ibid., 89.

18. J.H. Parry and Philip Sherlock, *A Short History of the West Indies,* 3rd ed. (London and Basingstoke: Macmillan, 1971), vii–viii.

19. Hall also questions the historical significance of the activities of Paul Bogle and of the civil disturbances at Morant Bay, describing them as merely a "local riot". Douglas Hall, *Free Jamaica 1838–1865: An Economic History* (Kingston, Jamaica: Caribbean University Press, 1976), 250.

20. Goveia, *Slave Society in the British Leeward Islands at the End of the Eighteenth Century* (Westport, Conn.: Greenwood Press, 1980), 245.

21. Melville Herskovits, *The Myth of the Negro Past* (New York: Octagon Books, 1964), 2.

22. Ibid., 297.

23. For the details of this intellectual debate see Lloyd Braithwaite, "Social Stratification in Trinidad", *Social and Economic Studies* 2, nos. 2–3 (1953): 6–175; M.G. Smith, *The Plural Society in the British West Indies* (Berkeley: University of California Press, 1965); Orlando Patterson, *The Sociology of Slavery* (London:

McGibbon and Kee, 1967); Lloyd Best, "Outline of a Model of Pure Plantation Economy", *Social and Economic Studies* 17, no. 3 (1968): 283–326; George Beckford, *Persistent Poverty* (Oxford: Oxford University Press, 1972). Significant contributions to this debate were also made by several American scholars, principally Philip Curtin, Sidney Mintz and Richard Price.

24. Edward Kamau Brathwaite, *The Development of Creole Society in Jamaica, 1770–1820* (Oxford: Clarendon Press, 1971), 309.

25. Ibid., 307.

26. Ibid., 307–9.

27. Brathwaite, *Contradictory Omens: Cultural Diversity and Integration in the Caribbean* (Kingston, Jamaica: Savacou Publications, 1974), 11.

28. Ibid., 25.

29. Ibid., 11.

30. Ibid., 53–54.

31. Ibid., 53.

32. Brathwaite, "Caliban, Ariel and Unprospero in the Conflict of Creolization: A Study of the Slave Revolt in Jamaica in 1831–32", in *Comparative Perspectives on Slavery in New World Plantation Societies,* ed. V. Rubin and A. Tuden (New York: New York Academy of Sciences, 1977), 42.

33. Brathwaite, *History of the Voice: The Development of Nation Language in Anglophone Caribbean Poetry* (London and Port of Spain: New Beacon Books, 1984), 5–6.

34. Ibid., 13.

35. Higman, *Writing West Indian Histories,* 6.

36. Ibid., 139.

37. Bridget Brereton, "Regional Histories", in *General History of the Caribbean,* ed. B.W. Higman, vol. 6, *Methodology and Historiography of the Caribbean* (London and Oxford: UNESCO/Macmillan, 1999), 331.

38. William Green, *British Slave Emancipation: The Sugar Colonies and the Great Experiment, 1830–1865* (Oxford: Oxford University Press, 1976), 28.

39. William Green, "The Creolization of Caribbean History: The Emancipation Era and a Critique of Dialectical Analysis", *Journal of Imperial and Commonwealth History* 14, no. 3 (1986): 149–50.

40. Ibid., 164.

41. Green's article was largely a continuation of his earlier attack on dialectical analysis in a scholarly exchange with Nigel Bolland. See Bolland, "Systems of Domination after Slavery: The Control of Land and Labour in the British West Indies after 1838", *Comparative Studies in Society and History* 23, no. 4 (1981); Green, "The Perils of Comparative History: Belize and the Sugar Colonies after Slavery", *Comparative Studies in Society and History* 26, no. 1 (1984); Bolland,

"Reply to William Green's 'The Peril of Comparative History' ", *Comparative Studies in Society and History* 26, no. 1 (1984).

42.   Richard Burton, *Afro-Creole: Power, Opposition and Play in the Caribbean* (Ithaca: Cornell University Press, 1997), 6.

43.   Ibid., 7n10.

44.   Ibid., 81n34.

45.   Karl Polanyi, *Dahomey and the Slave Trade: An Analysis of an Archaic Economy* (Seattle: University of Washington Press, 1966), 34. See also Melville Herskovits, *Dahomey: An Ancient West African Kingdom,* vol. 2 (Evanston: Northwestern University Press, 1967), 53.

46.   Brathwaite described Africa as "the existing submerged mother of the creole system". See *Contradictory Omens,* 6.

13

Creolization, Hybridity, Pluralism
Historical Articulations of Race and Ethnicity

Ileana **Rodríguez |**

[T]he term creolization . . . refers to a cultural process perceived as taking place within a continuum of space and time, but which, for purposes of clarification may be divided into two aspects of itself: ac/culturation which is the yoking (by force and example, deriving from power/prestige) of one culture to another . . . ; and inter/culturation, which is an unplanned, unstructured but osmotic relationship proceeding from this yoke. The creolization which results (and it is a process not a product), becomes the tentative cultural norm of the society. . . . Yet this norm, because of the complex historical factors involved in making it . . . is not whole or hard (crown: jewel: diamond), but cracked, fragmented, ambivalent, not certain of itself, subject to shifting lights and pressures.

– Edward Kamau Brathwaite, *Contradictory Omens*

I have always been very fond of the concept of creolization. Having been brought up under the sign of *mestizaje,* and being myself classified as a *mestiza* woman, when I came across the concept of creolization in the work of Edward Kamau Brathwaite, I felt a sense of comfort.[1] The reason for this was that whereas when I was growing up, in continental America *mestizaje* was a term that referred to a bio(social) condition – more biological than social, for it really made culture contingent upon race – *creolization* inverted the terms of the relationship, subordinating biology to culture and steering the discussion to the politics of culture.

To be a mestizo, when I was growing up, meant to me to be almost but not quite white. More precisely, being a mestizo was a way of purchasing my way out of being Indian. There was then, in the term, a double take, a sense of social aspiration and expectation alongside the awareness of a lack. It meant, as I said, almost but not quite, but it also brought up the in-between condition of a "neither nor" situation, as in neither white nor Indian. In continental America *mestizaje* meant in principle a "blood" mixture, a mixed breed, which was the product of rape, a perpetual reminder of colonial maltreatment of the subaltern indigenous by the dominant Spanish. A mestizo was a being born out of violence, a being deprived of the name of the Father, of the name of culture, of the father's rights, and in many ways he or she simultaneously carried the great slabs and slices of shame and stain of the conquering rights of European men. *Mestizaje* was thus a colonial sign, a walking and talking signifier.

But *mestizaje* was also an alien object within the culture of the indigenous, a constant reminder of an abuse, but an offspring that could ultimately be absorbed by the native communities. Words like *cholo* and *guacho,* as opposed to *ladino,* are indicators and symptoms of who absorbed whom – *cholo* and *guacho* into the subaltern, *ladino* into the elite. That was the negative side of the mestizo. Within the Spanish codes of honour and purity of blood, mestizos and ladinos were summoned to the edges and placed side by side with other troubled identities, such as those of *moriscos* and *conversos,* people belonging to Arab and Jewish cultures, people not truly *castizos.*

There is another meaning that runs through the genealogy of *mestizaje.* When Spanish *criollos* (one of the senses of the term *creole,* but not quite what the distinct grain of Brathwaite's thought signifies by it) struggled to achieve their independence from Spain, they used *mestizaje* as a banner to defend their rights to self-government. In nineteenth-century Latin America, *mestizaje* was the rallying cry that permitted the construction of what Antonio Gramsci theorized as the national-popular. But it was only in the works of José Martí that the term became the standard-bearer of an identity. He declared America to be mestizo America in his already classic piece entitled *Nuestra America.*[2] His idea has been extraordinarily generative, in that it helps cut through the arid wastes of a perception of the proper through the gaze of dominance. Mestizo America in Martí, as creole in Brathwaite, implies shifting the terms of value, accepting imperfection as a norm, regularizing and normalizing the tangled strands of the substandard and the depreciated. Thus the genealogy of *mestizaje* and *creolization* stands poised within the sociobiology of rape, and a highly charged political concept which provides the warrant for the construction of a popular bloc.

In the twentieth century *mestizaje* becomes in the United States a *Latino* buzzword, one which is more related to the concept of *négritude* such as this term was coined by Fanon. Mestizaje and négritude, as migrating concepts, come to embody a psychobiological syncretism, the epistemic signs people carry within themselves. Today both words have become sublated, and the discussion of ethnic identities has been played out within the domain of multiculturalisms. Paul Gilroy thinks this is symptomatic of the political conflicts of postmodernity, mainly in the overdeveloped countries, and a clear indicator that the discussion has moved away with glee from the feeble domain of the politics of bygone days as a problem played out in the everyday, an identity that is managed by the cultural industries of mass communication.[3]

Any Caribbeanists going over this ground will recognize that these meanings are also implicit in the word *creole*, as Brathwaite uses it.[4] For *creole* is ethnicity coupled with race, but it is also the possibility of a give-and-take which produces a new or altered being, a multiform orientation and positionality. Creolization is

> [a] model which allows for blood flow, fluctuations, the half-look, the look both/several ways; which allows for and contains the ambiguous, and rounds the sharp edges off the dichotomy . . . : [a] process which is particularly interesting since here we find an increasing reaction to external stimulus from the segmented orders as a whole.[5]

The difference between the two terms is that originally – that is, before *mestizaje* was steered into a different direction by Latinas in the United States – it was a term set up from above, whereas *creole* was from the beginning a concept worked from below, and one that absorbed, reflected and sublated the biological syncretism of ethnic mixtures and gave them a new cultural status and dignity.[6]

But it did more. Creolization was a proposal for the reorganization of society, a different way of understanding a temporal-social formation, and of advocating the already available sets of norms relative to the living textures of the national-popular life. These sets of norms coming from below not only opposed – or, rather, deconstructed – the norms from above but suggested a more organic normativity for Caribbean societies. *Creole* presented itself as a collective identity, as the possibilities for acknowledging a *we*. Brathwaite states it very clearly in *Contradictory Omens*, when he writes,

> The failure of Jamaican/West Indian society lay in the fact that it did not/could not fully recognize these elements of its own creativity **and so failed to complete the creolizing process** (p. 22). . . . This would have involved, above all else, **the acceptance of the culture of this black ex-African majority as the paradigm and norm for the entire society** (p. 30). . . . [However], at this point in time, faced with the fact of cultural incompleteness: none of us has been successfully acculturated to any one other, and the interculturation process is still in its early teens. We remain part creole, part colonial, seeking many-ancestorial conclusions. Our tides flow down the river, meet a holy but not wholly receptive sea. Hence the exiled natives, black albinos, **the snow was falling in the canefields** of the plural us (p. 55). . . . The "answer" to all this seems to inhere in recognition of the contradictions: the plural/whole, the cripple god, creative deprivation. But recognition, leading to "solution" cannot be an act of will (the sea anemone shrinking from the hurting hand) but miracle of tact and selfless grace: **explosure** (the uncurled bloom of light); **implossure** (firm but subtile feeding to the stem of origins), in distinction to **imposure** (imprint of the rule and ruler: imperson/personator). (p. 61)

In this respect creolization hit the neural system of colonialism, in proposing an ideology capable of constituting what Gramsci calls a popular bloc.[7] *Creole* in those days already undergirded all the possibilities of hegemony, and by hegemony I understand the moment of persuasion, the installation of moral authority and leadership. In its multidimensional character, hegemony stands for a degree of mastery across a wide spectrum of positions, and for that reason it could win a substantial degree of popular consent. *Creole* presented itself as the most salient description of a social formation, as a possible structure of organic governance from below, and, as I understood it when I first read it, it was the real thing: a historically produced condition out of which sets of discursive chains, clusters and fields of meaning could be worked out for the benefit of society at large. Had the idea taken hold of the political, it would have turned the world upside down.

When *creole* came up in the cultural market of the English Caribbean as an alternative signifier of the cultural politics of difference, the term in vogue in continental America was *transculturation*. Transculturation was also implicit in the word *creole*, but *creole* meant in excess of it. The genealogy of *transculturation* bears repeating here, because *transculturation* presents itself as an alternative to the word *acculturation*. *Acculturation* meant a one-way directional flow of culture and not, as Brathwaite proposes, a double articulation, a double vision, a multiple consciousness. Born out of the domain of anthropology in the Spanish Caribbean, *transculturation* was also a term inscribed in the study of black or African cultures. It was the Cuban anthropologist Fernando Ortiz who invented the term *trans-* to posit the dual articulation of cultures and to signal that the flow was at least in two directions, in a kind of give-and-take situation. Ortiz's own emphasis was black cultures and his interest resided more in what was called folklore, focused on religious syncretism but also thematizing other aspects of Cuban social formation such as music, dance and language. Ortiz excised negativity from Afro-American Spanish cultures and subjected national identities to a radical rethink. It was a cultural critic from Uruguay, Angel Rama, who lifted the concept from the field of anthropology and transplanted it to the studies of high culture. We can read his effort as establishing an articulation between the popular and the learned, the oral and the literate. But the relevance of the gesture is to bring discussions on ethnicity to bear on, or to serve as models for, theorizing national formations. For Rama the term was also a way of discussing uneven modernity, the migratory flows to the urban centres, and the creation of a periphery within the periphery. This is the series of time lags woefully spawned by modernity.

Thus, whereas *transculturation* was marking the route of a concept that originated in Afro-American culture and emptied into the philosophies of modernism and modernization, *creolization* was marking the territoriality of the diaspora, which was also the effect of modernization, but an effect that could move on to the domain of transmigration and globalization. *Creolization* was already built on the shaky grounds of positional identities within the perimeters of the national. But the two terms never met. Angel Rama preferred the term *négritude* to that of *creolization,* for reasons that probably had to do with the tradition of *mestizaje* and the discussion of ethnicity in the French Caribbean carried out by Fanon and Césaire, and by the Caribbean and African intellectuals nucleated around the journal *Présence Africaine*.[8] The continent was more ready to dialogue with a concept that would underline race over ethnicity rather than the other way around, and *creole* was certainly a more ethnically charged concept. Here I am invoking the distinction made by Stuart Hall between the two terms, *ethnicity* being a historically constructed *race*. "Ethnicity [he writes] acknowledges the place of history, language and culture in the construction of subjectivity and identity, as well as the fact that all discourse is placed, positioned, situated, and all knowledge is contextual."[9] And more than to culture, closer to the politics of culture. However, there is a moment in the history of cultural studies that the terms seem to cohabitate.

Creolization, mestizaje, transculturation – all seem to refer to the effects of colonialism and the mixtures it brought to the continent, and in the continent the terms were ways of bringing colonialism under the sway of modernism. Within this frame, *creolization* was the more left-leaning term, one that represented a radical epistemic rupture with the philosophies of accommodation and mediation expressed in the lukewarm concepts *transculturation* and *mestizaje*, and one that interrupted the linear logic of positivistic discourse. I see these last concepts as renditions of the politics of accommodation under the aegis of Western cultures, whereas I read *creolization* as a radical critique of Western epistemes, and for that reason, one to be first subsumed and sublated and then revitalized under a different name by the discussion of hybridity which followed in the debate. *Hybridity*, as discussed in the English bibliographies, stands on the shoulders of *creolization*.

Mind you, my attempt is to bring together and compare continental traditions that usually remain divorced. Our worlds, as Jose Antonio Portuondo used to say many years ago, do not communicate because we don't have a maritime industry to build ships, and so the islands perpetually turn their backs upon each other and we only communicate through the articulations of the metropolis. My attempt is also to bring together the strands of a discussion on race and ethnicity – two very tangled strands – that involve two sets of oppressed populations, the indigenous people of America and the African peoples of the diaspora. In this way *mestizaje* connotes the former and *creolization* the latter. *Hybridity* encompasses both. The term can be discussed in Spanish America through the work of Nestor García Canclini, and in Anglo America through the work of Homi Bhabha.

But before discussing hybridity, I want to point out the relevance of two other ways of articulating race and identity and of discussing the politics of the racialization of people. One of the terms is *heterogeneity*; the other is *subalternity*. I believe these two terms are relative, in that both *subalternity* and *heterogeneity* produce the discourses of differences whose trademark is that of a hermeneutical interruption.[10] Heterogeneity, such as it is studied by Antonio

Cornejo Polar, is that theatre in which alternative epistemologies meet in struggle. Two cultures can remain adjacent to each other, one side-by-side with the other, without ever being able to translate each other, and any attempt at translating one system into the other turns into a distortion. Cornejo gives as a foundational moment the meeting between Atahualpa and the priest Vicente Valverde at Cajamarca, Peru.

This moment marks the confrontation between the voice and the letter, and is characterized as a spoken dialogue between deaf people. Not only is there a language barrier, one speaking Quechua and the other Spanish, but there is also a basic disagreement about the letter of the law represented in Valverde's use of the Bible as the source of truth, legality and power. "The discovery of the book [writes Homi Bhabha] installs the sign of appropriate representation: the word of God, truth, art. . . . But the institution of the Word in the wilds is also an *Entstellung,* a process of displacement, distortion, dislocation, repetition."[11] Atahualpa rejects this law, and cannot even understand the act of reading. The book comes to be a sign of contention between two systems and two norms that are to remain split asunder for centuries, and, according to Bhabha, the book will turn delirium into the discourse of civil address, authority and order. And here we begin bordering the discussion of multiculturalism whose grounds are civil society and the public spheres. This same anxiety of possession of the voice by the letter is going to manifest itself throughout the history of Latin American high culture that Cornejo studies in the case of Peru. A novel like *The Storyteller* by Mario Vargas Llosa also refers to this recoiling of the subaltern cultures of orality into the wilderness, a movement which parallels the flight from the evil eye of whites that in Fanon breaks the black man's body.

I said that heterogeneity was a concept similar to that of subalternity, and what I meant is that in both heterogeneity and subalternity there is no mediation or negotiation or translation possible. The two terms basically represent that which is beyond grasp, representation and appropriation. And in this respect they stand for the *interruptus* of knowledge. Definitions of the subaltern quaintly hold hands with those of heterogeneity in that they fit what today is described in the jargon of the profession as ever-shifting grounds of culture, slippery signifiers, meanings always on the run.

Let me move now to the debate on hybridity. As I write today that concept has already been superceded by the discussion on multiculturalism, that is moving today into the arena of the public sphere and civil society. The questions now are related to consensus and persuasion. And here we have to tread very carefully, because we are engaging a very slippery customer. But at the close of the century, hybridity reigned supreme. In the work of Nestor Garcia Canclini hybridity is a postmodern condition, postmodern being a reflection on the modern. Hybridity for him comes right after the four tenets of modernization had reached their politically heuristic limit, and hence hybridity is a concept on the edge. What have come to an end are the projects of modernity understood as emancipation, expansion, renovation and democratization. As a result, Canclini defines hybridity "as a strategy of absorption, adaptation, reconversion, and replacement; it is a concept that seeks to dissolve the oppositions between modern and traditional, modern and postmodern, anthropological and sociological knowledges, and external and internal market structures".[12] For Bhabha, hybridity is the main vector for reading the cultures of the diaspora, colonialism and colonization. It basically consists in a project that moves away from the philosophies of fixity, tradition and origins into the moments of processes that are produced in the articulation of cultural differences. His idea is that it is in the in-between spaces, in the interstitial, where the strategies of selfhood and the new signs of identity are produced. He is, then, the poet of the in-between, of the in-excess-of, of cultural differences that split in the act of being articulated. His aim is to show how social differences are woven together and how this process constitutes an ongoing negotiation that seeks to authorize cultural hybridities.

To end, I will refer to the term *pluralism*. My point of departure is Stuart Hall, in particular his paper, "Pluralism, Race and Class in Caribbean Society".[13] The reason for my choice is that in this paper he discusses the meaning of "plural societies" (understood as conflictive and coercive), in contrast with the concept of "American pluralism" (which presumes cohesion, adaptation, accommodation and consensus). His way of arguing enables me to come to have some glimmer of an understanding of the virtues of creolization. Hall poses the problem of the norm as that practice which seems to reach a form of consensus which he also calls *creole*, and which links *creolization* to questions of hegemony and the creation of the popular bloc I outlined above. Again, what I find interesting about *creolization*, as a notion for thinking pluralism or multiculturalism, is that it avoids normalization from above (Western models). In Hall *creole* is a sign of the "ambiguity" of the cultural articulation, one that takes us back to the cultural accommodations dating to the period of slavery. In this respect *creole* and black are subsumed into each other and *creole* comes to invert the North American meaning of plurality, in that not the pure races (white Anglo-Saxon Protestants) but the mixed ones come to be postulated as a norm. Another big difference is the notion of majorities and minorities. In the Caribbean the notion of majority is black. According to Hall, whites develop "consensual" relations (or what he calls "imperative coordination") in which they are economically and politically hegemonic and so they constitute a consensus from above; whereas *creole* more aptly expresses "the will of the peoples" and, at the same time, it is the medium or broker and contingent concept which establishes what Ernesto Laclau calls the general form of fullness, within a field of dispersions and the presence of a totally unstable ground.

The genealogy of legitimacy is historical. Hall claims, and I agree with him, that " 'the plural society' model . . . tends to displace the historicity of the structure".[14] The works of Charles Taylor and Will Kymlicka are good examples of this situation. We must be aware of the displacement from a historical to a logical model of thinking which is a political divide affecting research strategies and areas. There is a necessity, it seems to me, to engage with logic, but not at the cost of historical specificity. And it is a necessity because the structures of governance are decided in that domain. Legitimation accounts for the structure of dominance, force and power, where force is understood in Laclau's sense as "an external source of a certain set of structural connections".[15] The internal connection is hegemony.

To close I want to say that I find it very provocative to read the central modern societies, mainly the North American and British societies, as creole or hybrid societies, where the notions of minorities and majorities are the major factors playing out a discussion on civil rights and citizenships in the era of globalization. In a way, *creole* is a way of globalizing the margins, a way of discussing the articulations of race, colour, class, national stratifications in both migrant and native populations – what Ralph Premdas calls the two societal contexts of the ethno-national and the migrant-minority varieties.[16] In this chapter I have clearly foregrounded the notion of *creole* and of *creolization* with the purpose of highlighting what for my generation represented a radical shift in the studies of culture within peripheral modern societies, and as a means of tracing the genealogy of the postmodern discussions of hybridity and multiculturalism. It is also my way of honouring the path-breaking work of Edward Kamau Brathwaite. I have not done justice to the concepts of *hybridity* and *pluralism,* but I have pointed to the directionality of the discussion. Hybridity, pluralism, and multiculturalism necessitate a bigger discursive space and time.

The efforts deployed in this discussion are all historically and regionally situated. The terms come to explain a condition of identity politics that begins with the process of colonization and the diaspora and ends in the era of globalization; they are terms that first connote race and biology and then move into the richer terrain of culture and politics. The debate over these terms denotes a way of contesting, affirming, explaining and debating the presence of populations within cultural articulations, but it is also a way of claiming intellectual authority over a domain. It is in fact the act of constituting a national intelligentsia, a way of producing a counterdiscourse. The terms are tools for organizing a universe of meaning alternative to that of colonialism and Western epistemes, but they are also a way of demonstrating how impossible it is to discuss one without the other. In so far as the difference between the terms reflects the differences between their historical moments, that difference is indicative of epochs and of the state of the question but also of political and poetic positionings. Some writers are more the students and scholars of Marxism, some others of liberalism, and yet others of deconstructionism. Some engage more the question of politics and the nation state, some others that of nation and culture, and yet others move into the denationalization that globalization seems to bring with it. But all in all they represent the curve from the modern to the postmodern, and from the national to the global.

Notes

1. Edward Kamau Brathwaite, *The Development of Creole Society in Jamaica, 1770–1820* (Oxford: Clarendon Press, 1971).
2. José Martí, *Tres documentos de Nuestra América*, ed. Roberto Romani Velazco (La Habana: Casa de las Américas, 1979).
3. Paul Gilroy, "British Cultural Studies and the Pitfalls of Identity", in *Cultural Studies and Communications,* ed. James Curran, David Morley, and Valerie Walkerdine (London and New York: St Martin, 1996).
4. "[Creoles are] all the ethnic groups which make up Caribbean society . . . moving through the period of settlement, through slavery and the post-emancipation period and the arrival of new ethnic immigrants, into the more recent

phenomenon of vicarious culture contact through tourist, book, magazine, film, television." Brathwaite, *Contradictory Omens: Cultural Diversity and Integration in the Caribbean* (Kingston, Jamaica: Savacou Publications, 1974), 204–5. In *Contradictory Omens* Brathwaite states that " 'Creole society' is the result therefore of a complex situation where a colonial polity reacts, as a whole, to external metropolitan pressures and at the same time to internal adjustments made necessary by the juxtaposition of master and labour, white and non-white, Europe and colony, European and African (mulatto creole), European and Amerindian (mestizo creole), in a culturally heterogeneous relationship" (10–11).

5. Brathwaite, "Caribbean Man in Space and Time", *Carifesta Forum: An Anthology of 20 Caribbean Voices*, ed. John Hearne (Kingston, Jamaica: Carifesta, 1976), 204–5.

6. See Gloria Anzaldúa, *Borderlands/La Frontera: The New Mestiza* (1987; reprint, San Francisco: Aunt Lute Books, 1999).

7. I am using the term in the Althusserian sense of that system of representation which enables us to bring together our imaginary relations to the real conditions of our lives.

8. See Lillyan Kesteloot, *Les écrivains noirs de langue francaise: Naissance d'une literature* (Bruxelles: Université libre de Bruxelles, Insitute de Sociology, 1965).

9. Stuart Hall, "New Ethnicities", in *Stuart Hall: Critical Dialogues in Cultural Studies*, ed. David Morley and Kuan-Hsing Chen (London and New York: Routledge, 1996), 446.

10. See Ileana Rodríguez, ed., *The Latin American Subaltern Studies Reader* (Durham and London: Duke University Press, 2001); and Rodríguez, ed., *Convergencia de Tiempos: Estudios Subalternos/Contextos Latinoamericanos: Estado, Cultura, Subalternidad* (Amsterdam and Atlanta: Rodopi, 2001).

11. Homi Bhabha, *The Location of Culture* (London and New York: Routledge, 1994), 105.

12. Ileana Rodríguez and Derek Petrey, "Hybrid Cultures: Strategies for Entering and Leaving Modernity", *MMLA The Journal of the Midwest Modern Language Association* 30, nos. 1–2 (Spring 1997): 135.

13. Stuart Hall, "Pluralism, Race and Class in Caribbean Society", in *Race and Class in Post-Colonial Society: A Study of Group Relations in the English-Speaking Caribbean, Bolivia, Chile and Mexico* (Paris: UNESCO, 1977), 150–82.

14. Ibid., 155.

15. Ernesto Laclau, ed., *The Making of Political Identities* (London and New York: Verso, 1993), 283.

16. Ralph R. Premdas, "Public Policy and Ethnic Conflict", Discussion Paper series, no. 12. Management of Social Transformations – MOST, UNESCO. Available online at www.unesco.org/shs/most.

14

The Prose of Creolization
Brathwaite's *The Development of Creole Society* and Subaltern Historiography

Leah **Rosenberg** |

> It was in language that the slave was perhaps most successfully imprisoned by his master, and it was in his (mis-)use of it that he perhaps most effectively rebelled. Within the folk tradition, language was (and is) a creative act in itself.
>
> – Edward Kamau Brathwaite, *The Development of Creole Society in Jamaica, 1770–1820*

At a job interview last year, I was asked why there is no subaltern studies group in the anglophone Caribbean. Since 1993, for instance, scholars in Latin American studies have explicitly adopted the name and project of subaltern studies; studies of "subalternity" in Palestine, Ireland, China and Africa have subsequently been published.[1] An appropriate response might have been to cite Edward Said's introduction to *Selected Subaltern Studies* (1988), in which he situates scholars of subaltern studies as belonging to a large group of intellec-. tuals from Asia, Africa, the Caribbean and Latin America who have challenged postcolonial forms of imperialism and oppression through cultural and intellectual action – a group including Ngugi wa Thiong'o, George Lamming, C.L.R. James and Gabriel García Márquez.[2] Caribbean scholars would have no reason then to adopt the name *subaltern studies*; they had been pursuing projects similar to subaltern studies at least since James's *Black Jacobins*.[3]

Not able to articulate this answer at the time, however, I began to consider whether Caribbean scholars in fact "did subaltern studies", and found what I thought were useful parallels between Ranajit Guha's foundational essay in subaltern studies – "The Prose of Counter-Insurgency" (1981) – and Kamau Brathwaite's equally influential *The Development of Creole Society in Jamaica, 1770–1820* (1971).[4] Both seek to address the hierarchy and inequality of post-independence society and culture through a revision of history that situates the disenfranchised majorities at the centre of historiography. Brathwaite's principle that creolization "was the single most important factor in the development of Jamaican society" placed the culture of Afro-creoles at the centre of Jamaica's history while countering both colonial histories and contemporary social science theories that presented slavery and plantation society as the defining forces in Jamaican society.[5] Similarly, Guha's project to "promote a systematic and informed discussion of subaltern themes in the field of South Asian studies, and thus help to rectify the elitist bias characteristic of much research and academic work" critiques both British colonial and nationalist historiography of India.[6]

This chapter is a preliminary examination of the value of setting subaltern historiography in relation to Brathwaite's historiography. It focuses on a predicament Brathwaite and Guha shared: writing the history of the dominated majority based on sources written by those that dominated them. Both historians believe that it is possible to extract much of the history of the subaltern from the documents of their oppressors. In fact, they have an uncannily similar approach to colonial discourse. They believe that historians can decode it or read it against the grain to extract critical information about subaltern culture and resistance. I seek first to demonstrate the striking parallel in their methods and, second, to illustrate that a comparison of the two historians allows us not only to see the power of their method but also its limitations.

There are, however, some important distinctions between Brathwaite's and Guha's projects. Guha contends that peasants contributed significantly to nationalism in India and that peasants survived and altered the conditions in which they lived; he seeks to establish their collective consciousness in rebellions, in order to liberate their history from the elitist narratives of colonialist and nationalist writers.[7] Brathwaite argues not only that Africans and Afro-

Caribbeans survived in Jamaica, but that they, more than other social groups, contributed to creole society. Guha's project explicitly attacks nationalist historiography for streamlining peasant history into an elitist nationalist narrative. Brathwaite is critical of post-independence nationalism that denies legitimacy to Afro-creole culture, but Brathwaite's own conception of creolization participates much more directly in a cultural nationalism than does Guha's conception of subaltern consciousness. As Nigel Bolland asserts,

> the cultural and populist aspects of the Creole-society viewpoint, with its emphasis upon the origins of a distinctive common culture as a basis for national unity, constitutes [*sic*] the ideology of a particular social segment, namely a middle class intelligentsia that seeks a leading role in an integrated, newly independent society.[8]

The third distinction I would like to highlight is in the historians' approaches to colonial discourse. Guha's article is an analysis of historical sources on peasant insurgency that provides a theory of colonial discourse strongly influenced by Roland Barthes and Antonio Gramsci; thus, his sources and reading strategies constitute one primary subject of his work. In contrast, rather than providing an explicit critique of colonial sources, Brathwaite's treatment of historical sources appears almost performative; he often places the reader in the position of historian by deluging her with citations, sometimes contradictory or unlabelled. The effect is to demonstrate some of the principles of Guha's theory of colonial discourse, such as the largely unified colonialist bias of these sources and the resulting difficulties in using them as evidence of subaltern experience.

Dipesh Chakrabarty tells the story that Guha received a grant to write on Gandhi and nonviolent resistance. Influenced by the Maoist peasant rebellion in Naxalbari as well as by Gramsci, Guha gave up the grant in order to write on violence.[9] In order to write this history of peasant insurgency, Guha had to rely on a variety of texts: colonial correspondence contemporaneous with the revolts, later English memoirs and histories, and Indian nationalist histories – what he denominates respectively as primary, secondary and tertiary discourse. These discourses provided elite history, first of the colonial state and then of the national elite: they were at root incapable of explaining the consciousness of peasant insurgents. Yet one could find the consciousness of peasants, Guha argued, if one learned how to read these highly encoded texts that melded interpretation seamlessly into apparently objective accounts.

Colonial discourses, in Guha's terms primary and secondary discourses, depicted peasant insurgency so strongly and exclusively from the perspective of the state that historical realities of peasants were literally turned upside down: "Islamic puritans" became "fanatics", "resistance to oppression" became "daring and wanton atrocities on the inhabitants". Guha defines these discourses as a "prose of counter-insurgency", concluding that "these documents make no sense except in terms of a code of pacification which, under the Raj, was a complex of coercive intervention by the state and its protégés, the native elite, with arms and words" ("Counter-Insurgency", 59). Nationalist historians also held that the elite was responsible for social change; they molded peasant resistance into an elitist and teleological history of resistance in which all peasant insurgencies "developed into the broad highway of India's struggle for freedom".[10] Guha's main concern is to refute the colonial stereotype of peasant insurgents as violent fanatics, and the nationalist portrayal of these same insurgents as primitive and superstitious people manipulated by a sophisticated elite.

In his analysis of primary and secondary accounts of the Santal rebellion (*hool*) of 1855, Guha found information to refute these stereotypes. Revolts had not been spontaneous but preceded by legal petitions and complaints; primary and secondary texts simply drop all mention of these legal protests from their explanation of the violence (Guha, "Counter-Insurgency", 55).[11] Thus Guha's first strategy seems simply to be a very careful reading of the prose of counter-insurgency. His second is reading against the grain. Taking his model from Mao Tse-tung, Guha establishes an apparently binary system in which what is "terrible" for the state is "fine" for the peasant insurgent. Thus if a colonial text asserts that fanatics intended to attack and commit atrocities, Guha learns that peasant Islamic puritans sought to punish their oppressors and to resist oppression (p. 59). Finally, Guha argues that all historiography is limited and skewed by its sources and the consciousness of the historian; it is the duty of historians to acknowledge this to their readers (p. 77).

Although Brathwaite's subject matter and objectives differ significantly from Guha's, he uses these two methods – a close reading of the colonial archive and a recoding of colonial sources – to establish the historical experience of the dominated majority. Guha employs the prose of counter-insurgency as evidence of Indian subaltern insurgency; in *The Development of Creole Society* Brathwaite employs evidence from English and local elite texts that constitute a discourse of anticreolization and counter-insurgency to write a history of Jamaican creolization and resistance. Many of the historical documents that Brathwaite uses as evidence – the histories of Bryan Edwards and Edward Long, the accounts of J. Stewart and J.B. Moreton, the diaries of Lady Nugent, Monk Lewis, governors and missionaries, the pages of the Royal Gazette – form part of English and local elite discourses on the West Indies.[12] These narratives are so unified in their central tenets that they are often formulaic. They present the "Great House" vision of Jamaica as a society dominated by large plantations and a clear colour-class hierarchy in which whites were wealthy and superior, browns were less wealthy and less superior, and blacks were least powerful and most inferior.[13] This emphasis on hierarchy and segregation seeks to minimize or, at the very least, condemn interracial social and cultural interaction. It is in this sense "a prose of anti-creolization".

The discourse is also ambivalent and contradictory. Writers de-emphasize the power of slaves but at the same time betray their fear of rebellion and of the influence of the Haitian revolution. Their general ambivalence about Afro-creoles results in deeply contradictory accounts of Afro-Jamaicans as both inferior and superior, repulsive and beautiful, deceitful and loyal. Brathwaite's ability to find evidence of creolization is in part enabled by this ambivalence and contradiction. It may have also been aided by the colonial perspective of the texts. Whether written by antislavery or proslavery writers, the texts are deeply invested in English colonial rule; accordingly, they represent Jamaicans and Jamaican culture as inferior to English citizens and English culture. Thus, though planters and their wives ought to have embodied the ideal of gentleman and lady in the local logic of white supremacy, English colonial writers often depict them as promiscuous, cruel and ignorant, mirror opposites of the English ideals. This particular contradiction was exacerbated by the growing opposition between pro- and antislavery factions during the period Brathwaite studies. This contradictory and ambivalent nature of colonial discourse, I think, is critical to both Guha's and Brathwaite's ability to extract information from it, but I don't think that either addresses this aspect of colonial discourse explicitly.

As Guha will ten years later, Brathwaite both recodes this discourse and uses its details to refute its explicit central tenet: in the case of Jamaica, that the great house model successfully kept Jamaica's nonwhite populations segregated and pacified. When an English colonial writer refers to a West Indian practice with moral and cultural disgust, Brathwaite sees in it a probable instance of creolization. Thus, when Lady Nugent expresses horror at white women speaking Creole, when Edward Long and many others condemn white creoles for eating pepperpot, when Moreton makes fun of white creoles' passion for dancing, when Stewart questions white creoles who dance to the "deafening noise of the drums", Brathwaite lists these as evidence of creolization (*Creole Society*, 302–3). Edward Long and Bryan Edwards attribute low birthrates among the enslaved population to promiscuity and polygamy; Brathwaite uses their accounts as evidence of widespread abortion as a form of resistance. J. Stewart complains of slaves' malingering and their neglect of their children's health; these Brathwaite takes as evidence of slaves' resistance to being "only 'labouring machines' " (p. 207). In missionaries' records of their failure to convert slaves, Brathwaite finds evidence of "a stubborn and remarkable resistance to Christian teaching" (pp. 256–57). In each of these cases Brathwaite decodes colonial discourse to produce a prose of creolization and resistance. In fact, these references to creole music, speech and religion serve to illustrate that creole practices were positive forms of culture and of resistance.

Like Guha, Brathwaite supplements decoding with detailed readings of archival material to find further evidence of creolization and resistance. Using figures from the *Jamaica Almanack* 1821 and Long's *History of Jamaica*, Brathwaite estimates that twenty-four thousand or 80 per cent of whites were not wealthy (*Creole Society*, 121, 135).[14] This finding constitutes a central foundation of Brathwaite's refutation of the "Great House" vision of Jamaican society, and his correlating argument that intercultural interaction was the most important dynamic in Jamaica society.

In addition, Brathwaite poses what may be his strongest challenge to colonial discourse by imitating the structure of many English histories and accounts of Jamaica. Like Edward Long's histories and countless other narratives, Brathwaite largely organizes his book according to the colour hierarchy: "Whites", "Other Whites", "Blacks", "the (Free) People of Colour". In colonialist histories, the hierarchy in the text articulates and legitimates the coordinated colour and class hierarchy. In contrast, Brathwaite uses these categories to invert the colonial hierarchy. Each section outlines the contribution of one social group. In Brathwaite's analysis, governors, the highest position in the colonial hierarchy, make no contribution to creole society, whereas those groups criminalized and overlooked by colonial writers prove the most significant contributors: Africans, skilled slaves, tradesmen, preachers, obeah-men and, finally, small-scale white settlers, whom Brathwaite names the "true pioneers" (*Creole Society*, 160, 150). (We should note that most of these categories are intermediary groups who would have a high degree of involvement with people in other social groups, and therefore are critical to Brathwaite's concept of creolization.) In Brathwaite's argument it is the segments of society who contribute most to society who have legitimate claim to define its culture. Thus, Brathwaite appears to construct a social hierarchy of legitimacy that fundamentally challenges the hierarchy embedded in the structure of colonial histories.[15] In imitating the form of colonial historiography, Brathwaite differs significantly from Guha and Chakrabarty. However, his imitative strategy illustrates his claim that creolization includes elements of imitation but that this "mimicry" is creative; in this case, it is also subversive of colonial discourse.[16]

As the previous example illustrates, Brathwaite doesn't simply use the colonial archive for numbers and examples. He imitates and incorporates it in ways that place the reader in the position of historian. In so doing, Brathwaite teaches the reader to read colonial discourse against the grain. He employs the specificity and abundance of colonial discourse to produce an almost physical impression on the reader. For instance, he reproduces the employments listed for whites in the Kingston Vestry jury lists:

> small merchants, lawyers, doctors, parsons and preachers, teachers, organists, clerks, tavern keepers, hostel keepers, police and night watchmen, fire-engine drivers and maintenance men, beadles, collecting constables, midwives, nurses, druggists, iron founders, masons, lumber measurers, lime-sellers, gunsmiths, brickmakers, brick-layers, cabinet-makers, milliners, plumbers, seamstresses, carpenters, cooks, pedlars, printers, saddlers, butchers, blacksmiths, gardeners, tailors, butlers, upholsterers, shipwrights, coopers, silversmiths, goldsmiths, coppersmiths, watchmakers and repairers, painters, pilots, shoemakers, sailmakers, wharfingers, vendue-masters (auctioneers), stationers, hairdressers, staymakers, joiners, bakers, coachmakers, dyers, etc. (*Creole Society*, 136)

Brathwaite's listing may simply, vigorously, call its readers to task, as if he is shaking us and asking energetically, "How can you believe in the great house model of Jamaica when there is all this overwhelming evidence of its inaccuracy?!" One appreciates the vigorousness of Brathwaite's tone when one considers the staying power of the myth of colour and class in Jamaica. Yet the enormity and detail of this list, particularly when read aloud, constitute a performance of the absurdity of this colonial myth, also representing a rhetorical strategy Brathwaite repeatedly deploys.

Throughout *The Development of Creole Society* Brathwaite nearly bombards readers with spectacular details from the colonial archive. I suggest that in this instance and others, Brathwaite teaches the reader the slipperiness, the horror, the overwhelming quantity and quality of colonial discourse. In discussing runaway slaves Brathwaite uses the detail of advertisements for runaway slaves to demonstrate that skilled slaves transcended the invisibility to which slavery condemned them. In just one paragraph he impresses us with slaves' visibility by citing in detail twelve different announcements for runaways. We learn of the "Marks of a large Sore, not perfectly cured, on the lowest Part of" the left leg of a man named Gloster, who was last seen by his master in a "Pair of black breeches and a Check Shirt"; of Susanna Baker who had "a black mark, like a fried sprat, on one of her elbows, and all her teeth broken from fighting"; of Adrian's height, his trade, the marks on his face; of how Romeo, an upholsterer, sent his wages home but absconded himself; and of the escapes, professions, clothing, language, and appearance of many others. Brathwaite continues Susanna Baker's story in the following paragraph: she was spotted on her way to Spanish Town with Billy, a runaway blacksmith; Brathwaite reminds us playfully of Susanna Baker's identity, noting in parentheses "she of the fried sprat on the elbow and the broken teeth" (*Creole Society*, 203). Brathwaite's extensive citation of and playful interaction with the descriptions suggest a method. To make enslaved individuals visible through colonial sources, the reader must experience the sources. In addition Brathwaite and the reader need to actively engage with these sources (hence, "she of the fried sprat on the elbow").

The reader must engage more actively with colonial discourse in the many instances throughout *The Development of Creole Society* in which Brathwaite inserts citations with little or no introduction, leaving the reader to discover the sources of the statements and to evaluate their significance. In a chapter on "Attitudes of Whites to Non-Whites", Brathwaite begins by asserting that the failure of the white elite to recognize black and brown Jamaicans weakened the entire Jamaican society; as a result, he comments briefly, stereotypes of African and Afro-creoles emerged. Without further comment he inserts six examples of these stereotypes, with no introduction or reference save the footnotes. Written by Long, Monk Lewis and J.B. Moreton, these passages demonstrate the extreme, dehumanizing and yet ambivalent terms in which English male writers depicted brown women and men. The passages are internally contradictory: Long claims that brown women are beautiful, "well-shaped" and "well-featured", but grow ugly early; that they are lascivious and vain but "in public remarkably decent", sensible, and "pay religious attention to the cleanliness of their persons". Moreover, the passages contradict each other: Long claims this interracial class is sterile; Lewis says they are fertile. The citations define brown Jamaicans as effeminate, weak, difficult, vain, ignorant, sterile and promiscuous. They also record the women's beauty, virtue and competence. Brathwaite does not acknowledge, much less explain, these contradictions. He comments only that whites preferred to see slaves as a mass, not as individuals (*Creole Society*, 177–78). Brathwaite's extensive citation demonstrates to the reader that evidence cannot be simply extracted from these texts, because the texts perform the ambivalence and contradictions of colonial discourse; they are lessons in the impossibility of using such sources to produce a straightforward history.

Brathwaite develops this technique of citation in *Contradictory Omens*, a text that applies the research of *The Development of Creole Society* to arguing for the recognition of predominantly Afro-Caribbean folk culture as a foundation for contemporary cultural norms. In fact, *Contradictory Omens* extends Brathwaite's technique of citation into something like a pastiche approach to argumentation. In it he cites extensively from opposing sides of arguments, and frequently leaves the reader to figure out who the speaker is (by turning to the footnotes at the back of the pamphlet). Colonial discourse is unmarked text; it does not usually introduce itself as a prose of counter-insurgency or of anticreolization. These are things the historian must decipher. Brathwaite's prose of creolization in *The Development of Creole Society* and *Contradictory Omens* reproduces these conditions for the reader, but it provides a model for decoding colonial discourse, as well as an answer key of sorts in the form of footnotes. The many times Brathwaite decodes and recodes texts act as reading lessons for the reader. For instance, Brathwaite teaches us to decode the prose of anticreolization when he finds evidence of creolization in the Jamaican language the governor's wife finds disgusting. In *Contradictory Omens*, Brathwaite may provide an explanation of this method when he contends that his "melange/montage style is as much omen as problem. . . . For **definition** (description fashioned into implement or tool) can only derive from a proliferation of images: a multiplication of complex probes: *a co-operative effort from us all*."[17] Here I emphasize that in Brathwaite's history, defining creole culture and society must derive from an *"effort from us all"*, and a significant element of that effort takes the form of deciphering Brathwaite's "proliferation" of citations.

Brathwaite's "melange/montage style", however, also suggests that the strategy of code switching he shares with Guha needs to be nuanced. In the chapter on "The 'Folk' Culture of the Slaves", Brathwaite presents one of the core foundations of his larger argument. Though he asserts that he will not enter into the debate about "African 'survivals', 'retentions', 'adaptations' and so on", this chapter uses historical accounts like Monk Lewis's journal and Long's *History,* as well as ethnographic and anthropological studies of the Caribbean and West Africa like M.J. Herskovits's *The Myth of the Negro Past,* to demonstrate that Afro-Jamaican folk culture derives in large part from West African cultural practices. To establish this retention, he recounts detail of rituals of birth and death, sexual and marriage practices, child rearing, religion, music, dance, dress and even furniture (*Creole Society,* 212).[18] Establishing the Africanness of Afro-Caribbean culture is of great importance to Brathwaite. He sees the African elements of Caribbean culture as contributing significantly to the development of creole society between 1770 and 1820. No less important to Brathwaite is the fact that Afro-Jamaican folk culture became the basis for national arts movements during the anticolonial period of nationalism and the first years of independence, when Brathwaite and other intellectuals sought to use art to complete the process of liberation begun and abandoned by political decolonization and nationalism. In short, "The 'Folk' Culture of the Slaves" is a key chapter for Brathwaite. In it he includes a critical but brief section on marriage and sexuality, "Sexual/Domestic Unions" – comprised of two citations, the first from Bryan Edwards and the second from Edward Long – which I cite in its entirety below.

(ii) Sexual/Domestic Unions

It is a truth well known, that the practice of polygamy, which universally prevails in Africa, is also very generally adopted among the Negroes in the West Indies; and he who conceives that a remedy may be found for this, by introducing among them the laws of marriage as established in Europe, is utterly ignorant of their manners, propensities, and superstitions. It is reckoned in Jamaica, on a moderate computation, that not less than ten thousand of such as are called Head Negroes (artificers and others) possess two to four wives.[19]

But

one only is the object of particular steady attachment; the rest, although called wives, are only a sort of occasional concubines, or drudges, whose assistance the husband claims in the culture of his land, sale of his produce, and so on; rendering to them reciprocal acts of friendship, when they are in want. They laugh at the idea of marriage, which ties two people together indissolubly.[20] (*Creole Society,* 215)

In the first citation Edwards claims that the African practice of polygamy has been transplanted in the West Indies and that as a result Afro-Caribbeans cannot be converted to Christian marriage. In this passage Edwards reveals that his underlying agenda is to defend slavery and to attack missionaries for attempting to convert slaves. After Edwards's citation, Brathwaite adds the word "But". Then he inserts a citation from Long, in which Long explains that male slaves have a "steady attachment" to only one woman and use all the others primarily for agricultural and domestic labour. This "But" signals that the two passages disagree with each other although, in fact, they concur. Long may wish to deny Afro-Jamaicans even the denomination of *polygamy* because it implies a type of marriage, however inferior Europeans may consider it, and therefore argues that Afro-Jamaicans are polygynous rather than properly polygamous. However, Long concludes in much the same way as Edwards: European, Christian marriage is anathema to slaves. The section on sexuality and domestic unions ends, and Brathwaite goes on to "(iii) Children". Though the section raises more questions than it answers, Brathwaite remains silent at this critical moment in his argument and lets Edwards and Long, the two arch-spokesmen of proslavery discourse, speak for him. Brathwaite contributes one word to the section, and that word is misleading. David Scott has written a brilliant and empowering critique of Brathwaite's reliance on cultural anthropology, suggesting historical imperatives that led Brathwaite to this approach as well as outlining its limitations and providing an alternative.[21] Here, I suggest that Brathwaite's silence and the implicit contradiction or confusion suggested by his "But" reflect the incoherence of his argument at this point.

This very incoherence makes the section a lesson in the art of creating a history of slave culture from the colonial archive. Brathwaite appears to treat the claims of Edwards and Long as he has other statements from the colonial archive: he inverts them. For Edwards and Long polygamy is a sign of the "terrible", of the cultural lack and inferiority of Africa and its diaspora; for Brathwaite it is "fine", evidence of cultural continuity between West Africa and Jamaica. In this case, however, I think we confront at least two complicating questions. First, I would ask, is polygamy "fine" in the way peasant insurgency or recognized forms of slave resistance are "fine"? I would judge most refusals of Christian marriage as resistance against an elitist class-and-colour hierarchy that has used Christian marriage as a prerequisite for social, economic and political power since the eighteenth century. Brathwaite, however, does not suggest this reading, so I doubt that he viewed polygamy as a form of resistance. Rather, Brathwaite strives to provide a historical argument for creole societies to accept and legitimate folk cultures, in order to establish more equitable and unalienated societies. Cultural nationalism was relatively quick to embrace many of the other forms of folk culture Brathwaite examines in this chapter, most importantly creole language and Afro-Christian religions, musical forms and dance. Cultural nationalism, however, neither embraced nor celebrated polygamy. In fact, it would be difficult to argue that polygamy – like creole language and Afro-Christian religions – is a cultural form of resistance that Jamaica needs to legitimate and institutionalize in order to establish itself as a healthy nation.

The second question I would ask is: Do these excerpts from Edwards and Long constitute evidence that enslaved Jamaicans were "polygamous"? My sense is that Brathwaite's code switching is weakened because he fails to take into account the racialized ideology of domesticity that informs the colonial texts he examines. Long and Edwards attribute the highly charged classification of polygamy to slaves' families. This may result not so much from slaves' family structures but from the imperatives of racial ideology that shaped these English narratives. This ideology distinguished between white and black, metropolitan and colonial, worthy and unworthy in large part on the basis of English middle-class domestic practices and gender roles; legitimate peoples and nations practised English middle-class norms of marriage and complementary gender roles. This ideology shaped the arguments of nearly all English discourse on the West Indies between 1770 and 1820, the period of Brathwaite's study. Within the terms of this ideology, polygamy was not a description of a type of family structure but a racially determined practice, a sign of the absolute difference and inferiority of Africans to Europeans. Polygamy and the domestic and political incompetence it signalled served to justify England's colonial rule. In sum, as exponents of this ideology Edwards and Long were bound to exaggerate claims of polygyny, and possibly to invent them. They were bound to use the term *polygamy* for apparentl polygynous black Jamaicans, but highly unlikely to use the term for polygynous white Jamaicans. Under the influence of this ideology, Long confidently asserts that African women slept regularly with orangutans.[22] In short, as scholars of colonial discourse have long told us, we cannot assume that Long and Edwards record historical realities or that all we need to do is to invert or transform the values and meanings they attribute to Afro-creole culture. Colonial discourse may be formed in large part by colonial reaction to subaltern action, but colonial discourse may react to these actions indirectly.

Guha's theory of reading against the grain and Brathwaite's practice of reading against the grain need to take the indirection of colonial discourse into account, because not all instances are quite so clear as that of the orangutans. It may be that their method too easily presupposes a specific result: if colonial discourse presents us with something terrible, they assume they will find something fine. The case of polygamy suggests that this is not necessarily so. These limitations have long been acknowledged; what is significant to my argument is that these two historians working in different decades on studies of very different colonies used the same approach, and that they did so at relatively early stages in their careers as subaltern historians. Their work laid the foundation for later scholars of colonialism like Ann Stoler and Dipesh Chakrabarty to produce more nuanced approaches to the colonial archive that would trace the ambiguities and conflicting elements of colonial discourse, as well as analyse the institutions and political alliances that produced particular colonial records and tensions.[23]

I would reiterate that placing Brathwaite's historiography in relation to subaltern studies helps us to see the implications of his engagement with colonial discourse. In *The Development of Creole Society* Brathwaite comments, "It was in language that the slave was perhaps most successfully imprisoned by his master, and it was in his (mis-)use of it that he perhaps most effectively rebelled. Within the folk tradition, language was (and is) a creative act in itself" (p. 237). Brathwaite would have been as accurate had he written, "It was in language that the postcolonial historian was perhaps most successfully imprisoned by colonialism, and it was in his (mis-)use of it that he perhaps most effectively rebelled." My goal in this chapter is to suggest that it may be useful to compare and contrast the ways in which historians of different postcolonies use and misuse colonial discourse, and effectively rebel.

Notes

1.   See Latin American Subaltern Studies Group, "Founding Statement", *Boundary* 20, no. 3 (1993): 110–21. For subaltern studies in other regions, see Vinayak Chaturvedi, ed., *Mapping Subaltern Studies and the Postcolonial* (New York: Verso, 2000), vii.

2.   Edward Said, foreword to *Selected Subaltern Studies,* ed. Ranajit Guha and Gayatri Spivak (Oxford: Oxford University Press, 1988), ix–x.

3.   C.L.R. James, *The Black Jacobins: Toussaint L'Ouverture and the San Domingo Revolution* (1938; rev. ed., New York: Vintage, 1989).

4.   Ranajit Guha, "The Prose of Counter-Insurgency", in *Selected Subaltern Studies,* 45–86; Edward Kamau Brathwaite, *The Development of Creole Society in Jamaica, 1770–1820* (Oxford: Clarendon Press, 1971). Both hereafter cited in the text.

5.   Brathwaite, *Creole Society,* 296. In addition to refuting colonial historians like Bryan Edwards and Edward Long who argued for the necessity and success of slavery's oppressive system, Brathwaite explicitly critiques: Orlando Patterson's assertion that Jamaica was defined by slavery; M.G. Smith's model of Jamaica as a plural society; V.S. Naipaul's vision of the Caribbean as condemned to failed imitation; and Monica Schuler's and Elsa Goveia's contentions that enslaved people on some level consented to slavery. Thus, like Guha, Brathwaite's history from below revises both colonialist historiography and the work of post-independence intellectuals.

6.   Guha, preface to *Selected Subaltern Studies,* 35.

7.   I do not want to draw too strong a distinction here, because Guha may not be saying that the subaltern classes are the single most important factor, as Brathwaite does, but he is striving to establish that their contribution to Indian history is significant and has been ignored. He writes, for instance, that colonial and nationalist narratives fail "to acknowledge, far less interpret, the contributions made by the people *on their own,* that is, *independently of the elite* to the making and development of this nationalism". See Guha, "On Some Aspects of the Historiography of Colonial India", in *Selected Subaltern Studies,* 39.

8.   Nigel Bolland, "Creolisation and Creole Societies: A Cultural Nationalist View of Caribbean Social History", *Caribbean Quarterly* 44, nos. 1–2 (March–June 1998): 4.

9.   Dipesh Chakrabarty told this story at an informal seminar in the History department, University of Florida, 27 September 2001.

10.   Suprakash Ray, *Bharater Krishak-bidroha O Ganatantrik Samgram,* vol. 1 (Calcutta: 1966), 340, quoted in Guha, "Counter-Insurgency", 76.

11.   Guha also designates certain cases of primary and secondary discourse as accurate. In this essay he accepts confessions of Santal insurgents about to be exe-

cuted as accurate, and uses these as evidence of the sincerity and specificity of spirituality to peasant resistance (p. 80).

12. Brathwaite's sources include: Bryan Edwards, *The History, Civil and Commercial of the British Colonies in the West Indies*, 3 vols. (London: Stockdale, 1794–1801); Matthew Gregory Lewis, *Journal of a West India Proprietor kept during a Residence in the Island of Jamaica* (London: John Murray, 1834); Edward Long, *The History of Jamaica*, 3 vols. (London: T. Lowndes, 1774); J.B. Moreton, *Manners and customs in the West India islands* (London: J. Parsons, W. Richardson, H. Gardner, and J. Walter, 1793); Maria Nugent, *Lady Nugent's Journal*, ed. Frank Cundall (London, 1907); J. Stewart, *An Account of Jamaica and its Inhabitants* (1808; reprint, London, 1844); and *The Royal Gazette* (Kingston, Jamaica: 1780–1837).

13. I am referring here to Lucille Mathurin Mair's use of the term "Great House" vision, in her "Historical Study of Women in Jamaica from 1655–1844" (PhD diss., University of the West Indies, 1974).

14. A less convincing example of this technique is the fourteen interracial marriages that Brathwaite locates in the parish of St Elizabeth between 1781 and 1813 (*Creole Society*, 188–89). Although Brathwaite asserts that these marriages are strong evidence of creolization, he found fewer than twenty interracial marriages for the fifty-year period of his study. This low number might equally well reflect the power of the taboo against interracial marriage.

15. Brathwaite does not exactly invert the colonial hierarchy. The nationalist foundation of Brathwaite's theory of creolization leads him to argue that the white creole establishment founded and maintained functional public institutions and contributed significantly to creole society (*Creole Society*, 267–68).

16. Brathwaite, *Contradictory Omens: Cultural Diversity and Integration in the Caribbean* (Kingston, Jamaica: Savacou Publications, 1974), 16.

17. Ibid., 6; emphasis added.

18. See M.J. Herskovits, *The Myth of the Negro Past* (New York: Harper and Brothers, 1941) and Martha Beckworth, *Black Roadways: A Study of Jamaican Folk Life* (Chapel Hill: University of North Carolina Press, 1929).

19. Long, *History of Jamaica*, 2: 414–15, quoted in Brathwaite, *Creole Society*, 215.

20. Edwards, *History*, 2: 175–76, quoted in Brathwaite, *Creole Society*, 215.

21. See David Scott, *Refashioning Futures: Criticism after Postcoloniality* (Princeton: Princeton University Press, 1999).

22. Long, *History of Jamaica*, 2: 364.

23. *Tensions of Empire: Colonial Cultures in a Bourgeois World*, edited by Frederick Cooper and Ann Laura Stoler (Berkeley: University of California Press, 1997) is a collection of essays that explore the complexities of colonial discourse and societies, examining the lack of coherence and the frequent conflict within colonial regimes and discourse as well as the complexity of identity categories produced

through relations between metropole and colonies. In *Rethinking Working-Class History: Bengal, 1890–1940* (Princeton: Princeton University Press, 1989), Chakrabarty bases his history of jute mill workers on an analysis of the institutions and political alliances that produced the very particular and unreliable records of the industry. These are merely examples of scholars whose work has developed and modified the strategies used by Guha and Brathwaite in the 1970s and early 1980s.

PART FIVE

Resurrecting the Human Face from the Archive

15

Resisting Representation
Locating Enslaved and Indentured Women's Voices in the Colonial Caribbean

Verene A. **Shepherd** |

Since the 1970s, and particularly during the 1980s, the tendency in Caribbean historiography has been to project the voices and experiences of enslaved and other exploited groups from the perspective of such groups and not simply to repeat the colonizers' perspectives. While there was continued focus on exploitation, the agency of enslaved and indentured peoples became much more important to scholars, especially within the context of a Caribbean region with heightened interest in postcolonial history. There was a frenzied search for "slave narratives" that would unambiguously catalogue the life stories of enslaved peoples and give them voice. This search was an attempt to capture black people's collective experiences, as well as to understand the critical role that oral tradition and resistance play in the history of people in the African diaspora, and has been of central importance to Kamau Brathwaite. These concerns resonate in his historical and literary works. His works have illuminated our understanding of the importance of finding forms of expression that retain and reflect African and Caribbean experiences. His seminal historical and literary works – for example, *The Development of Creole Society in Jamaica, History of the Voice* and "Jazz and the West Indian Novel" – all testify to the centrality of the folk, of folkways, folk language/nation language, folk music and expressions, in understanding Caribbean creole culture and aesthetics, in voicing the black experience and re-enacting Caribbean historical experiences. Since nation language comes from the folk tradition, (and this is clear from *History of the Voice*), Brathwaite sees West Indian poetry as a gradual approximation of that communal voice capable of capturing and expressing Caribbean folk experiences.[1]

It was this search for voice, in this case the voice of the subaltern, that informed the creation of the Text and Testimony Collective (TTC). This project, affiliated with the York/UNESCO Nigerian Hinterland Project, seeks to access the voices of those enslaved and indentured in the colonial Caribbean. Part of this mandate involves continuing the project of unearthing the articulated antislavery and anti-indentureship views of enslaved and indentured women that would act as a counter-discourse to writers who project the view that bonded women accommodated themselves more easily than men to forms of unfree labour, perhaps even reaping material and social benefits from slavery and indentureship. For example, there is a strong suggestion in Matthew Gregory Lewis's journal that enslaved women were contented with their status and that some of them were happy to know that Lewis was "their massa". The anonymous author of *Marly* also suggests that enslaved women encouraged white men's habit of living with black and coloured women as their mistresses.[2]

Similarly, despite the evidence that the Asian Indian woman's experience of emigration and indentureship was one of extreme hardship, exploitation and sexploitation, David Galenson, Pieter Emmer and David Northrup hold that emigration was of significant material benefit to those who left India.[3] Emmer, for example, argues that emigration was a vehicle of female emancipation "from an illiberal, inhibiting and very hierarchical social system in India".[4] His view echoes the early sentiments of Charles Doorly, Protector of Emigrants in the Madras Presidency, who, in a retrospective look at women's emigration in 1915, remarked, "I am convinced that emigration is a blessing to a large number of the women we send, and opens to them a way of escape from lives of misery, poverty and prostitution."[5] This perspective conflicts with Joseph Beaumont's and Hugh Tinker's neoslavery thesis, also articulated in the work of Rhoda Reddock, Jeremy Poynting, Jo Beall, Brij Lal, Rosemarijn Hoefte, Verene Shepherd, Marina Carter and Moses Seenarine.[6] The work done by some of these latter scholars reveals that even though the majority of Indian women arrived in the Caribbean as single, independent wage workers who were intent on bettering their lives (and some succeeded in this regard), wages were low and gender-discriminatory, and tasks sex-typed, giving an overall advantage to male workers. Women's childcare responsibilities also affected the time spent at work outside the home, and therefore the level of their wages. These economic facts, combined with clear evidence of sexual abuse and other forms of gendered tyranny towards Asian Indian women, determined that the overall conclusion of those who fall within the neoslavery school of thought would differ drastically from Doorly and Emmer's optimistic "material benefits" thesis. Indeed, after studying the fraudulent, deceptive, abusive and exploitative elements of the indentureship system, Jo Beall argued strongly that Indian women suffered "ultraexploitability", Rhoda Reddock that their whole experience was one of "freedom denied", and Jeremy Poynting that they experienced "multiple oppression".[7]

Indentured women's own views on how they experienced recruitment, shipment and indentureship are scarce, even scarcer than enslaved women's "narratives", but their twentieth-century letters and testimonies given at commissions of inquiry provide a glimpse into their experiences both on the passage from India and on the plantations.[8]

Influenced by Brathwaite's use of a variety of genres to capture the experiences of the subaltern, this chapter will use a sample of novels, historical narratives and testimonies from a nineteenth-century commission of inquiry to illustrate the problems inherent in any attempt to locate bonded women's voices. The structure will be chronological, with the discussion focused first on enslaved African women and then on an Asian Indian immigrant woman bound for colonial Guyana on the ship *Allanshaw*. Both cases demonstrate that despite the exploitation and sexploitation that characterized enslaved and indentured women's experiences in the colonial Caribbean, neither group was completely silenced but used body and voice in an effort to resist and destabilize systems of domination. However, it will be seen that the sources used are more ventriloquized accounts than first-person narratives, and thus need to be problematized.

Enslaved Women

In the case of enslaved women, evidence abounds to indicate that they did not accept their enslavement; that they had an antislavery stance. This is evident from the vast literature about their participation in all forms of resistance, armed revolts as well as day-to-day nonviolent acts of noncooperation.[9] Finding enslaved women's own (written) views about slavery is a more difficult task. Admittedly, we have available to us texts generated by enslaved peoples in the Caribbean; for the enslaved not only fought back, but wrote and spoke back as part of an ontological positioning with colonialism that placed slavery under their literary gaze, thus contributing greatly to the broad-based Atlantic antislavery literature. The enslaved understood and critiqued the dominant European scientific and intellectual dogma on the subject of race and slavery, and contributed to a counter-discourse that defeated enslavers' claim that the enslaved were beneath and indifferent to the intellectual discourses that surrounded them. Despite the endemic anti-intellectual culture bred by slavery, many Africans wrote important treatises, dictated autobiographical accounts, presented critical oral testimony to commissions of inquiry, and made arrangements for the recording and publication of a wide body of opinions which form an important part of the Caribbean literary tradition. Their views on slavery, for the most part, offer a counter-discourse to the racist and sexist assumptions of male writers like Thomas Thistlewood, Edward Long, Thomas Atwood and Cynric Williams, and the racist, elitist representations of women like Maria Nugent and A.C. Carmichael.[10] From the perspective of those interested in recovering enslaved women's voices specifically, one drawback of the available published accounts is that, from the Caribbean as a whole, most of these "slave voices" are those of enslaved men.[11] Indeed, apart from the contested narrative of Mary Prince,[12] and the letters of Dolly Newton and Jenny Lane,[13] few other "first-person" accounts of enslaved women have been uncovered for the British-colonized Caribbean. How, then, do we gain access to more enslaved women's voices?

I wish to suggest in this chapter that one solution to the problem of recovering the enslaved woman's voice is for us to increase current efforts to mine sources that ventriloquize their voices: contemporary historical and literary texts (including novels), newspapers, dictated letters and narratives, reports of commissions of inquiry, records of trials, and court records generally. Sceptical as we may be about their authenticity and the source of their authority, these sources may allow us to make some progress towards discovering what enslaved women thought about slavery as institution, their own status as enslaved labourers, slave society in general, the behaviour of their enslavers and the project of emancipation.

...   •   ...

The problems and pitfalls of ventriloquizing the black experience have, of course, been very widely discussed. Nevertheless, despite the problems and pitfalls, the use of second-hand, ventriloquized accounts of what enslaved women are supposed to have said and felt about their condition offers us a way out of the silence. Scholars such as Kamau Brathwaite, Barbara Bush, Hilary McD. Beckles, Bridget Brereton and Veronica Gregg, among others, involved in research on the social construction of the black woman, have already demonstrated the value of returning to contemporary published accounts – like *Lady Nugent's Journal* and the proslavery discourses of A.C. Carmichael and Edward Long – that centre slave societies.[14] In compiling *Slave Voices: The Sounds of Freedom* for UNESCO's Associated Schools' Project, Hilary Beckles and Verene Shepherd also made the decision to use a sample of ventriloquized accounts rather than exclude black women's antislavery views on the basis that "their narratives" did not exist and that we have mostly accounts of their actions and behaviour. For what it is worth, then, this chapter draws upon novels, travel narratives, historical texts and evidence presented at a commission of inquiry to illustrate further the possibilities.

The novels chosen have not been discussed widely in academic fora; the other texts have been more frequently discussed, but they are reread here with a view to discovering missed voices and stories. My focus is not so much on how the mostly white male authors represented black women negatively (as Henrice Altink,[15] Bush and others have explored), but on what they make these women say about their condition. My interest is to discover what light the sources throw on what women thought about control and punishment, their enslavers (including those who raped them yet called them their "mistresses"), motherhood and resistance. My use of novels may well be criticized on the basis that they are no more than romanticized, fictional accounts of the Caribbean slave system, but I decided to broaden the search to early novels because even though they fall within the genre of prose fiction, those published in the nineteenth century by authors who had personal experience of slave systems are quite close to being historical narratives and could, indeed, be said to fall into the realistic tradition. In any case, many of the contemporary works that claim to be "true/factual historical accounts" are themselves unrealistic inventions of the Caribbean, written without reference to the historical Caribbean – illustrating, according to Veronica Gregg, that the invention of the Caribbean as a European enterprise required little knowledge of the region and in fact depended upon "a willed ignorance".[16] Such narrative histories, then, are the politics of a process by which power and knowledge are constituted. The differences between fact and fiction that should unambiguously distinguish novels from contemporary histories and travel accounts are, therefore, not always obvious.

Enslaved "Women's Voices" in Novels

The three novels selected for this discussion are the anonymously authored *Marly, or a planter's life in Jamaica,* published in 1828; Cyrus Francis Perkins's *Busha's Mistress, or Catherine the Fugitive: a stirring romance of the days of slavery in Jamaica,* written in 1855; and Mary Gaunt's *Harmony, a tale of the old slave days in Jamaica,* published in 1933. All three are set on sugar estates in Jamaica.[17] There is no central enslaved female character in *Marly.* Indeed, the author hardly gives the enslaved women a voice, being more concerned with pursuing his romantic interest in the white creole woman Miss M'Fathom from Equity Hall Estate and reclaiming his inheritance on the Happy Fortune sugar plantation and Conch Shell Penn, properties of his late father in danger of falling into the hands of a dishonest agent/manager. However, as the author worked on Happy Fortune, we do learn a lot about the operation of the slave system in Jamaica through his eyes. He allows the women to endorse the practice of white men living with enslaved women, telling us that soon after he arrived in Jamaica, he was approached by "an elderly negro woman, accompanied by a young negro girl about sixteen or seventeen years of age, who she said was her daughter, requesting [me] to take this young girl for [my] wife – the girls who live with the white people being so called".[18] He tells us that he "declined the offer", but that such offers were repeated on other occasions, some of the women asking constantly, "Why massa Marly not take him one wife like oder buckras? Dere is him little Daphne, would make him one good wife – dere is him young Diana – dere is him little Venus – dere is him Mary Magdalene, and dere is him Phoebe."[19] While he represents himself as offended by the practice, he tells us that other white men had no such qualms about seeking out enslaved women as "wives". Although giving the impression that the women were collaborators in this practice, the text reveals a contrary tendency: enslaved women did not always allow themselves to be "chosen" against their wishes! When Mr Adams, the overseer of Water Melon

Valley, tries to seduce Delia she refuses his advances, much to the delight of other white workers on the property, who presumably have designs on her.[20] Such acts of opposition to slavery and the social behaviour of enslavers are not the dominant themes in this novel, however.

The central female character in *Busha's Mistress* is the quadroon, Catherine Brown, presented to us as the "mistress" of the overseer, Jackson. Nevertheless, Perkins gives space to other enslaved women: the mulatto Mary Ann Peach, George Waldy's "mistress"; Rosalie, the enslaved black woman who is instrumental in securing the services of an obeahman to "catch the shadow" of the old enslaved man, Williams, who was killed; and Jannette, an enslaved domestic on Wales Estate who is accused by Mary Ann of "keeping Waldy". The views of the female characters are quite often projected, at times through "their" Creole dialogue, at other times through the author's own narrated comments. Catherine, a loving mother of a child fathered by Busha Jackson, expresses her fear of the very same man; for he might have singled her out for his sexual pleasure, but he is, after all, an enslaver who, like all newcomers, is kind to the enslaved upon arrival, but changes soon afterwards. Catherine is reported to have said to the attorney of Greenside: "Mr Jackson use to treat the Negroes well at first but now he is too hard 'pon dem."[21] The result of refusing the sexual advances of Busha Jackson (ostensibly Catherine's lover) is outlined by Mary Ann Peach: Jackson tries to flog her publicly because she refused to leave George Waldy (overseer on nearby Maxfield Estate) and sleep with him. But, "said she", she already lived with "Mass George an' him nebba mek I want fe nutten, an him buy me from me mammy fair out"; so she could not leave him even if "Busha persecute me all de time", even putting her in the stocks. Upon hearing this tale, Catherine decides to leave "her" busha after being assured by the attorney that the busha could not "mek I lib wid him against me wishes". Despite Jackson's entreaties, Catherine leaves him to live with her aunt in the great house. Jackson's appeal for her to "come home" falls on deaf ears, Catherine on one occasion querying,

> Home? Home! Has a slave any home? He is here today and there tomorrow. He is sen' to work any property Trustee [the attorney] please, an' praps seld if Massa or young Massa owe money. Look at me sister Sarah!
>
> Me eber see him since de day marshall put handcuff on him an' drag him off de estate? An' didn't eberybody say Mr Hines was a rich man? De grave is de home for such as we.[22]

She goes on to express her regret that she has borne a child into slavery and sometimes wishes him dead. Jackson's reply, that if she behaves well he will buy her and the child, meets with a tirade from Catherine, who tells him that she has heard that promise before from him and other white men in relation to other women:

> It not today I hear the story talk of you buying me. S'pose you goin' buy me like Jack Mowatt buy Sally . . . buy him when him please an' sell him when he get tired of him. Is that mek Massa say him won't sell any of him people 'cept them is to be free. If you caan even buy me, you can buy de baby? If you get discharge 'spose I am to hand over to de nex Busha whether I like him or hate him. See Nancy Lewis, what she is come to . . . a gal dat use to wear shoes an' stocking when her fader was alive, an' could even read newspaper! I don' t'ink Nancy can all tell who is de fader of him two children. Tedder day me speak to him for him own good an' him say, "Pig ax him mumma wha' mek him mout' long so an' him mumma say 'ta' pick-ney tell yu mout' long so to."

Mary Ann is similarly promised her freedom by Waldy on one of her nocturnal visits to him at his new estate, Wales; his renewed promises to free her in order to hold on to her affection pacify her, even though she is clearly sceptical about the possibility.

Both Mary Ann and Catherine, despite their clear views about the poor treatment they receive at the hands of enslavers, at times even their own bushas, are made by Perkins to defend them staunchly. Catherine comes to Jackson's rescue when Waldy allegedly physically attacks him out of jealousy over Mary Ann; Mary Ann betrays her fellow enslaved to save Wales Estate from a planned Maroon attack, winning her freedom from the owner of the estate in the process. Catherine and Mary Ann team up to rescue Jackson, who has fallen on hard times after his dismissal from Greenside. With the help of the white woman, Mrs Arnold, Catherine leaves Jamaica for England to work as nursemaid for the Arnolds. While in England, she is set free, although this free status is contested by the authorities in Jamaica on her eventual return a few years after. She leaves her son to be educated in England, with some help from Vernon, who at one time worked as a bookkeeper on Greenside. But, according to her, she has never forgotten Jackson. The author also gives the impression that Jackson pined away after Catherine left. They eventually marry, and Catherine gains her freedom (in Jamaica, legally) from her former enslaver. This is, then, a tale of romance in a slave society; although we get a clear picture of enslaved women's discontent with their slave status, we also see clearly an attempt by the author to focus readers' attention away from the brutality and on to the so-called love relations between working-class white men and coloured enslaved women.

As in the other two novels, Mary Gaunt's *Harmony* contains a romantic plot. Maria Read, a white woman, daughter of a Portuguese woman and a male factor on the West African coast (Annamabu) is sold into slavery and arrives in Jamaica on the slave ship *Saucy Bell*.[23] Despite her protests that she is a free woman, she is bought by Marse Septimus Ridley and taken first to Harmony and then to Content. She eventually marries a white man, Jenkin Thole, who assumes that he is going to inherit Harmony from his father, Squire Thole. But old man Thole has two other sons of much the same age: Roger, by an enslaved woman named Hesba, and another by his white wife. During an outbreak of the pox on his estate, old man Thole's white baby son dies and subsequently he convinces his wife that Roger, who has survived the disease, is her son and heir to Harmony. He manages to ship Roger to England where he becomes educated, finally returning to Jamaica in 1817 where he is welcomed by all, including his mother, and proceeds to work alongside his father on Harmony, taking on all the racial prejudices of whites in a slave society. He eventually falls in love with Petronella, Ridley's daughter, and they plan a lavish wedding. Before the wedding, however, Squire Thole's deception is discovered and Jenkin Thole, who now realizes that he is the real heir to Harmony, proceeds to capture Roger and enchain him. Maria, Hesba and an enslaved man eventually help Roger to escape. Later on, Roger is freed officially after he betrays some slave rebels, revealing their plot to revolt.

The antislavery voices of women are muted in this novel. Maria does resist her shipment on the Middle Passage, and curses the men who sell and buy her. Says Gaunt, speaking through Ridley, "this girl faced the two men [Thole and Ridley] and called them every vile name she could lay her tongue to; looked them up and down, noted their weak points [baldness, etc] and gave them the benefit of her observation aloud".[24] The other enslaved women, for example Hesba, freed from field work because she has five children, are represented as having close relationships with the whites in the novel and as working towards making the estates and the lives of the whites run smoothly.

Historical Narratives

The nonfiction historical accounts discussed in this chapter are Bernard Senior's *Jamaica As It Was, As It Is, And As It May Be*,[25] Matthew Gregory Lewis's anecdotal record, *Journal of a West India Proprietor,* and Cynric Williams's *A Tour Through the Island of Jamaica* conducted in 1823 (the latter two perhaps more fittingly fall within the genre of travel literature).[26] Unlike Senior's text, Lewis's and Williams's texts are located between the two most significant moments in the eradication of slavery in the British-colonized Caribbean – 1807 (the abolition of the slave trade) and 1834 (the abolition of slavery and the beginning of the apprenticeship period) – and at the height of the antislavery campaign. Lewis and Williams seem intent on arguing the legitimacy of slavery and appeasing antislavery forces by stressing slave society's ameliorative possibilities and benevolent aspects. Lewis owns enslaved peoples, Williams does not, but neither seems to advocate immediate abolition. In fact, Williams is quite racist,[27] and seems bent on reassuring the English public that the enslaved in Jamaica are not as downtrodden as the English might be led to believe. Thus: "the public, or a portion of it, will have an opportunity of learning that Negro slaves are not worked and flogged alternately, at the option and caprice of their masters, as many good Christians imagine, who have signed petitions for emancipating them".[28]

Senior's account demonstrates the futility of amelioration, and the enslaved's insistence on freedom as manifested in the 1831 rebellion in western Jamaica. Both Lewis and Williams employ Jamaican Creole in their accounts, and both comment on enslaved women's activities. But they give more space to enslaved men's dialogue than to enslaved women's. Lewis, for example, tells us about the Eboe women: Psyche, Polly, Marcia, Phillis, Delia, Juliet, Venus, Whaunica, Bessie, Nancy, Philippa, Bridget, Christian, Minetta, Jenny, Amey, "mad" Catalina, Jug-Betty, and the mulatta Mary Wiggins. The women's antislavery positions are not brought to the fore through dialogue, though Lewis's reports of their actions indicate a rebellious set of women, "female demons" who constantly instigate what one "busha" terms "petticoat rebellions"[29] among field workers. Lewis, then, confines "women's voices" to innocuous happenings on the estate, their belief in obeah, their contentment with their lot, their attachment to their "massa" and attention to his welfare. Mary Wiggins, for example, is made to seem grateful that she had a "massa";[30] Polly is painted as being quite watchful of Lewis's health, closing the windows in the house when Lewis wanted them open, on the basis that "Night air not good for massa";[31] the "poor woman nearly 100 years old, and stone blind" insists on being taken to the great house so that she can touch "massa". When she has done so, she is reported to say "that was enough . . . now me hab once kiss a massa's hand, me willing to die tomorrow, me no care".[32] Venus, freed by Lewis's father, insists on getting agreement from his heir. She goes to Lewis to beg "massa so good as give paper" – that is, to formalize her freedom by signing the manumission paper – an indication that she wants to remain a free person and not be mistakenly pressed back into slavery under the new "massa".[33]

While admitting that enslaved field women can be rebellious, Lewis gives the impression that it only takes his threats to leave to subdue them. Thus, when he threatens them with harsh measures if they do not desist from their "petticoat rebellions", "to sell the most refractory and to leave for England and never return to Jamaica", he describes a penitent response: "all hands were clasped and all voices were raised, imploring me not to leave them, and assuring me that in the future they would do their work quietly and will-ingly".[34] He singles out two women, the cook and Philippa, who admonish those who are not loyal to "massa". To be fair, Lewis does express doubt that such a promise – to be loyal to "massa" and behave – would hold.

Cynric Williams's identity is not clear from his travel narrative, though we know he was from Hampshire, England, and he was identified with the Saints (English antislavery activists) by several characters in the text. The main female character in his narrative is the enslaved quadroon, Diana, who nurses him back to health after a bout of fever. He gives a little space also to: Diana's mother, who refuses to allow the planter by whom she had Diana to free her or to agree to have Diana sent away to England to be educated; the free-coloured lodging-house keepers in the major towns of Jamaica; Magdalene, who rendered an "ode to the buckras"; and several unidentified (unnamed) enslaved black women. With the exception of Diana, Williams hardly allows the women to "speak" for themselves, although enslaved men's narratives, especially those of Abdullah ("Dollar") and Ebenezer ("Sneezer"), are quite well represented in the text. When Diana does "speak", she is rep-resented as content with her situation. Only the enslaved African women seem to have an antislavery position, although Williams does not allow them to present this position through dialogue but through their actions. For example, among a party of enslaved peoples who were brought before the magistrate for misdemeanors was "one damsel in particular who in her defence said she had been harshly used, on one occasion getting 230 lashings at one flogging". The magistrate doubting this story, "the sable nymph without hesitation exposed her behind, whereupon there was no mark whatever; and it appearing that she had so done in derision and contempt, they ordered her a couple dozen".[35]

Another unnamed black woman, after a lashing by the driver, was said to have looked over her shoulder and said in a suppressed tone, but loud enough to be heard, "Go to h—ll", and walked off. But lest readers get the impression that this was a reflection of rampant antislavery and rebellious attitudes among the enslaved women in Jamaica, Williams hastens to add that the same woman admitted to him later that she was wrong and that her "massa" was really a kind man.[36] In fact, like Lewis, Williams stressed at several points in his text that the enslaved felt that they needed to belong to a "massa"; that it was all well and good for the antislavery activists in England to agitate for abolition but what would happen to the black person after that?

The final text is that authored by Bernard Senior, a retired military officer residing in England at the time he wrote his book, but who had resided in Jamaica for nearly twenty years, from 1815, and had been an active military officer who had helped to suppress the 1831 Christmas rebellion. His text is not positioned as a work of fiction. On the contrary, according to him "in the present work, fiction has been entirely discarded".[37] His objective was to "furnish the British public with a faithful account of the origin, progress, termination, and consequences of the insurrection which took place among the Negro slave population in the island of Jamaica, immediately after the Christmas of 1831".[38] But he wrote this text three years after the events transpired, and relied heavily on memory. On account of the specific objective of his book, Senior's narrative is a good way of finding out about enslaved women's participation in an armed revolt and in resistance generally; for, according to him in describing malingering, insolence and the attempt to enforce moral economy on the estate, "women as well as men were alike defaulters".[39] Dialogue does not abound in this text, and biographical details are sketchy, but we do get a profile of some enslaved women and their clear antislavery position. For example, Senior tells of the old, lame enslaved woman who acted as cook for the rebels, but who deliberately waylaid the troops with poisoned food in several iron pots as a way of entrapping them.[40] He also writes about Susan, who despite the dangers posed by a captain's detachment stationed near the plantation of Stracy, led a foraging party to the provision grounds to secure food for the rebels. On her apron were marked the words "My heart is fixed, I cannot change; I love my choice, too well to range."[41]

We learn from Senior about the runaway female rebel who, when accosted by the militia, feigned ignorance of the rebellion on the basis that she had run away before it broke out. She did say that she had heard that all the enslaved were to be freed as soon as the "Baptist parson" returned from England, and thought there was no harm in taking her freedom "a little before the time appointed".[42] Pressed about what she was doing in the woods and why she required so much water (several gourds full were discovered by a spring close to her hiding place), she said she was washing all of her clothes and wished to carry enough water for the purpose. Suspicious, the party bound her and threatened to treat her as a rebel if she did not tell the truth (they suspected that she was covering up the real reason for her presence in the woods). She became scared and promised to lead them to where rebels held some white women hostage. She then tried to lead them off course by taking a tortuous path. After the woman had successfully led the party astray for some time, the commander of the white troops became suspicious and held a gun to her head to force her to admit that she was taking them away from the hostages. She eventually relented and admitted that she had been leading them to the hideout of a well-armed rebel camp in the Cockpit Country that would have easily taken out the small group of white militiamen. The white women, who had been held for five days and nights under black sentries, were freed.[43]

The 1831 Christmas rebellion, of course, led Britain to realize that if emancipation did not come from above, it would come through the resistance of the subalterns. The Emancipation Act was therefore passed in 1833, to be effected in August 1834. After an unsuccessful attempt to delay full freedom by an apprenticeship period, "full free" was conceded in 1838. But the abolition of slavery did not end systems of domination. The landholding class did all in its power to deny the human rights and citizenship claims of the newly freed; they also imported additional labourers, mostly from India, to defeat the attempts of the formerly enslaved to secure higher wages and better working conditions.

The Indian Woman's Voice

The chapter shifts now to the post-slavery period, when indentured workers were relocated to the colonial Caribbean to re/place the Afro-Caribbean labourers. Indian women's own views about their exploitation and oppression are more abundant for the twentieth century than for the period of indentureship, when their voices were expressed through the pens and voices of others. Nevertheless, this chapter attempts to provide firm empirical data, by way of one woman's personal history, of Indian women's sexploitation.

Emigration officials had consistently denied that emigrant women were abused on nineteenth-century ships, and every effort was made to entice women to leave India in order to satisfy the stipulated forty-to-one-hundred female-to-male quota. Women were encouraged to emigrate because not only were plantation owners already familiar with women's productive labour, but they were also concerned that the sexual needs of the majority male workers be satisfied. Recruiting and shipping women, and avoiding any charge that their treatment replicated enslavement, were thus crucial concerns of the system. There is documentary evidence, however, that Indian women by no means had a smooth "ride" to the colonies, but rather were preyed upon by empowered males of various ethnicities, many of whom waylaid them in the area of the water closet (toilet). Their exploitation was related clearly to their gender, race, class and caste and, of course, to their status as bonded labourers. Firm evidence of such sexploitation comes from the case of the young Indian woman, Maharani, who was allegedly raped by sailors Oliver and Ipson and who subsequently died on the voyage of the *Allanshaw* from Calcutta to colonial Guyana in 1884.

Most of the documentary evidence used in the reconstruction of this episode comes from the over four hundred pages of correspondence generated by the investigation into the journey of the *Allanshaw*.[44] Briefly, during the early morning hours of 24 July 1885, Maharani, along with 660 other contract labourers, embarked at Calcutta on this sailing ship, owned by James Nourse and bound for colonial Guyana. Maharani did not complete her passage to the southern Caribbean: she was among the seventeen who died before the ship reached colonial Guyana. While the causes of death of sixteen of these people were ascertained and recorded unproblematically, Maharani's death was the subject of intense controversy, uncertainty and speculation. The surgeon-superintendent of the ship vacillated between "shock to the nervous system", "inflammation near the womb", "shock from shame" and "peritonitis" as the cause of death; a few fellow female emigrants attributed her death to "criminal assault", based on what Maharani allegedly told them before she died.

As a result of Maharani's ordeal, not one, but four official inquiries were launched into the voyage of the *Allanshaw:* one on the ship, one in St Helena (a revictualling stop), and two in colonial Guyana. At the last commission of inquiry, convened at the insistence of the Colonial Office, twenty-two witnesses, not all from the influential elite but including some of the emigrants themselves, gave evidence. Thus, at these inquiries, the bonded men and women themselves were allowed to speak. In general, indentured men's and women's voices were muted in the discourse of migration, so that normally, the task of writing the history and capturing the lived experiences of the subjects of the migration discourses is impeded by the depersonalizing, alienating system of emigration and indentureship. Of course, while we can now speak conclusively about Maharani's existence, her own voice was silenced, in that she did not live to relate her experiences directly to the various commissioners. On the other hand, the depositions of other emigrants, like the women Murti (or Moorti) and Mohadaya to whom she had related her ordeal, reflect her voice. Mohadaya testified:

> I came in the ship with Maharani. I have been in the colony before. I knew Maharani well. I do not remember when Maharani became sick. One day she told me that she had a pain in her hand. . . . She said she was very sick, that two sailors had connexion with her and that she was ashamed to tell me. . . . She said two sailors dragged her from the closet and had connexion with her on the deck. She said it was at night time. She described one sailor as having a red shirt and tattoo marks on the breast.[45]

Moorti testified similarly:

> I came on the ship Allanshaw. I knew Maharani. I went to see her one Friday evening. She was in hospital. I asked her what the matter. She said that two sailors dragged her from the closet and had connexion with her. She did not say that she had a pain in her belly. I did not ask her whether she cried out. She did not say anything to me about crying out. Maharani told me nothing more.[46]

Several other men and women gave similar testimonies. Nevertheless, what use was made of these voices? As Marina Carter describes in her work on

Mauritius, the depositions of the emigrants and immigrants were considered by officials as unacceptable at face value,[47] and they did not lead to a conviction of the sailors named as the perpetrators. In fact, a prevailing stereotype of lower-caste women as people of "low morals" was upheld. The treatment of the testimonies of the emigrants was related to class and race factors, as well as to the type of evidence that was needed to secure a conviction for rape in the nineteenth century.

What evidence was needed for a conviction? Clearly the investigators were looking for the perpetrator(s), eyewitness accounts, consistent depositions at the official inquiry rather than conflicting ones, medical evidence and some proof that Maharani had resisted the attackers. Merry Weisner's study of women and gender in early modern Europe notes that while rape was a capital crime in many parts of Europe (including England, whose customary laws on rape would have been patterned in the nineteenth-century Caribbean), convictions were more likely "if the victim [could] prove that she had cried out and made attempts to repel the attacker".[48] As the investigators claimed not to have found any of the "convincing evidence" they sought, the case was not settled to the satisfaction of the women who complained and some of the men who testified. Furthermore, at least two of the commissioners believed that Maharani had had consensual sex with the seamen. First, they read something sinister into the fact that Maharani had gone to the toilet by herself – though even the surgeon admitted that this was not an unheard-of occurrence – and that she had not complained to the *Babu* and *Sirdar* (Indian supervisors on board) about her ordeal. Second, they ignored the testimony of those who said that Maharani was a quiet, well-behaved girl who hardly fraternized. They preferred to believe those who hinted that she "had asked for it"; that she was promiscuous and might even have had a special man on board; that she had not raised an alarm. So, even though the commissioners found: men who fit Maharani's description of her attackers; people who linked one sailor in particular (Robert Ipson) to the crime; people who swore that Ipson had told them of his intentions to commit the act; deponents who swore that Maharani was a well-behaved girl; testimonies that Maharani had been prevented from raising an alarm because the attacker(s) had stuffed her sari into her mouth; unexplained gaps in the ship's log; contradictions between the post-mortem report and emigrants' testimonies; evidence that crew, officers and emigrants feared an outcome prejudicial to themselves and thus had been reluctant to tell all – two members ruled against Maharani: the chairman of the commission, Alexander, and Henry Kirke.

The conclusions in the official report of the commission of inquiry thus help to settle the question of why rape was discounted in the end (as such cases are even today). The erroneous ideology that non-elite women were "naturally promiscuous" was still alive and well in the late-nineteenth-century Caribbean; so was the racist view, held by men such as Kirke, that the Indians were unreliable witnesses. The crew maintained an ideology of racial, caste and gender superiority that clearly determined their lack of regard for the rights of the Indian women on the ship. The fact that persons found guilty of mistreating emigrants could (at least in theory) be dismissed from the service, fined, imprisoned or have their wages/gratuities reduced might also have been a factor shaping the nature of some of the testimonies. This might also help to explain both the denials that abuses had characterized the journey, the failure of the ship's surgeon and captain to log all acts of misconduct, and the surgeon's questionable post-mortem conclusions. That the crew were routinely warned against mistreating emigrants is not in doubt: when the crew was mustered as the *Allanshaw* pulled out of port, for example, they were reminded that they would lose one month's pay for every (proven) offence they committed against the emigrants. It is not surprising, therefore, that almost everyone who testified (even the five who had been logged or warned by the captain or surgeon about their behaviour towards the emigrants) swore that the crew treated the emigrants well, that the mortality rate was much lower than on other voyages, that no women were sexually abused, and that security was tight and efficient, making it hard for any woman to be sexually assaulted without being seen. Security was not impenetrable, however. Despite the assurances by the captain, surgeon and sirdar, some of the crew testified that in cold weather, the sirdars often abandoned their posts to seek warmth below deck, and some testified that the night in question was cold. The conflicting narratives of those called to testify were, therefore, another factor complicating the analysis of the case. Also dooming the case was the proplanter attitude of the agent-general of immigration and the anti-Indian attitude of Kirke, two influential members of the commission of inquiry in colonial Guyana who clearly did not wish to impede the flow of cheap labour from India to colonial Guyana.

An additional methodological problem is that the voices of the mostly illiterate Indians who testified were filtered through the pens of others. The testimonies of those who appeared before the commissions of inquiry were tran-scribed or recorded by official scribes, such as the secretary to the commission in colonial Guyana (and thus, like "slave narratives" and court records, in themselves problematic). Most of the emigrants could not even read the dep-ositions they were asked to sign, marking an "X" instead. Next to direct oral evidence, however, these transcriptions come the closest to revealing the voices of the subalterns. In this regard, the sources should not be viewed as any less trustworthy than the official documents on which so many books on post-slavery immigration to the colonial Caribbean are based.

Conclusion

While first-person narratives are ideal sources for studying the views and opin-ions of bonded people on a wide range of issues in American slave and inden-tureship systems, the paucity of written works by enslaved and indentured women need not destabilize the quest to find their voices and experience. Uncertain as we might be about their authenticity, we can find some clues through a closer reading of the second-hand, ventriloquized voices that can be found in contemporary works of fiction and history and in testimonies given at official inquiries. This chapter has not exhausted the sources that can be reread for clues, but has merely used a small sample to restart the conver-sation about where to find subaltern women's voices, and to demonstrate the ever increasing possibilities.

Notes

1. See Edward Kamau Brathwaite, *The Development of Creole Society in Jamaica, 1770–1820* (Oxford: Clarendon Press, 1971); *History of the Voice: The Development of Nation Language in Anglophone Caribbean Poetry* (London and Port of Spain: New Beacon Books, 1984); and "Jazz and the West Indian Novel", in *The Routledge Reader in Caribbean Literature*, ed. Alison Donnell and Sarah Lawson Welsh (London and New York: Routledge, 1996), 336–43.

2. See Matthew Gregory Lewis, *Journal of a West India Proprietor kept during a residence in the island of Jamaica* (1834; reprint, Oxford and New York: Oxford University Press, 1999); also *Marly, or a planter's life in Jamaica* (Glasgow, 1828).

3. See David Galenson, "The Rise and Fall of Indentured Servitude: An Economic Analysis", *Journal of Economic History* 44, no. 1 (March 1984): 1–26; Pieter Emmer, "The Great Escape: The Migration of Female Indentured Servants from British India into Suriname", in *Abolition and its Aftermath: The Historical Context, 1790–1916*, ed. D. Richardson (London: Frank Cass, 1985), 245–66; and David Northrup, *Indentured Labour in the Age of Imperialism, 1834–1922* (Cambridge and New York: Cambridge University Press, 1995).

4. Emmer, "The Great Escape".

5. Public Record Office, London (PRO), Colonial Office document (CO) 571/3, minute paper 54685, "Notes on the Methods of Recruiting Emigrants in the Madras Presidency", 6 November 1915.

6. Joseph Beaumont, *The New Slavery: an account of the Indian and Chinese immigrants in British Guiana* (London, 1871); Hugh Tinker, *A New System of Slavery: The Export of Indian Labourers Overseas, 1830–1920* (Oxford: Clarendon Press, 1974); Rhoda Reddock, "Indian Women and Indentureship in Trinidad and Tobago: Freedom Denied", in *Caribbean Freedom: Society and Economy from Emancipation to the Present*, ed. Hilary Beckles and Verene Shepherd (Kingston, Jamaica: Ian Randle, 1993), 225–37; Jeremy Poynting, "East Indian Women in the Caribbean: Experience and Voice", in *India in the Caribbean*, ed. David Dabydeen and Brinsley Samaroo (London: Hansib, 1987), 231–63; Jo Beall, "Women under Indenture in Colonial Natal", in *Essays on Indentured Indians in Natal*, ed. Surendra Bhana (Leeds: Peepal Tree Press, 1991), 89–115; Brij Lal, "Kunti's Cry: Indentured Women on Fiji Plantations", *Indian Economic and Social History Review* 22, no. 1 (1985): 55–72; Rosemarijn Hoefte, "Female Indentured Labour in Suriname: For Better or Worse?", *Boletin de Estudios Latinoamericanos y del Caribe* 42 (1987): 55–70; Verene Shepherd, "Emancipation through Servitude?", in *Caribbean Freedom*, 245–50; Marina Carter, *Lakshmi's Legacy: The Testimonies of Indian Women in 19th Century Mauritius* (Mauritius: Editions de L'Ocean Indien, 1994); Carter, *Voices from Indenture: Experiences of Indian*

Migrants in the British Empire (Leicester: Leicester University Press, 1996); and Moses Seenarine, "Indentured Women in Colonial Guyana", in *Sojourners to Settlers: Indian Migrants in the Caribbean and the Americas,* ed. Mahin Gosine and Dhanpaul Narine (Hamburg, Penn.: Windsor Press, 1999), 36–66.

7. Beall, "Women under Indenture"; Reddock, "Indian Women and Indentureship"; and Poynting, "East Indian Women in the Caribbean".

8. See, for example, Verene A. Shepherd, "Poverty, Exploitation and Agency among Indian Settlers in Jamaica: Evidence from 20th Century Letters", *Journal of Caribbean Studies* 14, nos. 1–2 (1999–2000): 93–115, and Shepherd, "Maharani's Misery: Narratives of a Passage from India" (paper presented at the conference Asian Migration to the Americas, Trinidad and Tobago, August 2000).

9. For evidence of enslaved women's antislavery activities see Lucille Mathurin Mair, *The Rebel Woman* (Kingston, Jamaica: Institute of Jamaica, 1975); Hilary McD. Beckles, *Natural Rebels: A Social History of Enslaved Black Women in Barbados* (New Brunswick, N.J.: Rutgers University Press, 1989); Barbara Bush, *Slave Women in Caribbean Society, 1650–1838* (Bloomington: Indiana University Press, 1990); Verene A. Shepherd, et al., eds., *Engendering History: Caribbean Women in Historical Perspective* (Kingston, Jamaica: Ian Randle, 1995), Beckles, *Centering Woman: Gender Discourses in Caribbean Slave Society* (Kingston, Jamaica: Ian Randle, 1999); and Shepherd, ed. and comp., *Women in Caribbean History* (Kingston, Jamaica: Ian Randle, 1999).

10. The Journals of Thomas Thistlewood, Lincolnshire Record Office, England; Edward Long, *The History of Jamaica,* 3 vols. (London, 1774); Thomas Atwood, *The History of Dominica* (London, 1791); Cynric Williams, *A Tour Through the Island of Jamaica* (London, 1826); Philip Wright, ed., *Lady Nugent's Journal of her Residence in Jamaica* (Kingston, Jamaica: Institute of Jamaica, 1966); and A.C. Carmichael, *Domestic Manners and Social Conditions of the White, Colored and Negro Population* (London, 1833).

11. See, for example, Paul Edwards, ed., *The Life of Olaudah Equiano* (New York: Longman, 1989); and Esteban Montejo, *The Autobiography of a Runaway Slave,* ed. Miguel Barnet and Alistair Hennessey (London: Macmillan, 1993). For a discussion of some of these texts see Verene A. Shepherd and Hilary McD. Beckles, eds., *Caribbean Slavery in the Atlantic World* (Kingston, Jamaica: Ian Randle, 2000), 821–67.

12. For a discussion of this narrative see Moira Ferguson, ed., *Mary Prince, The History of Mary Prince: a West Indian slave related by herself,* rev. ed. (Ann Arbor: University of Michigan Press, 1998).

13. See Beckles, *Natural Rebels.*

14. See Bush, *Slave Women in Caribbean Society*; Beckles, *Centering Woman*; Bridget Brereton, "Text, Testimony and Gender", in *Engendering History,* 63–93; and

Veronica Gregg, "The Caribbean (as a Certain Kind of) Woman" (paper presented at the conference Engendering History, University of the West Indies, Mona, Jamaica, 1993). See also Verene A. Shepherd, "Image and Representation: Black Women in Historical Accounts of Colonial Jamaica" (paper presented at the conference Black Women in the Old World and the New, University of Tennessee, September 1998).

15.   Altink is currently involved in a project to uncover the negative representations of enslaved mothers in contemporary writings. See " 'Belly-Women and Pickeniny Mummas': Language and Image in the Pro-Slavery Discussion about Jamaican Slave Motherhood, 1770–1838" (paper presented to the conference Discourses of Slavery and Abolition: Writing in Britain and Its Colonies, 1660–1838, 6–7 April 2001, Institute of Language Studies, University of London).

16.   Veronica Gregg, *Jean Rhys's Historical Imagination: Reading and Writing the Creole* (Chapel Hill: University of North Carolina Press, 1995), 11.

17.   *Marly* is set on an estate called Water Melon Valley (clearly a fictitious name), and *Busha's Mistress* (unpublished, written in 1855), on Greenside Estate in Trelawny. Cyrus Francis Perkins was a white Jamaican creole, born in Falmouth, Trelawny. He may have been attorney for Greenside Estate, property of the Cunningham family, and he obviously had intimate knowledge of Jamaican society during slavery. The author of *Marly* was not a creole, but was born in Scotland. Like Perkins, he worked on a sugar estate, but as a bookkeeper. Mary Gaunt's novel *Harmony* (London, 1933) roves between Content and Harmony estates. Unlike *Marly, Busha's Mistress* was never published as a novel but in 1911 was serialized in twenty instalments in an apparently short-lived Kingston newspaper, the *Daily Telegraph and Jamaica Guardian*. Paul Lovejoy, Verene Shepherd and David Trotman are currently involved in editing and introducing this novel for publication.

18.   *Marly,* 80.

19.   Ibid., 133.

20.   Ibid., 148.

21.   Perkins, *Busha's Mistress,* chapter 1.

22.   Ibid., chapter 2.

23.   Gaunt, *Harmony,* 13–19.

24.   Ibid., 19.

25.   Bernard Senior, *Jamaica As It Was, As It Is, And As It May Be* (London, 1835).

26.   Lewis, *Journal of a West India Proprietor;* Williams, *Tour Through the Island of Jamaica.* Lewis was born in London in 1775. He inherited Cornwall and Hordley sugar plantations in Jamaica from his father, who died in 1812. It was after his two visits to his newly acquired plantations in Jamaica in 1815–16 and 1817–18

that he wrote this work, which was published many years after his death from yellow fever in 1818. Not much is known about Cynric Williams, although he may have been associated with the church.

27. Observe the following: "Diana in tears looked almost beautiful, in spite of her brown face." Williams, *Tour Through the Island of Jamaica*, 48.

28. Ibid., iv.

29. Lewis, *Journal of a West India Proprietor*, 87.

30. Ibid., 46.

31. Ibid., 52.

32. Ibid., 212.

33. Ibid., 83.

34. Ibid., 88.

35. Williams, *Tour Through the Island of Jamaica*, 339.

36. Ibid., 13.

37. Senior, *Jamaica*, iii.

38. Ibid., 1.

39. Ibid., 171.

40. Ibid., 206–7.

41. Ibid., 212.

42. Ibid., 215.

43. Ibid., 216–17.

44. CO 384/160, Irving to Granville, despatch no. 56, 1 March 1886, and enclosures.

45. CO 384/160, Mohadaya's testimony, ff. 36–38.

46. CO 384/160, Moorti's testimony, f. 39.

47. For her views on the use of testimonies and depositions, see Carter, *Lakshmi's Legacy*; *Voices of Indenture*; and, with James Ng Foong Kwong, *Forging the Rainbow: Labour Immigrants in British Mauritius* (Mauritius: S.N., 1997).

48. Merry Wiesner, *Women and Gender in Early Modern Europe* (Cambridge and New York: Cambridge University Press, 1993), 50.

16

The Links of a Legacy
Figuring the Slave Trade to Jamaica

Douglas B. **Chambers** |

Introduction

In the summer of 1791 a young enslaved man named Brutus ran away from his new master in the Black River area of St Elizabeth parish, on the leeward side of Jamaica. Brutus's master noted that this slave, who had been purchased from a dealer on behalf of an absconded owner, claimed to be a creole but was assumed to be African born. As the current master wrote in the published advertisement, Brutus "calls himself a Creole, but is supposed to be from Africa, as he talks both the Eboe and Coromantee languages *very fluently*".[1]

Although Brutus may have claimed a creole birth to enhance his status, or indeed his price,[2] if he was in fact African born it is noteworthy that he found it necessary or useful to learn not just one but two African languages "very fluently". Furthermore, if Brutus was indeed born in Africa, and presumably in the hinterland of either the Gold or the Calabar coast (likely among either Akan or Igbo peoples), then he would have learned one language (while retaining the other, natal, one) after surviving the Middle Passage. Or, if this man was a creole, as he clearly claimed, and perhaps had one parent from each African region, then each would have taught their son their own ancestral tongue, with all three maintaining them as living languages. Finally, assuming that Brutus knew who he was and where he was born, perhaps he learned to speak both Eboe and Coromantee precisely because, like plantation Creole ("nation language") and English, those two particular African languages were in everyday use in Jamaica in the last quarter of the eighteenth century?

In any of these potential historical cases, this young runaway man (who was not known to speak, for example, Mandingo and Fon, or Moko and Mondongo, or Chamba and Kongo, and so forth) and the broader circumstances of Brutus's linguistic dexterity call out for questioning. They also question many of the reigning assumptions about "creolization" in the Caribbean. And that this so-called Brutus spoke both Eboe and Coromantee during the high tide of the importation of Africans to Jamaica, the last cresting wave of primary creolization, is especially significant.

Grounding Historical Creolization

The basic principle of the concept of creolization, as originally conceived in the 1970s, was that displaced Africans in the Americas were "strangers" in a strange land. As such they were forced to make themselves anew in the crucible of slavery. The pioneering scholar Kamau Brathwaite saw the process as a multilinear one, in which generic Europeans and Africans, whites and blacks – in unequal relation to each other – created a new society from the cultural confrontation of these mutually antagonistic arrivants. Whites dominated and blacks resisted, and all in the peculiar context of the slave plantation. The variety of human responses among the slaves, and also presumably among the whites, resulted in a *cultural continuum*. This historical cultural reality ranged from conservative ancestralism to adaptive pragmatism to self-effacing and self-serving mimesis.[3]

In a much less subtle, though perhaps more influential formulation, at least for those writing about North America, Sidney Mintz and Richard Price focused on the centrality of the Middle Passage experience, on the supposed randomness of the slave trade, to argue that any population of displaced Africans constituted a heterogenous "crowd" rather than a culturally conversant "group". In the face of atomism and amid the oppression of slavery they managed, in largely *ad hoc* ways, to create an essentially new community and a novel culture. However, they also somehow managed to preserve a loosely shared or generically "African" style (cultural grammar).[4]

For Brathwaite the locus of this process of cultural construction was the plantation; for Mintz and Price it was aboard the slave ship(s). In both of these views, however, the Atlantic was a barrier rather than a bridge, and "Africa" largely a vague and generic space rather than the site of specific, generative human cultures.

Both approaches opened new vistas on the remarkable creative adaptation of people caught in cruelly oppressive circumstances, whose cultural creativity belies the older assumption of the "damage" or "catastrophist" school (from Frazier through Elkins, and beyond).[5] And yet they both still relied (unwittingly) on a whole set of assumptions that can only be termed catastrophist. Each relies on the trope of Tribe, the metaphor of the Middle Passage, the symbol of Seasoning, the mnemonic of Mimesis. As Brathwaite wrote,

> The nature of their capture in West Africa, their transport, sale and "seasoning" in the West Indies is crucial to an understanding of this [cultural "conformity"]. Slaves in Jamaica came from a wide area of West Africa. . . . mainly from the Gold Coast and the Niger and Cross deltas. They were an agricultural non-literate people, with a political and social background based on the tribe, the clan, and the village. They were uprooted from this context on capture, and further disorientated at the trading forts on the West African coast, on the ships of the "middle passage", and when sold and distributed on their arrival in Jamaica. *Creolization began with "seasoning"* – a period of one to three years, when the slaves were branded, given a new name and put under apprenticeship to creolized slaves. During this period the slave would learn the rudiments of his new language and be initiated into the work routines that awaited him.[6]

Ironically, whereas Mintz and Price asserted that such survivors expected to experiment, that cultural dynamism and change were the only constants in these early slave communities, Brathwaite argued that the plantation slaves, "like most people wholly involved in agricultural or industrial routine, were also conservative, disliking, even fearing, change; becoming attached to places and/or persons with whom they had identified themselves".[7] In what he later termed "negative creolization", or the rejection by blacks of cultural influences of "the Other" (whites), Brathwaite evoked this conservative, Africanesque end of the creole continuum, which he called *nam* (from *nyam,* "to eat"). In his own aspect as a postmodern griot, Brathwaite breathtakingly conjured how the essential nature of the "African capsule or circle culture" encouraged "the slave" to continue to be

> aware of an active relationship with the life/force/cosmos through priests, ritual observance, charms ("fetish"), sacrifice/propitiation ("obeah"); and this continued to influence all other aspects of his life/expression, though many of the more public forms of this (e.g. *jonkonnu*) were limited and eventually eroded; while other life-forms (politics, economics and several aspects of the arts, for example) were truncated and submerged; and all were legislated against. What was "permitted" is what (*parts of wholes*; "creolized", watered down versions) pleased the local establishment. So the masks had to become less "ugly", drum-beat less complex, dances more "formal" less "frenzied". But obeah and the obeahman persisted despite the legislation increasingly secularized; true; increasingly commercialized; increasingly malfunctioning and malevolent in many cases; but still the religious *nam* remained; nourishing the "cults", distracting attention from the priests.[8]

Beginning from and within this Africanesque end of the continuum, historical creolization was most likely to have been a group phenomenon. To restore the lost links of black Atlantic legacies we must now reimagine the basic cultural and historical contexts in which a self-identified creole runaway, like our Brutus from 1791, could learn to speak "very fluently" not just one but two African languages in western Jamaica. As chronology is the key, we must also recognize that this man's time represented the precise historical moment when the slave trade to Jamaica was dominated by people of these two neo-African nations (Eboe, Coromantee). Not all people of Atlantic African ethnic backgrounds were equally represented in these creolizing slave communities. As such, to recapture the agency of particular African groups, to forge the links of these half-forgotten legacies, we must focus on the roles and resources of those peoples most heavily represented in various times and diasporic places, to account *historically* for the development of regional creole slave subcultures.

Since the 1990s historians have been (re)turning to a conception that sees Atlantic Africa as the birthplace of African-American culture, as the spring of creolization, rather than the slave ship or the plantation, *per se*. Specifically, historians have been disaggregating Africa in order to perceive particular African ethnic or identity groups. Through the use of new research tools and increased mastery over the numbers of the transatlantic trade, over the sources, origins and distributions of masses of enslaved Africans in time and space, once again the Middle Passage is becoming a historiographical bridge rather than a conceptual barrier to diasporic understanding.[9]

Sufficient control over the numbers enables us to attempt again to grasp that the flows of captives were not random, but rather multilinear, circling with clusters and waves and even at times floods of peoples from basically similar ethnic backgrounds to defined regions in the Americas. At times these whirlpools of people "reafricanized" whole regions.[10] But even if Mintz and Price were right, it remains a problem of interpretation to explain how such populations of purported strangers, supposedly expecting to experiment, raised their children to conserve what had become distinctively Afri-regional folk cultures.

Upon returning to Jamaica in 1785, the chronicler Bryan Edwards provided a hint of an explanation – that is, the solidarity of prior and newer African arrivants from the same ancestral regions. In an underappreciated passage, he noted,

> I was surprised to find the old-established Negroes, when young people newly arrived from Africa were sent among them, request, as a particular instance of favour and indulgence to themselves, the revival and continuance of the ancient system [of receiving newcomers by adopting them]; assuring me they had the means of supporting strangers without difficulty. Many who thus applied, proposed each of them to adopt one of their young country-folks in the room of the children they had lost by death, or had been deprived of in Africa; others, because they wished, like the patriarchs of old, to see their sons take to themselves wives from their own nations and kindred; and all of them, I presume, because, among other considerations, they expected to revive and retrace in the conversation of their new visitors, the remembrance and ideas of past pleasures and scenes of their youth. The strangers too were best pleased with this arrangement, and ever afterwards considered themselves as the adopted children of those by whom they were thus protected, calling them parents, and venerating them as such.[11]

The multilinearity and contingency of historical creolization as a cultural process, and one at first among the various kinds of Africans and their children, as well as whites (though in a relatively limited way), is what made for a creole continuum within what Brathwaite finally termed a "prismatic" society.[12] The emerging cultural continuum was given further impetus by the appearance of a third caste: mixed-race people, the browns, who were perhaps the ultimate creoles and of course the most pragmatic, at least from a modern perspective.

To ground historical creolization we must guard against the facile reversion to the antediluvian search for static survivals, reactionary retentions, chimerical carryovers and so forth. And yet the Atlantic crossing experience, as traumatic as it was, did not simply obliterate the captives' memories of how to do things, to act, to be "people"; nor did it kill the spirits. The ubiquity of the belief of diasporic Africans that upon their physical death they would return "home" suggests that they collectively saw themselves as exiles, rather than outcasts. And though much of what made the culture of the slaves distinctive was creolism, adapting what was familiar and adopting what was functional, none of this happened in a cultural vacuum. Very little happened simply randomly.

Of course enslaved people had to be flexible, had to be pragmatic. The quest for control over one's surroundings suggested by the plethora of omens and the importance of signs in archaic African-American vernacular cultures throughout the diaspora expresses in ideological terms the vulnerability of oppressed people to events and decisions out of their control. But again, it seems unlikely that in any one region individuals simply made these all up on the spur of the moment. By drawing on loosely shared ancestral traditions, slaves in particular regions created living common cultural traditions that were distinctive. Their immediate descendants then elaborated them into various regional African-derived *historically* creole societies.

Figuring Imports of Slaves to Jamaica

As the Jamaican scholar Mervyn Alleyne noted, the "regional and ethnic provenance of Africans is crucial to the reconstruction of the cultural history of Jamaica, but it is extremely difficult to know". Impressive research in the 1960s had begun to clarify the picture, at least in broad strokes, though little was done subsequently to refine either the total estimates or the chronology of the importation of various groups to the island.[13] Therefore, by the 1990s scholars such as Alleyne, who diligently searches for the influences of Africans in both historical and contemporary Jamaican culture, tended to focus attention on those groups whose influences were most obvious (like the Coromantee/Akan), or which reflected commonly held modern beliefs about past influential groups, thus at times overlooking history to validate myth.[14]

Estimates of the total number of Africans taken to Jamaica vary significantly. Curtin offered a total estimate of nearly 750,000 Africans imported between 1655 and 1807, but with no decennial breakdowns. New and detailed work by David Eltis for the seventeenth century, and a reliance on Orlando Patterson's corrected figures from the official lists of Stephen Fuller (1788), yield a higher estimate of about 890,000 slaves.[15] Combining figures from Eltis with Patterson's Fuller series and new numbers from the Trans-Atlantic Slave Trade (1999) database[16] for 1776–1810 yields an even higher estimate of nearly 950,000 Africans landed on the island, or about one-quarter more than Curtin's initial estimate. As the total TSTD figure of about 913,000 "disembarked" is based on detailed documentary sources, is less than the highest revised estimate and yet is in general a great improvement over Curtin's figures in that the data can be organized into five-year intervals, the TSTD figures should be accepted as definitive.

Table 16.1   Competing Estimates of Total Slaves Imported to Jamaica 1655–1810

Curtin[a]		TSTD[b]	
1655–1701	88,000	1656–1700	64,038
1702–1725	64,000	1701–1725	125,338
1726–1750	128,000	1726–1750	144,057
1751–1775	172,500	1751–1775	225,057
1776–1791	123,100	1776–1790	129,129
1792–1807	171,900	1791–1810	225,132
	747,500		912,884
Revised			
1662–1700	95,029		
1702–1775	497,879		
1776–1810	354,261		
	947,169		

[a]Curtin, *Atlantic Slave Trade*, 160.
[b]"Disembarked"; organized to compare with Curtin.

Therefore, it is highly likely, or at least plausible, that some 950,000 Africans were taken to Jamaica. The vast majority were in the eighteenth century, and especially after 1750, although significant imports of slaves did occur prior to 1703. Some significant proportion of these captives, however, were re-exported, trans-shipped to merchants and masters in other colonies. It would appear that some 225,000 Africans were re-exported, nearly half before 1750. But, as we shall see for the trade to Jamaica as a whole, even the re-export trade in recently imported slaves does not appear to be exactly random.

Figures are known for the long century after 1702, and overall about one-quarter (26.4 per cent) were re-exported between 1702 and 1807. But before 1750 re-exports comprised fully 40 per cent of slaves imported, and at times well over 50 per cent. After 1751, however, the proportion of Africans re-exported fell to 20 per cent or less (see table 16.2).

It is also likely that before 1750 (and especially 1706–40), merchants and planters financed their dramatic expansion of the slave trade to Jamaica by reselling substantial portions of their human cargoes. They may well have done so selectively.

Table 16.2   Estimates of Slaves Re-Exported from Jamaica, 1702–1807[a]

Years		
By Decade	No. Re-Exported	% of Imported[b]
1702–1710	8,436	16.9
1711–1720	24,941	52.4
1721–1730	33,155	52.1
1731–1740	26,978	63.5
1741–1750	14,545	22.4
1751–1760	11,146	14.3
1761–1770	9,889	11.6
1771–1780	24,372	25.4
1781–1790	26,333	27.7
1791–1800	6,200	16.6
1801–1807	17,800	26.4
	223,795	26.4
By Defined Period		
1702–1750	108,055	40.1
1751–1785	56,935	18.4
1786–1807	58,805	21.9

[a]After Patterson, *Sociology of Slavery*, 289–91 (for 1702–90); and Curtin, *Atlantic Slave Trade*, 26 (for 1791–1807).
[b]The percentage of imported is the percentage of the number "disembarked" in each decade, from TSTD.

For example, the shipping records suggest an unusually large proportion of shipments from the Bight of Benin to Jamaica before 1750. And yet, other than a few place names (such as Whidah Estate) and occasional references to "Whydaw" and "Papaw" slaves,[17] there is little evidence of Aja/Fon or Gbe (Popo) cultural influences in Jamaica. There is no record of *vodoun* or *Legba* or other cultural artefacts derived from folk habitus in this part of West Africa, even though captives from within and without Whydah (Ouidah), Ardra, Dahomey numerically dominated shipments in what Alleyne called the "formative period" (*c.*1660–1700).[18] Rather, it seems that the early reliance of Jamaican merchants on re-exporting fully four in ten African arrivants in this early period, when such highly regarded Slave Coast shipments held a momentary prominence in the Jamaican trade, was anything but accidental. And then in the first forty years of the eighteenth century, Africans from the Gold Coast began to arrive in substantial numbers. Jamaican planter-merchants apparently financed this new wave of "Coromantee" slaves by re-exporting others from the Bight of Benin. After a decade of relatively massive imports from the Gold Coast, in 1711 Jamaican merchants turned to re-exporting a majority of the Africans they imported, and continued to do so for the next thirty years (to *c.*1740). As Africans from the Slave Coast constituted by far the second most numerous imports (nearly one-third), after those from the Gold Coast (about 40 per cent), it seems that such "Popo" were resold, rather than the "Coromantee". In fact, after 1750, when re-exports declined by half (as a percentage of arrivants), imports from the Bight of Benin declined even more precipitously.[19]

Patterns of Provenance

In order to make sense of the slave trade to Jamaica, to figure it properly (and to *figure it in*), we must move beyond relying upon global numbers, totals only, as well as simply arbitrary intervals, those round numbers of twenty-five-year periods and turns of centuries. As importantly, we must transcend a simplistically developmental model, or overcome the assumed primacy of a single "formative period", an initial cultural hegemon to which all subsequent African latecomers were subject.[20] Instead, we must pay close attention to chronology, to the reality of waves of groups of enslaved people who washed up on the various shores of the island at different times, adding particular elements to the ongoing bricolage of slave culture. We must, in short, constantly break it down and aim even for event-level analysis.[21]

Of course there is a certain surface utility in figuring the overall coastal breakdowns, the gross percentages, especially for Jamaica. In general there has been an assumption of Gold Coast predominance in an Akan-centric historiography, itself largely resulting from an over-reliance on Maroon cultural/social/ideological artefacts as representative of "the African" in folk Jamaican culture. Overall, however, a sample of nearly 760,000 Africans embarked for Jamaica shows that those from the Bight of Biafra actually outnumbered those from the Gold Coast. Of Africans landed on the island, those from Biafra were the most numerous, followed by captives originating in the hinterland of the Gold Coast, with those from west-central Africa (Congo and Angola) a distant third. Something like 300,000 of the sample of 915,000 Africans disembarked in Jamaica during the slave trade originated in the Bight of Biafra; another 250,000 were taken from the Gold Coast. In short, overall totals suggest that, contrary to the traditional historiographical emphasis, there were measurably more "Eboe" (Biafran Africans) than "Coromantee" in Jamaica, especially after 1750 (see tables 16.3 and 16.4).

Table 16.3   Known Coastal Provenance (Disembarked)[a]

1650–1810	N = 651,323	
Coast	Number	Percentage
Bight of Biafra	218,007	33.5
Gold Coast	179,451	27.6
West-Central Africa	109,002	16.7
Bight of Benin	77,741	11.9
Greater Senegambia[b]	66,579	10.2
South-East Africa[c]	543	–

[a]Based on TSTD query: "Full time period and Where slaves embarked = [Gold Coast, etc.] and Imputed region in which greatest number of slaves disembarked = Jamaica." Rank ordered.

[b]Following the Senegalese historian Boubacar Barry, I have grouped together Senegambia, Sierra Leone and Windward Coast into "Greater Senegambia"; Barry, *Senegambia and the Atlantic Slave Trade*, trans. Ayi Kwei Armah (Cambridge: Cambridge University Press, 1998). Alternatively one could call the region "Upper Guinea", following Walter Rodney, *A History of the Upper Guinea Coast, 1545 to 1800* (Oxford: Oxford University Press, 1970). For supporting documentation from Charleston, South Carolina advertisements and notices, see Elizabeth Donnan, ed., *Documents Illustrative of the History of the Slave Trade to America*, vol. 4 (1935; reprint, New York: Farrar, Straus and Giroux, 1969), 312n14, 373n2, 412n11, 428, 442n4, 477n5. See also George Brooks, *Landlords and Strangers: Ecology, Society, and Trade in Western Africa, 1000–1630* (Boulder: Westview Press, 1993).

[c]Principally Mozambique and Madagascar.

Table 16.4   Estimated Nominal Totals, Landed[a]

A. 1650–1810	N = 914,902
Bight of Biafra	306,492
Gold Coast	252,513
West-Central Africa	152,789
Bight of Benin	108,873
Greater Senegambia	93,320
South-East Africa	915
B. 1750–1810	N = 579,318
Bight of Biafra	233,465
Gold Coast	152,361
West-Central Africa	85,160
Greater Senegambia	61,987
Bight of Benin	46,345
South-East Africa	–

[a]Based on TSTD query: "Full time period and Where slaves disembarked = Jamaica"; to which are applied the frequencies from the sample in table 16.3. Rank ordered.

Regarding Biafran Africans and their collective cultural influences in Jamaica, earlier scholars like Brathwaite and Alleyne recognized that Igbo (and other Biafrans) were numerous. And yet, partly for reasons that are understandable, the effort has been to explain away their presence by arguing that they were "not culturally influential".[22] This has tended to be the case even though today, for example, the Accompong Maroons still have a box-drum that they call "Ebo drum"; historiographically, the vivid presence of "Eboe" slaves in the documentary sources has been largely overlooked. Why has no one studied the Igbo-dominated 1816 slave insurrection in the Black River area, in which some 250 African conspirators elected a "King of the Eboes"? When this "king" was hanged, he died declaring that "he left enough of his countrymen to prosecute the design in hand, and revenge his death upon the whites". Indeed, one of the other leaders escaped from the Savanna-la-Mar jail, and when later recaptured he was "found concealed in the hut of a notorious Obeah-man".[23] Cultural artefacts like obeah (compare with archaic Nri-Awka Igbo ôbia, "doctoring") and the ubiquitous "arsenic bean" in c.1800 Westmoreland parish (that is, Calabar bean, *Physostigma venemosum*), the latter apparently having been abandoned and forgotten by the twentieth century, and the observation by Edward Long in 1769 (as chronology is the key) that "several new masks appeared: the Eboes, the Papaws, &c. having their respective Connús", have all remained research paths not taken.[24]

New evidence from the remarkable TSTD (quinquennia series, "embarked"[25]), suggests that there were deeper patterns in the provenance of Africans taken to Jamaica. Combining these patterns with the tempo of importations, one may see four periods in the slave trade to Jamaica. The first, from 1661 to 1695, was marked by relatively small numbers – an average of about 9,150 per quinquennia – though it was relatively well documented.[26] The greatest proportion came from the Bight of Benin (37 per cent), followed by west-central Africa (28 per cent), and the Bight of Biafra (19 per cent); Africans from the Gold Coast were a tiny proportion (9 per cent).[27]

The second period was from 1696 to 1750. This era saw a great expansion in the Jamaican trade, averaging over 31,000 per quinquennia (or nearly 6,250 per year), but was relatively poorly documented.[28] And though there was a continuing clustering of slaves shipped from the Slave Coast, this period saw a massive shift towards the importation of slaves from the Gold Coast. Of the sample of nearly 120,000 Africans with a "known" provenance, those from the Gold Coast now comprised 37 per cent of imports, while those from the Slave Coast fell to less than a quarter (24 per cent).

The third period, from 1751 to 1785, saw a further increase in the annual numbers of people imported, even with the disruption of the two great colonial wars in those decades (the Seven Years' War and the American Revolution). Imports to Jamaica rose to almost 10,500 per year (52,000 per quinquennia), and it was an era that was very well documented.[29] There was a continuing strong presence of Gold Coast slaves (nearly 105,000 or 34.6 per cent). But more importantly, this was an era in which Gold Coast shipments were concentrated – that is, over half (51.4 per cent) of *all Africans from the Gold Coast* were shipped in the thirty-five years after 1750. This concentrated wave of Gold Coast Africans was matched by the dramatic appearance of slaves from the Bight of Biafra (nearly 100,000 or one-third of the total for the period), and the equally dramatic disappearance of Africans shipped from the Bight of Benin.

The fourth period, from 1786 to 1808, saw a peak in the average numbers of slaves shipped to Jamaica, with more than 13,300 shipped annually (61,500 per quinquennia). This was also the best-documented period, with nearly 94 per cent of slaves shipped with a recorded provenance. From the Gold Coast

Table 16.5 Periodization in the Jamaica Slave Trade: Numbers and Annual Averages, 1661–1808

	1661–1695	1696–1750	1751–1785	1786–1808
Embarked	64,035	343,538	364,417	307,914
Provenance (known)	48,614	118,827	302,582	288,403
Annual Average	1,830	6,246	10,412	13,388

Table 16.6 Percentage of Africans Imported by Coastal Provenance, 1661–1810: Quinquennial Series[a]

	1661–1695 N = 48,614	1696–1750 N = 118,827	1751–1785 N = 302,582	1786–1810 N = 288,403	Total 1661–1810 N = 758,426
Greater Senegambia	5.80	6.60	13.9	7.40	9.80
Gold Coast	9.30	*37.20*	*34.60*	17.6	26.90
Bight of Benin	*37.40*	*23.70*	10.7	5.30	12.40
Bight of Biafra	18.90	15.90	*32.60*	*48.3*	35.10
West-Central Africa	*28.30*	16.30	8.30	*21.50*	15.80
SE Africa	0.04	0.04	–	–	–

[a]After TSTD. The numbers in italics represent statistical waves or predominant clustering.

came nearly 51,000 slaves, which would have extended the cultural impacts of earlier arrivants, but their presence was swamped by a massive flood of other Africans from the Bight of Biafra, nearly 140,000 in this one generation. Indeed, in this ultimate quarter-century came over half of all Biafran Africans (52.4 per cent), almost certainly heavily Igbo, who were taken to Jamaica. It is noteworthy that this period also saw the appearance of west-central Africans, comprising about one-fifth of the total, and those 62,000 who were shipped also represented over half (51.6 per cent) of all those shipped from those coasts to the island. But again, in this last period, Biafrans dominated imports to Jamaica.

Waves of Numbers/Numbers of Waves

The first step in using these waves of slave-trade numbers to get at questions of proximate cultural influence is to identify periods of clustering of Africans imported from a particular coast. The crudest measure is simply the percentage of the known total of imports, as above; a more meaningful measure is the proportion of slaves from that coastal region imported in a particular period. Both of these approaches were utilized in the paragraphs above. But they can also be measured against each other.

For example, west-central Africans seem to be particularly important in the initial period (1661–95), when they were 28.3 per cent of the sample. However, that number was only 11.5 per cent of *all the slaves* taken from west-central Africa to Jamaica. At the other temporal end (1786–1808), even though peoples from this same broad region were just over a fifth of slaves imported, that same cohort represented more than 50 per cent of west-central Africans shipped to the island. Hence they were highly concentrated. One could more rightly say that the number of slaves from west-central Africa during the last period constituted a wave, because of the disproportionate number taken in that relatively short time-frame. And they were likely to have arrived with a greater potential influence, because they were concentrated in a relatively short period.

Such obvious waves – that is, when the proportion of Africans from a coastal region imported in a particular interval (as measured against the total for that coastal region) is far greater than the overall or average percentage of all slaves imported for that time period – can be a useful tool for perceiving the potential for cultural influences beyond the gross frequencies. For example, though slaves from Greater Senegambia in the third period (1751–85) were only 14 per cent of Africans imported, that number represented 57 per cent of slaves taken from that coast to Jamaica. At first blush the 14 per cent figure would be easily overlooked; but well over half of all peoples taken from Greater Senegambia to Jamaica arrived in this one short generation. In general, when half or more of the Africans from one region are taken in one generation, then one should see that flow of forced migrants as a potential wave of cultural actors, even if their proportion of the total imports was relatively small.

Another measure, more precisely statistical though not without its limitations, is more exact and more dynamic, and is called a *distribution index*. This statistical measure is a comparison of frequencies, and hence a ratio. Given an overall average percentage, one may ask whether at any particular time interval the proportion of imports is representative (proportionate, as if random) or clustered (disproportionate). Thus one may compare the two basic frequencies: a) the percentage of Africans imported from a particular coast for that interval (proximate frequency); and b) the mean percentage for the whole period. If X equals the proximate frequency and Y equals the mean percentage of the total, then Z = the ratio of X to Y $(X/Y=Z)$. If Z is greater than 120 (or 20 per cent more than expected), then the number of captives from the defined coast could be termed disproportionately large; I call this a *pulse*. The higher the ratio (Z) the more disproportionate the number imported, and thus the stronger the pulse. Using a quinquennial series, two or more pulses constitute a *wave*. For an annual series, a pulse is an isolated year of disproportionate imports; a cluster is a few such consecutive years; a wave is a set of clusters. In defining a wave, the number of years within the interval that are pulses must be greater than one every other year (that is, over 51 per cent), and with a Z-ratio of over 120. Again, the higher the Z-ratio, the more disproportionate (non-random) the numbers imported, and the stronger the wave.

Using this method to make a distribution index for Jamaica yields some very interesting results. I used an annual series ("embarked"), with the criteria described above, and applied the method to Africans from each of the five defined main coasts. My findings support and amplify the periodization I propose in table 16.5. The annual series underscores the puzzling early importance of Africans from the Bight of Benin (1679–1730) as well as west-central Africa (1665–1701), the shift to Gold Coast slaves in the first third of the eighteenth century (1703–27) and their continuing significance in the second half of the century (1748–90), the emerging presence of Biafran Africans in the second quarter of the century (1729–46) and their disproportionality even at the very height of their numerical dominance (1773–1808), and that even west-central Africans experienced short but intense waves of imports (1723–49, 1792–1803). In short, a rough schema suggests a dual Benin/west-central African cultural dynamic in the seventeenth century, followed by an almost continuous wave from the Gold Coast in the eighteenth century, with several lesser waves (including Biafran, Greater Senegambian, west-central African) in the middle decades and then a veritable tidal wave of Biafran Africans in the final generation (1773–1808).

Table 16.7   Estimated "Waves" by African Coastal Region: Annual Series[a]

Bight of Benin	1679–1730		
	N = 43,616		
	Z = 297		
West-Central Africa	1665–1701	1723–1749	*1792–1803*
	N = 15,907	N = 13,312	N = 56,326
	Z = 181	Z = 163	Z = 218
Gold Coast	*1703–1727*	*1748–1790*	
	N = 31,403	N = 119,449	
	Z = 178	Z = 126	
Bight of Biafra	1729–1746		*1773–1808*
	N = 11,124		N = 187,031
	Z = 133		Z = 128
Greater Senegambia		*1750–1777*	
		N = 40,701	
		Z = 176	

[a]The periods listed in italics were probably the most influential in the development of the creolizing slave communities.

Beyond the general numbers of waves, it is also important to look at patterns of distribution. The TSTD also contains some very suggestive data on the geographical distribution of shipments of imported Africans. A comparison of leeward and windward ports, though a relatively limited (if rather large) sample, suggests that Africans from different coastal regions tended to be delivered to different parts of Jamaica. It is possible to compare distributions in the two basic parts of the island after 1751. The most striking differences are the very small percentages of Bight of Benin and west-central African slaves landed in leeward ports, versus the tendency of shipments from the Bight of Biafra to be sent to the western parts. Whereas Biafran Africans comprised just under 30 per cent of slaves landed in windward ports (1751–75), in those same years in leeward ports they made up nearly half of slaves landed. The tendency to send Bight of Biafra shipments to the western ports became more pronounced in the last generation (1776–1808), when they represented nearly 70 per cent of African arrivants (see tables 16.8 and 16.9).

Furthermore, even though new Gold Coast slaves were sent in large numbers to the island, they were clustered in the windward areas in the same gen-

Table 16.8   Percentage of Africans Landed at Windward Ports, by African Provenance, 1701–1810

	Greater Senegambia	Gold Coast	Bight of Benin	Bight of Biafra	West-Central Africa	SE Africa
1701–1750 N = 46,149	4.30	34.90	15.30	24.20	20.40	1.00
1751–1775 N = 110,731	16.9	33.20	12.20	29.30	8.50	–
1776–1810 N = 256,858	5.90	22.40	6.20	43.10	22.30	–
1701–1810 N = 413,738	8.60	26.70	8.80	37.40	18.40	–

Table 16.9   Percentage of Africans Landed at Leeward Ports, by African Provenance, 1751–1810

	Greater Senegambia	Gold Coast	Bight of Benin	Bight of Biafra	West-Central Africa	SE Africa
1751–1775 N = 8,567	11.80	36.60	3.30	48.40	–	–
1776–1810 N = 49,296	10.8	16.60	3.80	68.20	0.60	–
1751–1810 N = 57,863	10.9	19.60	3.70	65.30	0.50	–

eration. And in the 1776–1808 period, when the majority of west-central Africans were taken to Jamaica, they were landed almost exclusively in the east (or at least, almost none were landed in the west); it is perhaps to this period that we should look to see the beginnings of *kumina*, for example, which even today is best known on the windward side of the island north of Kingston.[30] These non-random distribution patterns would have further concentrated certain groups of Africans in different parts of Jamaica, contributing to a sense of cultural localism.

Given the patterns of importation, it is also interesting that twentieth-century Afro-Jamaican kumina included within it a nation called "Ibo", which is typical of latecomers who incorporate other African peoples already there, rather than of first-comers who exclude later arrivants. For example, in Cuba, among traditionalists, even today one generally should not be initiated into the Calabar-derived *abakuá* masqueing society if one had been previously initiated into the Yoruba-derived *Regla de Osha* (*"santería"*); however, an *abakuá* could become a *santero*, no problem.[31]

The Question of Ethnicity

One of the most vexing questions of all, of course, is just who those groups of Africans were. While the TSTD, and other sources, clearly demonstrate the likelihood of clustering of peoples through time and space, the shipping data speak only to general African coastal origins. Detailed analyses of the histories of each coast's hinterland in the slave-trade era are required to estimate the distributions of ethnic groups taken into the diaspora. The issue is compounded by the fact that people regrouped after the Middle Passage. They reinvented themselves, and forged new collective identities that were African-derived (or neo-African).[32]

Americanists, however, have a potentially powerful documentary source to work with, though one which for the Caribbean has been largely ignored: fugitive slave advertisements. One of the signal contributions of these advertisements is the ability to get the actual "named groups" among diasporic Africans, to move beyond generalized coastal designations to the ethnic groups themselves. While there is a plethora of named ethnies (ethnic groups) in any New World setting, it appears that everywhere the vast majority of African-born slaves rather quickly subsumed their local natal associations into more generalized, perhaps regional, certainly diasporic collective identities.[33]

A small but statistically illustrative sample of nearly 3,100 fugitive African-born slaves in Jamaica (mostly 1776–1817) suggests some important patterns.[34] The paid advertisements and, from the 1770s, parish workhouse lists routinely include mention of the runaway's putative "country" or "nation". It is clear from the workhouse lists that the terms used to denote these "countries" were largely elicited from the captured runaways, rather than simply imposed by the white supervisors. It is also clear that in any district (and indeed in other colonies), the vast majority of these named Africans, roughly 80 to 90 per cent, fell into just a relative handful of ethnic designations, usually about ten. Diasporic terminology was most common for the major named groups; the fewer the number in a group, the more likely they were to identify themselves in strictly local terms, or in terms of subethnies.

For example, in the Jamaican data set there are a total of thirty-seven examples of African ethnonyms. However, just nine groups make up 93 per cent of the Africans with a specific ethnic provenance. Furthermore, when grouped into imputed coastal provenances in order to compare with figures from the TSTD, for any coastal region usually only two named groups predominate. Therefore, the superficial super-heterogeneity of Africans in Jamaica before *c.*1820, upon closer examination, actually gives way to signficant clustering, within both the named groups themselves and the putative coastal provenances (see tables 16.10 and 16.11).

Table 16.10 Major Diasporic Ethnies among Jamaican Runaways, 1718–1817

N = 3,090

Group	No.	Percentage	Coastal Provenance
Eboe	550	17.8	Bight of Biafra
Congo	499	16.2	West-Central Africa
Mungola	392	12.7	West-Central Africa
Mandingo	389	12.6	Greater Senegambia
Moco	358	11.6	Bight of Biafra
Coromantee	329	10.6	Gold Coast
Chamba	169	5.5	Gold Coast[a]
Nago	109	3.5	Bight of Benin
Popo	81	2.6	Bight of Benin
	2,876	93.1	

[a]Chamba are often placed in the Bight of Benin, though internal evidence from the Jamaican data set clearly suggests that Chamba were associated with the Gold Coast; other evidence suggests that these basically were Mossi peoples.

Table 16.11   Major African Ethnies, by Imputed Coastal Provenances, 1718–1817

N = 3,090

	No.	Percentage
Greater Senegambia		
N = 471		
Mandingo	389	82.6
Canga	65	13.8
Others[a]	17	3.6
Gold Coast		
N = 578		
Coromantee	329	56.9
Chamba	169	29.2
Wakee	51	8.8
Other[b]	29	5.0
Bight of Benin		
N = 191		
Nago	109	57.1
Popo	81	42.4
Oban	1	0.5
Bight of Biafra		
N = 915		
Eboe	550	60.1
Moco	358	39.1
Others[c]	7	0.8
West-Central Africa		
N = 934		
Congo	499	53.4
Mungola	392	42.0
Angola	32	3.4
Others[d]	11	1.2
SE Africa		
N = 1		
Madagascar	1	100.0

[a]Bambara, Bona, Bruman, Fulah, Bassoo, Brass-pan, Cago, Kissie, Manhabba, Otto, Sacum.
[b]Succo, Banda, Fante, Asante, Gold Coast.
[c]Ottam, Calabar, Malabar.
[d]Soso, Wanga, Cango, Mayow.

Conclusion

New evidence on the transatlantic slave trade, in conjunction with largely untapped documentary sources such as fugitive slave advertisements, may help to untangle the links in Jamaica's African legacies (to turn Franklin Knight's phrase around).[35] The emerging patterns from longitudinal analyses also serve to challenge some important assumptions, including those about the proportions of various groups taken as slaves, their distributions over time and space, the historical relation between numerical predominance and cultural dominance, and not least, the whole idea that the "formative period" culturally was necessarily the earliest one (that is, the latter seventeenth century).

Rather than assuming a cultural analogue to the ideal theory of linguistic creolization (pidgin-creole-koiné) – that is, creative invention out of absolute necessity among strangers; elaboration; then approximation; or birth/ life/death – there are other linguistic theories and metaphors. I suggest that "second language acquisition" theory, or how newcomers change a language even as they acquire it, and "waves" which ebbed and flowed may be particularly helpful in figuring the slave trade to Jamaica, as elsewhere in the black Atlantic world.

That a young male fugitive slave in the Black River area of St Elizabeth in 1791 should speak both Coromantee and Eboe "very fluently" (as well as English and/or nation language, presumably) really should not surprise. Assuming that he was born c.1770, he came of age in a time when Africans from the Bight of Biafra and the Gold Coast dominated the slaves imported to Jamaica. Furthermore, whereas Biafran Africans tended to be concentrated in the western part of the island, in the mountains there were communities of Maroons (such as Accompong and Trelawny) that were strongly Coromantee-influenced. The remarkable point about this fugitive Brutus – that is, that he was (or at least claimed to be) a creole – is actually less remarkable if we simply assume that creoles too found it necessary or useful to learn the languages of those African groups which predominated in their area: in this case Igbo and Akan (Twi). Of course, the maintenance of such linguistic communities among the enslaved people in the last decades of the eighteenth century itself runs counter to the current orthodoxy on "creolization".

At about the same time as Brutus enters the historical record, a white visitor to Jamaica (J.B. Moreton) recorded the lyrics of a song, now famous.

Usually it is referenced as an evocation of the separation from Africa, and of the restrictions imposed by bondage in Jamaica. It is curious that the song, which calls the names "Ebo" and "Guinea" and "Congo", does not call out "Coromantee" (though it keeps a polysyllabic rhythm with "Kingston" and "England"). At first I read it in the conventional sense, too:

> If me want for go in a Ebo,
> Me can't go there!
> Since dem tief me from a Guinea,
> Me can't go there!
>
> If me want for go in a Congo,
> Me can't go there!
> Since dem tief me from my tatta,
> Me can't go there!
> If me want for go in a Kingston,
> Me can't go there!
> Since massa go in a England,
> Me can't go there![36]

But now when I read this passage, I sense a living geography: an equivalence of Ebo and Congo and Kingston and England. In this piece they exist at the same level of direct consciousness. I am struck by the symmetry, if indeed "Eboe" Africans were clustered to leeward and "Congo" Africans to windward, with Kingston in the middle. Perhaps the mental topography here is descriptive of Jamaica *c.*1790, and the absence of "Coromantee", presumably embodied in the Maroon towns of the mountains, is not accidental? In any case, with the new tools at our disposal such as the Trans-Atlantic Slave Trade Database, and older still-fugitive ones like runaway slave advertisements, we may more clearly define the historical links in Jamaica's prismatic African legacy. And unlike the enslaved people themselves, if we "want for go in a Ebo" then *we can go there.*

Notes

1. *Royal Gazette* (Kingston, Jamaica), 4–11 June 1791; emphasis added. Included in Douglas B. Chambers, ed., "Abstracts of Jamaican Fugitive Slave Advertisements, *c.*1791–1814: A Compilation from Original Sources" (manuscript, 1999; copy on deposit with Special Collections, Main Library, University of the West Indies, Mona, Jamaica).

2. In the period 1770–1820, whites valued creole slaves at three times the price of Africans, largely because they were already seasoned, and thought to be "sensible"; Edward Kamau Brathwaite, *The Development of Creole Society in Jamaica, 1770–1820* (Oxford: Clarendon Press, 1971), 164–65.

3. Ibid., passim. See also Brathwaite, "Caliban, Ariel and Unprospero in the Conflict of Creolization", in *Comparative Perspectives on Slavery in New World Plantation Societies,* ed. Vera Rubin and Arthur Tuden (New York: New York Academy of Science, 1977), 41–62; also Brathwaite, *The Folk Culture of the Slaves in Jamaica,* rev. ed. (London: New Beacon Books, 1981), in which he puts more emphasis on African cultural and social influences in creolizing Jamaica.

4. Sidney W. Mintz and Richard Price, *The Birth of African-American Culture: An Anthropological Perspective* (Boston: Beacon Press, 1992); orig. publ. as *An Anthropological Approach to the Afro-American Past: A Caribbean Perspective* (Philadelphia: Institute for the Study of Human Issues, 1976).

5. See E. Franklin Frazier, *The Negro Church in America* (New York: Schocken Books, 1963); and Stanley M. Elkins, *Slavery: A Problem in American Institutional and Intellectual Life* (Chicago: University of Chicago Press, 1959).

6. Brathwaite, *Creole Society,* 298; emphasis added. Cf., with very similar descriptions for Africans taken to colonial North America, Allan Kulikoff, "Uprooted Peoples: Black Migrants in the Age of the American Revolution, 1790–1820", in *Slavery and Freedom in the Age of the American Revolution,* ed. Ira Berlin and Ronald Hoffman (Urbana, Ill.: University of Illinois Press, 1983), 153–54.

7. Brathwaite, *Creole Society,* 299.

8. Brathwaite, "Caliban, Ariel and Unprospero", 56.

9. See David Eltis, et al., eds., The Trans-Atlantic Slave Trade: A Database on CD-ROM (Cambridge: Cambridge University Press, 1999); Philip D. Curtin, *The Atlantic Slave Trade: A Census* (Madison: University of Wisconsin Press, 1969). See David Eltis, "The Volume and Structure of the Transatlantic Slave Trade: A Reassessment", *William and Mary Quarterly* 58, no. 1 (2001): 17–46. See also other recent slavery databases, including Gwendolyn Midlo Hall, ed., *Databases for the Study of Afro-Louisiana History and Genealogy, 1699–1860* [CD-ROM] (Baton Rouge: Louisiana State University Press, 2000). For a series of critiques of

anthropological creolization along these lines, see various papers in David Buisseret, et al., eds., *Creolization in the Americas* (College Station, TX: Texas A&M University Press, 2000); and Verene A. Shepherd and Glen L. Richards, eds., *Questioning Creole: Creolisation Discourses in Caribbean Culture* (Kingston, Jamaica: Ian Randle; Oxford: James Currey, 2002).

10.   For earlier works, sample Melville J. Herskovits, *The Myth of the Negro Past* (New York: Harper and Bros., 1941); Robert Ferris Thompson, *Flash of the Spirit* (New York: Vintage, 1983); Margaret Washington Creel, *"A Peculiar People"* (New York: New York University Press, 1988); Joseph E. Holloway, ed., *Africanisms in American Culture* (Bloomington: Indiana University Press, 1990); Gwendolyn Midlo Hall, *Africans in Colonial Louisiana* (Baton Rouge: Louisiana State University Press, 1992). And, more recently, compare Linda Heywood, ed., *Central Africans and Cultural Transformations in the American Diaspora* (Cambridge: Cambridge University Press, 2002); James H. Sweet, *Recreating Africa* (Chapel Hill: University of North Carolina Press, 2003); Douglas B. Chambers, *Murder at Montpelier: Igbo Africans in Virginia* (Jackson: University Press of Mississippi, 2005); Gwendolyn Midlo Hall, *African Ethnicities in the Americas* (Chapel Hill: University of North Carolina Press, 2005).

11.   Bryan Edwards, *The History, Civil and Commercial, of the British Colonies in the West Indies,* vol. 2 (Dublin, 1801 ed.), 155.

12.   Brathwaite, "Caliban, Ariel and Unprospero", 42.

13.   Alleyne, *Africa: Roots of Jamaican Culture* (Chicago: Research Associates School Times Publications, 1996), 37. See also Orlando Patterson, *The Sociology of Slavery* (Rutherford, NJ: Fairleigh Dickinson University Press, 1969). In large part, in his discussion Alleyne simply reused Curtin's number, though without direct attribution: cf. Alleyne, *Africa,* 40, and Curtin, *Atlantic Slave Trade,* 160.

14.   Alleyne, *Africa,* 28–57.

15.   Curtin used a variety of largely arbitrary intervals: see *Atlantic Slave Trade,* 71, 140, 160. See David Eltis, *The Rise of African Slavery* (Cambridge: Cambridge University Press, 2000), 28; see also Eltis, "The Volume and African Origins of the British Slave Trade before 1714", *Cahiers d'Etudes africaines* 35, nos. 2–3 (1995): 618. Compare with Patterson, *Sociology of Slavery,* 289–92.

16.   Hereafter referred to as TSTD.

17.   For examples see National Archives of Jamaica, Accounts Produce or Crop Accounts, 1B/11/4; and Registers of Returns of Slaves, 1B/11/7. See also William Beckford, *A Descriptive Account of the Island of Jamaica,* vol. 1 (London, 1790), 216; Bryan Edwards, *History, Civil and Commercial,* vol. 2, in *After Africa,* ed. Roger D. Abrahams and John F. Szwed (New Haven, Conn.: Yale University Press, 1983), 69–70.

18.   Alleyne, *Africa,* 41.

19. Many of these may have been sold to St Domingue, and also clearly some were sent to French Louisiana; Gwendolyn Midlo Hall, personal communication, October 2001. See the nearly 350 slaves in Louisiana notarial and parish records whose origins were given as Jamaica; Hall, ed., *Afro-Louisiana History and Genealogy, 1718–1820* [digital database; accessed 26 March 2002], available at http://ibiblio.org/laslave.

20. See, for example, Robert P. Stewart, "Akan Ethnicity in Jamaica: A Re-Examination of Jamaica's Slave Imports from the Gold Coast, 1655–1807", *Maryland Historian* 28, no. 1/2 (2003): 69–107.

21. For attempts along these lines, see John Thornton, "The African Experience of the '20 and Odd Negroes' Arriving in Virginia in 1619", *William and Mary Quarterly* 55, no. 3 (1998): 421–34; Lorena S. Walsh, "Chesapeake Slave Trade: Regional Patterns, African Origins, and Some Implications", *William and Mary Quarterly* 58, no. 1 (2001): 139–70; Randy J. Sparks, "Two Princes of Calabar: An Atlantic Odyssey from Slavery to Freedom", *William and Mary Quarterly* 59, no. 3 (2002): 555–84; the papers in Paul E. Lovejoy and David V. Trotman, eds., *Trans-Atlantic Dimensions of Ethnicity in the African Diaspora* (London: Continuum, 2003); Chambers, *Murder at Montpelier*.

22. Alleyne, *Africa*, 53.

23. Matthew Lewis, *Journal of a West India Proprietor*, ed. Judith Terry (1843; reprint, Oxford: Oxford University Press, 1999), 143, 144. For an account of the incident, see 138–44.

24. For "arsenic bean" see Lewis, *Journal*, 208; Douglas B. Chambers, "Ethnicity in the Diaspora: The Slave-Trade and the Creation of African 'Nations' in the Americas", *Slavery and Abolition* 22, no. 3 (2001): 30, 38n41. The bean may not have been known by the mid-twentieth century, as per Colin Palmer, personal communication, 2002. Edward Long, *The History of Jamaica*, vol. 2, quoted in Abrahams and Szwed, *After Africa*, 229.

25. "Embarked" figures are the numbers of Africans estimated taken aboard ship, and though they perforce are larger than those "disembarked" (landed), they can serve as a useful proxy, including for coastal provenance. Because the TSTD database is configured to emphasize "embarked" numbers, especially for figuring breakdowns by coastal provenance, those numbers will be used here.

26. Exact figures are: 64,035 embarked, of which 48,614 had a known provenance; the annual average was 1,830.

27. The remainder were widely scattered among Senegambia, Sierra Leone, Windward Coast, and southeast Africa (Madagascar and Mozambique).

28. That is, there was a much lower proportion of Africans with a known coastal provenance. Of 343,538 embarked, only 118,827 or 34.6 per cent were "known", though this is still a quite large sample for statistical purposes.

29. Some 83 per cent of those embarked had a known coastal provenance.

30. For kumina in St Thomas parish, see Alleyne, *Africa*, 92–93.

31. Interviews with various abakuá and santeros in Regla, Havana and Guanabacoa, Cuba, June–July 2000.

32. For recent arguments along these lines see Chambers, "Ethnicity in the Diaspora", 25–39; and the collection of papers in Lovejoy and Trotman, *Trans-Atlantic Dimensions of Ethnicity*.

33. For example, among the nearly 9,000 records with specific African ethnicity information in colonial Louisiana records, there are 217 possible examples of African ethnonyms, of which 91 are identifiable; yet, a relatively small list of about 15 comprise the vast majority of Africans. See Gwendolyn Midlo Hall, *African Ethnicities in the Americas*, 78 and passim. For a theory of diasporic ethnogenesis that seeks to explain the divergence between continental and diasporic African ethnonyms, see Chambers, "Ethnicity in the Diaspora".

34. These are part of a data set of some 7,500 runaway slaves I have compiled for Jamaica: Chambers, ed., *Jamaican Runaways, 1718–1817: A Compilation of Fugitive Slaves* (manuscript, 2003). This collection is from advertisements and workhouse lists in four newspapers: *Weekly Jamaica Courant* 1718–54; *Cornwall Chronicle* 1776–79, 1781–86, 1792–95, 1811–14, 1816–17; *Jamaica Mercury* 1779–80; and *Royal Gazette* 1791–92. There are substantial gaps in coverage, especially the second quarter of the eighteenth century (1730s–1750s) and 1796–1809. Within the general period data exist for a total of thirty-eight years; based on these numbers, I estimate that at least 25,000 runaway slaves are likely to have been advertised or otherwise listed in extant Jamaican newspapers between *c.*1718 and 1834.

35. Margaret E. Crahan and Franklin W. Knight, eds., *Africa and the Caribbean: The Legacies of a Link* (Baltimore: Johns Hopkins University Press, 1979).

36. J.B. Moreton, *Manners and Customs* (1790), 153, quoted in Brathwaite, *Folk Culture*, 20.

17

The Arabic Manuscript of Muhammad Kabā Saghanughu of Jamaica, c.1820

Yacine **Daddi Addoun** and Paul E. **Lovejoy**

An Arabic manuscript wrongly thought to be fragments of the Qur'ān written down by "a Young Mandingo Negro" is currently on deposit in the Baptist Missionary Society (BMS) papers, Angus Library, at Oxford University.[1] From internal evidence, however, it is clear that the manuscript is a treatise on eschatology, praying, marriage and ablutions. It is a poignant statement of life under slavery as a Muslim, revealing a deep faith and attempts to maintain Muslim customs while trying to explain the enforced and prolonged ordeal of slavery. The treatise is divided into two sections that appear to be distinct books; we have given the manuscript the title *Kitāb al-salāt* ("The Book on Praying"). The significance of the manuscript is twofold. First, it demonstrates that Arabic scholarship continued into the diaspora, in this case among a small group of Muslims in Jamaica; second, the book reveals the strategy of some Muslims in protecting their religious customs against the pressures to conform to the racialized slave regimes of the Americas. Muslims may have continued to practise their religion under slavery, but it was increasingly difficult to do so.

The author is identified as Muhammad Kabā Saghanughu, who lived on the coffee estate of Spice Grove in the mountains of Manchester parish, west of Mandeville. Spice Grove, and hence the author, were owned initially by Robert Peart (who died in 1797) and then by his children, Edward and John Peart.[2] Kabā lived there from the time of his arrival in Jamaica as a slave in 1777 when he was initially known as Dick, until his death in 1845. Although a committed Muslim, he joined the Moravian mission church and was baptized on 17 October 1813 under the Christian name of his deceased master, Robert Peart. At the time, the Moravian mission church was at Carmel, below the escarpment on which Spice Grove was located. Before his conversion Kabā had several mystical experiences, in the form of dreams, and suggestive of the mystical *sūfī* background of his Islamic upbringing in West Africa. He went to the Moravian mission on 24 January 1813 to seek the intervention of the Reverend John Lang, who had been the missionary at the Carmel station since 1805, in a crisis at Spice Grove. According to Kabā,

> My Massa told me to cut down the gardens belonging to our Negroes and to let his cattle run into them. Now this is very hard and I have . . . in my mind whether I should obey him in this case or rather take a flocking [*sic*]. Whatever you say I will do.[3]

His master at the time was James Robinson, who had married the widowed Mrs Peart and taken over the management of Spice Grove. Robinson owned the neighbouring cattle pen of Nottingham. The marriage of Robinson and Mrs Peart combined property amounting to many hundred acres, including several coffee estates and cattle pens. Upon Robinson's death, the properties passed to Mrs Peart's son, Edward.

In his appeal to Reverend Lang, Kabā complained that the enslaved population of Spice Grove was being denied customary rights in land use that had been recognized under the management of the original owner, Robert Peart, and hence rights that dated back to the period before 1797. The Pearts were resident proprietors (unlike many sugar planters), raising their family in the highlands of Manchester – a most picturesque setting, with a prevailing breeze, above areas threatened annually by serious hurricane damage and disease. It is instructive that when Kabā was baptized he took the name of none other than his deceased master, instead of the name by which he was actually known: Dick. It was as if he was asserting the persona of his deceased master in upholding the rights of the community, which he clearly represented. He received his first communion on 24 September 1815. His children, Helena, Belinda and Robert, were also baptized in 1815, and his wife, Mary Ann,[4] received communion on 25 August 1816. Although Kabā, alias Robert Peart, was still known as "the Mahometan", he rose steadily in the eyes of the Moravians, even writing a report in Arabic on the manner of delivering religious instruction to slaves.[5] By 1816 Reverend Lang was referring to Kabā as "Br. Robert our Helper from Spicegrove", signalling that Kabā had achieved the status of "elder" in the Moravian mission hierarchy.[6] Indeed, Kabā's close association with the Moravians was a factor in the decision to move the Moravian mission from unhealthy Carmel to Fairfield, which was located on the escarpment adjacent to Nottingham Pen and Spice Grove.

By the time Kabā died in 1845, he had passed through the hands of several owners, because he outlived them. After the death of his first master, Robert Peart, he belonged to John Robinson, who married Robert Peart's widow, and then to Edward Peart (Robert's son), who was his master until the Emancipation Decree of 1834. Kabā consciously chose the name of his deceased master, clearly relating his identity to issues of community.[7] Although Kabā has previously come to the attention of scholars who have studied enslaved Muslims in the Americas, until now it has not been recognized that he was the author of the manuscript discussed here, or that he was associated with other Muslims in the hills of Manchester.[8]

The manuscript, fifty folios in length, was written with brown ink on cheap, lined notebook paper; it was clearly written in Jamaica, some time before late 1823 and perhaps many years earlier. It is not known if this is the original manuscript or a copy, although internal evidence suggests that the manuscript might well have been two separate texts, and repetition that seems the result of a copying error rather than style or necessity raises the possibility that this manuscript is a copy. Moreover, the note attributing the text to "a Young Mandingo Negro", while Kabā was in fact well advanced in years in 1823, also suggests that it may be a copy. The binding on the text is old, now brittle, made of thick cowhide, with a rectangular strip cut to overlap the notebook and sewn on at the back. It is perhaps comparable to leather bindings in West Africa. The current binding appears to have replaced the original paper card cover. The cowhide binding may well have been made in Jamaica, and was added to preserve the manuscript, clearly demonstrating the value that the original owner put on the text, whether this is the original text or a copy.[9] No other copy is known to exist.

The note written at the "back" of the *Kitāb al-salāt* in English is dated 11 March 1824, the date the manuscript was apparently received at BMS headquarters in London; this establishes that it was not only written before late 1823, but that the notebook was also bound by that date, at least. It is likely, therefore, that the present version was written in c.1820 or earlier, by someone who had access to Baptist notepaper – perhaps after Thomas Godden became the pastor at Spanish Town in 1819, but there are various ways in which the paper could have been obtained.[10] Various preachers associated with the Baptists, most especially George Lewis, visited the Manchester mountains regularly, and he or another itinerant Baptist may have provided the notebook for this particular copy.[11] Lewis was a close friend of Kabā, and hence it is perhaps most logical that Lewis was the source of the notebook in which Kabā's text was written, or copied.

Kabā's relationship with George Lewis is particularly noteworthy. Like Kabā, Lewis came from the upper Guinea coast and had been taken as a slave to Jamaica, but unlike Kabā Lewis then went to Virginia, where he remained in slavery and converted to Christianity, becoming a Baptist. Lewis subsequently returned to Jamaica, and a Miss Valentine of Kingston became his owner. Lewis then became an itinerant merchant travelling the countryside as Miss Valentine's agent. Lewis earned a local following as a preacher, using his mobility to visit different plantations. He was at Spice Grove frequently, at least as early as 1815, although he was not popular with managers of the coffee and sugar estates. In 1816 the overseer at Spice Grove "was determined to take up George Lewis & put him to jail;"[12] however, Kabā was instrumental in raising funds to help Lewis purchase his freedom from Miss Valentine,[13] which must have exacerbated the tension with Robinson. Lewis is most likely the source of the notebook used for *Kitāb al-salāt*, although he probably obtained it from Reverend Godden or another Baptist missionary in Kingston.

The *Kitāb al-salāt* is difficult to read: it is blurred in parts, and Muhammad Kabā seems to have had difficulty in accurately pronouncing some words, which is revealed in numerous mistakes in his writing. At least the Arabic with which he was familiar seems to have been the colloquial form common in West Africa at the time. The fact that the author was not a native Arabic speaker is clear, especially in the grammar, or lack of grammar, which makes some passages difficult to understand. In addition, some words are not readily intelligible, and probably could only be understood by someone familiar with the way the author spoke and pronounced words. The errors of spelling, grammar and vocalization present major problems in deciphering meanings, further suggesting that the author was not a practised writer, probably because he did not have much opportunity in Jamaica. For example, he wrote "al-Bukari" instead of "al-Bukhārī", "ta'yala" instead of "tāla", and "'Ashuma'anna" instead of "'Uthmān". Some words are difficult to decipher, such as "sakīdatu". The construction of sentences is also problematic.

Muhammad Kabā's *Kitāb al-salāt* contains two sections that focus on prayer and the rituals associated with praying; there is additional and important information in each section that suggests the level of instruction among Muslims in Jamaica in the early nineteenth century. The first section concerns the classical subject of eschatology, and is in the form of speeches and exhortations about desire and fear, which are equated with heaven and hell. The second section focuses on ablutions before praying, the place of praying and what to pray, but in the middle is inserted a marriage contract. This mix of different subjects relating to what it takes to be a Muslim may have been used as a manual of instruction, providing an example of how Islamic marriages may have been consecrated in Jamaica under slavery, and how Muslims attempted to retain other rituals and details of their religion.

In the first section Kabā addresses the "*Jamā'atu 'l-muslimīna wa 'l-muslimāt*" – that is, the community of Muslim men and Muslim women – three times: the first part of the speech implores people to submit to Allāh, the second concerns "the matter of the tomb", and the third addresses the obligation of Muslims to pray five times daily. This part of *Kitāb al-salāt* is a series of exhortations for prayer, emphasizing Friday but, curiously, not mentioning the main Friday prayer itself, which is commonly a large communal gathering (*salāt al-jumu'a*). Kabā writes, for example, "Whoever prays the dawn prayer [*fajr*] on a Friday, it is as though he prayed with 'Ali b. Abī Tālib [cousin and son in law of the Prophet]". He then discusses situations in which prayers are missed, referring to *Kitāb al-Munabbihāt* of Ahmad b. 'Alī b. Hajar al-'Asqalānī, and singling out *hadīth* attributed to 'Abd Allāh b. al-Mubārak. He cites the *Sahīhs* of Muslim and Bukhārī, two classic books on *hadīth* (the traditions of the Prophet). He mentions several prophets and their qualities. He refers to the ending of the world and the eternity of the other world. He discusses the tomb, the straight path, and death, using as examples Solomon and others who had once lived in this world but died nonetheless. He identifies the signs of the end of the world, painting a grim picture of how people will perspire excessively when the world is ending; although people will seek out each and every prophet to ask for intercession, none of these save Muhammad is capable. The author then admonishes readers to follow the straight path, and warns them of the questions that will be asked; people must pass the test. Apparently as a symbol of legitimacy, he states that he finished the book on a Friday. As verification, he notes that people whom he identifies as "Jews" referred to him by his Muslim name, Muhammad Kabā Saghanughu.[14]

Kabā inserts several important comments that help to put his *Kitāb al-salāt* in perspective with reference to the condition of enslaved Muslims in the Americas, and specifically in Jamaica. His confession that he has lost touch with the tradition of scholarship and instruction available in West Africa is particularly poignant and revealing:

> I do not know anything of the knowledge of *al-Bahr*.[15] My memory [reason] is cor-
> rupted. I am not finding science. I have started asking for pardon day and night. I
> ask for pardon for every situation [. . .] I have learned these words from Shayhk
> Bābā al-Fakīru. . . . The speech [book] ends, as Abū Madyan said, end.[16]

While the significance of this concluding commentary requires fuller discussion than is presented here, it should be noted that Kabā was aware of his isolation, and hence the manuscript and other evidence of Islamic instruction should be situated within the context of slavery and not be glorified as a "survival" or evidence of power, other than spiritual.

The second section or book, like the first, begins with the phrase "In the name of Allāh Most gracious, Most Merciful", the standard opening of any important document. This section, like the first, ends with a colophon. However, the second section or book inexplicably has what appears to be a marriage contract, inserted without transition or explanation. This contract ends with "It was correctly [done] by the hands of Almami in the religion of Allāh." The text mentions Is-hāq b. 'Alī al-Dāramī,[17] Muhammad Mā and 'Isā Ayay Mālikī, and refers to testimonies involving wives, including the first wife of al-Hājj Walāti, Fatīma, the second wife, Zaynab, and the third wife, Maryam. He then returns to the subject of ablutions and what to say when performing them, and then what to say while praying. Kabā provides a formalized ending for the manuscript, concluding, "The speech is finished [. . .], book of Kabā Saqanuqu."

Despite weaknesses in style and form, Kabā's *Kitāb al-salāt* is clearly not composed of portions of the Qur'ān, which other evidence indicates was in fact available to Muslims in Jamaica, having been written down from memory at least once.[18] This manuscript is proof that the Muslim community managed to preserve knowledge of texts familiar to the Qādiriyya brotherhood [*tarīqa*] of West Africa, many of which Kabā cites from memory. The style of preservation reveals an educational format that was common in West Africa, particularly among those associated with the Qādiriyya. Indeed, the manuscript is solid evidence that the Qādiriyya, as a *sūfī* order, was to be found in Jamaica in the early nineteenth century, and clearly reflects an attempt to preserve this particular system of instruction.[19]

The *Kitāb al-salāt* is a commentary and instructional manual on Islam, with references to a deep and sophisticated tradition of education and transmission. It is equally clear that the author was the leader of a Muslim community in Jamaica, despite the impediments to remaining in touch with much of his Islamic heritage and its institutions. Despite the chain of transmission in leadership that is reminiscent of West Africa, Kabā did not have access to the books or to the intellectual apprenticeship associated with the Qādiriyya in West Africa. Nonetheless, Kabā, Abū Bakr al-Siddīq and other Muslims successfully maintained a sense of community as Muslims, communicating in writing, even as they had to disguise their Muslim identity through the use of Christian names, hiding behind the cloak of evangelical missionary Christianity. They used the spoken word to convey a message of accommodation and adherence to Christianity, while they used written Arabic and identifying symbols, such as names, to claim their religious autonomy and spiritual superiority as Muslims. An Arabic grammar and the Qur'ān were essential for the preservation of the community of believers, hence their request to Magistrate R.R. Madden in 1834 for these essential tools of instruction.[20]

The author states his name at the end of the first section of the manuscript, and again at the end of the second section, as Muhammad Kabā Saghanughu.[21] The name reveals much about his background and his relationship to his homeland in West Africa. Muhammad, the name usually given to the first-born son by Muslims, is easily recognizable as Muslim. Indeed, this is stated in the account of Muhammad Kabā's life as recorded by Madden: "The first son, he says, is always called Mohammed".[22] The Moravian minister J.H. Buchner considered Kabā "by birth a Mandingo".[23] According to Angell, Kabā "was born in a place called Bouka, in the Mandingo country, nine days' journey from the sea-side, and near the country of the Fouhlahs, the capital of which is Timbo".[24] Bouka is to be identified with one of the Saghanughu towns in the region of Worodugu, south of Kong, Jenne and Timbuktu and east of Futa Jallon, where kola nuts were obtained for the markets of the savanna.[25] Kabā is a common patronymic among Mandingo and other Muslim Manding in the western Sudan, in fact constituting a clan of the Jakhanke, the merchant and clerical diaspora in the Greater Senegambia region.[26] The Jakhanke were active in Futa Jallon, the neighbouring gold fields of Bambukhu, and along the routes further into the interior.[27] The Saghanughu were an important clerical family among the Jakhanke. They were noted for teaching the Islamic sciences, and were associated with the tradition of scholarship founded by *shaykh* Sālim al-Sūwarī in the late fifteenth century.[28]

Although Muhammad Kabā identifies himself twice in the text, the covering note on the *Kitāb al-salāt*, in English, states that the text was written by "a Young Mandingo Negro" and came to the attention of Reverend Godden in Spanish Town, apparently through "a Negro named Brailsford", who was a deacon in the Baptist church in Kingston, where James Coultart was the minister.[29] There is no further identification of the "Young Mandingo Negro" or Brailsford, but if the author was Muhammad Kabā Saghanughu, he was not young in 1824 (he was sixty-eight). He had been absent from West Africa at least forty-six years by that time, having left in about 1777. Indeed, the author's lament that he was losing his memory confirms his claim that he had been long removed from Africa. Hence the "Young Mandingo Negro" may only have been the person who gave the manuscript to Deacon Brailsford, or he could have been someone who had copied the manuscript, as was common in the system of education among Muslims in West Africa.

Despite this apparent confusion, the author is the same person as "Mahomed Caba", alias Robert Peart, alias Robert Tuffit,[30] who came to the attention of Magistrate Madden in 1834. On 7 October 1834 Benjamin Angell, "one of the most respectable inhabitants" of Manchester parish and owner of Adam's Valley, sent Madden a letter informing him of an unusual Muslim elder who was literate in Arabic, and whom he had come to know, apparently through the Moravian mission at nearby Fairfield.[31] Angell forwarded Kabā's letter to Madden because the magistrate had taken a personal interest in the Muslims he had discovered, to his surprise, among the enslaved population. Madden had notably befriended Abū Bakr al-Siddīq, who had been born in Timbuktu and had grown up in the commercial centre of Jenne, on the Niger River southwest of Timbuktu. After Madden took an interest in al-Siddīq, he attempted to arrange for his emancipation, which initially proved difficult. However, after his efforts were reported in the Kingston *Herald*, Madden was able to convince al-Siddīq's master to free him. The incident appears to have been widely known at the time.[32] Thereafter Madden collected considerable information on Muslims in Jamaica, including the correspondence between al-Siddīq and Kabā. Madden later published al-Siddīq's autobiography and introduced him to the Royal Geographical Society, unsuccessfully attempting to secure his employment as a guide for future British expeditions in West Africa.[33]

Otherwise, where Kabā came from is a mystery, his identified home, Bouka, not being recognized. His father was "Abon loo de Kadri" (apparently a representation of 'Abd al-Qādiri), and was a wealthy merchant, a common occupation of the Kabā clan. According to what Madden was told, Kabā's father "was a substantial yeoman, possessing 140 slaves, several cows and horses, and grounds producing quantities of cotton, rice, and provisions, which he exchanged for European and other commodities brought from the coast by Higglers [merchants]".[34] The Kabā, and specifically the Saghanughu, belonged to the Qādiriyya brotherhood in the western Sudan, and while the Qādiriyya was closely associated with the *jihād* movement, the Kabā were known to oppose *jihād*; instead, they propagated a quietist and tolerant tradition that was partially related to the fact that their commercial communities tended to be in areas where non-Muslims were in the majority.[35] Moreover, Kabā was captured near an unnamed town where his uncle lived, another of the many towns in the western Sudan in which there were Saghanughu clerical families – but, again, the exact location cannot be identified.[36]

Muhammad Kabā was well educated, according to his own testimony, "partly by his father, but principally by his uncle, Mohammed Batoul, who was a great lawyer, and had designed him for the same profession". According to Buchner, Kabā

> was taught to read and write, and early initiated into the Mahometan faith, being designed for an expounder of their law. When about twenty years of age, he went on a visit to his uncle, previous to his entering "the great school of Timbuctoo" to finish his studies. While there [at his uncle's] he was waylaid, and carried down the coast to be sold. His relations endeavoured to ransom him, but in vain: he was brought to Jamaica: this was about the year 1777.[37]

From the manuscript it is clear that Kabā had studied the basic subjects: Qur'ān, *hadīth*, *fiqh*. He refers to the *Sahīhs* of Muslim and Bukhāri, both books on *hadīth*, and he cites 'Abd Allāh b. al-Mubārak, mentioned in *Kitāb al-*

Munabbihāt. He refers to *shaykh* Bābā al-Fakiru, who seems to have been one of his teachers, and to the classical scholar, Abū Madyan (*c.* AH 509–594, that is, *c.* AD 1115–1198).[38] These references suggest a standard Islamic education as instituted by the Qādiriyya in West Africa.[39] According to John Hunwick, the style of scholarship focused on a "core curriculum" consisting of the *Muwatta'* of Imam Mālik, the *Shifā'* of Qādī 'Iyad b. Mūsā, and the *Tafsīr al-Jalālayn*.[40] It is possible that Mohammed Batoul is to be identified with Muhammad al-Mustafā b. 'Abbas, the famous Saghanughu cleric who died in 1776–77, the same year that Kabā was enslaved. Muhammad al-Mustafā's tomb at Boron, in northern Côte d'Ivoire, is a place of pilgrimage to this day.[41]

Both the names Kabā and Saghanughu establish the author's connection with the Jakhanke and the Qādiriyya. In the western Sudan the Qādiriyya was associated both with the *jihād* movement and with a quietist, pacifist tradition. The Kabā were associated with this latter quietist tradition that advocated accommodation with local rulers and non-Muslim societies.[42] Moreover, the examples of marriage in the *Kitāb al-salāt* include a reference to Is-hāqī b. 'Ali al-Dārami. The Darame were associated with the holy town of Gunjur in Senegambia. According to Lansine Sanneh, "the Darame clerics were treated as the heirs-apparent of al-Hājj Sālim [shaykh Sālim al-Sūwarī] . . . and fathered numerous saints . . . , jurists, ascetics . . . , and scholars".[43] While the context of the reference in *Kitāb al-salāt* is unclear, it nonetheless further establishes a connection between the Muslim community of Jamaica and the Qādiriyya, further connecting Kabā with this branch of Islamic scholarship.

Although it has not been possible to identify either Kabā's family's home or that of his uncle, the points of reference should be noted. The location with respect to Timbo (the capital of Futa Jallon), the distance from the sea, and the association with a route to Timbuktu suggest that Kabā came from one of the towns in what is now northern Côte d'Ivoire, where the Saghanughu had founded numerous communities before the mid-eighteenth century. These communities were located to the east of Futa Jallon, about nine days from the coast, and in the region that was known as "Mandingo" country. Instead of reaching Timbuktu, Kabā was taken across the Atlantic. Ironically, Kabā came to live near another "Tombuctoo", one of the estates owned by Angell, whose testimony has been noted above.

As Kabā's text makes clear, there were Muslims in Jamaica who were literate, and to some extent this elite was using the written word in a script indecipherable to the white masters as a means of "secret" communication that offered potential for sabotage and resistance. In 1831 Kabā allegedly had in his possession a document that was deemed sufficiently incriminating that his wife destroyed it at the time of the 1831 Christmas rebellion. This pastoral letter (wathīqa) "exhorted all the followers of Mahomet to be true and faithful if they wished to go to Heaven, etc.";[44] other than this exhortation, the contents of the letter are not known. Kabā's wife feared that its contents would be interpreted as support for the 1831–32 uprising, and so she destroyed it. The letter was supposedly written in West Africa, which, if accurate, reveals a considerable degree of communication linking the Jamaican community with West Africa. As Ivor Wilks has observed, we do not know what Muslims in diaspora were able to learn about the momentous events in West Africa relating to the jihād movement. If the pastoral letter is dated to 1826–27 and was an exhortation to religious observance, then it might well have been incriminating. The letters between al-Siddīq and Kabā seem conspiratorial, which is to be expected in a slave regime.

Muhammad Kabā and Abū Bakr al-Siddīq appear to have known each other, although for how long is not known. Madden learned that the two men "for some time past [had] carried on a correspondence".[45] Madden realized that both Kabā and al-Siddīq maintained a commitment to Islam, despite verbal assurances of Christian belief, which is clear in the letter from Kabā forwarded by Angell to Madden. Although the original Arabic has not been located, Kabā reportedly wrote,

> In the name of God, Merciful omnificent, the blessing of God, the peace of his [P]rophet Mahomet. This is from the hand of Mahomed Caba, unto Bekir Sadiki Scheriffe.[46] If this comes into your hands sooner or later, send me a satisfactory answer for yourself this time by your real name, don't you see I give you my name, Robert Tuffit [Peart],[47] and the property is named Spice Grove. I am glad to hear you are master of yourself, it is a heartfelt joy to me, for Many told me about your character. I thank you to give me a good answer, "Salaam aleikoum". Edward Donlan, I hear of your name in the paper: the reader told me how so much you write.[48]

In congratulating Abū Bakr al-Siddīq on receiving his freedom, the letter reveals Kabā's continuing commitment to Islam, despite his association with the Moravians.

When Angell approached Madden in 1834, he suggested that Kabā's "short and simple annals . . . may not be uninteresting to you".[49] He could not have more greatly understated the significance of the "annals". Kabā, alias Dick or Robert Peart, had lived at Spice Grove for fifty-seven years by that point. He remained there for such a long time that his influence must have been considerable. He held a privileged position with the Moravians, being appointed "Helper" – that is, an elder. Because of his prominence, Spice Grove must have become a centre of Islam in Jamaica, even under cover of the Moravians. According to Angell, Muhammad Kabā "has always borne an irreproachable character, and maintained a high place in the estimation of his employers".[50] This evaluation, in the context of Jamaica under slavery, suggests that Kabā did not drink or otherwise behave in a way that would defile the conscience of a devout Muslim. Such behaviour was consistent with the teachings of the Moravian Brethren as well. The reference to his character, combined with the way in which his book reflects his knowledge of Islamic literary tradition and the style and substance of his correspondence with Abū Bakr al-Siddīq, seem to suggest more. Kabā was certainly capable of running a Qur'ānic school, and from the evidence he likely would have attempted to do so. Yet there is no evidence of such a school at Spice Grove at this point – other than the possibility of the manuscript being a copy, which might indicate tutoring, at least (copying being a standard pedagogical technique of West African Islam, and the Qādiriyya in particular).[51]

In his investigations, Madden had inadvertently stumbled on a small Muslim community that had existed in Jamaica since at least the end of the eighteenth century and that identified itself as Mandingo.[52] It is instructive that Muhammad Kabā addressed the "community of believers" ("jamā'at al-muslimīna wa 'l-muslimāt"), using the phrase three times. Bryan Edwards had learned of the presence of Mandingo clerics in Jamaica in the eighteenth century, and other contemporary observers also noted their presence and their identification with Islam elsewhere.[53] It remains to ask if there were connections between Muslims in Jamaica and Muslims elsewhere in the Caribbean and North America; the existence of a pastoral letter that was supposedly written in West Africa suggests that there is reason to believe that some communication occurred. The Trinidad community was particularly well organized in the 1820s and 1830s, under Mohammed Bath and others. The Muslim leaders claimed that there were no Muslims in Trinidad who were still enslaved at the time of emancipation in 1834, a far different situation than in Jamaica, where al-Siddīq and Kabā were both slaves.[54] In Trinidad, as in Jamaica, Muslims were generally known as Mandingo, which suggests a parallel that may have been reinforced by direct communication. As elsewhere in the Caribbean and in North America, Mandingo were identified with Islam. There were similar communities of "Mandingo" in the United States, Antigua and probably elsewhere.[55]

Abū Bakr al-Siddīq answered Kabā's letter of congratulations on 18 October 1834, addressing him "dear countryman", and asking for his prayers and for the prayers of the community, noting, "whenever you wish to send me a letter, write it in [the] Arabic language; then I will understand it properly".[56] Abū Bakr al-Siddīq recounted the principal details of his life, from his birth in Timbuktu to his education in Jenne, and the good fortune that he had experienced in Jamaica despite slavery, attributing his fate to God. He expressed allegiance to Britain and its king, and called for unity within the Muslim community. He asked Kabā to pray for his former master, who under Madden's pressure had voluntarily freed Abū Bakr al-Siddīq, without financial compensation. Apparently there was hope for the same treatment for other Muslims, thereby holding the hope of release from the period of apprenticeship that was to last until 1838.

In the *Kitāb al-salāt* Kabā talks about losing his memory, reflecting a preoccupation with his ability to cite Islamic texts accurately. There are some indications of efforts to communicate with other Muslims, and thereby attempt to sustain Islamic scholarship. At least, as described above, sometime after 1827 he came into the possession of a pastoral letter that his wife deemed sufficiently incriminating to destroy in the anxious times of 1831–32. As the *Kitāb al-salāt* demonstrates, Kabā may have had difficulty remembering his Islamic education, but the book also clearly demonstrates that he tried his best to sustain his faith and convey the teachings of Islam to other Muslims. The manuscript is a remarkable testimony to the memory of this Muslim, its many citations and quotations evidence of Kabā's education and retentive abilities. Usually in writing a treatise on praying a scholar would have access to classical texts, which Kabā did not, relying instead on what he could remember, and then not writing it down until more than twenty years after last having had access to a library.

Appendix

The Kitāb al-salāt of Muhammad Kabā Saghanughu of Jamaica c.1823[57]

First Part

In the name of Allāh, Most gracious, Most Merciful. Allāh's blessings and peace be upon our Master Muhammad – His Prophet – and his family and companions [. . .]

Allāh Almighty said: "Be wary of Allāh [. . .] and perform your prayers day and night [even] when people are asleep." You sleep but God does not sleep. You sleep but the devil does not sleep. You sleep but the angels do not sleep. O [brother], wake up, because sleep is a waste; because you will regret it. You will regret it. O community of Muslim men and women [yā Jamā'at al-Muslimīna wa-'l-muslimāt], think about the matter of this world. This world must be submission to Allāh because Allāh said: "He who obeys Allāh and His Prophet will enter paradise for ever and he who disobeys Him and His Prophet will enter hell forever."[58]

The Prophet in the book [. . .] said: "Whoever prays the dawn prayer [fajr] on a Friday, it is as though he prayed with 'Ali b. Abī Tālib,[59] may Allāh be pleased with him. Whoever says the prayer of noon [duhr] on a Friday, it is as if he prayed with 'Uthmān b. 'Affān,[60] may Allāh be pleased with him. Whoever says the prayer of the afternoon ['asr] on a Friday, it is as though he prayed with 'Umar b. al-Khattāb,[61] may Allāh be pleased with him. Whoever says the prayer after sunset [maghrib] on a Friday, it is as though he prayed with Abū Bakr al-Siddīq,[62] may Allāh be pleased with him. Whoever says the prayer of the night ['atama or 'isha']; 'atama and 'isha' are the same;[63] it is as if he prayed with Muhammad, Allāh's blessings and peace be upon him."

The Prophet said: "Whoever performs the five prayers washes five times a day. Will he remain dirty? [Likewise], he who says the five prayers will remain [. . . .]"[64]

The Prophet said: "He who does not say his prayers; it is as if he [. . .] his mother inside the Ka'ba." The Prophet said: "Whoever [. . .] his mother inside the Ka'ba is [closer?] to the blessing of Allāh." The Prophet said: "[Delaying the prayers will delay] four things: sleep in the tomb, delaying the weighing of deeds and delaying the resting in paradise."[65] 'Abd Allāh b. al-Mubārak[66] said in a book entitled *Al-Munabbihāt*:[67] Four [voices] will speak for everyone: Angels will speak about the soul; the [. . .] will speak about the flesh; the parents will speak about the material world [?]; the tyrant by his deeds. The pious people said in the book of Muslim[68] and Bukhārī,[69] Allāh will compensate four [kinds of people] through [the fate of] four [Prophets]: the slave by Joseph; the poor by Jesus; the sick by Job; the rich by Solomon, Allāh's blessings and peace be upon them.[70]

This world lasts only one hour because Allāh Almighty said: "All that is on earth will perish but will abide [for ever]; the face of thy Lord Full of Majesty, Bounty and Honour."[71] This world is a house for the one who does not have a place in paradise.[72] This world is carrion, who asks for it is like a dog. The things of this world are insignificant; they are [the objects of] vanity, for people who have illusions. The afterworld is the place of happiness. Do not hold this world on your heads. And do not prefer [. . .] to [. . .] because [. . . .] O community of Muslim men and Muslim women Think about the matter of the tomb; because the tomb is dark, and its secret is obedience to Allāh; because the path [*sirāt*] is darkness, and its secret is charity.[73]

O community of Muslim men and Muslim women Think about the matter of death. Did it not come to Solomon, son of David, who possessed the world and its comforts? He died. Was not it the case of Alexander the Great, Bū-'l-Qarnayn,[74] [who] possessed the world and its comforts? He died. Was it not the case of Namrūd son of Kan'ān who possessed the world and its comforts? He died. Was it not the case of the king [. . .] who possessed the world and its comforts? He died. Was it not the case for the ones who preceded us and the ones who will come after us? Everybody will die.

The day of judgment when the trumpet will be blown, they will cry in their tombs [. . .] line by line. They will stand in five places. Each one lasts one thousand years. On the first day of the end of the world, the sun will be a span of one hand above the heads of people.[75] [. . .] Their heads will hurt seventy times more. People will say "my head, my head, my head". People will not recognize their parents and parents will not recognize their children, because the judgment day is [the day] when people pay their debts.

People will sweat all over their bodies.[76] Some will feel the sweat on their legs, some on their feet, some on their navels, some on their knees, some on their thighs, some on their [. . .], some on their [. . .], some on their hips, some on their bellies, some on their chests, some on their [. . .], some on their necks, some on their lips, some on their faces, some on their heads. Some will sink in their sweat like [. . .] sinking in water.

When people are exhausted of waiting, and after they have faced so much hardship, they will ask for intercession.[77] They will go to Adam; they will tell him: "O Adam, intercede for us this day. The [test of] endurance and the fear of punishment have exhausted the people. [Their minds have gone]. Their children look old, and the elders look young [senile]." Adam will say: "I cannot [do anything] today."

They will go to Noah, and they will tell him: "O Noah, intercede for us this day. The endurance and the fear of punishment have exhausted the people. [Their minds have gone.] Their children look old and the elders look young." Noah will say: "I cannot [do anything] today."

They will go to Abraham, and they will tell him: "O Abraham, intercede for us this day. The endurance and the fear of punishment have exhausted the people. [Their minds have gone.] Their children look like old and the elders look young." Abraham will say: "I cannot [do anything] today."

They will go to Moses, and they will tell him: "O Moses, intercede for us on this day. The endurance and the fear of punishment have exhausted the people. [Their minds have gone.] Their children look old and the elders look young." Moses will say, like his brothers: "I cannot [do anything] today."

They will go to Jesus ['Isā], and they will tell him: "O Jesus, intercede for us on this day. The endurance and the fear of punishment have exhausted the people. [Their minds have gone.] Their children look old and the elders look young." Jesus will say, like his brothers: "I cannot [do anything] today."

They will go to Muhammad, Allāh's blessings and peace be upon him, and they will tell him: "O Prophet of Allāh, intercede for us on this day. The endurance and the fear of punishment have exhausted the people. [Their minds have gone.] Their children look old and the elders look young."

The Prophet of Allāh will then fly and will land above the throne. He will fall down [. . .] in front [of Allāh]. [He] will tell him, "O Prophet of Allāh, raise your head. There is no prostration and no bowing on this day. You ask, [and] I will give. Today, you get what you were promised."

The Prophet will say: "The endurance and the fear of punishment have exhausted the people. [Their minds have gone.] Their children look old and the elders look young."[78]

Today is the day of separation between the ones who will be happy and the ones who will be punished. Allāh will give orders to the angels [. . . .] They will bring earth. He will expand it under their feet [. . . .] No injustice will be committed on it. They will carry him and walk the distance of five hundred years.

Hell will be put in a huge hole whose opening will be suspended on the top of people. All the people will tremble. The Prophet of Allāh will take the opening of hell with one hand and will fly with it five hundred years. Snakes and scorpions will take the sinners among the people and fly to fire. The snakes are as big as cows and scorpions as [. . . .] Even when the snakes and scorpions are biting for one year no poison will enter the body.

People will be given books [of their deeds]. The ones who receive their books with their right hands will be the winners. Angels will lift them above the crowds. They will tell them "O so and so, son of so and so, [you are granted] happiness, no sadness thereafter."

The ones who get their books from behind their backs, with their left hands, are the corrupt ones. The angels will lift them above the crowds. They will tell them. The angels will lift them above the crowds. They will tell them:[79] "O so and so, son of so and so, [you are condemned] to misery, no happiness thereafter." They will bring the balance and it will go down. [They weigh] the deeds of people. The ones who [are] good will be safe. The ones who [are] bad are the corrupt ones.

They will follow the path [sirāt], which is situated on the top of hell. The path is thinner than a hair [. . . .] You never find such a darkness. It has seven corners.

On the first corner, people will be asked about their prayers. If they performed them, they will pass; otherwise, they will fall into hell. On the second corner, people will be asked about alms. If they provided them, they will pass; otherwise, they will fall into hell. On the third corner, people will be asked about the fasting. If they performed it, they will pass; otherwise, they will fall into hell. On the fourth corner, people will be asked about the pilgrimage. If they performed it, they will pass; otherwise, they will fall into hell. On the fifth corner, people will be asked about the obligations to parents. If they performed them, they will pass; otherwise, they will fall into hell. On the sixth corner, people will be asked about the rights of the gathering [of the community] [haqq al-majlis]. If they performed them, they will pass; otherwise, they will fall into hell. On the seventh corner, people will be asked about the rights of worldly existence [haqq al-dunyā]. If they performed them, they will pass; otherwise, they will fall into hell.[80]

'Uthmān stands on the beginning of the path, 'Umar on one side, 'Alī in the middle, Gabriel on the other side, and Abū Bakr at the end of the path. Until the last person of the nation [*umma*] of the Prophet of Allāh, blessings and peace of Allāh be upon him, will pass.

Some people will pass on the path like lightning; others will pass like wind, others will pass like birds; others will pass like [. . .] of horses; others like [. . .]; others will walk like [. . .]; others will make it to the end of the path walking on their knees; some will stand on the path [. . .]; some will follow the path on their bellies like snakes. Some will cross the path in one year; others will cross it in one thousand years. All the people will follow the path according to their deeds.

The book is finished. The last day of writing by the hands of the '*abd* [slave or person] is Friday. The Jews refer to the name of the one who owns the writing as Muhammad Kabā Saqanuqu [Saghanughu]. I am Muhammad Kabā Saqanuqu. I do not know anything of the knowledge of *al-Bahr*.[81] My memory [reason] is corrupted. I am not finding science. I have started asking for pardon day and night. I ask for pardon for every situation [. . . .]

I have learned these words from Shayhk Bāb al-Fakīru, who said: "Whoever hides knowledge [will be bridled with a bridle of fire]."[82] "End." The speech [book] ends, as Abū Madyan[83] said, end.

Second Part

In the name of Allāh, Most gracious, Most Merciful.

Section. The obligation of ablutions [*wudū'*]: pure water, clean [*tāhir*] clothes, clean prayer ground.[84] The Prophet of Allāh avoided praying in the lair of the lion or in his path, [. . .], near tombs, [. . .] in the doorways of houses, [. . .], in the place of coitus [*mawdi'u al-wat'*], the places of unbelievers, and [. . . .][85]

Ablutions are made with water whose colour has not changed, and water [. . . .] The conditions of using sand ablutions [*tayammum*] are absence of water, being sick and not being able to wash; then one can use *tayammum*.[86] [. . .]

When one bows [*raka'a*], one should say: "Glory and praise be to the sublime Lord." When prostrating one should recite the following: "Glory to God. I abused myself, and did wrong. Grant pardon to me [. . . .]"[87]

O Allāh, bless Muhammad and the family of Muhammad three times. O Allāh, bless Muhammad and the family of Muhammad three times. Praise be to Allāh Who permitted to us what is permitted and forbade fornication and [created man] from water, and established lineages and marriages. Your God is Most Powerful.[88]

I take you, O Angels of God and Muslim men and Muslim women who are present here, as witnesses that the son of so and so wants to contract a marriage between so and so and the daughter of so and so. We married her to him according to the obligation of Allāh, the traditions [sunna] of His Prophet, and the acts which saints regard as acceptable.

Then [reciting] three times, "Have we not expanded thee thy breast" until "Turn thy attention".[89]

Her dowry is declared, received with grace, and [even, if necessary] her divorce with benevolence. Allāh may bring between us and the married couple, [love], happiness, richness, and worthy offspring, for the umma [community] of Muhammad, Allāh's blessings and peace be upon him.

May Allāh grant pardon to me, to my parents, their parents, our brothers, the brothers of our brothers, our kinsmen, the kin of our kin people, our teacher, the teacher of our teacher, for all the Muslim men and Muslim women and pious men and women; all of them, the ones who are alive and the dead ones. You are the Most Powerful. May God bless Muhammad, Allāh's blessings and peace be upon him.

It was correctly [done] by the hands of Almami [imām, leader of the community] in the religion of Allāh and the religion of the Prophet, Allāh's blessings and peace be upon him. This is a duty, the obligation of all Muslim men and Muslim women, from Adam to Muhammad and from Muhammad to the end of time.

[In accordance with] the sunna of your Prophet [O brother], this act of writing [the contract] is for the sake of Allāh and the Prophet. There are three concerned witnesses – Is-hāq b. 'Alī al-Daramī,[90] Muhammad Ma 'Isā, Iyāyi Mālikī. Certified between him and his wife [wives?] the name of the first wife of Hajj Walātī [. . .] Hajj Walātī Fatīma, the second Zaynab, the wife of Hajj Walātī, the third Maryam, the wife of Hajj Walātī; that it will be proof between us and them, in this world until the day of judgment, Allāh willing; no doubt about Him, He who [has] doubts about Him is an unbeliever [kāfir].

Section: The obligation of ablutions [wudū']. It is an obligation for all, the ones who are at the age of puberty [mukallaf] among the umma of Muhammad.

In the name of Allāh: what [to say/think] [niyya] when performing ablutions three times:

O Allāh, make me eat from [. . .] of paradise, O Allāh [. . .] from the fruits of paradise. O Allāh, make my face white as the white face of the pious and the virtuous people, and not as dark as the darkness of unbelievers and hypocrites, for the holiness of Muhammad, Allāh's blessings and peace be upon him. O Allāh, give me my book with the right hand, three times. O Allāh, protect my head from the trouble of the day of judgment, three times. [I will hear] with attentive ear three times. O Allāh, hold my feet on the path as you hold the feet of the pious and good people, three times. And not weaken my feet on the path as you weaken the feet of the unbelievers and hypocrites, for the sake of Muhammad, Allāh's blessings and peace be upon him.[91]

After the *tayammum* and ablutions, [one has to say]: I bear witness that no God exists but Allāh, alone with no associates, and bear witness that Muhammad is His servant and His Messenger.[92]

And calling for the prayer, you say in prostration three times: "Glory and praise be to the sublime Lord." Upon bowing you say three times: "Glory to God. I abused myself, and did wrong. Grant pardon to me." You recite the goodness of Allāh.[93]

By the prayer of dawn, submissiveness [*qunūt*],[94] "O Allāh we ask your help and seek your forgiveness, we believe in you, we ask your pardon, we abandon ourselves to you, we retire to you, and we cast off the people who [disobey] you. O Allāh we worship you and pray for you. We prostrate before you, we flee to you, we [. . .], we hope for your mercy. We fear very much your punishment. Your punishment will fall on the unbelievers."[95] End.

This is the obligation of the five prayers for the Muslim men and Muslim women of the *umma* of Muhammad, Allāh's blessings and peace be upon him.

The speech is finished [. . .], book of Kabā Saqanuqu.

Acknowledgements

We would like to thank several people for their assistance, including James Robertson, who introduced us to the manuscript and assisted our research, as well as providing comments on an early draft. Maureen Warner-Lewis also examined the Moravian Papers in the National Archives in Spanish Town and provided us with numerous leads. Sultana Afroz discussed her research on the history of Muslims in Jamaica with us, offering useful advice. We also thank various people at Spice Grove, especially Willy Robinson, who provided us with additional information and accompanied us to the cemetery on the estate. Support for this research came from the Social Sciences and Humanities Research Council of Canada and the York/UNESCO Nigerian Hinterland Project.

Notes

1. The manuscript is filed in the James Coultart Papers, Baptist Missionary Society Collection, Angus Library, Regent's Park College, Oxford University. It is listed in Kenneth E. Ingram, *Sources of Jamaican History, 1655–1838: A Bibliographical Survey with Particular Reference to Manuscript Sources*, vol. 1 (Zug: Inter Documentation, 1976), 525, where it is incorrectly identified as "a part of the Koran", following the description on the manuscript itself. The manuscript is filed with the papers of James Coultart, who was the Baptist minister in Kingston from 1817 to 1829; see John Clark, W. Dendy, and J.M. Phillippo, *The Voice of Jubilee: A Narrative of the Baptist Mission, Jamaica, from its Commencement; with Biographical Notices of its Fathers and Founders* (London: John Snow, 1865), 147–60. The American Southern Baptists, who transferred the BMS collection to microfilm, appear not to have copied the manuscript (personal communication, James Robertson, 13 April 2001). We wish to thank Audra Diptee for digitalizing the manuscript.

2. Robert Peart, Esq., a magistrate and colonel in the Jamaica Regiment during the Maroon War of 1795–96, was buried at Spice Grove, his tombstone giving his date of death as 1 January 1797, when Kabā had been there for twenty years. Two portraits, one of Peart and the other of Mrs Peart holding a small child, are in the possession of Willy Robinson, Spice Grove. For details on the Peart prop-

erties, see the map collection in the National Library, Kingston, especially: Nottingham Pen (M90), showing the boundary with Spice Grove, surveyed in 1800, and at the time belonging to John Peart; Lincoln (M112); Oatlands (M147), owned by Edward Peart in 1828; Manchester parish, 1838 (M258), showing various Peart properties. Also see St.E.846 which shows the locations of the great houses at Nottingham and Spice Grove. Spice Grove, Nottingham and Lincoln were contiguous, and in turn bordered Fairfield, where the Moravian mission was relocated in 1823. Also see Jamaica Almanack, 1811–1840, for references to the Peart properties, the number of enslaved inhabitants on the estates, and the acreage. We have also consulted the wills and inventories in the Island Records Office, Spanish Town.

3. John Lang, diary, F–1 – Fairfield, entry 27, Moravian Papers, National Archives, Spanish Town, Jamaica; also quoted in Maureen Warner-Lewis, "Religious Constancy and Compromise among Nineteenth Century Caribbean-Based African Muslims" (paper presented at the conference Slavery, Islam and Diaspora, York University, Toronto, 2003).

4. According to Warner-Lewis, "Religious Constancy", Mary Ann was originally named Peggy; she died on 17 January 1860 (citing Moravian Papers, Fairfield, D2, 1860, entry 1).

5. Lang diary, 27 August 1817.

6. Warner-Lewis, "Religious Constancy", citing Lang's diary for 1816.

7. For a biographical account of Kabā and his importance to the Muslim community in Jamaica before 1845, see Yacine Daddi Addoun and Paul Lovejoy, "Muhammad Kabā Saghanughu and the Muslim Community of Jamaica", in *Slavery on the Frontiers of Islam*, ed. Paul Lovejoy (Princeton: Markus Wiener, 2004); Warner-Lewis, "Religious Constancy"; and Michael A. Gomez, *Black Crescent: The Experience and Legacy of African Muslims in the Americas* (Cambridge: Cambridge University Press, 2005), 50–56.

8. See especially Ivor Wilks, "Abū Bakr al-Siddīq of Timbuktu", in *Africa Remembered: Narratives by West Africans from the Era of the Slave Trade*, ed. Philip D. Curtin (Madison: University of Wisconsin Press, 1967), 152–69. See also Sylviane A. Diouf, *Servants of Allāh: African Muslims Enslaved in the Americas* (New York: New York University Press, 1998), 55–56, 58–59; Allan D. Austin, *African Muslims in Antebellum America: A Sourcebook* (New York: Garland Publishing, 1984), 525–83; Austin, *African Muslims in Antebellum America: Transatlantic Stories and Spiritual Struggles* (New York: Routledge, 1997), 41; Sultana Afroz, "The Unsung Slaves: Islam in Plantation Jamaica: The African Connection", *Journal of Muslim Minority Affairs* 15 (1994): 163–64; Afroz, "From Moors to Marronage: The Islamic Heritage of the Maroons of Jamaica", *Journal of Muslim Minority Affairs* 19 (1999): 161–79; and Afroz, "The *Jihad* of 1831–1832:

The Misunderstood Baptist Rebellion in Jamaica", *Journal of Muslim Minority Affairs* 21 (2001): 232, 234, 236. For an overview, see Michael Gomez, *Exchanging Our Country Marks: The Transformation of African Identities in the Colonial and Antebellum South* (Chapel Hill: University of North Carolina Press, 1998); and Gomez, *Black Crescent*, 47–90.

9.   We wish to thank James Robertson for his description of the binding.

10. For a discussion of Godden's ministry in Jamaica, see Clark, Dendy, and Phillippo, *Voice of Jubilee*, 43–47, 166–70.

11. See, for example, John Clarke, *Memorials of Baptist Missionaries in Jamaica* (London: Yates and Alexander, 1869), 9–33; Clark, Dendy and Phillippo, *Voice of Jubilee*, 33–43; and various documents in the Moravian Papers, especially Lang's diary (February 1805 to November 1819), Fairfield, Q–7, and the various diaries of the Negro Congregation, 1824–25, 1826, 1827, 1828, 1829, 1831, 1835, 1836, 1841, 1843 (Fairfield, J–9, J–19, H–2, Q–8, Q–9, Q–10, J–14, J–15, J–16, J–12).

12. Lang Diary, 4 March 1816, quoted in Warner-Lewis, "Religious Constancy".

13. For a discussion of George Lewis and his connection with Kabā, see Warner-Lewis, "Religious Constancy". It is even possible that Lewis was originally a Muslim, since he came from the upper Guinea coast, and the relationship between Lewis and Kabā suggests a sense of shared community that may have derived from shared religion.

14. This reference to "Jews" may be to Benjamin Angell, and there were also estates owned by the Cohen family in the area.

15. He refers to the scholarship of one of his teachers, who is otherwise unnamed.

16. For the doctrinal and poetic works of Abū Madyan Shu 'ayb b. Husayn al-Ansārī, see Vincent J. Cornell, comp. and trans., *The Way of Abu Madyan: The Works of Abu Madyan Shu'ayb* (Cambridge: Islamic Texts Society, 1996).

17. According to Lamin O. Sanneh, the Darame clerics were the religious heirs of shaykh Sālim al-Sūwarī and therefore Qādiri like the Kabā clan; see Sanneh, *The Jakhanke: The History of an Islamic Clerical People of the Senegambia* (London: International African Institute, 1979), 19–20.

18. R.R. Madden, *A Twelvemonth's Residence in the West Indies, during the Transition from Slavery to Apprenticeship*, vol. 1 (1835; reprint, Westport, Conn.: Negro University Press, 1970), 99. For a discussion of Madden's career, see Edward J. Mullen, introduction to *The Life and Poems of a Cuban Slave*, by Juan Francisco Manzano (Hamden, Conn.: Archon, 1981), 4–12.

19. On the Qādiriyya, see Sanneh, *Jakhanke*, 38–43.

20. Madden had been appointed stipendiary magistrate in 1833 to oversee the emancipation of the enslaved population. He had previously travelled to Constantinople in 1824 and had lived in Egypt in 1825–27; see *Twelvemonth's Residence*, 1: 29.

21.   The author writes "Saqanuqu", a colloquial rendition – more properly,
      Saghanughu.

22.   Madden, *Twelvemonth's Residence*, 2: 135.

23.   J.H. Buchner, *The Moravians of Jamaica: History of the Mission of the United
      Brethren's Church to the Negroes in the Island of Jamaica, from the Year 1754 to 1854*
      (London: Longman, Brown, 1854), 50–51.

24.   B. Angell to Madden, Manchester, Jamaica, 7 October 1834, quoted in Madden,
      Twelvemonth's Residence, 2: 134.

25.   For the Saghanughu towns, see Ivor Wilks, "The Transmission of Islamic
      Learning in the Western Sudan", in *Literacy in Traditional Societies*, ed. Jack
      Goody (Cambridge: Cambridge University Press, 1968), 162–97. We wish to
      thank Ivor Wilks for discussing the possible location of Bouka, and Pierre Kipré
      for information on the foundation of the two towns of Bouaké in the interior of
      Côte d'Ivoire, one of which is located near Boron, but in both cases (the modern
      town of Bouaké north of Abidjan and the one near Boron) the towns are said to
      be of recent foundation. The location near Boron, if confirmed, would increase
      the likelihood that Kabā's uncle was the famous Qādiri cleric whose tomb is
      located there. Sylviane Diouf identifies Bouka with Bouna, which is south of
      Jenne but not near Futa Jallon; see *Servants of Allah*, 55. Afroz claims that Bouka
      was near Timbuktu, apparently mistaking Timbo, capital of the "Foullah coun-
      try", for Timbuktu; see *"Jihad* of 1831–1832", 232. In an earlier paper we identi-
      fied Bouka with Boké, located on the Rio Nunez, at the coast; see "The Arabic
      Manuscript of Muhammad Kabā Saghanughu of Jamaica, *c*.1823" (paper pre-
      sented at the second Conference on Caribbean Culture, University of the West
      Indies, Mona, Jamaica, 9–12 January 2002). After consultations with Ivor Wilks,
      we now favour a location in the interior, as outlined here.

26.   On the Kabā clan of Jakhanke, see Sanneh, *Jakhanke*, 38–43. Kabā is also a family
      name that is found in upper Guinea among Maninka Mori, or Muslim Maninka.
      The Kabā family founded the Maninka Mori capital city of Kankan (we wish to
      thank Walter Hawthorne for this information). There were a number of Kabā
      who ended up in slavery in the Americas. See, for example, the account of
      Lamine Kabā, who was born in Futa Jallon in about 1780 and was taken to the
      southern United States in about 1807, obtaining his freedom in 1834; see
      Austin, *African Muslims Sourcebook*, 415, and the account of Ibrahima Kabwee
      [Kabā] from Kankan, in ibid., 434–36. Also see Wilks, "Abū Bakr al-Siddīq",
      152–69. Sultana Afroz argues that the name Kabā has significance as "a symbol
      of Islamic unity, [as it] is the first house of Allāh initiated by Prophet Ibrahim".
      However, she is referring to *ka'ba*, which is entirely a different word, and her
      argument ignores the prevalence of Kabā as a patronymic in West Africa. See
      Afroz, *"Jihad* of 1831–1832", 236.

27. For Futa Jallon in this period, see Boubacar Bary, *Senegambia and the Atlantic Slave Trade* (Cambridge: Cambridge University Press, 1998), 99–102, 148–50; and Sanneh, *Jakhanke*, 94–105.

28. Ivor Wilks, *Forests of Gold: Essays on the Akan and the Kingdom of Asante* (Athens: Ohio University Press, 1993), 21–22; Wilks, "Islamic Learning", 162–97; Wilks, "The Saghanughu and the Spread of Maliki Law: A Provisional Note", *Research Review* (Institute of African Studies, University of Ghana) 2, no. 3 (1966); and Wilks, "The Juula and the Expansion of Islam into the Forest", in *The History of Islam in Africa*, ed. Nehemia Levtzion and Randall L. Pouwels (Athens: Ohio University Press, 2000), 95–103. On the dating of al-Sūwarī, also see Sanneh, *Jahankhe*, 18. Also see Yves Person, *Samori. Une Révolution Dyula*, vol. 1 (Dakar: IFAN, 1969), 131–49. Also see Ivor Wilks, *Wa and the Wala: Islam and Polity in Northwestern Ghana* (Cambridge: Cambridge University Press, 1989), 98–100; and John O. Hunwick, *Arabic Literature of Africa*, vol. 4, *The Writings of Western Sudanic Africa* (Leiden: Brill, 2003), 540, 550–52.

29. Coultart Papers, BMS Collection, Oxford.

30. The name Tuffit appears in a letter from Kabā to Abū Bakr al-Siddīq, apparently transcribed from Arabic, which states: "I give you my name, Robert Tuffit, and the property [where I live] is named Spice Grove"; see Madden, *Twelvemonth's Residence*, 2: 133. The name Tuffit may derive from some confusion over the transliteration of Peart into Arabic and its subsequent translation back into English, but otherwise is not explained. It should be noted, however, that Angell is credited with using both names, Tuffit and Peart, but this may have been Madden's insertion.

31. Madden, *Twelvemonth's Residence*, 2: 133. Angell purchased Adam's Valley in 1818; see the survey map, November 1818, M 18, National Library of Jamaica, Kingston. By 1821 Adam's Valley was a small coffee estate with 4 people in slavery and 21 livestock; his wife owned Providence, which had 54 enslaved people and 6 stock; see Return of Givings-In, Proprietors, Properties etc. Given to the Vestries for Quarter Ending March 1821, *Jamaica Almanack* 1822, 31. In 1832 Angell not only owned Adam's Valley, which then had 96 enslaved residents and 20 stock, but also Tombuctoo with its 18 slaves and 8 stock, Mayfield with 61 slaves, and Top-ham, with 3 slaves and 54 stock (Return of Givings-In, Proprietors, Properties etc. Given to the Vestries for Quarter Ending March 1832, *Jamaica Almanack* 1833, 143). Both Angell and Kabā were associated with the Moravian mission at Fairfield, which is probably how Kabā's letter came into Angell's possession. By 1840 Adam's Valley was one of only four outstations for the Moravian mission; see *Jamaica Almanack* 1840, 39. For Kabā's connection with the Moravians, see the diary of John Lang (1805–17) and subsequent

diaries of the Negro Congregation, Moravian Papers, National Archives, Spanish Town, Jamaica.

32. See Madden, *Twelvemonth's Residence*, 2: 131. Al-Siddīq's manumission was recorded on 9 September 1834 in Kingston; see Manumission Book 69, commenced 8 February 1834, 1B/11/6/40, Jamaica Archives, Spanish Town. His owner had been Alexander Anderson, who freed him without compensation in the face of Madden's pressure.

33. Madden, *Twelvemonth's Residence*, vol. 2. For a discussion of al-Siddīq's autobiography, see Wilks, "Abū Bakr al-Siddīq", 152–69.

34. Madden, *Twelvemonth's Residence*, 2: 135.

35. Sanneh, *Jakhanke*, 38–43.

36. For the Saghanughu network, see Wilks, "Islamic Learning".

37. Buchner, *Moravians of Jamaica*, 50–51.

38. Cornell, *Way of Abu Madyan*.

39. Wilks, "Islamic Learning", 192.

40. Hunwick, *Writings of Western Sudanic Africa*, 550–51.

41. Wilks, "Saghanughu and the Spread of Maliki Law".

42. John Hunwick, "Toward a History of the Islamic Intellectual Tradition in West Africa Down to the Nineteenth Century", *Journal of Islamic Studies* 17 (1997): 9; Wilks, "Islamic Learning", 168–70; Sannah, *Jakhanke*, 14–27, 38–43; and Wilks, "Mallams Do Not Fight the Heathens: A Note on Suwarian Attitudes to *Jihad*", *Ghana Studies* 5 (2002): 215–30.

43. Sanneh, *Jahanke*, 19–20.

44. The dating of this letter is subject to interpretation. According to Angell, Kabā "has referred me to a known, though anonymous, correspondent", to verify Kabā's claim that "about three years ago [that is, 1831], he received from Kingston, by the hands of a boy, a paper written in Africa, forty-five years previously [1789]. He knew it to be of this date, as the paper purported to have been written in the forty-third year of the age of the King, Allaman Talco, who was thirty-five years old when he (R.P.) [that is, Kabā] left the country". According to Wilks ("Abū Bakr al-Siddīq", 163–64), it is likely that the reference is to the forty-third year of the thirteenth century of the Muslim calendar, which would date the letter to 1827–28. Almami Talco has not been identified, although at the time the Almami of Futa Jallon was Bubakar; see Bary, *Senegambia and the Atlantic Slave Trade*, 148–50.

45. Madden, *Twelvemonth's Residence*, 2: 133.

46. The significance of the term "Sherrif" should be noted, often referring to merchants from Morocco in this period.

47. It is suggested here that Tuffit is a corruption of Peart, as translated into Arabic and retranslated into English.

48. Madden, *Twelvemonth's Residence*, 2: 133.

49. Ibid., 134.

50. Ibid.

51. Madden, *Twelvemonth's Residence*, 2: 142–47, letter to William Rainsford, Benjamin Cochran, Benjamin Larten, and Edward Donlan (Abū Bakr al-Siddīq), Kingston, 15 October 1835.

52. On the Manding/Mandingo in the African diaspora, see Sylviane Diouf, "Devils or Sorcerers, Muslims or Studs: Manding in the Americas", in *Trans-Atlantic Dimensions of Ethnicity in the African Diaspora*, ed. Paul Lovejoy and David Trotman (London: Continuum, 2002).

53. Bryan Edwards, *The History, Civil and Commercial, of the British West Indies*, vol. 2 (London: 1819), 71–73. Also see Cynric Williams, *A Tour through the Island of Jamaica, from the Western to the Eastern End, in the Year 1823* (London: Thomas Hurst, Edward Chance and Co., 1827). Elsewhere see, for example, the report of the Mandingo Muslim in St Croix, named Benjamin, who died in 1796. He supposedly joined the Moravians in 1779; see John Holmes, *Historical Sketches of the Missions of the United Brethren for Propagating the Gospel among the Heathen* (Dublin: R. Napper, 1818), 326; and Christian G.A. Oldendorp, *A Caribbean Mission: C.G.A. Oldendorp's History of the Mission of the Evangelical Brethren on the Islands of St. Thomas, St. Croix, and St. John*, originally published 1770, ed. and trans. Arnold Highfield and Vladimir Barac (Ann Arbor: Karoma Publishers, 1987).

54. Paul Lovejoy and David Trotman, "Creating the Community of Believers: African Muslims in Trinidad, *c.*1800–1850", in *Trans-Atlantic Dimensions of Ethnicity*. Also see Warner-Lewis, "Religious Constancy".

55. Lovejoy and Trotman, "Community of Believers"; Gomez, *Exchanging Our Country Marks*, 59–87; Diouf, *Servants of Allāh*; and Afroz, "Islam in Plantation Jamaica", 159–60.

56. Madden, *Twelvemonth's Residence*, 2: 136–37.

57. Translation by Yacine Daddi Addoun.

58. Verses of this sort appear in the Qur'ān in several places, but not in this form. Cf., for example, Qur'ān 4:13–14; 57:17; 72:23. The version used here is Abdullah Yusuf Ali, *The Holy Qur-ān: English Translation of the Meanings and Commentary, revised and edited by The Presidency of Islamic Researches, Ifta, Call and Guidance* (Al-Madinah: King Fahd Holy Qur-ān Printing Complex, 1410 [1989/90]).

59. Cousin and son-in-law of the Prophet and the fourth caliph.

60. The third caliph.

61. The second caliph.

62. The first caliph.

63. Muhammad Muhsin Kan, *The Translation of the Meanings of Sahih Al-Bukhari,*
    Arabic-English (Al-Madina Al-Munawwara: Islamic University Press, n.d.), 314.

64. Ibid., 301. The *hadīth* number 506 has almost the same meaning.

65. This appears to be from Ahmad b. ʿAlī b. Hajar al-ʾAsqalānī (AD 1372–1449),
    Al-Munabbihāt min aqwāl Rasūli 'l-Lāhi sallā 'l-Lāhu 'alayhi wa-sallam, wa-'l-
    sahāba wa-'l-hukamā' wa-'l-shu'arā (Beirut: Dār al-Kitāb al-Jadīd, 1987), 17. A lit-
    eral translation of ʿAsqalānī's text is as follows: "Who leaves four [actions] until
    four [situations] will go to paradise, sleeping until the tomb, pride until passing
    the balance, resting until passing the path, enjoyment until being in paradise."

66. ʿAbd Allāh b. Mubārak (*c.*736–97) is the author of several books, among them a
    book on *hadīth*. See al-Imām ʿAbd Allāh b. al-Mubārak, *Musnad 'Abd Allāh b. al-*
    Mubārak wa yaīlh kitābu al-birr wa al-sila, ed. Dr Mustafā ʿUthmān Muhammad
    (Beirut: Dār al-Kutub al-ʿilmiyya, AH 1411 [AD 1991]). See also J. Robson, "Ibn
    al-Mubārak", in *The Encyclopaedia of Islam,* by H.A.R. Gibb, et al., vol. 3 (Leiden:
    J. Brill, 1960), 879.

67. This appears to be a reference to Ahmad b. ʿAlī b. Hajar al-ʾAsqalānī,
    Al-Munabbihāt. See note 65.

68. Abū 'l-Husayn Muslim b. al-Hajj al-Qushayrī (AD 821–875).

69. Muhammad b. Ismāʾīl al-Bukhārī (AD 810–870).

70. ʿAsqalānī. *Munabbihāt,* 17.

71. Qurʾān 55: 26–27.

72. ʿAsqalānī. *Munabbihāt,* 29.

73. Ibid., 19.

74. Cf. W. Montgomery Watt, "Al-Iskandar", in *Encyclopaedia of Islam,* 4: 127.

75. See the same description in Ibn al-Mubārak, *Musnad,* 51.

76. Ibid.

77. Ibid., 53–4; similar to the *hadīth* with difference in wording.

78. For this passage of intercession, see ʿAbd Allāh b. Ahmad, Maqdisī, *Kitāb al-riqqa*
    (Beirut: Dr al-Kutub al-ʿIlmiyya, 1994), 217.

79. These two sentences are repeated in the original, perhaps by mistake.

80. It should be noted that the question of *jihād* is not raised.

81. *Al-Bahr* literally means *sea* but refers specifically to any man of science, or one
    who displays a wide range of knowledge.

82. This last sentence is crossed out in the original.

83. Abū Madyan Shu ʿayb b. al-Husayn al-Ansārī (AD 1115–1198).

84. Ibn Abī Zayd al-Qayrawānī, *Matn al-Risāla* (Beirut: Dār al-Fikr, 1996), 13–14.

85. Ibid.

86. Ibid., 19–21.

87. Ibid., 25–28.

88. Reference to chapter 15, *sūrat al-Furqān*, 54: "It is He Who has created man from water: then has He established relationships of lineage and marriage: for thy Lord has power (over all things)". See *Qur'ān*, 1048.

89. Chapter 94, *sūrat al-sharh*: "1. Have we not / Expanded thee thy breast? / 2. And removed thee / Thy burden / 3. The which did gall / Thy back? / 4. And raised high the esteem / (in which) thou (art held)? / 5. So, verily, / With every difficulty, / There is relief: / 6. Verily, with every difficulty / There is relief / 7. Therefore, when thou art Free (from thine immediate task), / Still labour hard, / 8. And to thy Lord / Turn (all) thy attention". See, *Qur'ān*, 1974–75.

90. According to Sanneh, the Darame clerics were considered the heirs of al-Ḥājj Sālim Sūwarī and are associated with the holy town of Gunjur; see *Jakhanke*, 19–20.

91. This section shows what to say or think when performing ablutions, following the order of the parts of body one washes: mouth, nose, face, arms, head, ears and feet. Qayrawānī does not mention this in his *Risāla*.

92. Qayrawānī, *Risāla*, 18.

93. This is called *tashahhud* and is recited silently when seated: "All Salutations are due to Allāh and all Prayer and everything pure. Peace be upon thee, O Prophet, and the mercy of Allāh and His blessings; and peace be on us and on all righteous servants of Allāh. I bear witness that Muhammad is his servant and Messenger". See the Arabic text and this translation in *Salat: The Muslim Prayer Book* (Islamabad and Surrey: Islam International Publications, 1997), 42. See also the variants of tashahhud in Muhammad Nāsir al-Dīn al-Albānī, *sifat salāt al-Nabī sallā 'l-Lāhu 'alayhi wa sallam, mina al-takbīri 'ilā 'l-taslīmi ka'annka tarāhā* (Bayrūt: Manshūrāt al-Maktab al-Islāmī, AH 1389 [AD 1969]), 172–82. Also see Qayrawānī, *Risāla*, 28.

94. *Qunūt* is a text recited during the prayer of dawn.

95. *Salat: The Muslim Prayer Book*, 64. On *qunūt* see Albānī, *sifat salāt al-Nabī*, 191–97.

18

Religion and Sociopolitical Protest in Jamaica
Alexander Bedward of the Jamaican Native Baptist Free Church, 1889–1921

Veront M. **Satchell** |

Introduction

Resistance to oppression in the Jamaican colonial society has had a long tradition, dating back to the earliest era of the slave plantation economy.[1] Every
period of the island's history "involved a crisis of opposition to the system
which in its very act of struggle and confrontation helped not only to liber-
alise the system, but in human/social terms, helped us [Jamaicans] to transform ourselves".[2] Tackey's rebellion, which erupted in St Mary in 1760 and
came to engulf the entire island, taking the government over eighteen
months to suppress; Sam Sharpe's revolt of 1831, which forced Britain to con-
cede to abolish the system of slavery; Paul Bogle's revolt of 1865; and the mass
protests of the 1930s are but a few examples.[3]

These protest actions against the system, referred to as "Black Power"
actions by Brathwaite, were the most dramatic manifestations of resistance.
But beginning in the late eighteenth century, there was the development of a

movement described by Brathwaite as a humanitarian revolution, a quieter, less documented but no less significant social change taking place in the island, via religion.[4]

> Since about [1795] the new confidence of the slaves was not only being expressed in military/guerrilla activity but in the revitalisation of their own Afro-Jamaican religious culture into a creolised variation of Christianity known variously as the Black Native or Spiritual Baptist Church. . . . Dreams, and visions . . . were reintro- duced as an essential aspect of the Black Church; water baptism was reinterpreted back into African magico-religious symbolism (river, spirit, passage).[5]

This religion was Afro-Christianity, which refers not only to the formal doc- trinal practices and beliefs preached by white European-Christian missionar- ies, but also to a cultural expression and self-awareness, focused through "religion" but living itself through a whole complex of other activities and practices.[6] This was not worship or adoration in the European-Christian sense but rather in a form of spirit-contact, or possession by God, expressed in danc- ing, drumming, speaking in tongues, prophesying, in the revivalist, vodoun, shango, pukumina or West African religious sense.[7]

Worshipping in this way, within a cultural style that they understood, gave the oppressed people a sense of freedom and dignity which they would not otherwise have had. This religio-cultural freedom led the black missionary preachers quite easily into more terrestrial and humanitarian claims to free- dom as well. Having a fundamentalist theology of the Bible that could be politically radicalized, black preachers, unlike their white counterparts, came to view Christianity as a liberating force. Christianity was seen in a holistic way. The Spirit was not separated from the World or the Word from the Flesh.[8] Thus they could argue that God, as God of justice, equity and truth, could not have ordained the type of physical oppression and exploitation being heaped on them by the colonial masters. This was seen as contradictory to Christianity; consequently Christianity became the starting point for political activity and resistance. Biblical texts such as "If the Son therefore shall make you free you are free indeed" (John 8:36), "there is neither Greek nor Jew, there is neither bond nor free" (Gal. 3:28), "It is for freedom that Christ has set us free. Stand firm then and do not let yourselves be burdened again by a yoke of slavery" (Gal. 5:1), and popular hymns such as "Take force by force! Take force by force!" and

> We will be slaves no more,
>
> Since Christ has made us free,
>
> Has nailed our tyrants to the cross,
>
> And bought our liberty[9]

came to be interpreted by black religious leaders and their followers as rallying calls for resistance against oppression.

During the late nineteenth and early twentieth centuries there was no shortage of apocalyptic and potentially subversive religious leaders in Jamaica who were prepared to challenge the status quo, but as Burton points out, it took the career of the remarkable Reverend Alexander Bedward and his Jamaica Native Baptist Free Church, one of the island's several revivalist churches, to bring the radical energies of Jamaican Afro-Christianity to their peak.[10] Following in the tradition of earlier black Caribbean religious preachers and missionaries such as George Lisle, Moses Baker, Sam Sharpe and Paul Bogle, Bedward emerged as one of Jamaica's loudest voices of protest against the colonial government and the inherent racism in colonialism during the late nineteenth century.[11] His charisma and scathing messages against injustice, discrimination and oppression so appealed to the black majority that his popularity and that of his church burgeoned throughout the island as well as abroad. His overwhelming influence over the black lower classes, coupled with his anti-white-upper-class rhetoric, posed a serious threat to the colonial government and to the political stability of the colony. Not surprisingly, the government embarked on a long but successful campaign of harassment against him. In the end he was defeated. He was arrested, tried and found guilty of lunacy and was confined to the lunatic asylum where he eventually died.

Bedward was born sometime around 1859, probably on Mona Estate in the parish of St Andrew. He came from a poor family and had very limited formal education. As an adult he worked on Mona Estate as a cooper. Prior to his ordination to the ministry of the Jamaica Native Baptist Free Church, he was a member of the Wesleyan/Methodist church. Notwithstanding his avowed religious affiliation, he confessed that in his early life he had committed every sin except murder. He claimed that early in his life he "was attacked by some mysterious disease which local doctors were unable to cure". In 1883, at age twenty-three, he migrated to Panama, as so many lower-class Jamaicans were doing, to gain employment and to see if the change in environment would improve his health. He returned to Jamaica in 1885, but he claimed that within a few days disease, burdens and oppression, both physical and spiritual, had so beset him that he had to return to Colón, this time vowing never to return to Jamaica.[12]

However, he alleged that immediately upon arriving in Panama he had two visions, which were in effect his call to ministry. In the first vision he was ordered by a man to return to Jamaica: "If you stay here you will die and lose your soul, but if you return to Jamaica, you will save your soul and be the means of saving others." In the second he was told by a man to go to August Town: "Submit yourself to Mr Ruderford for instruction, with fasting then be baptised for I have a special work for you to do."[13] He returned to Jamaica immediately and in January 1886 he was baptized. In 1891, at the age of thirty-two, he began his public ministry in the Jamaica Native Baptist Free Church.

In 1893 Bedward reputedly got divine instructions to build a house for the service of God. In June 1894 the cornerstone was laid at Union Camp, August Town, which was to become the headquarters of the church.[14] Bedward's personality became so inextricably wound up with the movement that it came to be called *Bedwardism*, and its followers, *Bedwardites*. Under Bedward's leadership the Jamaica Native Baptist Free Church was transformed from just another revivalist church to its final position as a mass politico-religious movement, the prototype of nationalist movements and, as such, forerunner of the pan-Caribbean nationalist movement of the early twentieth century. Undoubtedly his activities formed part of the wider liberation struggles among peoples of Africa, Asia and Latin America against colonialism and imperialism during the nineteenth and twentieth centuries, and were a continuation of the earlier Afro-Jamaican religious struggle against oppression.

In a rigidly defined social structure based on class and colour, responses to Bedward inevitably varied along class lines. To the white and coloured upper classes Bedward was enigmatic – vilified yet feared. On the one hand he was a schemer, an extortionist, a religious fanatic, a lunatic and a monomaniac; on the other, he was a threat to their privileged position. To the several thousands of rural and urban lower-class black Jamaicans, however, he was prophet, shepherd, healer and deliverer from racial injustice, inequality and oppression. For them he was Jesus Christ who had returned to earth in the flesh to end white oppression. Bedward himself declared that he was the reincarnation of "the word made flesh", dwelling among the Jamaican lower-class black population with a mission to preach the good news to the poor and liberate the oppressed (John 1:1, 14; Luke 4:18). His message was one of action. For him the time had come for the black majority to rise up and crush the white minority and take control of their destiny. If this was not done, he exclaimed, "hell will be your portion".[15]

Despite his virulent attacks on racial discrimination and white minority rule, Bedward is recorded in the annals of Jamaican history as the lunatic from August Town who attempted to fly. This portrait of Bedward in Jamaica's colonial history is unfortunate and needs correcting; this chapter attempts that corrective. It argues that in so far as Bedward's activities attracted the attention of the highest level of authority in the land, forcing them to discredit and silence him, he cannot be dismissed simply as a lunatic. Bedward must be considered a politico-religious nationalist, a political priest who, in a society marked by racial discrimination, economic oppression and social and political inequality for the black majority, valiantly challenged white minority rule on behalf of the oppressed, under the guise of religion.

II

Jamaica, during the period under review, was shaped by the phenomenon of plantation slavery. On this foundation was built a socioeconomic structure marked by racial oppression and inequity. White European values and biases permeated the entire society. During slavery a few whites and coloureds owned and controlled the means of production. Blacks were the enslaved and, being associated with powerlessness and poverty, occupied the bottom of the social hierarchy. On emancipation in 1838 the power relationship remained unchanged, despite the fact that 218,530 slaves, representing over 80 per cent of the population, were made free citizens. Very little provision was made for them to start their new life or to acquire wealth. They were not given any land, social amenities were almost nonexistent in their communities, and their political rights and privileges were extremely circumscribed. In fact, it was expected that upon emancipation they would be transformed into a proletariat, and so continue to work on the plantations as wage earners. Land in this agrarian society, however, was extremely important; it was tied to political participation, upward social mobility and economic independence. Land acquisition was therefore seen by the formerly enslaved as the means of redressing their poor socioeconomic status. However, to acquire land was difficult since, in general, land remained concentrated in the hands of the few, and most landholders refused to sell. Notwithstanding, by differing means many former slaves gained access to land and set themselves up as peasant farmers.[16]

The government and large landholders viewed this growth of a black peasantry with alarm and apprehension, as it was seen as unhealthy for the economic development of the island, but there was very little that could be done to prevent the rapid expansion. The growing numbers of black small landholders made them the majority of the electorate, and soon their votes began influencing the complexion of elected members to the House of Assembly,[17] a development which disturbed the British imperial government but which it could do little to arrest at that time.[18] The general view of the Colonial Office was that, given the bigotry and continued administrative mismanagement by the local assembly, the situation would soon come to a head, thus enabling Britain to avoid the greater disaster: black majority rule (perceived as premature) in the island.

Developments during the 1860s soon presented the imperial government with the opportunity to effect the political changes it had envisaged from very soon after emancipation as necessary for the political stability of the island. The economic depression facing the world during the 1860s had its effect on all classes in Jamaica. However, the government sought to pass the burden on to the peasant and working classes through increased taxation. Wages were drastically reduced and land became increasingly difficult to acquire. Appeals were made to the highest authority, but to no avail. This untenable situation led to open conflict in the celebrated Morant Bay Rebellion in October 1865, led by Paul Bogle, a deacon in the Native Baptist Church. The result of this revolt was its brutal suppression, withdrawal of the old constitution with its representative politics, and the introduction of full Crown Colony government. This meant that the island was governed directly from England through the governor, assisted by officials recruited from Britain, and with the governor's nominees, selected primarily from the planter class, forming the Legislative Council.[19] The black majority, now disenfranchised, had little political representation.

During the last quarter of the nineteenth century full Crown Colony government was modified to allow for "wider representation".[20] A few black middle-class professionals – including Alexander Dixon, elected in 1899; S.A.G. Cox, a barrister; and Robert Love – gained access to the Legislative

Council through elections under a franchise based on property and income. Few, however, acted as agents of the lower-class black masses; most became absorbed in the system, aspiring to be black Englishmen, and to many the concept of black nationalism was alien.[21] Marcus Garvey stated, "When a black man did occasionally rise in the social hierarchy he adopted white culture, featuring himself 'other than black' and thinking 'from white and coloured mind'. "[22] Joy Lumsden, in her discussion on the psyche of the black middle class, argues that

> although they believed in the equality of the black and white races, they accepted almost without question, that European civilisation was at that time superior to anything found elsewhere in the world. They therefore asserted their equality with the whites by insisting that [middle class professional] blacks were capable of reaching the standards of European civilisation.[23]

This was a part of the make-up of Robert Love, the most significant figure in Jamaican politics between 1890 and 1910. A Bahamian-born Anglican priest, Love came to Jamaican via Haiti. He soon rose to prominence as journalist, editor of the *Jamaica Advocate* (a weekly which essentially was the voice of black Jamaicans), orator and politician. He worked assiduously for the election of black candidates to the Legislative Council; he himself was elected to that body in 1906. But despite his avowed black consciousness, his greatest desire was to be English. In 1897 he wrote that he was convinced that the best hope for black people lay within the British legal and political system, and his job was to encourage them to strive to take their rightful place within the system: "We desire to be English. . . . In spite of some faults which we see and feel, there is much that is good and sound in the great heart of England, and we have confidence in her good intentions . . . let us work as English men and win as English men."[24]

The entry of these black middle-class professionals into representative politics, therefore, made little difference in the lives of the black lower classes. Rather than identifying with the struggles of the black masses, the black middle-class politicians strived to distance themselves from the masses, in their desire to become accepted as Englishmen.

The Jamaica Constabulary Force, a paramilitary unit, was established during this period to suppress and prevent any political uprising. At the same time the new government instituted land policies aimed at addressing the disorganized state of land tenure, and initiated economic policies geared

towards the plantations. These policies had a positive impact on the plantation economy but adversely affected the lower classes. Several small landholders were ejected as squatters from their bona fide holdings; small land
holdings had now become more difficult to acquire, and wages were severely
depressed. The overall result was the demise of the peasantry and a resuscita-
tion of the plantations. The lower classes, having very little prospect of surviving in their homeland, opted to migrate overseas to seek out a better way of
life. Between 1880 and 1940, 336,500 lower-class Jamaicans migrated overseas; 80 per cent of this total left between 1880 and 1920.[25]

The black lower classes, then, were left leaderless and humbled, with few
avenues for appeal. The island had no mass-based political party, there was no
apparent political leader of the majority of the population, and, with a strong
police force, overt political protest was almost impossible. What the masses
had, however, was their radical Afro-Christian religion – but this too came
under attack from the establishment during this period, especially since Afro-
Jamaican religious leaders were quite correctly implicated in almost all previous acts of rebellion. In essence, Afro-Jamaican Christianity was viewed by the
upper classes as dangerous and subversive; consequently, the state and the
mainstream churches made efforts to stem the tide of

> religious excesses to which the Afro-Jamaican masses were by now believed to be
> congenitally subject. . . . The Anglican Church increased its number of churches
> from 89 in 1868 to 212 in 1900, with places for 70,000 worshipers two thirds of
> them regularly filled; in addition there were 96 mission stations in the fourteen
> parishes. The Methodists, Moravians, Baptists, Presbyterians made similar efforts to
> strengthen their hold on the existing colored middle class and the emerging black
> lower class as well making inroads into Afro-Jamaican masses. In their vast major-
> ity, however, the black lower classes remained outside but not uninfluenced by the
> mainstream churches, participating in one or more of a variety of popular religious
> forms ranging from the wholly non-Christian Kumina . . . through the barely
> Christianised Convince cult, to the overlapping forms of Revivalism that in time
> would be given the names Pocomania, Revival Zion and Tabernacle.[26]

Norris, in agreeing with this position, posits that it is not contradictory to
argue that Jamaicans have adopted Christianity without abandoning the traditions of African religious rituals. Pukumina, Zion and other revivalist cults
embodied biblical Christian as well as African concepts. The adherence of the
black lower classes to these religious forms indicates that they satisfied a deep

social need in this oppressed community.[27] For generations, economic and social privations had made black Jamaicans come to rely more on deliverance from above, since experience had taught them that it was totally unrealistic to expect it from below. Having nothing in common with and no chance to express themselves in British-oriented public life in Jamaica, which was the exclusive preserve of the elite white and brown classes, lower-class blacks resigned themselves to their new world, where their religion became not just an outlet for their talents or an escape from their hard life but also a principal focus of cultural opposition to socioeconomic and political oppression. This was the socioeconomic and political culture out of which Bedward and the Jamaica Native Baptist Free Church emerged.

III

The history of the Jamaica Native Baptist Free Church did not begin with Bedward but rather with Harrison "Shakespeare" Woods, an African American who arrived in Jamaica sometime during the nineteenth century. He settled in the parish of St Andrew and soon gained fame as a prophet. In 1889, after convening a meeting in Papine Pasture in that parish, he selected and ordained twelve men and twelve women to be elders of the gathering. These were the early beginnings of the Jamaica Native Baptist Free Church, and these persons its first elders.[28] Woods then left the area, but not before appointing Robert Ruderford from the Baptist church and Jos. Waters from the Wesleyan church as his chief elders in charge of the fledgling church. Woods had predicted earlier that a healing fountain would be opened up in the Hope River near August Town, but that the man who would rule it was not yet ready. Bedward was to become that man.[29]

Healing and baptism became the two most important pillars of Bedwardism. On these pillars Bedward – with the help of one V. Dawson, a former Baptist gospel worker – built up an elaborate organization, with camps all over the island, to the extent that it became the largest and most important revivalist group in Jamaica.[30] Persons of both genders and from all walks of life – peasants, artisans, labourers, wage earners, as well as the unemployed – became converts of Bedward through healing and baptism.[31]

It is felt, however, that the healing ministry coupled with Bedward's messages of deliverance, more than any other factors, attracted lower-class Jamaicans to the Jamaica Native Baptist Free Church. In December 1891

Bedward declared that the spirit had informed him that the water from the Hope River could be turned into medicine for the body and soul:

> [D]e Lord takes me by the han' and leads me to a place in the 'Ope River and says to me 'Bedward, my prophet dip up dis water, pour it into a big Spanish jar, bless it an' whosoever drink shall be healed in body an' soul . . . once I made water wine, behold I now make water medicine. And you, have I ordained my dispenser, watchman, shepherd and trumpeter.'[32]

The healing stream, part of the Hope River which runs through the eastern border of August Town, thus became the cornerstone of the movement. "People from every part of the island are either visiting the spot or having the water sent them in the belief that it possesses the power to heal the multitudinous diseases that affect humanity."[33]

The first formal step into Bedwardism was baptism. In Bedwardism, however, baptism had both religious and political significance. It meant much more than the washing away of sins and the transforming of the sinner into a child or elect of God, who in solidarity with the others vowed to fight against evil. Baptism into Bedwardism came to encompass the fight against the evil of socioeconomic and racial oppression; hence at each baptismal service Bedward exhorted the baptized that through baptism they were transformed into the elect of God, to bring an end to white oppression forced on them by the government and the whites.[34]

Healing and baptismal services together took place on the banks of the Hope River, and hundreds of persons from all over the island and from abroad (including Cuba, Colón and Costa Rica) journeyed to August Town to be baptized by Bedward or to bathe in or drink from the healing stream and thus be cleansed in body and soul. Those who could not make the trip had the water taken to them. One newspaper, commenting on the overwhelming hold Bedward and the healing stream had on the population, stated,

> Ten, fifteen, twenty thousand or more of the Negro population of the island gathered on the banks of a little glen near the village of August Town. They have made the pilgrimage thither the majority of them on foot, from all parts of the country. There are people of all ages and social conditions, the women being the more numerous.[35]

In towns, villages and hamlets people were acclaiming Bedward prophet, healer and deliverer, as more and more converts came to be baptized. An observer commented, "There was not a square mile of Jamaica that had not yielded at least a dozen souls into the strong arm of Bedward to be baptised. August Town had now become a Mecca."[36] Branches of the church sprang up throughout Jamaica and overseas. Missionaries were to be found in Costa Rica, Port Limon and Colón (Panama), and Cuba, working among lower-class Jamaicans who had migrated to those places. During the heyday of Bedwardism the movement attracted a membership of over seven thousand. The census figures indicate that the movement was active in every parish except Trelawny; it was, however, more popular in the eastern parishes than in the western. This figure seems very conservative, given the extremely wide influence this movement had among the lower-class population.[37] But given the inherent white bias in Jamaican society, which encouraged a negative attitude towards things black and African, it is quite likely that many Bedwardites, responsive to social pressures, refrained from declaring themselves as such. No figures for the overseas membership have been found, but judging from the large numbers of lower-class Jamaicans who had migrated overseas and the fact that Bedward sent missionaries to work among them, it can be assumed that the membership was substantial. Given the appeal of Bedward's message to the oppressed lower classes, it can also be conjectured that membership included lower-class citizens of those countries as well. Bedward had now internationalized his activities.

IV

It is without doubt that Bedward was remarkably charismatic, and his appeal among the lower-class population was without equal at that time. But what was his appeal? Was it the healing stream or was it his message of deliverance? Pierson, commenting on Bedward's personal appeal, remarked, "The mystique that enabled Bedward to become a charismatic leader may be complex – the prophetic descendant of 'Shakespeare', his assured manner, his message of assurance and healing, and the latent Black Nationalism that was developing caused him to attract thousands."[38] Post argues that "Bedward's movement was not only a religious one, its doctrines had profound political implications as well, and it challenged established authority both ecclesiastical and secular".[39] Elkins posits that Bedwardism was "the nursery of black ideas" which was to develop after World War I, when militant New World Africans in the West Indies began a general struggle for political and social emancipation, their efforts infused with a nationalist spirit.[40] Bedward and Bedwardism, according to Burton, not only "provide[d] a vital link in the continuity of protest from Morant Bay onwards; they also prepared the way for the still more subversive worldview of Rasta Farianism".[41] Pastor Roman Henry, one of Bedward's lieutenants, claimed in a personal interview that Bedward had a divine mission to free black people, not just in Jamaica but wherever blacks were held in bondage. Referring to Genesis 49:10, Henry argued that "the sceptre, the sword and the lion or crown were stolen from the black man by the British and kept in England; these things were later returned to Ethiopia to the black man. If Bedward had not come those things would not be returned to the black man."[42]

An analysis of Bedward's leadership, his religious activities and his forthright messages indicates quite clearly that he was not merely a religious preacher of the earlier European-Christian missionary type who stressed submissiveness and conservatism and an acceptance of present circumstances in the hope of a better life in the world to come. Neither was he akin to the later American Pentecostals who, with a negative appraisal of society and a pessimistic outlook for the future, became apolitical, conservative, a "bulwark of the status quo".[43] Bedward saw himself as the political advocate for, and the voice of, the marginalized and oppressed black majority.[44] His sermons, which were blatantly political and at times subversive, attracted the attention of the colonial government, resulting in a protracted conflict between himself and the colonial authorities who were bent on suppressing him. He and his church were placed under strict surveillance by the government, with strong detachments of police officers at services to monitor his activities. In January 1895, after preaching one of his most powerful sermons of protest, he was arrested for treason and sedition. In this sermon, based on chapter 16 of St Matthew's gospel, he openly described the whites as hypocrites, robbers, thieves and liars, the Pharisees and Sadducees whom Jesus warned his disciples against:

> Brethren, the bible is difficult to understand. Thanks to Jesus, I am able to understand it and I, servant of Jesus will tell you. The Pharisees and Sadducees are the white men, and we (the black masses) are the true people. White people are hypocrites, robbers and thieves. They are all liars. The ministers of religion are rogues and vagabonds. Hell will be your portion if you do not rise up and crush the white men. The time is coming; I tell you the time is coming. There is a white wall and a black wall and the white wall is closing around the black wall; but now the black wall is stronger than the white wall and must crush it. The governor is a scoundrel

and robber; the governor council pass laws to oppress the black people, take their money from their pockets and deprive them of bread and do nothing for it. Tell the ministers that I say that they are all scoundrels; that they fill the almshouses, hospitals and prisons. I have a sign that the black people must rise. Remember the Morant Bay war? The only thing to cure all diseases is this, the Mona water, bless by me first. The governor can't stop me; the police are here and I defy them to arrest me.[45]

A sermon as highly inflammatory and vitriolic as this one, to a large body of oppressed persons from a man as influential as Bedward, could not have been taken lightly by the government – especially since reference was made to the bloody Morant Bay Rebellion, which had been perceived as a "race war". In essence Bedward was inciting the oppressed to take action against their oppressors; this was indeed sufficient to have him arrested. The governor acted quickly and decisively – though tactfully, in fear of the people – to arrest Bedward. Every precaution was taken to ensure the successful suppression of any resistance from Bedward or his followers. Accordingly, at three o'clock on the morning of 22 January, a strong detachment of police personnel (comprising four white police inspectors, a few detectives and thirty policemen, all wearing side arms and carrying rifles) went to August Town and arrested him. The warrant for his arrest charged him with being "[a] wicked, malicious, seditious and evil disposed person".

There was no resistance. Bedward's only remark at his arrest was, "You take me like a thief in the night." He was handcuffed, strapped to a buggy and taken to the Half Way Tree police station where he was placed in jail, to appear the next morning before Mr Vendryes, resident magistrate. At the hearing the magistrate ordered trial on 22 April and ordered that Bedward be remanded in custody without bail. Thus for three months Bedward remained behind bars, unable to mobilize his flock to subvert the peace. Notwithstanding this, on the day of the trial over six hundred of his followers vigorously demonstrated outside the courthouse, some throwing stones at the mounted orderlies.[46]

The trial of 22 April is instructive, as it demonstrates quite forcefully the judicial injustices that prevailed in this colonial society. Witnesses for the prosecution comprised only two persons: a white newspaper reporter and a police inspector. For the most part they gave a rehash of a newspaper account of Bedward's speech. A physician was called to testify on Bedward's health; he reported that Bedward was suffering from mental intoxication and amnesia.

Lawyer for the defence, Philip Stern, in his closing remarks to the jury, attacked racial injustice and implored them to "rise above selfishness and resist despotism and cruelty even to a dog or Negro".[47]

The jury agreed that Bedward had uttered seditious language, but it found him not guilty of the charges on the grounds of insanity. Consequently, Bedward was immediately sent to the lunatic asylum, reputedly for treatment, but in reality for incarceration since the asylum was little less than a prison. The decision was appealed to the circuit court, on the grounds that the verdict of not guilty should have been a general verdict and under the sedition law did not provide for detention on the grounds of insanity. Bedward's lawyer got a writ of *habeas corpus* ordering his immediate release. His arrest and subsequent release canonized him in the sight of his followers. On his return to Union Camp he continued his politico-religious activities, but in a somewhat subdued manner. In the first sermon after his release he declared that the scribes had made false accusation against him, although he had not spoken against the queen, the governor and high folks but against clergymen and physicians: "They tried to cause disturbance and injury against me and to crush me."[48]

The colonial authority had now successfully quelled Bedwardism. From this date through 1920, Bedward and Bedwardism appeared to be in retreat. There is no doubt that the government, through the use of its constituted force, had made significant gains in suppressing and defeating Bedward and the movement. But this retreat, however, must also be seen in relation to the emergence and development of the Universal Negro Improvement Association (UNIA) led by another Jamaican, Marcus Garvey, a spirited black nationalist. This overtly political movement with its powerful doctrine of racial pride, black consciousness and black self-help, and its international cry of "Africa for the Africans at home and abroad", came to overshadow Bedward and Bedwardism. In light of Garvey's black nationalism and anticolonial stance aimed at ending white oppression, it would appear that Bedward could now take a more religious position; his political mission was to be continued in the UNIA. Pastor Henry, in his comments on the impact of the Garvey movement on Bedwardism, stated that the two movements were complementary. The UNIA, he claimed, was the political vanguard for black liberation, while the Jamaica Native Baptist Free Church was the religious vanguard. Bedwardites were also Garveyites. "I am a Garveyite, a Bedwardite, an African, an Israelite",[49] Henry declared. Burton argues further, however, that this apparent torpidity in Bedwardism and indeed in radical Afro-Christianity was also the result of the rise of Pentecostalism in Jamaica:

> Afro-Christianity was itself profoundly transformed by a new wave of Pentecostal missionaries . . . both black and white, from the United States. . . . Beginning with the founding of a Jamaican branch of the Holiness Church of God in 1907 Pentecostalism rapidly became the dominant religion of poor Jamaicans, especially of working women.[50]

Although Bedward's political overtones were somewhat subdued, he remained extremely influential among the masses. His strong influence over the people is demonstrated in an allegation that after he preached a sermon on faith, many of his followers attempted to fly. This awesome sway that Bedward had over the people continued to bother the government. Cognizant of his nationalist sentiments, the government maintained that he and the movement were potential threats to the stability of the society.[51] Consequently, Bedward continued to experience intense harassment from the colonial officials, whose sole aim was to permanently defeat the movement. Numerous clashes between the colonial authority and Bedward resulted. It was alleged that at one of his meetings members physically assaulted a police constable. Bedward's ownership of land, like that of so many other lower-class Jamaicans at that time, came under dispute. The commissioner of lands challenged Bedward's rights to the landholding he had held in August Town. Bedward claimed that he had to strongly defy authority: "the police Inspector and soldiers with guns and pistols come to my place and told me to get out; but I refused to do this, because I told them it was my home where I had lived for thirty-three years".[52]

This continued conflict and tension between Bedward and the government came to a head in December 1920, when Bedward declared himself to be Jesus Christ, saying that he, like Elijah, would ascend to heaven in a flaming chariot on 31 December of that year, returning three days later to take his faithful followers to glory. He would then rain down fire upon those who were not among the elect, and destroy the whites. He instructed his followers to gather at Union Camp to witness this ascension. Thousands residing throughout the island and abroad gathered at the camp in obedience to him. The governor, in response to this mass gathering and in anticipation of a revolt against the constituted authority by the people, dispatched a strong police presence to ensure that no civil disturbance took place. Although no physical ascension occurred, his adherents journeyed back home undaunted in their belief in prophet Bedward.[53]

In April of the following year, Bedward decided that he would make a manifestation. He announced that on 27 April he and all his followers would march into the city of Kingston to do battle with the enemies, presumably the whites. Gripped by fear, the governor, Sir Leslie Probyn, assessed the situation as volatile and dangerous. To avert any possible disturbance of the peace he decided that there would be no march and that Bedward would be permanently silenced.[54] In the meantime Bedward summoned his followers to August Town to prepare for this momentous march. He also sent a messenger to the city to get permission to hold a public meeting; this request was flatly refused by the authorities. The police were sent to August Town to prevent the march. In defiance of their bidding Bedward replied angrily, "Do you know who I am? I am the Lord Jesus Christ. Must I obey you and disobey my father?"[55]

Sir Leslie, in panic, immediately convened a meeting at Kings House with the attorney general and the inspector of police to decide on how the situation and Bedward should be handled. The meeting agreed that if Bedward were to march, he should be met with the strongest joint police-military party available and that he should be arrested on two trumped-up charges: assaulting a constable and a district constable whilst they were acting in the execution of their duties, and threatening to commit a breach of the peace in Kingston and inciting others to do so. These charges were indeed farcical; the first charge was for an alleged offence committed some long time prior, and the second was anticipatory – it had not occurred. Sir Leslie, in the meantime, dispatched a telegram to the resident magistrate, Mr Sam Burke, with specific instructions for him to go to August Town with the necessary force and fire power to read the Riot Act. Burke was also instructed to fire into the crowd if the march proceeded, in order to stop it. This is clear evidence of the fear Bedward had created among the authorities, and the extent to which they were willing to go in order to suppress him.

Early in the morning of 27 April Bedward and approximately eight hundred of his followers – peasants, carpenters, tailors, shoemakers, dockers, bakers, butlers, labourers and the unemployed – started their march to Kingston. The marchers were dressed in clothes of full white and armed with small wooden crosses and palm leaves; they proceeded, singing "Onward Christian Soldiers". As they marched Sam Burke, with about sixty well-armed police officers drawn from Sutton Street, Half Way Tree and Matilda's Corner police stations and a detachment of an equal number of soldiers from the Royal Sussex Regiment, waited in ambush at the old Mona Estate works yard, ready to intercept the marchers. On reaching the works yard the Bedwardites were met by Burke and the joint police-military force who diverted them off-course, escorting them to the Half Way Tree courthouse. Bedward and five others, who had claimed that Bedward was Jesus Christ, were locked up, while the others were arrested under the vagrancy law: "[b]eing able to labour and habitually abstaining from work". The onus of proof was on the accused.[56] This was a convenient law under which to charge these marchers, and in general a very useful means of class control.

Burke summarily tried the group in batches of ten and was able to deal with nearly three hundred defendants in less than three hours, all of whom were found guilty. The remaining five hundred were sent home without trial.[57] The execution of justice was extremely swift; the defendants had no time either to defend themselves or to get legal advice or representation. The swiftness of the justice, or injustice, prompted questions in the Legislative Council. The elected member of the council for St Catherine, the Reverend Mr Young, in commenting on the procedure argued that the exhibition in court did not savour of British justice because the people were given no opportunity to defend themselves: "The whole thing looked like a lynch law. All the people were charged under the vagrancy law yet some were imprisoned while others were freed . . . was vagrancy proven among them?" He further questioned whether, if one of the established churches had ordered its members to march to Kingston, they would have been similarly treated: "Would they be charged under the vagrancy law and imprisoned? It was high time the executive see that justice was meted out to the masses irrespective of religion."[58] In view of this protest, the governor pardoned all the convicted men and women.

Bedward and the five others were brought to trial on 5 May. Bedward's case was called for trial first. Witnesses for the Crown were a medical doctor, the sergeant major of police, two police officers and a census taker, who alleged that he had been beaten up by Bedward. On the evidence of the doctor Bedward was freed of the charges on the grounds of lunacy. But that was not the end of the matter, because Bedward was to be brought back into court a short time after, to be tried on a charge of lunacy – "a person of unsound mind wandering at large". Before this, however, the case involving the five others was called. They were acquitted, but on freeing these five the magistrate made clear his intentions regarding how Bedward would be dealt with. He remarked, "I may tell you at once that Bedward your leader is going to the asylum and when that person whom you believe to be Jesus Christ is locked up in the asylum, you will realise how foolish is your belief."[59]

There was indeed a well-devised plot to have Bedward permanently silenced, a plot which was executed with the greatest of ease. Bedward, amid his jubilant adherents, was on his way home, but on reaching Half Way Tree Square, a short distance from the courthouse, he was apprehended and arrested by Sergeant-Major Williams, armed with a warrant for Bedward's arrest on a charge of lunacy. A befuddled Bedward was before the magistrate for the second time within the day. The two main witnesses were the doctor who had just declared Bedward a lunatic and Sergeant-Major Williams. Both stated that Bedward had declared himself Jesus Christ, the saviour of the black race, and that he had attempted to ascend to heaven. Justice was again swift; on the strength of the evidence, Bedward was found guilty and sentenced to the Kingston lunatic asylum, without being given the chance to defend himself. He was to spend the last ten years of his life in that institution; he died on 8 November 1931.[60] In contrast to the case of his followers, there was no voice of protest raised at this glaring act of injustice, indicating that all in established society were united in their abhorrence of this man.

Chevannes, in summing up the entire Bedward episode, stated,

> The breath was knocked out of Bedwardism and before it could recover, its leader was safely put away in the lunatic asylum. The effect was shattering. Many followers remained faithful to bury him ten years later, and then quietly await his return, but for most the movement was dead. Bedwardism received a mortal blow in its struggle on behalf of the oppressed people. A black wall rose up to crush the white wall, which was closing in around it, but was crushed instead.[61]

The *Daily Gleaner,* which had waged relentless war against Bedward, had this to say on the abrupt manner in which his mission had ended: "It is sad that a man who had such a wonderful influence over the lower strata of the community . . . today is an inmate of the lunatic asylum, shorn of all his glory, a broken and discredited man, such is the hand of fate."[62] According to Post, "Those who defied Colonial Authority were dismissed as vagrants or mentally sick."[63]

According to Burton, this final arrest and incarceration of Bedward was climactic, in that it signalled the beginning of the depoliticization of Afro-

Christianity in Jamaica, bringing to an end the long tradition of radicalism and militancy the movement had come to be noted for. This struggle was to be continued by the Rastafarian movement and Marcus Garvey and the UNIA, but Afro-Christian radicalism was to be profoundly undermined by the more conservative and apolitical American Pentecostalism.[64]

Conclusions

Alexander Bedward is of immense significance in the development of racial awareness and consciousness and political mobilization in Jamaican society. Following the tradition of strong religio-political leaders in Jamaica, under the guise of religion Bedward challenged the status quo on behalf of the majority black Jamaican population who, like himself, had no voice in political decision-making. He introduced new levels of organization and new symbols of unity and power among the black lower classes. As an indigenous response to the colonial situation, he represented a real force of change. Of course, Bedwardism, like most other liberation movements of the time, failed to accomplish its immediate goals since it was suppressed and defeated, but according to Ray these resistance movements did not fail to achieve a broader purpose. In most instances, they stimulated a new historical awareness which later ushered in the nationalistic consciousness of the pre-independence period.[65]

Notes

1. Edward Kamau Brathwaite, *The Development of Creole Society in Jamaica,
    1770–1820* (Oxford: Clarendon Press, 1971), 252.
2. Brathwaite, *Nanny, Sam Sharpe and the Struggle for People's Liberation* (Kingston,
    Jamaica: Published by API for the National Heritage Week Committee, 1977), 4.
3. See Michael Craton, *Testing the Chains: Resistance to Slavery in the British West
    Indies* (Ithaca: Cornell University Press, 1982); Gad Heuman, *The Killing Time:
    The Morant Bay Rebellion in Jamaica* (London: Macmillan, 1994); Don Robotham,
    The Notorious Riot: The Socio-Economic and Political Bases of Paul Bogle's Revolt,
    Working Paper no. 28 (Kingston, Jamaica: Institute of Social and Economic
    Research, 1981); Claus F. Stolberg, ed., *Jamaica 1938: The Living Conditions of the
    Urban and Rural Poor* (Kingston, Jamaica: Social History Project, Department of
    History, University of the West Indies, 1990); O. Nigel Bolland, *On the March:
    Labour Rebellions in the Caribbean, 1934–1939* (Kingston, Jamaica: Ian Randle,
    1995); Patrick Bryan and Karl Watson, *Not for Wages Alone: Eyewitness Summaries
    of the 1938 Labour Rebellion in Jamaica* (Kingston, Jamaica: Social History Project,
    Department of History, University of the West Indies, 2003).
4. Brathwaite, *Creole Society*, 252, 265.
5. Brathwaite, *Nanny*, 21.
6. Ibid.
7. Brathwaite, *Creole Society*, 254; Thomas C. Holt, *The Problem of Freedom: Race,
    Labour and Politics in Jamaica and Britain, 1832–1938* (Kingston, Jamaica: Ian
    Randle, 1995), 289–91; Richard D.E. Burton, *Afro-Creole: Power, Opposition and
    Play in the Caribbean* (Ithaca: Cornell University Press, 1997), 10.
8. Brathwaite, *Creole Society*, 258.
9. Quoted in Brathwaite, *Creole Society*, 255.
10. Burton, *Afro-Creole*, 116; Katrin Norris, *Jamaica: The Search for an Identity*
    (London: Oxford University Press, 1969), 16.
11. Boukman, leader of the 1794 slave rebellion in St Domingue (later Haiti), was a
    vodoun leader; vodoun rituals were fully integrated in this struggle. Sam Sharpe,
    slave and Baptist deacon, led the decisive Christmas slave rebellion of 1831
    which forced Britain to emancipate the slaves in the British West Indies; Paul
    Bogle, leader of the Morant Bay Rebellion in Jamaica in 1865, was a Native
    Baptist deacon.
12. Roscoe M. Pierson, "Alexander Bedward and the Jamaica Native Baptist",
    Lexington Theological Quarterly 4, no. 3 (July 1969): 68.
13. Ibid., 69.
14. Ibid., 70.
15. "Bedward Arrested on a Charge of Sedition", *Daily Gleaner*, 22 January 1895, 3,

6; "Alexander Bedward the Supposed Crazy Bedlamite Has Been Arrested",
Colonial Standard, 23 January 1895, 1, 2.

16.   Veront Satchell, *From Plots to Plantations: Land Transactions in Jamaica,
1866–1900* (Kingston, Jamaica: Institute for Social and Economic Research
[ISER], 1990), 37–39.

17.   Gad Heuman, *Between Black and White: Race, Politics and the Free Coloreds in
Jamaica 1792–1865* (Westport, Conn.: Greenwood Press, 1981), 118–24.

18.   See Henry Taylor, "Memorandum Submitted to the Cabinet on the Course to be
taken with the West Indian Assemblies", 19 January 1839, Public Record Office
(PRO), London, Colonial Office, CO318/169; also reproduced as a pamphlet,
available in the Main Library, University of the West Indies, Mona, Jamaica.

19.   "All powers, functions and duties, heretofore . . . exercised by the executive
committee . . . are hereby transferred to, and vested in the governor." Law 8 of
1866, A Law for making Alterations in the Law consequent on the Constitution
of the Legislative Council. See Richard Hart, *From Occupation to Independence*
(Kingston, Jamaica: Canoe Press, 1998), 84.

20.   By an order-in-council of 19 May 1884 the constitution of Jamaica was
amended, making provisions for nine elected members of the Legislative
Council. The franchise was restricted to males possessing an income of £150
from land, or £200 partly from land and partly from an office or business, or
£300 arising from an office or business provided that such voters paid annual
direct taxes or export duties not less than ten pounds. In 1886 the franchise was
extended to males who had paid a land tax of not less than ten shillings, or not
less than one pound ten shillings in other taxes. Jamaica Law 20 of 1884;
Jamaica Law 21 of 1884; Hart, *From Occupation to Independence,* 99–100, 102–8.

21.   The first political organization to express Jamaica's nationalistic aspirations was
the National Club, launched in March 1909 by S.A.G. (Sandy) Cox; Hart, *From
Occupation to Independence,* 99–100, 102–8.

22.   Garvey to R.R. Morton, 29 February 1916, quoted in W.F. Elkins, *Black Power in
the Caribbean* (New York: Revisionist Press, 1977), 2.

23.   Joy Lumsden, "The Roots of Race Consciousness in the Career of Dr Robert
Love" (seminar paper presented March 1983, Department of History, University
of the West Indies, Mona, Jamaica), 23–24. See also Joy Lumsden, "A Forgotten
Generation: Black Politicians in Jamaica, 1884–1914", in *Before and After 1865:
Education, Politics and Regionalism in the Caribbean,* ed. Brian Moore and Swithin
Wilmot (Kingston, Jamaica: Ian Randle, 1998), 112–22.

24.   Love to J.E. Bruce, 30 July 1897, J.E. Bruce Collection, Schomburg Center, New
York Public Library, quoted in Lumsden, "Roots of Race Consciousness", 24.

25.   Satchell, " 'Squatters or Freeholders?' The Case of the Jamaican Peasants during
the Mid-Nineteenth Century", *Journal of Caribbean History* 23, no. 2 (March

1991): 164–77; Satchell, *From Plots to Plantations*, 63–78; Louleita Evans, "Patterns and Trends in Out Migration, Jamaica, 1880–1940" (final-year undergraduate research paper, University of the West Indies, Mona, 1994), 26.

26. Burton, *Afro-Creole*, 116.

27. Norris, *Jamaica*, 16; see also Alston Chevannes, "Jamaican Lower Class Religion: Struggle Against Oppression" (MSc thesis, University of the West Indies, 1971), 47; and Burton, *Afro-Creole*, 10.

28. Pierson, "Alexander Bedward", 68.

29. A.A. Brooks, *History of Bedwardism or the Jamaica Native Baptist Free Church, Union Camp, August Town, St. Andrew JA., B.W.I.* (Kingston, Jamaica: The Gleaner Co., 1917), 7.

30. Sundkler argues that healing activities in Revivalist churches must not be understood as just another kind of religious eccentricity on the part of primitive people who do not grasp what Christianity means. The fact that this healing message attracts ever-increasing numbers shows that it appeals to a very real and vital need. A holistic approach is taken to healing, thus physical healing cannot take place without procuring religious sanctions. See Bengt Sundkler, *Bantu Prophets in South Africa* (London: Oxford University Press, 1961), 236.

31. Compare Zin Henry's view that the movement was "in fact a camp of unemployed and discontents, being indoctrinated under the guise of religion, with hostility to and rejection of the society of the day"; Henry, *Labour Relations and Industrial Conflict in Commonwealth Countries* (Port of Spain: Columbus Publishers, 1979), 20.

32. Brooks, *History of Bedwardism*, 12.

33. "The Healing Spring of Mona: A Visit to August Town", *Daily Gleaner*, 14 September 1893, 7.

34. W.F. Elkins, *Street Preachers, Faith Healers and Herb Doctors in Jamaica, 1890–1925* (New York: Revisionist Press, 1977), 18.

35. *New York Sun*, 13 November 1893, n.p.

36. "Bedward, Alexander", The Bedward File, National Library of Jamaica, Kingston.

37. *Jamaica Population Census* (Kingston, Jamaica: Government Printing Office, 1941). The population censuses of 1911 and 1921 attest to the islandwide sway of this movement, and the tremendous influence the movement had on the people. According to the 1911 census there were 1,135 members; in 1921, 1,309 members.

38. Pierson, "Alexander Bedward", 71.

39. Ken Post, *Arise Ye Starvelings: The Jamaican Labour Rebellion of 1938 and Its Aftermath* (The Hague: Institute of Social Studies, Martinus Nijhoff, 1978), 7.

40. Elkins, *Street Preachers*, 18; Elkins, *Black Power in the Caribbean*, 1.

41. Burton, *Afro-Creole*, 119.

42. Pastor Roman Henry, interview by author, August Town, Jamaica, January 1981.

43. Randall J. Stephens, "Assessing the Roots of Pentecostalism: A Historiographic Essay", *The American Religious Experience* [web site; cited June 2002], http://are.as.wvu.edu/pentroot.htm.

44. Sundkler, in his discussion on black religious leadership in racist South Africa, makes the point that a successful leader "is a big, bulky brave man. Conspicuous wherever he goes and who receives acclamation of the masses as a matter of right. Bravery is tested mainly in the struggle against white domination. The leader emerges conscious of being a Moses freeing his people from slavery." Sundkler, *Bantu Prophets in South Africa*, 107.

45. John Lanigan's report and testimony at Bedward's court hearing in the St Andrew Resident Magistrate Court, reproduced in the *Daily Gleaner*, 24 January 1895, 2; editorial, *Colonial Standard*, 25 January 1895, 2; see also "Interview with Bedward", *Daily Gleaner*, 22 January 1895, 1, 3, 6.

46. "Bedward Case", *Colonial Standard*, 25 April 1895, 2; "Bedward Pleaded Not Guilty", *Colonial Standard*, 30 April 1895, 2; "The Release of the Prophet", *Colonial Standard*, 28 May 1895, 4.

47. Elkins, *Street Preachers*, 13, 14.

48. Ibid., 14.

49. Henry, interview.

50. Burton, *Afro-Creole*, 119–20.

51. The government's position is understandable, since by this date nationalist sentiments among blacks had been fairly well developed in the British Caribbean. The British rulers were by now well aware that their hold on the British Caribbean was being threatened. Elkins, *Black Power in the Caribbean*, 3.

52. Elkins, *Street Preachers*, 16.

53. Ibid.

54. See "His Excellency the Governor's Orders", Bedward File, National Library of Jamaica, Kingston.

55. "Lord Bedward, His Chief Lieuts. And Hundreds of his followers were made Prisoners by Police Yesterday", *Daily Gleaner*, 28 April 1921, 1.

56. Ibid.

57. Elkins, *Street Preachers*, 17.

58. "Lord Bedward", *Daily Gleaner*, 28 April 1921, 1.

59. "Bedward Again Arraigned", *Daily Gleaner*, 5 May 1921, 6.

60. Ibid.

61. Chevannes, "Jamaican Lower Class Religion", 26.

62. "Bedward Again Arraigned", *Daily Gleaner*, 5 May 1921, 6.

63. Post, *Arise Ye Starvelings*, 34.

64. Burton, *Afro-Creole*, 118–19.

65. Benjamin C. Ray, *African Religions: Symbol, Ritual and Community* (Englewood Cliffs, N.J.: Prentice Hall, 1976), 155.

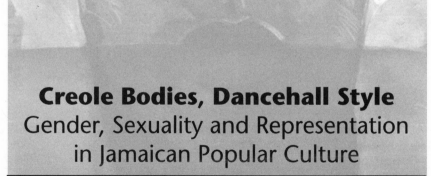

PART SIX

Creole Bodies, Dancehall Style
Gender, Sexuality and Representation
in Jamaican Popular Culture

19

"Love Punaany Bad"
Negotiating Misogynistic Masculinity in Dancehall Culture

Donna P. **Hope** **|**

Introduction

> Under patriarchy, men are the arbiters of identity for both males and females
> because the cultural norm of human identity is, by definition, male identity – mas-
> culinity. And, under patriarchy, the cultural norm of male identity consists in
> power, prestige, privilege, and prerogative as over and against the gender class
> women. That's what masculinity is.[1]

This chapter represents a part of my ongoing interrogation of dancehall culture in Jamaica and my recent interest in the intricacies of gender, in particular Jamaican masculinities, in the discourse of the dancehall. In this context
dancehall masculinities are intricately bound up with a (post) colonial ethos
that simultaneously harks back/across to Britain, the (former) motherland,
while trading with the ebb and flow of metropolitan life and culture in the
global superpower, the United States, but remaining grounded in the African-
influenced aesthetics and culture of contemporary Jamaican life. Here
Brathwaite's discussion of creole society is particularly relevant in the post-

colonial mêlée of contemporary Jamaican life and the ongoing identity negotiations in the dancehall. For Brathwaite, " 'Creole society' is the result of a
complex situation where a colonial polity reacts, as a whole, to the external
metropolitan pressures, and at the same time to internal adjustments made
necessary by the juxtaposition of master and slave, elite and labourer, in a culturally heterogeneous relationship."[2]

Within the postcolonial structure of Jamaican society, traditional gender
politics are overtly subscribed to within dancehall culture; their epiphenom-
ena are transmuted through the lyrical representation of what is labelled by
"decent" Jamaican society as "vulgar", "slack", anti-(male)-homosexual and
misogynist lyrics. However, based on my research within the cultural space
that is dancehall, I argue that these lyrics reveal much more than simply a
culture or group actively engaged in the dissemination of violent, anti-(male)-
homosexual, sexually explicit and misogynist lyrics. Indeed, the existence of
what has been labelled homophobia, I argue, may be more correctly analysed
as a kind of "femmephobia", where same-sex relationships, particularly those
between two men, are viewed as having the power to feminize men. This
"femmephobia" is rooted in an overwhelming fear of the power of the feminine other on the part of men, in their quest for masculine identities.
In Jamaica this discourse speaks to some core issues affecting not only the
masculine and feminine identities in the dancehall dis/place,[3] but also a
broader framework of masculine and feminine identities in Jamaica. This
chapter will, however, focus on the popularized claim that dancehall culture
is misogynistic.

Politics of Gender

In many societies like postcolonial Jamaica, gender stratification operates in a
framework of patriarchy that can be clearly defined as a system or society
reflecting values underpinning the traditional male ideal. It is masculinism in
a political context, and is supported by all the institutions operating within
that system or society. One should note here that patriarchy is not only male
dominance in its strictest sense, but also a persistent ideology of male super-
ordination that both men and women maintain consciously and unconsciously. In this system, both men and women are victims.[4]

Based on the historical experiences of Caribbean peoples, slavery as a system has been seen as the main social experience on which rests the foundation of contemporary ideologies and relations of society. The creolization and mulatto society which resulted from African slavery and European colonialism means that while other oppressive features may be peculiar to these Caribbean societies, race and class have been identified as the two dominant factors intersecting with gender. These have been noted in the colonial legacy and, it is argued, still effectively inform contemporary gender relations.

Coming out of slavery, indentureship, colonialism and postcolonialism were creolized issues of sexuality and identity that were effectively tied to the race/class (colour) and gender hierarchy. The process, which began around the sixteenth century, of defining women and nonwhites as savage, uncontrollable and uncivilized provided an opening for the domestication and exploitation of these groups. Within this framework women and black people were credited with unnatural and insatiable sexual urges that needed the control and guidance of men – originally, white men.

In the Caribbean context of slavery, white men were placed at the helm, and particular notions of sex and sexuality were effectively created and perpetuated. For example:

- black women had no morals and were content to breed, dropping children almost at will;
- black women were strong like animals – they could work in the fields all day and then work in bed all night;
- black women had insatiable and unnatural, animal-like sexual urges
- black men were well endowed, with large penises;
- black men did not understand fatherhood in its Eurocentric sense, but preferred to have many women and many children;
- white women had to be safeguarded from the lusty attentions of black men;
- on the other hand, neither were white men safe from the animal-like lust of black or coloured women, who apparently had some strange hold over them sexually.

Black people, men and women, were stereotyped as sexual animals, driven by insatiable sexual desires and in need of constant supervision.

In contemporary Jamaica the creolization of gender in a racialized class system still operates. Concepts of beauty and ugliness, ideas of good speech or bad speech still depend on their proximity to what is a white, Eurocentric ideal. Jamaican women are reminded that beauty, as defined by the Miss Jamaica (World) and Miss Jamaica Universe beauty contests on an annual basis, still rests on a close approximation to the European phenotype, coupled with high social positioning.

Where sexuality is concerned, the madonna/whore syndrome is transformed by these additional factors to produce the race/class-influenced *ghetto slam* (that is, ghetto sex) ideology. One obtains a ghetto slam from a *trang* (strong) black woman from the lower or working class or from the inner city – a black, lower-working-class phenomenon. This woman is perceived as possessing the physical attributes that make her suitable for engagement in overtly physical displays of sexual activity – large breasts, large posterior, big frame – together with the social positioning that makes her more accessible for use or abuse by men. The often lighter-skinned, more feminine upper/middle-class counterpart is perceived as too ladylike and pure for engagement in any overtly physical displays of sexual prowess, on the one hand, and less accessible, on the other. As concepts of beauty consistently strive towards the European ideals of softness, clear (that is, light) skin and soft flowing hair, the *browning* (or lighter-skinned Jamaican woman) continues to hold pride of place, with those not so light skinned using harsh bleaching agents (in the lower classes), dermatologist-approved skin lighteners (in the middle/upper classes), or marriage (middle/upper classes) to attain this ideal. Issues of identity are also reflected in statements like "My ooman mus have hair pon har head" (My woman must have hair on her head). A woman who cannot lay claim to the soft, flowing tresses (natural, chemically altered or extensions) defined as feminine in a Eurocentric context is considered less than feminine by some.

Notions of sexuality also impact on Afro-Jamaican men, especially those at the lower socioeconomic levels who have limited access to the symbols of real power. A real man is one who can act as traditional hunter and provider. He is able to access the symbols of masculinity as wealth and power – money, brand-name clothing, flashy cars, beautiful women – with very little effort. For the man who cannot access these symbols, issues of sex and sexuality attain primacy in laying the foundation for definitions of his identity. It may be argued that this phenomenon is a throwback to the freelance stud of the slavery and colonial era. However, because of their tenuous place in the relationships of production, many black men have little real power over their women. Ongoing research in the dancehall dis/place shows that the concept of a *wukka man* (worker man)[5] who *have nuff gyal inna bungle* (has many girls in a bundle)[6] is actively subscribed to by men and women who find themselves precariously placed on the edge of the race/class/gender nexus.

As the socioeconomic tensions deepen, these groupings find themselves with increasingly diminished access to the traditional and emerging symbols of social mobility and power in Jamaica, including socioeconomic background at the middle or upper levels, high levels of education and a white-collar career, among others. For the women, meaningful monogamous relationships are traded for polygamous liaisons with "powerful" men. Power here is sited, for example, in the man's perceived social status in his community. The resident don, area leader, druggist[7] and dancehall deejay are examples of such men. This power is not always only economic, but may also extend to the legitimacy, respect, authority or fear which this man generates, enjoys or invokes in his community or the wider Jamaican society. For the men, other more accessible and ideologically placed sites are often utilized.

Defining Dancehall Masculinity: Courting/Conquering the Feared *Punaany*

The masculine gender role is one that arguably encodes behaviours, attitudes and conditions supported by stereotypes and ideals that maintain a system of power and benefit for men. At its most extreme, therefore, masculinity is power over women with the sexual relationship at the core. For Afro-Jamaican men with little access and few links to the relations of production, who are positioned in a precarious socioeconomic space, more and more emphasis is placed on rooting their masculine identities through the extreme manifestation of masculinity: the conquering of and dominance over the female, since at the root of masculinity is the sexual relationship between men and women. Clatterbaugh speaks to Franklin's identification of at least five types of black masculinities in the United States that seek to grapple with their marginalized existence within an oppressive social and political structure. This is also related to Majors and Billson's work on "cool pose", a ritualized form of masculinity entailing behaviours, scripts, physical posturing, impression management and carefully crafted performances that deliver a single, critical message: pride, strength and control.[8] The marginalized African-American man can be easily paralleled with the marginalized (black) working-class man in Jamaica.

The former lives in a racist society, while the latter's life is structured based on a rigid hierarchy of race, class and colour. For these men in Jamaica, the use of sex and sexual symbols to create a highly sexual(ized) masculinity is dominant as a site of empowerment, a way to assert manhood and symbolize one form of masculinity. In the male-dominated dancehall in Jamaica, this is translated into the courting, conquering and dominance of female sexuality, femininity and women. Arguably, this is an instance of patriarchy's operation at its most elemental, basest and most sexual level, often labelled misogyny.

In the dancehall dis/place, the lyrical emanations abound, courting and/or conquering the *punaany* (vagina). At the level of courtship, the lovers of punaany sing its praises:

> Love punaany bad, love punaany bad, love punaany bad, mi a punaany guinea-gog
> [I love vagina very much (rept.), I am a vagina master];[9]

and

> Punaany too sweet, it too sweet, it too sweet
> [Vagina is unbearably sweet (nice), (rept.)][10]

At the other extreme the conquerors, through sexual violence and threat of violence, wage a lyrical war against this manifestation of femaleness:

> Jack it up, cock it up, dig out di red
> [Lift it up, hoist it up, dig out the red(ness)];[11]

and

> Mi have di agony, man mi have di agony, mi have di agony girls dem remedy.
> [I have the agony, oh yes I have the agony, I have the agony, the remedy (cure) for the girls (women)].[12]

In August 1988, at the second staging of Dancehall Night, under the auspices of the premiere reggae show of the time, Reggae Sunsplash, held at the Bob Marley Performing Centre in Montego Bay, Jamaica, treatises engaged in either courting or derogating femininity and the punaany took centre-stage and reached a deafening crescendo. The dancehall dalliance with "lewd and slack" lyrics extolling the positives or negatives of the female sex and female sexuality during the previous year, 1987,[13] had been honed and perfected through 1988. Encouraged by the interactive response and support of dancehall affectees,[14] both in sales and accolades at dancehall events, the deejays (both male and female) at Reggae Sunsplash 1988 "were guilty of singing praises or savagely criticising the size, shape and colour of the female anatomy which found favor among male and female members of the oversized crowd".[15] The crowd at Dancehall Night 1988 was estimated to be about fifty-six thousand at peak time (1:30 a.m.).

For the male courtier/conqueror, the punaany must be subdued by any means and at all costs. It must be conquered before it becomes too powerful and results in the subjugation and submission of men and the corruption or elimination of their masculinity. Here, the feminine other becomes a trophy whose conquest bequeaths an overtly masculine identity to the marginalized male.

As argued earlier, the intersection of the race/class/gender variables forces a man with limited or no access to true power or resources to define his maleness, his identity, through the most available and accessible avenues legitimated under Jamaican patriarchy. These include sex, sexuality and male dominance of women at its most physical and extreme point of manifestation. The dancehall, with its heavy concentration of actors from the marginalized dis/places of Jamaica (such as the inner cities of Kingston), provides a powerful stage for the creation, re-creation and symbolization of these manifestations in a lyrical, as well as real, sense.

For example, the man who can become a babyfather (that is, sire children) multiple times lays claim to high levels of masculine identity as a potent and virile man. Concerns about the economic and emotional welfare and upbringing of his numerous offspring are avoided and negated in the precarious economic landscape of the confined dis/place. Further, the impact of his sexually promiscuous activities on the lives of women is of little or no concern to such a man.

Misogynistic Masculinity in the Dancehall

Contemporary and popular claims for high levels of misogyny in the dancehall dis/place deserve more in-depth research and analysis to unearth the underlying sociopolitical, cultural and gendered imperatives that result in this popularized discourse of gender. As argued in the foregoing, the central issue in this misogynistic dialogue in the dancehall is male identity and male sexuality at the expense of that dreaded other, femininity. The researcher who engages in more than a cursory glance or, as in this instance, outright immersion in the dancehall discovers that male dancehall adherents cannot be classified as women-haters in a literal sense. While the lyrical output of the dancehall at one end may signify elevated levels of misogyny amongst its producers and adherents, it is clear that other lyrical output and behaviour signify that these same producers and adherents also revere the manifestation of woman as mother and nurturer. Many of these men are products of single-parent families headed by mothers, grandmothers, older sisters, aunts and so forth and, therefore, a great deal of reverence is sited around the manifestation of "Mother".

There are popular examples, such as successful dancehall artiste and two-time Grammy winner Shabba Ranks's consistent praise of his own mother, Mama Christie, in both his lyrical outpourings and his interview sessions. Shabba's rise to superstar status was accompanied by his efforts to improve his mother's standard of living by remodelling her home in the inner-city community of Seaview Gardens, since she refused to move to an upscale residential area. Another popular dancehall deejay, Bounti Killa, is also known for his lyrical exhortations about his mother, Miss Ivey, and at times refers to himself as "Miss Ivey laas son" (Miss Ivey's last son). Like Shabba Ranks, Bounti Killa's rise to stardom and his access to economic wealth have also been paralleled by his moving his mother out of the inner-city community in which he had been raised and into a modern apartment at the expensive Oaklands Complex on Constant Spring Road in Kingston. Bounti Killa's perception of his mother, Miss Ivey, and his love and respect for her are encoded in the following treatise:

> Mama she's not in a good mood the basket inna mi kitchen running out of food
> [Mama, she is not in a good mood because the basket in my/our kitchen is running out of food]
> Papa can't find no excuse, him drink out wi money gamble and lose
> [Papa cannot make any excuses because he spent our money on liquor/alcohol and also gambled and lost it all]
> Mama can't find the next dime, she might can buy rice but not the meat kind
> [Mama cannot find the next dime/cent, maybe she can buy some rice but not meat]
>
> Through the wickedest struggle Mama nuh leave us,
> [Throughout the harshest times, Mama did not leave us]

She stand by mi side, Mama – Daddy grieve us,

[She stood by our side, Mama – Daddy caused us pure grief]

She make sure say water inna mi thermos,

[She made sure that she provided resources for me]

So mi know Miss Ivey stand out all purpose

[Therefore, I know that Miss Ivey is special]

To make dat ooman happy, I am anxious

[I am anxious to make her happy]

And when dat ooman down is like it mek mi feel nervous

[And whenever she is depressed/unhappy it makes me nervous]

She teach me to be honest and righteous

[She taught me to be honest and righteous]

And to be educated and famous

[And to become educated and famous]

Mi nah go push har round like a clown inna circus

[I will not treat her disrespectfully as I would a circus clown (idiot)]

Sincerely love ah give har surplus

[My love for her is sincere and abundant]

An everything mi own har name wid nuff plus

[And I have made her a co-owner of everything I possess]

Mama she's not inna good mood, the basket . . . [repeat stanza 1]

Mama should get a medal, that's the way I feel,

[I believe that Mama should receive a medal]

She teach me to be honest, don't steal,

[She taught me to be honest and not to steal]

She tek up di bible pon har knee wheh she kneel

[Whenever she knelt to pray she would place the bible on her knees]

And to the Almighty Jah mi Madda appeal

[And appeal (cry out) to the Almighty Jah for help]

It's real

[Believe me, it is true]

Mama she's not inna good mood, the basket inna. . . [repeat stanza 1][16]

Bounti Killa's foregoing exhortations, and Baby Wayne's cries of "Mamaaa" in the following dancehall hit, underpin the view of many both within and without the dancehall that Mama, the nurturer, will stand by one's side through thick or thin:

Bout them haunted, kill man an' get wanted
[Stating that they were haunted (bad), they killed a man and became wanted (by
the police)]
An mi nuh response fi yuh an nuh lawya bizness. . .
[And I am not responsible for you and any business with lawyers]

Mamaa! Hear murdera a cry,
[Mamaaa! Listen to the murderer cry]
Ah pure teardrops and wata come out a him eye
[A lot of teardrops and water are falling from his eyes]
Mamaa! Hear murdera a bawl,
[Mamaa! Listen to the murderer bawl]
Deh a courthouse an hear him name call. . .
[He is at the courthouse and has heard his name called]

Mamaa! Come check mi regula,
[Mamaa! Come and visit me (in prison) regularly]
Bring mi tootpase, mi soap an nuh lef mi dinna. . .
[Take my toothpaste, my soap and do not leave my dinner]

Mamaaa! Come tek mi out ya,
[Mamaa! Come and take me out of this place]
Cause bad bwoy have mi dung yah a spin propella . . .
[Because bad boys/men have me down here (in prison) like a spinning propeller
(that is, they are torturing me mercilessly)][17]

I argue, therefore, that while select examples of dancehall lyrics and culture
may encode misogynistic elements, the overall labelling of the dancehall as
totally misogynistic arises from isolated examinations of these particular lyrics
and cultural practices that emanate from the dancehall. These examinations
are themselves essentially flawed, as many are sited only around the language
utilized in describing the male attempt to court/conquer the feared punaany,
and also manifested in treatises about the *matey/ie* or *skettel*.[18] Closer examination of the lyrics themselves, together with discussions with dancehall song
creators, disseminators and consumers, reveal that these manifestations are
symbols utilized by the male in his attempt to court, conquer, subjugate and
ultimately defeat that feared other, the female. This multiple discourse treats
the female sex organ in various lyrical, physical and sexual positions, using
names like *punaany, pum pum, cratches, panty meat, renkin meat, vagi, good hole,
tight underneath, tight and good,* and *ukubit.* It also treats with various manifes-

tations of women as *wife, babymother, matey/ie, skettel, gyal, she* and *ooman*, among others. The ultimate aim in this quest is the ascendancy and empowerment of a particular form of masculine identity. This masculine identity is negotiated via a route that wrests power (sexual and otherwise) from the feminine other, resulting in the upliftment of an intensely heterosexual, polygamous and ultimately powerful form of male identity.

In this arena, not all manifestations of woman become sexual conquests, since the manifestation of woman as mother cannot be viewed as bearer of the sexual vagina, the feared punaany, but rather as the bearer of the nurturing womb – a positive space. The battle for male ascendancy and power against the feminine other, therefore, has to be sited in male-female intimate relationships with sexual partner, girlfriend, babymother, spouse or wife – that is, with the bearer of the sexual vagina, the feared punaany.

Conclusion

In the dancehall dis/place, therefore, the selective usage of language/lyrics to court, conquer, subjugate and defeat the feared punaany, on the one hand, is coupled with language/lyrics that revere and uplift the womb and the mother as a site of positive femininity whose role is to nurture masculinity. This duality of the male-female discourse in Jamaican dancehall music speaks to the simultaneity of the love-hate relationship that is an ongoing part of the masculine engagement with the feminine other. Kerr's discussion of the conflicting attitudes within Jamaican male identity identifies forced weaning as one socializing pattern that results in the strong ambivalence that Jamaican men have towards women.[19] This ambivalence is played out in their strong, permanent attachment to their mothers and their high levels of promiscuity in relation to their spouses. While this socializing pattern may be partly responsible for this duality in male-female relations, the dancehall discourse speaks more clearly to the varied masculinities that arise from the cultural split and multiple socializing patterns in Jamaica, as well as to the tenuous linkages that different masculinities have with real social and economic power.

Brathwaite notes that creolization was a cultural action or social process that affected both elites/masters and labourers/slaves.[20] This concept of creolization is reflected in the dichotomy that exists in Jamaican culture and life, where the elite classes continue to maintain a broad divide between high and low cultural and social practices. The pervasive cultural dichotomy that Brathwaite identifies as the result of slavery and creole society remains in contemporary, postcolonial Jamaica. The "high culture" of the educated middle classes is polarized against the "low culture" of the unwashed masses of the inner cities of Kingston, St Andrew, St Catherine and the lower classes of Jamaica as a whole. Dancehall culture, as the contemporary manifestation of this "low culture", is actively creating and re-creating the tensions that operate in Jamaican society. This is played out in the field of popular culture, where the dancehall, as ghetto and lower-working-class culture, works to both produce and reproduce varied and competing forms of personhood in Jamaica.

Consequently, to label the entirety of lyrical discussion and cultural performance around women in the dancehall as totally misogynistic is erroneous. This removes the focus of these male-female discussions away from their true site, which is a creative negotiation of multiple masculinities as part of the lived realities of the actors in the dancehall dis/place. This erroneous labelling draws on Eurocentric notions of feminism and seeks to reorient dancehall discourse around a feminist discourse on the overt and covert use of violence against women as part of the symbols that are encoded in the dancehall. It gives little or no credence to the cultural, social and economic realities of life in postcolonial Jamaica that provide the cultural crucible of intense lack, unending creativity and an intense belief in a better future by any means for many Jamaican men.

In conclusion, therefore, the key role of sex and sexuality in underpinning masculine identities at different levels in postcolonial Jamaican society is still primary. It becomes more important in a context where material resources are increasingly denied or inaccessible to particular groups of Afro-Jamaican men in urban and rural communities. The action of traditional hierarchies of race/class/colour on the creation and representation of multiple masculinities results in extreme lyrical and symbolic discourses in the dancehall dis/place, that simultaneously revere and denigrate the feminine other, the punaany, in an effort to uplift these men and seek their empowerment.

Notes

1. John Stoltenberg, "Toward Gender Justice", in *For Men Against Sexism: A Book of Readings,* ed. Jon Snodgrass (Albion, Calif.: Times Change Press, 1977), 74–83, quoted in Kenneth Clatterbaugh, *Contemporary Perspectives on Masculinity: Men, Women and Politics in Society,* 2nd ed. (Boulder: Westview Press, 1997), 41.

2. Edward Kamau Brathwaite, *The Development of Creole Society in Jamaica, 1770–1820* (Oxford, Clarendon Press, 1971), xvi.

3. Donna P. Hope, "Inna di Dancehall Dis/Place: Sociocultural Politics of Identity in Jamaica" (MPhil thesis, University of the West Indies, 2001), 11–13. The term *dis/place* was developed and refined during research for my MPhil. In this thesis, *dis/place* is used to impute sociocultural and political meanings to the space which dancehall culture occupies in Jamaican society; it provides a working framework within which to locate overlapping symbols of power and domination, as well as the ongoing struggles within dancehall. The term incorporates three main sources. First, the literal English meaning of the word *displace;* second, the Jamaican Creole use of the term *dis* to mean the English *this;* and third, the Jamaican Creole use of the term *dis* as slang for *disrespect(ful)(ed).* My working definition of *dis/place* is:
   this disrespectful place where we have been placed; this place where we are consistently disrespected and mistreated; this place where we are consistently denied our legitimate human rights"; "this place where we are denied access to resources"; "this place where our identities are negated" and even more importantly, "this place from within which we are forced to re-create and claim our resources, identities, personhood and self-esteem by any means.

4. Pat Mohammed, "Nuancing the Feminist Discourse in the Caribbean", *Social and Economic Studies* 43, no. 3, special issue, ed. Brian Meeks (September 1994): 135–67.

5. A *wukka man* or *worker man* refers to a man who displays skill and prowess in his sexual dealings with his women. These men are perceived as ideal sexual partners, and many openly flaunt several romantic/sexual partners.

6. "Nuff gyal inna bungle" (many girls/women in a bundle) describes the multiple sexual/romantic relationships or liaisons of a traditional wukka man, don or other male who is perceived as attractive by women based on his sexual prowess or access to resources.

7. *Don* is a title of distinction afforded to men considered to be of high social, political and economic status in Jamaica, particularly among individuals of the lower socioeconomic levels and in the inner-city context. It grounds its definition around the label given to Mafia overlords of the kind immortalized in the movie *The Godfather,* but orients itself around localized symbols of political and narcopolitical linkages in Jamaica. Many dons have been accused of illegal or

extralegal activities in Jamaica. As a part of this masculine group, a *druggist* or *drug don* engages in the importation/exportation/dissemination of illegal narcotic drugs such as marijuana and crack/cocaine.

8. Clatterbaugh, *Masculinity,* 162–63; Clyde W. Franklin, II, " 'Aint I a Man?' The Efficacy of Black Masculinities in America", in *The American Black Male: His Present Status and His Future,* ed. Richard G. Majors and Jacob U. Gordon (Chicago: Nelson-Hall, 1994), 3–19;
    Majors and Janet Mancini Billson, *Cool Pose: The Dilemmas of Black Manhood in America* (New York: Lexington Books, 1992).

9. Shabba Ranks, "Love Punaany Bad", *c.*1988.

10. Lecturer, "Punaany Too Sweet", 1987.

11. Spragga Benz, "Jack It Up", *c.*1994. *Di red* or *the red* refers explicitly to the moist, red labia of the vagina; in the dancehall this also refers to the very essence of what is considered feminine. The redness of the labia denotes a healthy, strong vagina and by extension a healthy, strong, aggressive woman whose submission/subjugation is symbolized by the forceful, painful removal and negation of the healthy red of the labia.

12. Red Dragon, "Agony", 1989.

13. Admiral Bailey's "Punaany" was voted the number-one hit in the dancehall and also in the wider society, based on compilations of the Jamaica Broadcasting Corporation's (JBC) weekly Top 40 charts.

14. In my work in the dancehall, the *affectors* are defined as the creators of dancehall culture and the *affectees* as the consumers of dancehall culture. See Hope, "Inna di Dancehall Dis/Place" for an in-depth discussion of these categories and their subcategories.

15. See "Attack on 'Punaany' ", *Weekend Star,* 19 August 1988, 1.

16. Bounti Killa, "Mama She's Not in a Good Mood", *c.*1990.

17. "Mama" by Baby Wayne, *c.*1990.

18. In the dancehall dis/place *wife* refers to woman no. 1, or the currently legitimate spouse/babymother of a man. In very rare instances does it refer to a married woman. *Matie,* from the English word *mate,* refers to the sweetheart or "other woman" engaged in an extramarital or extrarelationship affair with another woman's spouse. The matie is seen in a negative light as a woman with a huge sexual appetite who lures men into sexual relations, often against their will. In the dancehall dis/place the term *skettel* incorporates the most negative sites of feminine derogation. This manifestation of woman is located at the base of the female-female hierarchy, even below the offending matie. Literally defined, the skettel is a woman with loose morals, easily available for sex to any and all men.

19. See M. Kerr, *Personality and Conflict in Jamaica* (London: Wilmer Brothers and Hannam, 1963).

20. Brathwaite, *Creole Society,* 297.

20

Jamaica's Emerging Tradition in Film
Presenting the Female Body
in Dancehall Queen

Rachel **Moseley-Wood** |

In the editor's note to a special edition of *Review* on Latin American film, Jerry W. Carlson emphasizes that the "Boom" in Latin America occurred not only in novels but in narrative as well, pointing out that since the 1960s Latin America has been producing a body of feature films and documentaries that has been every bit as innovative and diverse as its more widely recognized prose fiction.[1] Unfortunately, the same has not been true of the anglophone Caribbean. More than thirty years after the success of *The Harder They Come*, the first feature film to emerge out of Jamaica, the film industry in this part of the region is still struggling to realize its potential.

But it is perhaps unreasonable to compare the film industry in Latin America with that of the anglophone Caribbean. Film does not exist in a social vacuum, and apart from the differences in size of populations and, therefore, audience size, there are a number of mitigating factors that account for the very different directions which film has taken in these two regions.

According to Julianne Burton, political developments in Latin America after World War II brought about significant shifts in film production that reflected a growing awareness, particularly among the younger generation, of social and economic inequalities.[2] This led to a redefinition of the role of film, Burton explains, in which film became valued not only as entertainment but also for its social function, and the priority given in the Hollywood model to technical and commercial concerns was fiercely rejected. Experimentation led to the consideration of new models, such as Italian Neorealism, and the emergence of new conceptual frameworks in the 1960s such as Third Cinema, Cinema Novo or New Cinema, and "imperfect cinema".

In Cuba the establishment of the Cuban Institute for Cinematic Art and Industry (ICAIC) after the 1959 revolution meant that local film production could benefit from financial support from the state, and also that film production would be linked to the revolutionary process. Further, the 1961 blockade imposed by the United States cut off access to Hollywood movies, forcing Cuban audiences to become familiar with other types of films. Speaking in an interview in 1977, Cuban filmmaker Tomás Gutiérrez Alea stated,

> Initially it seemed that this cutting off of the feature film supply was a disaster. Our public was thoroughly accustomed to those films. But I think it was actually a great boon for us. . . . They have come to accept and understand other film languages, other approaches to filmmaking.[3]

Alea points out as well that Cuba was in a unique position in that the state, through the ICAIC, controlled local film production as well as what was shown on cinema screens in Cuba; therefore, "what we see is in fact what we choose to see. This is another way to educate the public."[4]

In contrast, filmmakers in the anglophone Caribbean have not been the beneficiaries of state funds, and Caribbean audiences' enthusiastic and easily accommodated consumption of the Hollywood product has meant that local films not only have to compete with Hollywood but are likely to be rejected by local audiences if they move too far beyond familiar narrative patterns and models. It is almost redundant to state that funding, as one of the most challenging obstacles to film production and distribution, places enormous pressure on the filmmaker to realize a profit, but it is important to bear in mind that economic factors have significantly affected the types of films that have been produced in Jamaica, the anglophone Caribbean's most significant producer of films to date.

Unlike the films coming out of Cuba and Latin America, which have been used as social instruments and which have emerged out of a spirit of experimentation, innovation and diversity, Jamaican films have been decidedly populist, aiming to appeal to the widest possible audience. This in itself poses certain problems for the Caribbean filmmaker, however, because of the way in which the Caribbean has traditionally been presented in the cinema of the largest and probably most lucrative market, the United States. The Caribbean has long been used as a location for the shooting of Hollywood feature films, due to its topography and proximity to North America. As suggested by Michael Thelwell's searing analysis, however, many of the earlier movies shot on location in Jamaica constituted "a classical expression in cinema of the colonial relationship first developed in literature", in which the Jamaican people "appeared as extras in crowd scenes or in brief cameos as picturesque native types or servants of one sort or another: human exotica, local color". Thelwell states further,

> In each [film] the Jamaican landscape and people represented a visually dramatic backdrop against which white "movie stars" . . . could disport themselves at the center of vehicles of foreign design and even more foreign intention. As I recall, these films were very different each from the other, having in common only two qualities: an infinite forgettability and the marginalization of all things Jamaican.[5]

Keith Warner also concludes that Hollywood films have tended to offer stereotyped perspectives of the Caribbean, in which Caribbean people are often relegated to nonspeaking roles of service and subservience. Many of these films, he points out, were meant primarily for American audiences who "hardly knew, or even cared, where the Caribbean was". They were "largely gazes from the outside, giving viewers on occasion the impression of seeing a travelogue meant to promote tourism in the islands".[6] Marginalization and stereotyping of the Caribbean persona continues, Warner notes, in more recent Hollywood films such as *Cocktail*, a 1988 film starring Tom Cruise, and even to some extent in the very popular *How Stella Got Her Groove Back* (1998).[7] To satisfy the expectations of the foreign audience, therefore, may be to deny the reality of home.

In some ways the Caribbean filmmaker is facing the same paradigm shift and reorientation that Edward Kamau Brathwaite identified for Caribbean writers and poets decades ago when he pointed to the need to seek a voice, perspective and rhythm that was essentially Caribbean:

> We are more excited by English literary models. . . . And in terms of what we write, our perceptual models, we are more conscious (in terms of sensibility) of the falling

of snow for instance – the models are all there for the falling of the snow – than of the force of the hurricanes that take place every year. In other words, we haven't got the syllables, the syllabic intelligence, to describe the hurricane, which is our own experience; whereas we can describe the imported alien experience of the snowfall.[8]

Brathwaite's own response to this challenge led him to the concept of *nation language* and led him, in his own poetry, to develop and create new forms, as well as experiment with existing forms in order to change and transform them so that they spoke more clearly and more precisely to the Caribbean cultural experience and reality. His early experimentation led to poems like "The Dust",[9] in which he captures the cadence of Bajan speech, and "The Cracked Mother", in which the broken lines of the poem, repetition and the evocation of the movement of the seesaw combine to evoke the rhythms of the ocean:

See?
She saw

the sea
come

up go down
school children

summer-
saulting in the park.

See?
Saw

what on the sea
water?[10]

However, the Jamaican filmmakers' attempts to experiment with narrative forms and develop and create a new filmic vocabulary that speaks more clearly to the Caribbean reality and experience are hampered by the factors referred to earlier, which do not present difficulties for the poet. Restricted by market and other economic considerations, lacking the catalyst of political change and the ideologically driven impetus to explore the social function of film, Jamaican filmmakers have found it difficult to break away totally from the narrative models of dominant cinema.

Despite the difficulties, however, there have been interesting and encouraging developments. For the Jamaican filmmaker, music has been one means of striking a happy medium between commercial considerations and cultural authenticity; music has allowed Jamaican films to successfully cross audiences by using an element of the culture which has become globally recognized but which continues to speak strongly to the reality and cultural traditions of its place of origin.[11]

Music performs this task successfully in the 1998 Jamaican film *Dancehall Queen*,[12] which exposes the social and economic realities of the Jamaican urban underclass and plunges the viewer into the world of the Jamaican dancehall, a musically based culture that has become known around the globe. Even as dancehall music identifies the film as culturally and aesthetically Jamaican, however, the struggle to emerge from the limitations of the commercial imperatives and the perspectives of dominant cinema is at play in the film, and is apparent in the film's representation of the female.

Dancehall Queen depicts the struggle of Marcia, a street vendor and single mother of two, to break free from the cycle of poverty of the Jamaican inner city. As she struggles for economic stability Marcia realizes that she must take control of her life and become self-reliant if she is to provide for her family. She discovers the dancehall as a space of opportunity within the limited choices presented to women in the ghetto, and undergoes a physical transformation that will allow her to challenge the reigning dancehall queen, Olivene. This rivalry culminates in a dance contest, which Marcia wins. The physical transformation which accompanies Marcia's entry into the dancehall mirrors a series of other changes in her life, including the exploration and expression of her sexuality and the transformation of her relationship with her daughter.

The film attempts to challenge conventional ways of seeing the female body and female sexuality, as well as conventional attitudes towards the display of sexualized images of the female body, by interrogating the presumption of power in the male gaze. The film's failure, however, to fully disrupt and dislodge patriarchal perspectives and successfully dismantle inscribed relationships of power in the gaze ultimately hinges on its inability to move beyond the perspectives and concerns of dominant cinema, and results in a narrative that is marked by contradictions.

Dancehall Queen constructs the dancehall as a female-centred space, in opposition to the patriarchal structures of power and authority that define the ghetto which Marcia inhabits. At the very beginning of the film, the city is established as a violent, brutal place where men hold power. In the opening scene, Marcia and Priest (one of the villains of the movie) vie for possession of a space on the sidewalk from which to sell their goods. Priest's refusal to move even in the face of Marcia's previous "possession" of the spot, Marcia's rejection of a bystander's appeal for compromise, and the deciding factor in the power struggle – the show of force by Marcia's ally (Sonny) – all indicate that violence, brute strength and aggression define the structures of power. Priest further proves this when he kills Sonny, taking the contest of strength and machismo to an unexpected level of cold brutality that shocks even street-smart Marcia.

In doing so, Priest becomes an image of threat. His distinctive appearance – red hair, gold tooth and, in particular, his oddly coloured eyes – is an appropriation of the feminine; signs which in the dancehall are markers of the feminine art of decoration, become in Priest's hands indications of menace and danger. Larry, the local don, is Priest's counterpart in this respect, as he is also portrayed as a man of violence and threat. An old family friend who is addressed as "Uncle" by Marcia's children, Larry forces himself on Marcia's daughter, Tanya, as repayment for his financial support of the family. Not surprisingly, therefore, when Marcia craftily pits the two men against each other, they "resolve" the conflict through violence, thus allowing Marcia to claim victory by using the very element that has fuelled male ascendancy as the weapon of its destruction.

The ghetto's discourse of violence, terror, confinement and control is defined as patriarchal and defines the woman (Marcia) as victim. This discourse is denounced and subverted by the dancehall's opposing discourse of creativity, hedonism, and sensual and ritualistic movement. The audience is introduced to the first dancehall scene by the voice of a deejay who chants, "Remember, whoever make the gun make a wicked thing . . . devil!", in a clear denunciation of violence.

The dancehall is further defined as an alternative to the ghetto-city's discourse of violence and control by establishing itself as a site of female subversion. Because there seems to be no discrimination and few criteria concerning body shape, size or appearance, the dancehall opposes the concept that the female body should conform to a single, carefully defined ideal. By opposing the ideal of the tall, super-slim model that is held up to women by the Western mass media and the beauty pageant (other sites for female display), the dancehall instead embraces female diversity. Indeed, if there is a preference in the dancehall it would seem that it is for the larger woman. In one scene Marcia's brother, Junior, teases a rather large dancehall patron about her typically skimpy, skin-tight outfit. She is neither embarrassed nor self-conscious, but rather asserts the beauty of her body and her right to wear beautiful and revealing costumes. There also seems to be no strict requirement of age or great emphasis on youth in the dancehall, so that Marcia – still quite young, but the mother of two – can successfully participate. In addition, the dancehall is depicted as a safe venue for female display. Despite the women's pose of eroticism, the male patrons do not violate the performers' personal boundaries.

The dancehall further suggests itself as a site of female subversion as it attacks the madonna/whore dichotomy that often marks conventional patriarchal representations of the female. In direct contravention of patriarchal values, *Dancehall Queen* elevates and celebrates a type of costuming that has traditionally been associated with prostitution and sexual availability, and a representation of female sexuality that has been vilified by conventional morality. The revealing costumes of the dancehall, the purpose of which is to display and emphasize the erotic qualities of the female body, are in the film allotted the acceptance that was once granted to such forms of masculine adornment as the codpiece. The film attempts to push the limits of acceptability by validating these representations of the female body which have traditionally been forbidden and negatively labelled as "dirty", crass and vulgar. Carolyn Cooper points out that in the dancehall the deejays' slackness ("crude and often insulting wordplay pronouncing on sexuality and sexual antagonism"[13]) is potentially a politics of subversion: "a metaphorical revolt against law and order; an undermining of consensual standards of decency. It is the antithesis of Culture."[14] The erotic costumes and movement of the dancehall can also be regarded as performing a similar function by challenging conventional standards of "decency", feminine decorum and dress, and by privileging an aesthetic of excess and overstatement.

There is also an element of carnival in the film's rendering of the dancehall, in its emphasis on creativity, abandon and the ritualistic, as well as in its attempt to subvert the received hierarchy of values and signs surrounding the female body. Also reminiscent of the carnival is the way in which the dancehall is seen as providing the opportunity for women to assume a pose or wear a mask of exaggerated eroticism that might not be permissible in their "real" or other lives.

Commenting on the importance of the motif of disguise, role playing and shifting identities in the films *Dancehall Queen* and *Babymother,* Carolyn Cooper describes the dancehall as

> a potentially liberating space in which working-class women and their more timid middle-class sisters assert the freedom to play out eroticized roles that may not ordinarily be available to them in the rigid social conventions of the everyday. The dancehall, thus conceived, is an erogenous zone in which the celebration of female sexuality and fertility is ritualized.[15]

Cooper also points to the complex transformations and metamorphoses that occur in filmic representations of the dancehall:

> The film medium becomes a locus of transformation in which the already fantastic culture of the dancehall assumes extraordinary status once transferred to the screen. In both films, one set in Jamaica, the other in the U.K., the disguises of the dancehall – the hair, clothes, make-up and body language that are assumed – enhance the illusion of a fairy-tale metamorphosis of the mundane self into eroticized sex object.[16]

While critics of the dancehall define this display of sexuality in negative terms, it is clear that *Dancehall Queen* attempts to endow it with legitimacy and authority. Cooper points out that although the affirmation of the pleasures of the body in the dancehall is often misunderstood as a devaluation of sexuality, it can in fact be theorized as an act of self-conscious female assertion of control over the representation of her person.

A fundamental difficulty occurs, however, when the erotic display of the dancehall is interpreted or captured by the camera with the intention of communicating its liberating and revolutionary potential for women. While it certainly is possible to communicate this using film, to do so means that the director must move beyond what Laura Mulvey describes as mainstream film's coding of the erotic into the language of the dominant patriarchal order, in which "[i]n a world ordered by sexual imbalance, pleasure in looking has been split between active/male and passive/female. The determining male gaze projects its fantasy onto the female figure, which is styled accordingly."[17] The dancehall, constructed in the film as a site where a variety of looks converge on the female figure, is perhaps a complicated, but potentially exciting, space in which to explore the politics of the pleasure of looking at the female.

Bibi Bakare Yusef's reading of *Dancehall Queen* asserts that the film does move beyond the patriarchal language of dominant film by challenging the active/passive polarization of the performer and audience. She suggests that rather than passive onlookers, the audiences in the film, specifically in the contest scenes, are active participants in the performances, as their role as spectator does not dominate their role as active participant:

> Those performing witness and respond to the mood of the crowd and those in the crowd mimic the prowess of the performers. Consequently, that which is being performed, female agency and eroticism, is disrupted and affected equally by those on stage and those before it in a joyous transfer and cross transfer of voluptuous capacity. The visual spectacle of a performing female body gyrating before the crowd is, therefore, not merely a spectacle.[18]

Bakare Yusef suggests that in the film's contest scenes, the distance or gap necessary for objectification closes, and the performer ceases to be an externalized object and a fetishized mode of activity that implies and enforces an equal and attendant mode of fascinated passivity on the part of the audience. Because there is no distance or elimination between the stage and the active audience, she argues, the audience is much more like a crowd, a site for potential activity and engagement:

> The dancehall queen represents the audience as a representation of themselves. The performing woman embodies and mirrors her community. In this sense the embodied agency of the dancehall queen involves an erotics of community. The community of the crowd is folded within her every movement. Her dancing body is the subject of the performance and the means by which the crowd can reciprocate by expressing its own identity. As an erotic site the stage performance, therefore, allows for the jubilant celebration of female carnal power as a unique opportunity afforded by the culture. This celebration does not slip back into pornographic images because the community itself is presented within the audience. The crowd contains celebrating women as much as appreciative men. An erotics of community replaces pornography because both sides of the stage are engaged in active dialogue or communion.[19]

Both Cooper and Bakare Yusef point to the element of homoeroticism in the dancehall performance, with Bakare Yusef noting that part of the pleasure and enjoyment the (largely female) audience derives from the dance is from the recognition and celebration of the erotic in the female and consequently, in themselves.

This interaction between dancer and audience occurs in several instances elsewhere in the film, but is not as developed or as intense as in the contest scene. In one scene Beenie Man, a performer, calls Olivene and Marcia to dance on stage with him during his performance. In another scene Olivene is dancing at the centre of a group of admirers, who not only watch her appreciatively but are also dancing themselves as they watch.[20]

However, even as it poses the dancehall as a site for the expression of female sexuality and, as Bakare Yusef suggests, of female carnal power, the film's very definition of eroticism remains bound up in, constrained and circumscribed by conventional patriarchal ideas of what is erotic in the female, and of how female sexuality should be presented. *Dancehall Queen*'s attempt to validate the display of female sexuality is rooted in its elevation of a particular, stylized presentation of female sexuality that is prevalent in the dancehall, its insistence on the authority of this presentation, and the assertion of women's enjoyment in participating in this type of display. The film's weakness is that it does not attempt to interrogate this received image as a definition of female sexuality that has been imposed on the female body and constructed by male desire, nor does it attempt to pose an alternative definition of eroticism or an alternative means of display.

As such, the dancehall as a subversive space is compromised because it is informed by male desire. This is illustrated in Larry's response to Marcia when she assumes the costume of the dancehall. Previously Larry thought her unattractive and was more interested in her daughter, Tanya, but when Marcia is dressed in her dancehall outfit, complete with wig and make-up, Larry does not even recognize her and refers to her as the "sexy bitch". In the disguise of the dancehall queen Marcia captures his gaze, attention and wallet, something she could not do as Marcia the street vendor. Larry's spontaneous reaction to Marcia – "those legs lead straight to heaven" – suggests that for him she has been transformed into a kind of idealized version of female sexuality. But this idealization denotes a negative quality: she is not merely sexy, she becomes the "sexy *bitch*".

This description, which becomes the term Larry uses to identify Marcia's other (dancehall) identity, reveals the male's ambivalence towards female sexuality, as it associates Marcia's sexuality and desirability with negative connotations. Larry's response forces one to weigh his idealization of Marcia's sexuality against the form which her transformation takes, and to question whether that form has been inspired and fuelled by Marcia's inner sense of her own sexuality or by what she knows to be the expectations and desires of the male consumer. Indeed, Marcia admits to Tanya that "This ain't me", and that the sexy bitch image is not her true self. Rather, she regards her transformation as a means of coping with harsh economic realities, as part of a strategy for survival. By assuming the image or disguise of the sexy bitch Marcia is able to exploit or cash in on what patriarchal society demands and expects of her. She recognizes that as a street vendor her opportunities to make money are limited, but clothed in the costume of the dancehall she is able to exploit more fully the asset most prized by patriarchal society – her body – because as the sexy bitch she conforms to the male's idealized version of a desirable woman. As her friend Winsome remarks of Olivene, the reigning dancehall queen, "The girl only paint up her face and wine up her batty and she have money, she can buy anything." Cooper also points out that it is not the promise of sex and romance that causes Marcia to assume the role of dancehall queen; it is rather the prize money, which guarantees a measure of economic independence, however temporary.[21]

Undeniably, there is a strong element of pleasure in the masquerade for Marcia. She is excited at the prospect of dressing up for the dancehall and enjoys the process of transformation. She also enjoys the feeling of power which the masquerade allows, as she observes the effect she has on Larry. She is delighted when he gives her a cell phone, as she tells a friend how good it feels to get an expensive gift from a man. The gift, an expression of Larry's approval of her newly presented body, confirms that he regards the female body as a commodity, and represents an investment that he expects will eventually lead to sexual access to that body.[22]

In addition, Bakare Yusef's reading of the role that crowd response and the involvement of the audience play in establishing a dynamic between dancer and audience becomes problematic when placed within the context of the cinema audience. Although, as Bakare Yusef asserts, two-way interaction between performer and audience occurs within the film, as it does in a live situation, such interaction cannot be duplicated between the film and its audience in the cinema. Bakare Yusef describes in some detail the cultural differences in audience response. Indeed, Caribbean audiences tend to respond to films and movies as if they were live entertainment.[23] Even though such an active response may enhance the cinematic experience, it is based on an illusion, for no matter how loudly the audience shouts, cries or screams it cannot have a direct bearing or effect on the performance of the actors nor on the outcome of the film. In the cinema we are presented with a *fait accompli* to which we may respond but which (unlike the live performer) cannot in turn respond to us. Dialogue between performer and crowd, in its true sense, is not possible in the cinema, because we are shouting at a performer who cannot hear, far less react, to our response.

Athough the audience in the cinema may respond (like the contest audience *within* the film) to Marcia's performance, that sense of exchange and reciprocal pleasure between performer and audience cannot be duplicated, even though the illusion is created (as we in the cinema identify with and cheer along with the crowd at the contest) that Marcia is responding to our pleasure and excitement. The concept of an "erotics of community", therefore, while certainly applicable to the contest scenes within the film, does not fit quite so comfortably into the context of the scene being viewed by the cinema audience.

It is also apparent that the gaze of the cinema audience, unlike that of the (live) crowd, is controlled and directed by the look of the camera. In the contest scenes, despite there being an identical response from the crowd to the two performers, the camera tends to view Olivene from a different perspective than that from which it views Marcia. When viewing Olivene the language and vocabulary of the camera are the same as when it views the performers in the earlier dancehall scenes: close-ups and medium shots dominate and the camera tilts upward, viewing the dancer's body from below. When viewing Marcia's performance, however, the camera pulls out from its previous tight shots and moves into medium and long shots. In effect, when viewing Marcia the camera attempts to mimic the look of the crowd, but persists in viewing Olivene with the gaze of the voyeur. In *Dancehall Queen,* therefore, except when it views Marcia, the camera's mediation between the viewed subject and the audience disrupts the idea of the dancehall as a celebratory site of female sexuality and carnal power. Cooper's assertion that the affirmation of the pleasures of the body in the dancehall can also be theorized as an act of self-conscious female assertion of control over the representation of her person is not applicable to the female dancehall performer who is viewed through the eye of the camera. In such a situation it is (the person behind) the camera, not the performer herself, who controls how she is represented.

As the camera looks at Olivene with the gaze of the voyeur it emphasizes the blatant sexual quality of her performance. Olivene, the dancehall veteran, shows the agility and flexibility that in the dancehall is likened to sexual performance. She frequently grasps her pubic area and opens her legs wide. In contrast, Marcia's performance, while also erotic, with much swaying of the hands and hips and movement in the bottom, is not as bluntly sexual as Olivene's. Yet it is Marcia who wins the contest. Certainly by dancehall standards, however, she has not performed better than Olivene. In fact, judging particularly from previous dancehall scenes, it is the type of dance that Olivene performs that is regarded most highly in the dancehall. The outcome of the contest (ignoring for the moment the conventions of the genre which dictate that Marcia, the underdog and star, must win) suggests that there is value in subtlety, that a dancehall performer can be appealing, pleasing and provocative without having to resort to flagrant display. But to assert this, to advocate subtlety, is to undermine and reject the idiom of the dancehall, which is defined by exaggeration and conspicuous displays of sexuality.

The vocabulary of patriarchy, displayed in the way the camera views Olivene, is evident in other scenes in the film as well. In the first dancehall scene Marcia herself is the observer, when she goes to the club to check out the latest dances and fashions. This scene illustrates vividly the ability of the camera to interpret and impose meaning. The dances performed in this scene emphasize the sexuality of the female dancers: sexually suggestive movements and positions are imitated, and some women grasp their pubic areas. The camera views these dancers and dances in such a way as to further emphasize their sexual quality. When the camera looks at the female dancers, it shows mainly dismembered body parts: the focus is on the breasts, the frontal pubic area and the buttocks in particular. Close-ups and medium shots are often used for the female dancers, as well as shots in which the camera tilts upward, viewing the female dancer from below so as to emphasize her body while calling attention away from her face. During the sequence the camera moves from Marcia's face, watching intently, to close-ups of the dancers. As she watches she attempts a few steps and moves. Although she is an observer, and a careful and intent observer at that, Marcia's look is not that of the male. This is borne out by her lack of response to and apparent disinterest in the erotic suggestions of the dance images. Marcia's face reveals not the slightest sign of arousal or sexual desire. She appears to be studying the dances from a purely "technical" perspective, as she tries to learn the moves.

Although Marcia's gaze must be defined as something other than male, in this scene the gaze of the camera is decidedly voyeuristic. Indeed, this scene demonstrates the power and ability of the camera to impose the look and gaze of the voyeur on the cinema audience. For although Marcia, as live witness, watches the dancing from a nonerotic perspective, the camera translates the activity for us, the cinema audience, into an exercise in titillation.

In the next dancehall scene Marcia has moved from observer to participant. The change in status is marked. Gone are the jeans and baggy shirt; Marcia is now dressed in her brand-new dancehall outfit, complete with wig and shades. In this scene the photographer at the club is entranced with this new face. Marcia, now the participant and performer, glows in this attention as she smiles, dances and poses *for the camera*. She is made the centre of attention because the eye of the (photographer's) camera is turned on her. However, when another dancer catches the photographer's eye, he turns his back on Marcia to photograph her rival. Marcia is immediately deflated, feels rebuffed and leaves the dance floor, soon to declare that she is going home.

In this scene the look of the (movie) camera is duplicated by the gaze of the photographer who is armed with his own (still) camera. As participant, Marcia must now compete with other dancers for the attention of the male gaze, which in this scene is symbolized by the photographer. Within this context dancing becomes an activity that is not sustained solely by notions of personal pleasure or expression: it becomes a display or performance which is validated by the gaze of another or others. The gaze for which the women in the dancehall often compete, however, is not the type of observation displayed by Marcia in the initial dancehall scene, in which attention is captured by the technical elements of the movement; it is, rather, the gaze of the male spectator who is moved and affected by the erotic display, as typified by the photographer in the club. As he photographs Marcia the photographer smiles appreciatively; Marcia smiles back in return, tilting her head downwards and peering over her shades in an affected pose often used in flirtation rituals. When he turns to photograph the other dancer the photographer again smiles broadly and eagerly. Clearly, there is an important difference in the way the photographer looks at the dancers as opposed to the way Marcia looked at them as an observer. Indeed, the photographer reveals the intent and purpose of his gaze when he follows Marcia to the bar to inquire whether she has a man.

The film, however, also challenges the photographer's apparent authority as holder and representative of the male gaze, when it positions him during the contest scenes as a member of the audience. As Marcia dances on stage, arms outstretched as if to draw in and embrace the celebratory, participatory audience, the photographer is busily taking photographs of the dancer, somewhat out of sync with the rest of the crowd, which is enthralled with and participating in the performance. In addition, there is a brief shot of another camera man, a videographer in the audience who watches Marcia and Olivene through a video camera. The significance and authority of his gaze (and the presence of the camera) is suggested when we see, within the same sequence, Marcia's younger daughter and Tanya's boyfriend watching the performance at home on the television. The video camera is not only "seeing" and interpreting the performance for those at home, but also broadcasting Marcia's "secret" identity: "That's your mother?" exclaims Tanya's boyfriend in disbelief. The movement between the videographer at the performance and the television screen in Marcia's home (in effect the videographer's translation of the performance) again reveals different ways of looking at the two performers, Olivene and Marcia. Other types of gazes are also evident. In the second dancehall scene there is a brief interplay between two women: one stalks by, head held aloft in an exaggerated expression of aloof disinterest in the gaze of another, while the woman whom she attempts to ignore looks at her in a pose that exaggerates both the act of looking and the expression of amazement.

In the actual dancehall, while significance and importance is attached to the look and response of the largely female crowd/audience, it is often the gaze of the aroused male for which the women compete. The structured contest with its ordered performances on a stage, as depicted in the film, is not the most common form of participation in the dancehall, and yet the contest crystallizes the component of female rivalry that not only exists in the dancehall but also appears to feed its growth and very creativity. The stage show also underscores the fact that economic gain has a large part to play in this rivalry. This is precisely why the male gaze in the dancehall acquires such primacy and significance: because it is supposedly backed by money. For, in the dancehall, the capture of the male gaze is often equated with the securing of male patronage, as occurs with Marcia and Larry. In the context of the competition male patronage has been replaced by prize money, thus eliminating the need to attract the gaze of the male and allowing for the elevation of the look of the crowd/audience. The distinction between the gaze of the male and the celebratory look of the crowd is reflected in the two aliases Marcia acquires when she enters the dancehall: Larry refers to her as the "sexy bitch", but she is called "mystery lady" by the dancehall crowd.

The expensive dancehall costumes not only represent female creativity, therefore, but are also financial investments designed to catch the eye of the male spectator (again, as Marcia does with Larry). In this way, then, the idea of female display in the dancehall as a form of female power and authority is undermined, because it appears to be derived, in part at least, from the male structures of commerce in which females compete against each other for the gaze and attention of the male and his patronage. Indeed, this is Marcia's ostensible reason for entering the dancehall in the first place: financial gain. It appears, then, that an important component that informs such female performance and display is the desire to fulfil and then exploit male desire, not the female's reading and construction of her sexuality. Far from being free of male influence, therefore, the film depicts the dancehall as a site defined in part by commerce in which the female body is used as a commodity. Marcia acquires her new-found confidence not by rejecting or rebelling against the capitalistic patriarchal structures and values of the male ghetto, but rather by becoming a participant within the male capitalist economy, by using her body as capital and maximizing its profitability by conforming to the demands of the consumer.

As a performer in the dancehall Marcia remains bound within and conforms to the discourse of the male ghetto-city. She has gone full circle, and finds herself in the same position into which she once forced her daughter: that of using her body as an economic investment. Marcia wins the prize money, so she will not have to sleep with Larry, or any other man, but in order to win the contest she had to undergo a process in which she shaped and transformed her body into that representation that the male has deemed satisfactory and appropriate. In this light Marcia's physical transformation becomes an expression of the Cinderella syndrome.[24] The prize (in this instance money, not a husband) is only attainable, however, after the woman has reshaped her body into the required social role.

Dancehall Queen's attempt to construct the dancehall as a subversive space for women is complicated by its depiction of male influence and authority, which converge to dictate and inform female expression. The repeated images of disembodiment and separation associated with the female body in the dancehall are also in conflict with the attempt to use the dancehall as the space in which Marcia achieves wholeness. Thus, the linking of Marcia's movement towards subjecthood and self-realization with her entry into the dancehall becomes contradictory. The plot, which insists on the autonomy of the heroine, attempts to counteract the underlying contradictions of the visual images which repeatedly define the woman as object, by having Marcia ultimately reject the dancehall and bequeath her trophy to Olivene but retain the prize money as her ticket to a better life. Marcia uses the dancehall as a means towards an end, not as an end in and of itself. At the end of the film she removes and puts aside the mask of the sexy bitch and the mystery lady, and emerges from the dancehall as Marcia, the street vendor, resuming her place beside the push-cart. Her real triumph, therefore, is not simply winning the contest; it is rather the transformation that the experience has brought about: a new-found self-confidence, a relationship with her daughter that is based on mutual respect, and a recognition of herself as a worthwhile member of the community.

The film's retention of the vocabulary of patriarchy, in both the ideological conception and the visual presentation of the female performer in the dancehall, compromises the attempt to pose the dancehall as a subversive and liberating site for women within patriarchy, thus mitigating the revolutionary potential of this cultural space. Such unqualified radical statements are kept firmly in check by the film's adherence to the narrative forms of dominant cinema, and its attendant intention to appeal to a popular audience, as signalled by its formulaic ending. Despite the contradictions, however, *Dancehall Queen* must be credited with exploring and exposing a cultural space in which the female plays a prominent role, and, through this, contributing to the discourse on female representation, female sexuality and its display. The very contradictions in the film force audiences to confront their own views and presumptions concerning the display and viewing of the female body.

Notes

1. Jerry W. Carlson, "Guest Editor's Note", *Review: Latin American Literature and Arts*, no. 46 (Fall 1992): 4.
2. Julianne Burton, introduction to *Cinema and Social Change in Latin America: Conversations with Filmmakers*, ed. Julianne Burton (Austin: University of Texas Press, 1986), x–xi.
3. Tomás Gutiérrez Alea, "Beyond the Reflection of Reality", interview by Julianne Burton, in *Cinema and Social Change*, 126.
4. Ibid., 125.
5. Michael Thelwell, "The Harder They Come: From Film to Novel", in *Ex-Iles: Essays on Caribbean Cinema*, ed. Mbye Cham (Trenton: Africa World Press, 1992), 177.
6. Keith Q. Warner, *On Location: Cinema and Film in the Anglophone Caribbean* (London: Macmillan, 2000), 41.
7. Ibid., 59–62. Warner describes *Cocktail* as a tourist-oriented film in which nearly every black face belongs to a waiter, a hotel maid or some such worker. While he allows that *How Stella Got Her Groove Back* does challenge certain stereotypes, namely the older man–younger woman liaison, he points out that it also perpetuates the tourist-brochure image of Jamaica as a place for sun, sand, sea and sex.
8. Edward Kamau Brathwaite, "History of the Voice", in *Roots* (1986; reprint, Ann Arbor: University of Michigan Press, 1993), 263.
9. Brathwaite, "The Dust", in *The Arrivants: A New World Trilogy* (Oxford: Oxford University Press, 1967), 62–69.
10. Brathwaite, "The Cracked Mother", in *The Arrivants*, 180–81.
11. The commercial function of music in Jamaican films is somewhat controversial. Kenneth Harris describes *The Harder They Come*, widely recognized as one of the best films to emerge from the anglophone Caribbean, as "produced for the purpose of selling records and directed by a man (Perry Henzell) who boasts of having made four hundred commercials". Harris, "Sex, Race Commodity and Film Fetishism in *The Harder They Come*", in *Ex-Iles*, 211.
12. *Dancehall Queen*, dir. Don Letts and Rick Elgood, 96 min., Island Digital Media, Island Pictures, 1998, DVD.
13. Paul Gilroy, *There Ain't No Black in the Union Jack* (London: Hutchinson, 1987), 188, quoted in Carolyn Cooper, *Noises in the Blood: Orality, Gender and the 'Vulgar Body' of Jamaican Popular Culture* (1993; reprint, London: Macmillan, 1994), 141.
14. Cooper, *Noises in the Blood*, 141.
15. Cooper, " 'Mama Is That You?': Erotic Disguise in the Films *Dancehall Queen* and

Babymother" (paper presented at the nineteenth annual University of the West Indies Conference on West Indian Literature, Georgetown, Guyana, 2000).

16. Ibid.

17. Laura Mulvey, "Visual Pleasure and Narrative Cinema", in *Feminisms: An Anthology of Literary Theory and Criticism,* ed. Robyn R. Warhol and Diane Price Herndl (New Brunswick, N.J.: Rutgers University Press, 1996), 436.

18. Bibi Bakare Yusef, "Fanon Can't Dance: Antiphonies of the Gaze in *Dancehall Queen"* (paper presented at Reggae Studies Unit Film Seminar Series, University of the West Indies, Mona, Jamaica, March 1999). The extracts are taken from an audio recording of the seminar done by the Radio Education Unit, University of the West Indies, Mona.

19. Ibid.

20. Brathwaite also makes note of the revolutionary potential of the crowd in his description of the 1972 Kingston premiere of *The Harder They Come*: "At the premiere, the traditional order of service was reversed. Instead of the elite moving from their cars into the Carib cinema, watched by the poor and admiring multitude, the multitude took over – the car park, the steps, the barred gates, the magical lantern itself – and demanded that they see what they had wrought. 'For the first time at last' it was the people (the raw material), not the critics, who decided the criteria of praise, the measure and grounds of qualification". Brathwaite, "History of the Voice", 296n44.

21. Cooper, "Mama Is that You?".

22. Larry used a similar strategy with Tanya, Marcia's daughter. After contributing to her education he demanded sex with the teenage girl, an exchange which Marcia initially condoned. As the sexy bitch, Marcia manipulates Larry by first enticing and then frustrating and humiliating him when she reveals her true identity.

23. This is graphically illustrated in the Rialto scene in *The Harder They Come,* in which movie patrons shout and jump out of their seats to cheer the star, totally disrupting the classic image of the quiet, silently attentive cinema audience with eyes slavishly glued to the screen.

24. Promotional material actually described *Dancehall Queen* as "a modern-day Cinderella story, with no Prince Charming, but one very strong Jamaican woman".

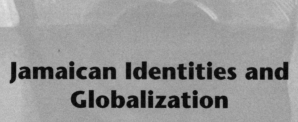

PART SEVEN

Jamaican Identities and Globalization

Citizenship, Subalternity and Cyberspace

21

Citizenship and Subalternity of the Voice within Globalization
Dilemmas of the Public Sphere, Civil Society and Human Rights in the Periphery

Robert **Carr** |

[Creoles are] all the ethnic groups which make up Caribbean society . . . moving through the period of settlement, through slavery and the post-emancipation period and the arrival of new ethnic immigrants, into the more recent phenomenon of vicarious culture contact through tourist, book, magazine, film, television.

– Edward Kamau Brathwaite, *Contradictory Omens*.

The [holding] cell which [held eighteen males who had been rounded up off the street] was about 8ft by 7ft in size [and] was extremely hot due to the congestion. There was very little air available and this was only accessible through small holes in a metal door for the cell. The cell had no windows and they were surrounded by concrete walls. Water dampened the floor and in order to quench thirst, perspiration and water dripping from walls had to be used as no drinking water was made available to them. He also testified that one man had to drink his own urine in order to quench his thirst. After being released from the cell for lunch at 1:00 p.m. on Friday, they were never fed again and were locked up thereafter without further release until Saturday morning [when three of them were found to have died].

– Testimony in the wrongful death suit brought against the Jamaican state on behalf of Agana Barret, 1992.

The Public Sphere as a Forum

In an unpublished article on the question of citizenship and the rights of the people (*derechos de gente*), Latin Americanist Ileana Rodríguez analyses the spaces in which indigenous Guatemalan activist and Nobel Peace Prize Laureate Rigoberta Menchú engages with the public sphere at the level of globality, that is, within the halls of the United Nations and other key forums of the West. For Rigoberta, "civil society [means] a group of organisations that represent the socially marginal groups without rights to juridical citizenship but with well-established cultural citizenships".[1] I bring this up to introduce the idea of the public sphere as a forum, and to raise questions about the politics of the constitution of the public sphere in its history, identity, ethnicity, class, nation, and in relationships to the state, state-formation and the international division of labour. Kamau Brathwaite's body of work has consistently reminded us that these concerns are at the core of the sociopolitical and therefore cultural construction of creole societies and of social justice. Brathwaite also raises questions of how these factors bear down on who can speak, whose voice counts as speech, in many ways an issue taken up by Gayatri Spivak in "Can the Subaltern Speak?" and revisited in *A Critique of Postcolonial Reason*.[2] Caribbean societies are divided in many ways – uptown versus downtown, brown versus black, elite versus subaltern – and these divisions, as Brathwaite has argued, have come to define the ways in which Caribbean societies have been administered and dominated, emerging from the initial onslaught of colonial times to the present day. Creole represents the push and pull along multiple vectors that Brathwaite sees as incomplete, as the struggle continues between a culture of the black/African masses and the British colonizing system. In this context the politics of culture is loaded with the culture of politics. While it is present in poetry and in notions of aesthetics (Brathwaite's famous notion of a British uproar following a BBC interview in which Prince Charles declares the supreme beauty of Nina Simone or the Hottentot Venus), I want to follow strands of these ideas in their political and juridical instances, in raising questions of human rights, social justice, the public sphere and those dead bodies on whom order is predicated.

Such questions press directly on Jamaican society as, war-weary in many ways, it enters the twenty-first century. At a conference on human rights in Jamaica convened by the United Nations Development Programme (UNDP) on 7 December 2001, the minister of national security for Jamaica called for an "open debate" on breaches in human rights by the Jamaican security forces. He regarded the level of the existing debate about such breaches by the security forces as a sign of the health of the civil debate and the respect for human rights in Jamaica.[3] The state, the minister went on to argue, exists for the purpose of guaranteeing the rights of "citizens" but, he noted, this capacity rests on the ability of the state to maintain law and order. That capacity is under severe threat in parts of Jamaica's territory, as has been amply documented by Jamaicans for Justice, by Families Against State Terrorism (FAST), by the Centre for Population, Community and Social Change at the Mona campus of the University of the West Indies, by Amnesty International, by Human Rights Watch, by the World Bank and others.[4]

For the minister, the state's existence qua state is in dire jeopardy, and law and order are the solutions to its stabilization, on the basis of which the state can then move towards guaranteeing the rights of the citizenry. This takes us into the realm of law and criminality, and the relationship between these two concepts and the state. For the minister, this is where the political questions of citizenship in Jamaica rest today. It was left to the working-class founder of FAST, Yvonne Sobers, to raise (after the minister had left, unfortunately) the issue of in whose name, and over whose corpse, do states claim to found law and order out of chaos in the name of preserving the rights of citizenship. Nazi Germany and the Taliban, she argued, operated on the same principle of corpses → order. I would add that the Israeli regime's genocidal policies towards the Palestinians have followed the same tragic route. In those regimes the proper constitution of the state is predicated on the dehumanization and brutalization (where not extermination) of a mass, one individual at a time, in the name of the citizenry, law, order, the function of the identification of the criminal, and the special place reserved for the criminal in law, nationally and internationally. And in each of these cases, as in Jamaica, the extremity of the state is masked and normalized, and the public mindset of the relative elite is characterized, on the one hand, by a desire to not fully know, to be ignorant, helpless, inert – or, on the other, we bestow unconcealed support.

Subalternity, the Underclass and the West Indian State

This raises the question of subalternity, because by definition, the subaltern is one on whose domination citizenship and the state are founded.[5] To illustrate this we can look at the colonial system for a West Indian subaltern study.

Under this system white equalled citizen, black equalled slave, then subject; the former the subject of law and order, the latter the object of law and order. Rebellions and riots of the subalterns across the islands, in tandem with the bankruptcy of the plantation system and the political-economic shifts in the paths of international capital away from mercantilism towards free trade, began to change that strategy, until we arrive at globalization and the situation we face today. This historical political-economic shift from mercantilism to free trade to globalization is critical to understanding the conceptual shifts from slave to underclass to subaltern. *Underclass* was a term central and appropriate to Marxist analyses of modes of production under nineteenth-century industrialization. Under globalization the *subaltern* as a political and social subject is constituted by a persistent and definitional "exclusion or limitation"[6] that interrupts the narratives of history that for us begin in colonization and continue in the twenty-first century. This shift from underclass to subaltern would necessarily include the development of colonial administrative structures and the constitutions of the "people" under colonialism, segue into nationalism and the nation state, and then culminate in neoliberalism, postnationalism and the growing threats to the state.

The conceptual shift to the subaltern thus registers the changing position and conceptualization of the black underclass, and the relationships between that class and state and nation formation in our region. This shift will have important effects that will become central to my argument about the state under threat, the constitution of the nation, civic debate, and the subaltern. In *Contradictory Omens* Brathwaite states that

> "Creole society" is the result therefore of a complex situation where a colonial polity reacts, as a whole, to external metropolitan pressures and at the same time to internal adjustments made necessary by the juxtaposition of master and labour, white and non-white, Europe and colony, European and African (mulatto creole), European and Amerindian (mestizo creole), in a culturally heterogeneous relationship.

and his logic holds true here.[7] These adjustments have come to include the don system, the informal economy, and the rise of a coalition of force that effectively rules substantial swathes of the Jamaican diaspora, anchored in the Kingston ghettos as a base, but with a triangulated reach that incorporates both the United Kingdom and New York. I will argue that under globalization creole culture from below takes on brutal incarnations.

I need to introduce one more set of ideas concerning the don system and structures of masculinity before I can come to my thesis, which ties all these disparate strands together and which makes what I know will be a heavily controversial point. The underclasses within the underclass that come to define the terms of the new structures will also emerge in this analysis of the social scientific literature documenting the struggle for governance and governability in twenty-first-century Jamaica. Sistren, as historiographers, will close my case against the postcolonial state.

The don system in Jamaica is well known and understood within the island. It is a system in which a gang leader has risen to the status of community leader, and from there, through the gang, comes to dominate all aspects of community life, especially in politics, economics, welfare and justice. The don system's grip on everyday life in the ghettos – or rather, the "garrison communities" Horace Levy describes[8] – is also well understood and well documented. Dons are frequently drug and/or arms dealers, who wield total power through gangs of young men aged roughly fourteen to twenty-five, and who often die before they are thirty. The men and women in the don system lead a brutal life that brutalizes communities, but the system also provides security – the minister's portfolio – to those in the ghetto through retaliative violence that is part of daily life but is "ordered" – in the Foucauldian, forensic and military senses – by the don system. We could say that because it serves this function, it is vigorously sustained and loudly defended by the people in the ghetto communities.

The dons provide employment to those who aspire to US-style consumerism in a society which considers entire neighbourhoods criminal and abandons their inhabitants to their fate. This is not a metaphor: persons applying for jobs who live in these areas are refused employment on the basis of their street address alone. The same is true, it ought to be said, for Trinidad, and so this speaks to a Caribbean problem – that is, our capacity and our habit of categorizing entire populations as disposable, as objects of law and order whose bodily presence on our streets is a sign of their inherent criminality and difference, as "subaltern".

What, then, is the place of the voices of these communities, and these dons, and these gang members, and those within these communities whose voices are not heard? We come full circle to the question of citizenship, of the public sphere, to the question of criminality and law and order, and on whose back law and order is predicated. We need to ask who pays the price of their lives – in quality and in quantity – for the preservation of order by the Jamaican neoliberal state.

My thesis is as follows: *Endemic to the question of the state is who is allowed to enter the public sphere and this, together with male gender identity formation, has brought the Jamaican state to a crisis from which it may never fully recover.* The public sphere, as Habermas defines it, is that place where "civil society is discussed and it is within it that public discourse is 'a notion of procedural rationality and its ability to give credence to our views in the three areas of objective knowledge, moral practical insight, and aesthetic judgement' ". Further, "the notion of the public sphere is thought of as a neutral space where equality is practised through discourse".[9] Is this the public sphere of which the minister/state speaks?

For such definitions cut to the very heart of the questions I have about the key terms of the discourse of states and the current status of the state in post-colonial Jamaica. Who is the citizen who is the subject of that state, and who is the object of the battle over state control? The presence and operational strategies of the don system by themselves muddy the waters; the open collusion of politicians with the don system underscores the turning upside-down of the (neo)liberal principles on which the concepts of civic debates, the public sphere, and citizenship are premised, and takes us to the question now of human rights, on which the whole concept of civil society rests.

For centuries the black subaltern population has been the object of law and order. These spaces – the citizenry/subjects of law, and the subaltern/objects of law beneath the radar – have both been historically dominated since slavery by men, our historians of Caribbean slavery tell us.[10] This system of male domination has taken us to the questions raised by Errol Miller in his analysis of the men of the black underclass, and the ways in which Caribbean societies are comprised of brown and white elites who control government and the economy and who predicate their power on the suppression of the men of that underclass.[11] This amounts to an unbroken history of exclusion from the category of citizenship and its privileges – fairness before the law, concern over a decent education, concern over the voice of these people in thinking about the Subject of the state, life expectancies, sanitation, human waste control, running water, electricity – and the list goes on.

The premises upon which masculinity is defined, including its Caribbean and more particularly its Jamaican brand, are in direct conflict with submission to such treatment by the state in the face of the growing prosperity of the "uptown" – read relative elite – community. Male gender identity, already sim-mering within the domains of its authority, thus explodes into the public sphere in the don system, which is the threat to the state that has the minis-ter and many Jamaicans so worried. The don system is nevertheless perform-ing many state functions within the ghetto community, and thereby providing relief from the very government which wants to stake a claim to allegiance but which has not managed to provide what the don system has: some security from rape, robbery and random killings, a steady income, money for school fees, school books and school uniforms, money for doctor's bills and medication, and so on. It is this that has eroded the state: the failure of the state to provide the protections of citizenship subtended by the social pact has led to the very impasse that has the government decrying criminal-ity and unleashing the security forces on the ghettos. On the one hand, the political mission of the government unleashes these assaults on the ghetto communities to take territory and seize ammunition. On the other hand, members of parliament then attend the funerals, shake the hands of, and meet with the very leaders of the system they decry as the undoing of law and order – an undoing that requires the arming of the security forces to take ter-ritory, which means defining communities as zones of conflict and then killing people caught within those zones, which killings are then debated in the public sphere and civil society.

Citizenship: The State and Human Rights

We confront, then, the question of who is included in the public sphere and in the debate over human rights and citizenship raised by Dr Glenda Simms at the UNDP conference with which I began this chapter. As Vasciannie has argued, the questions of citizenship and of human rights are addressed in Jamaica through the terms of the United Nations' Universal Declarations of Human Rights, the treaties signed to ratify those declarations into national law, the question of the state and its survival as predicated on the triangle of the liberal state, the subject of law and the object of law – all terms addressed in the debate.[12] But in fact, on the other side of domination, the questions of citizenship and of human rights revolve around the foundational question of who is a human being. This is foundational because it is only those included in the category of human being who qualify for citizenship.

This question of who is a human being is vital, and will be the central issue of the rest of this chapter. The answers to that question uncover multiple levels of conflict – we could say war, in some cases – over access to the category. At the bottom of the heap – in this chapter and by way of raising, in the end, questions of the structure of the public sphere and civic debate in Caribbean societies – will be prisoners, gay men and persons who are HIV-positive. On the way we will address male gender identity and its role in the link to citizenship and the denial of citizenship between brown Jamaica and black Jamaica. This will take us to the question of the place of women and "woman" within subaltern Jamaica, and the question of citizenship within the nascent state challenging the state; the place of the homosexual in that nascent state through an analysis of Chevannes's work on masculinity and Levy's work on the workings of the nascent state;[13] and the role of brutality in relationship to citizenship within all these spheres.

These considerations argue that the threat to the state comes from the state's failure to know, address and resolve these problems as they grew. The international division of labour and the global trade in drugs now provide the base for the ghetto economy, and from there a platform for the rise of a criminal bourgeoisie that dominates the ghetto, takes the territory, and establishes its own cultural norms for the rule of law, that is, hegemony.[14] For the state, these men must be processed and imprisoned, coming under the rule of law as the prisoner, and this is often the case.

But then consider the relationship between the state and the prisoner which is imputed by the testimony in the second epigraph to this chapter. That testimony is a description of the brutal social pact the state imposes on the subaltern who finds himself in the grip of the rule of law, the object of a violently dehumanizing interpretation of order, despite legal commitments and public exhortations of peace and justice as fundamental to a good society and as the rights of all human beings. On the back of these abuses, the creole state will confront the new creole subaltern bursting out of the private sphere of the ghetto into the public sphere of state politics and international trade.

Who, then, will qualify as a human being at the end of the brief incursion allowed by the pages allotted to this chapter? In closing, I will argue that Sistren, in two testimonials in *Lionheart Gal*, warned us all of what was to come, but the state did not listen to the stories of murder, rape, poverty, and arms that they were telling as they were documenting for us the birth of the don system.[15] This documentation of private subaltern lives as public political history bring us back, finally, to the question of who speaks in the public sphere, and the question of the voice as a political concept, as central to who is a human being, and so to human rights – a concept central to Brathwaite's *oeuvre* – and the future of the neoliberal state.

In his contributions to cultural analysis Brathwaite has posed *creolité* as the emergence of the voice of the colonized with the complex structures that bear down upon it. He writes,

> [T]he term creolization . . . refers to a cultural process perceived as taking place within a continuum of space and time, but which, for purposes of clarification may be divided into two aspects of itself: ac/culturation which is the yoking (by force and example, deriving from power/prestige) of one culture to another . . . ; and inter/culturation, which is an unplanned, unstructured but osmotic relationship proceeding from this yoke. The creolization which results (and it is a process not a product), becomes the tentative cultural norm of the society. . . . Yet this norm, because of the complex historical factors involved in making it . . . is not whole or hard (crown: jewel: diamond), but cracked, fragmented, ambivalent, not certain of itself, subject to shifting lights and pressures.[16]

In what follows I point to the emergence of the creole subaltern state out of these processes with a growing force in the twenty-first century, as the power of the formal state is threatened by the very forces of the underclass that gave it its strength in the twentieth-century waves of nationalism.[17]

Inside the Jamaican Subaltern State

The don system, in which the don represents the bourgeoisie complete with Mercedes Benzes and multiple mansions, has become a subaltern state – although this is clearly an oxymoron, given the definitions of the subaltern I outlined above.[18] It is precisely the emergence of such an oxymoron which has brought the Jamaican state to a crisis. For no state can protect its citizens, its territory and its economic interests without arms – and these men are very good at procuring arms, and high-powered ones at that, as witnessed in the summer 2001 eruption between the security forces and armed gang members across the Kingston Metropolitan Area and centred in Tivoli Gardens, in the now infamous West Kingston. That the economic base is the global trade in drugs is no accident, because the global trade in drugs is a highly profitable trade flowing from the periphery to the metropolis. This trade is also under

the control of men in the periphery, and is a major source of employment
and capital accumulation for those in the periphery who have been left out of
the traditional markets of the neoliberal state, and who have formed a thriv-
ing economy officially referred to as "informal", in contradistinction to the
formal economy managed by the Jamaican state. This informal economy is
the last chance for those whom formal society brands the unemployable. Such
pacts between the subaltern and the international drug trade mean this subaltern state has made an international pact to serve the interests of its citizens, for whom it provides security and access to education, health care and
so on. The eruption in the summer of 2001 also suggests that the dons are
quite capable of working in tandem, pointing to a model of postmodern feu-
dalism as the dominant political structure of the Jamaican ghetto. We will
come back to this at the end of the chapter.

For now we can turn to the brutal epigraph – a fragment of a legal brief
from Jamaica, 1992 – that opened this chapter. The chain of history proves
revealing: faced with the fruits of state policy from the days of slavery when
the estate was the state, to post-emancipation subjugation under colonialism,
through to the postcolonial state positing law and order on the subalternization of the poor and the elevation of the brown and white locals to the status
of the elite, the state then responds through the "security forces" by further
brutalizing poor men at the lower end of Jamaican society as inherently sus-
pect of criminal activity. "Criminal" becomes the category for the citizens of
the subaltern state. Thus the police can round up eighteen men and lock them
in a closed cell until three of them are dead, and the state has to be sued
before it will acknowledge a wrongful death. Agana Barret, one of the men
who died in that lock-up, was not a citizen of the Jamaican state, in the sense
of his having human rights the state was obliged to respect. His life had no
meaning for the state; he was not a human being. He was an object of the law,
as were all the men locked in that cell. That is the Jamaican state at work, in
the name of law, order, and the protection of human rights for the citizenry
proper. Where could such concepts of what these terms mean come from? The
traditional answer is, we learned to be brutal because we had brutal teachers.[19]
However, I think we need to look more closely at Caribbean constructions of
masculinity.

In her essay "Liberal Ideology and Contradictions in Caribbean Gender
Systems", V. Eudine Barriteau raises the following key questions that help me
to build my argument:

What are the choices men make in the construct of their masculinity?

How does the State relate to men?

What are the gender ideologies men subscribe to?

What are the contents of the concept and construct of Caribbean masculinity?

Does the former include a definition of masculinity as total control and power over women [that is, brutality and the denial of human rights]?[20]

The work of Barry Chevannes and Janet Brown, Horace Levy, and Caroline Moser and Jeremy Holland provides some answers.[21] For in the Gender Socialization Project, in the Contribution of Caribbean Men to the Family study, in Chevannes's *Learning to be a Man,* and elsewhere, we encounter critical strands organizing daily life, the home, gender socialization, and thus community politics (as studied by Levy and by Moser and Holland), and thus the politics internal to the subaltern and Jamaican states.[22] Two of these strands are most important for my argument.

One: men must rule women and households, and violence is acceptable in maintaining this hegemony. The Chevannes, Moser and Holland, and Levy studies refer to the extent to which violence and the threat of violence structure gender relations. "Beatings are commonplace", Levy writes, as "the man's response to the woman's quarrelling".[23] Levy also reports that in garrison communities, women can be raped or gang-raped for dating a man from enemy territory, or in retaliation in the war between men for territory and for shares in the drug trade, or, as Crawford-Brown documents, in making men men. Crawford-Brown recounts the story of a young boy forced by the don in his community to watch his peers gang-rape a young girl from the community because he was too "soft".[24] Masculinity is here conceived through the brutal subalternization of a young woman from the ghetto community who is categorized as an object of the subaltern state in making men worthy of citizenship.

Two, following from the brutally sexist logic of the first: men must not be soft, not be women, because that is degradation, expressed in the worst-case scenario as homosexuality, a walking abomination. In *Learning to Be a Man,* Chevannes's informants make it clear that the spectre of homosexuality leads to threats of being thrown out of the family home onto the street. One group of Jamaican informants implied to the researchers "that they killed homosexuals".[25] Further, Chevannes argues that this "intensity of revulsion" stems from gay men's becoming "antiman, againstman", and so poor communities "reduce them to the status of women". This move "effectively treats them as people who need not be taken seriously" and renders them "the objects of behind-the-back jokes ridicule [sic], which are liable to become front-to-face abuse in conflicts conducted in public".[26] Men in these communities, as has since been documented, thus also reserve the right to violently exclude gay men from the category of human beings born with equal human rights.[27]

This homophobic violence is also extended to those believed to be HIV-positive, as other studies have shown.[28] The reduction of certain categories of human beings, in territory controlled by the subaltern state, to "less than" status becomes both systemic and associated with the feminine or with contamination. "Hostility towards homosexuality and the fear of being contaminated by homosexuals" were themes repeatedly encountered by the research team led by Brown and Chevannes.[29] We confront here the normalization of inequality amongst human beings, with accompanying implications for access to human rights.

These same ideas of what constitutes a man and how a man maintains order are also held by the security forces of the state. This is one answer to the question of how policemen could come to be such that they could lock eighteen men in a concrete cell, eight by seven feet, with no windows, ignoring their pleas for three days until three people are dead – and never a charge brought against any of the detainees. For the police, these men are not human beings.

The brutal, dehumanizing machismo shown by the state in the form of the police also sets the terms internal to the subaltern state: (1) it must be ruled by men; and (2) women, gay men and those believed to be HIV-positive are three of the categories who are not the equals of the heterosexual men who rule. This macho attitude feeds into the love of gun-play that is the province of men, into the subordination of women, and into the expulsion and brutalization of gay men. The sophistication of the weaponry, the numbers of dead, the categories of the dead, the names of the men who are leading the skirmishes become central to negotiating the borders between the Jamaican and subaltern states. And here, in negotiating these borders, the treaties and declarations of human rights ratified by the Jamaican state do not hold.[30] But even in the absence of a hot skirmish, the cold war within the ghetto communities and between the ghetto communities and the state rages on, with mounting casualties. The voice of the representative from FAST, raising the question we frame here of "who is a human being?", thus cuts both ways.[31]

The Jamaican Subaltern State in a Global Perspective

But let us look again at what I have been calling the subaltern state, and have also referred to as a coalition of postmodern feudal territories. Both of these descriptions, I would argue, are correct, and both are as anomalous as they are oxymoronic. I want to add a third critical element, which is the international character of the don systems. In this way, the systems are networks that stretch from Jamaica to New York and back, as well as from Jamaica to London and back, as just two of the many nodal points involved.[32] In this way, armed and brutal with no respect for human rights themselves, the leadership in the subaltern feudalistic state is also an international network spanning the West, a network that organizes and wields power in the way that the al-Qaeda network organizes and wields power, although by no means to the same extent or with the same sophisticated objective. When the World Trade Centre, as the centre of the financial megalopolis of the West, was demolished and three thousand people killed, and the Pentagon, as the military headquarters of the only remaining military superpower, was attacked, it was clear that the rules of war had changed in multiple ways. For our purposes in trying to understand the impasse in the Jamaican state, what stands out is that whereas previously states declared war on states, and there were rules of engagement which privileged minimal loss of life for each state and maximum damage for the people of the opposing state, here it was a network – not a state – declaring war on the United States, and suicide – not survival – in the name of the cause was central to the rules of engagement.

This, I would argue, mirrors what the Jamaican state faces within its territory as a by-product of history, identity, class, nation, relationships to state and state-formation and the international division of labour, as these have played out on the national terrain. Superseding states are networks of power with rules of engagement that break with the paradigms of modernity. This is mirrored in the structures and interrelationships of the megacorporations that dominate the neoliberal economies. This, I would argue, is "globalization from below", rather than the globe-trotting of activists protesting the World Trade Organization. It is telling that the brutal effects of these historical political-economic developments are felt most in the periphery – Jamaica in our case, others, in the case of al-Qaeda.

The Crisis of the Jamaican State

Let me close with a glance back to where the description of this Jamaican debacle emerged. I have argued elsewhere that it is documented in Sistren's *Lionheart Gal*,[33] and it is a point I think sufficiently important to bear reiterating here in closing. In Sistren's text the politicization of the ghetto, and the transformation of the new ghetto men of the democratic socialist People's National Party and the new men of the arch-conservative capitalist Jamaica Labour Party into armed, misogynist guerrilla gangs is documented by two separate witnesses. There too, the transformation of gentle community men into armed and dangerous parasites demarcating political affiliation into friendly and enemy territory, and the managing of excursions into enemy territory for murder and rape, are documented. This, it was said, was the work of the Jamaican state. It is this allegation by the subaltern historians that leads Obika Gray to analyse the Jamaican state in terms of parasitism in its relation to the urban poor.[34]

When the politicians changed their minds about the usefulness of the armed guerrilla bands they had created to fight for political control over the ghettos, the monster men and the brutal society they had created in the ghetto became part of the growing trade in cocaine, itself a global network established in the 1970s when, we are told, globalization as we know it today really began to take off.[35] As Sistren documents in *Lionheart Gal,* the political parties used the ghetto as the battleground for political ideologies that were the proper province of the public sphere as Habermas defined it.[36] These men and women dying for the political futures of Jamaica's political elite and their control over the state were not allowed into the public sphere; rather, they were used as pawns in an international Cold War game to gain leverage in that arena. When the politicians attempted to jettison their political operatives back into the ghetto, relying on the shroud of subalternity and the denial of their inclusion as citizens, these men and women found that their survival depended on alternative alliances.

As Spivak argues, the future of subalternity, the voices of the subaltern are merely co-opted, "the rhetoric of their protest . . . constantly appropriated" in political war games.[37] Now, as we saw in the Jamaican election rhetoric of 2001–2002, gender and sexuality have entered the public debate through accusations of homosexuality – that is, in the accusations from both sides of a covert homosexuality (from the Jamaica Labour Party) or its repudiation in "logging on to progress" (from the People's National Party), "logging on" just as the popular dancehall track of the time called for "logging on" to the beating of gay men. Both sides agree on one issue: that Jamaican politics, like Jamaica's broader public sphere, is no place for men who are like women. The state process of realizing democracy by holding free and fair elections thus includes at its core reiterations in the debates within the ranks of the official state of the contamination of a man being perceived as like a woman, a configuration we saw earlier as normalizing violent inequality in gender and sexual socialization in the subaltern state.

In Jamaica the game of co-optation played in the 1970s with the bodies and lives of subalterns, a game whose rules are the brutal rules of Jamaican masculinity as defined by brutal Jamaican men, have come back to threaten the survival of the state at the beginning of the twenty-first century. Sistren were crystal clear in their warnings, but the failure of the state to recognize the damage done by the violence of the constitution of the citizen, of male subjectivity, of subalternity, is propelling us as a test case into the new paradigms developing across the globe in the periphery.[38] For subalternity, I would argue, is the architecture of globalization, and foundational to the process. Globalization is actually dependent on subalternity, and, I argue, the problem we face is one incarnation of a global phenomenon exacerbated by the strategies of the World Trade Organization, the behaviour of the megacorporations of the legal global economy, and the failure of nation states in the periphery.

Finally, we confront layers upon layers of brutality permeating the state and state pacts, through civil society, down into the subaltern community, that come back to threaten the existence of the state. Circling back to the primary issue of human rights, we can take the last step and close with the following understanding. In West Indian postcolonial societies we have given ourselves permission, in the public sphere and in our civic debates, to excuse entire populations from the category of human beings, and therefore from citizenship. Lloyd Barnett provides a partial list and brief descriptions of the breaches of human rights that are part and parcel of civic society in our countries; his example is Jamaica. Stephen Vasciannie raises the issue of the category of prisoners with which I opened this discussion.[39] As a culture we hold up the Bible, in the public as well as in the private sphere, claiming it gives us the right to constitute and then declare entire categories of people disposable, not human beings. With the emergence of HIV over the past two decades, we have made health status a criterion describing another category of disposable people. Prisoners, gay men, HIV-positive people: as a society, we greet such people with a brutal subalternization and look the other way.

This violence structures our society, even as we attempt to privatize it and ignore it. Gender studies reminds us that the private is political. In this instance, the fragmentation of our societies and the denial of the rights of citizenship have come back to bring the state into crisis. The citizens of this state need to understand that this child is our own.

Notes

1.   Ileana Rodríguez, "Western Texts, Indigenous Histories: Translations, Prophesies, Secrets and the Discussion on the Public Spheres, Cultural Citizenship, and *Derecho de Gentes*" (unpublished manuscript, 2001), 6.

2.   Gayatri Chakravorty Spivak, "Can the Subaltern Speak?", in *Marxism and the Interpretation of Culture,* ed. Cary Nelson and Lawrence Grossberg (Urbana, Ill.: University of Illinois Press, 1988), 271–313; Spivak, *A Critique of Postcolonial Reason: Towards a History of the Vanishing Present* (Cambridge, Mass.: Harvard University Press, 1999).

3.   See Dr the Honourable Peter Phillips, minister of national security, "Main Address". It seems only fair to recognize that Phillips walks a tightrope not of his own making, and that his acknowledgement of the public sphere and civic debate is itself a step forward. The conference was hosted at the UNDP office in Kingston, Jamaica, 7 December 2001.

4.   See, for example, Horace Levy, comp., *They Cry "Respect"! Urban Violence and Poverty in Jamaica* (Kingston, Jamaica: Centre for Population, Community and Social Change, University of the West Indies, 2000); Caroline Moser and Jeremy Holland, *Urban Poverty and Violence in Jamaica* (Washington, D.C.: World Bank, 1997); Amnesty International, *Jamaica: Killings and Violence by Police: How Many More Victims?* (ai-index AMR 38/003/2001), available at http://web.amnesty.org/library/pdf/AMR380032001ENGLISH/$File/AMR3 800301.pdf; and Obika Gray, "Rethinking Power: Political Subordination in Jamaica", in *New Caribbean Thought: A Reader,* ed. Brian Meeks and Folke Lindahl (Kingston, Jamaica: University of the West Indies Press, 2001), 210–31.

5. For a genealogy from the perspective of Latin American subaltern studies, see John Beverley, "The Im/possibility of Politics: Subalternity, Modernity, Hegemony", in *The Latin American Subaltern Studies Reader*, ed. Ileana Rodríguez (Durham, N.C.: Duke University Press, 2001), 47–63.

6. Ibid., 50.

7. Edward Kamau Brathwaite, *Contradictory Omens: Cultural Diversity and Integration in the Caribbean* (Kingston, Jamaica: Savacou Publications, 1974), 10–11.

8. Levy, *They Cry "Respect"*.

9. Rodríguez, "Western Texts", 7.

10. See Hilary McD. Beckles, "Historicizing Slavery in West Indian Feminism", in *Rethinking Caribbean Difference*, ed. Patricia Mohammed, a special issue of *Feminist Review* 59 (Summer 1998): 34–56; and Beckles, *Centering Woman: Gender Discourses in Caribbean Slave Society* (Kingston, Jamaica: Ian Randle, 1999).

11. See Errol Miller, "Gender and the Family: Some Theoretical Considerations", in *Gender and the Family in the Caribbean*, ed. Wilma Bailey (Kingston, Jamaica: Institute of Social and Economic Research, 1998), 1–31.

12. Stephen Vasciannie, "Human Rights in Jamaica: International and Domestic Obligations" (paper presented at the Human Rights Day Roundtable, UNDP, Kingston, Jamaica, 7 December 2001).

13. See Barry Chevannes, *Learning to Be a Man: Culture, Socialization and Gender Identity in Five Caribbean Communities* (Kingston, Jamaica: University of the West Indies Press, 2001); and Levy, *They Cry "Respect"*.

14. Gray sees this as the urban poor protecting itself and contesting state power as parasitic ("Rethinking Power").

15. Sistren, with Honor Ford Smith, *Lionheart Gal: Life Stories of Jamaican Women* (London: Women's Press, 1986).

16. Brathwaite, *Contradictory Omens*, 6.

17. See Robert Carr, *Black Nationalism in the New World: Reading the African-American and West Indian Experience* (Durham, N.C.: Duke University Press, 2002).

18. Interestingly, Gramsci, who developed the political concept of the subaltern, made the point that "[t]he subaltern classes, by definition, are not unified and cannot unify until they are able to become a state" (*Selections from the Prison Notebooks*, ed. and trans. Quintin Hoare and Geoffrey Nowell [New York: International Publisher, 1971], quoted in Beverley, "The Im/possibility of Politics", 49). Beverley points out that this was the project of communism, as "it was the (necessary) function of the party to enable the subaltern to take state power" (ibid.).

19. Beverley, citing Mahmood Mamdani, repeats this argument in addressing this issue.

20. V. Eudine Barriteau, "Liberal Ideology and Contradictions in Caribbean Gender Systems", in *Caribbean Portraits: Essays on Gender Ideologies and Identities,* ed. Christine Barrow (Kingston, Jamaica: Ian Randle in association with the Centre for Gender and Development Studies, University of the West Indies, 1998), 452.

21. See Janet Brown, et al., "Caribbean Fatherhood: Underresearched, Misunderstood", in *Caribbean Families: Diversity among Ethnic Groups,* ed. Jaipaul L. Roopnarine and Janet Brown (Greenwich, Conn.: Ablex Publishing, 1997), 85–113; Levy, *They Cry "Respect"*; and Moser and Holland, *Urban Poverty.*

22. See Brown, et al., "Caribbean Fatherhood"; and Chevannes, *Learning to Be a Man.*

23. Levy, *They Cry "Respect",* 38.

24. Claudette Crawford-Brown, *Who Will Save Our Children? The Plight of the Jamaican Child in the 1990s* (Kingston, Jamaica: Canoe Press, University of the West Indies, 1999).

25. Chevannes, *Learning to Be a Man,* 144.

26. Ibid., 220, 221.

27. Robert Carr, "On 'Judgements': Poverty, Sexuality-Based Violence and Human Rights in 21st Century Jamaica", *Caribbean Journal of Social Work* 2 (July 2003): 71–87.

28. Carr, "Stigma, Coping and Gender: A Study of HIV+ Jamaicans", *Race, Gender and Class,* special issue on The Intersection of Race, Gender and Class in Social Service and Social Welfare. 9.1 (2002): 122–44.

29. Chevannes, *Learning to Be a Man,* 144.

30. See Amnesty International, *Killings and Violence by Police*; and Vasciannie, "Human Rights in Jamaica".

31. See Levy, *They Cry "Respect"*; and Moser and Holland, *Urban Poverty.* Beverley also speaks of "intra-subaltern" violence, which was very much at the root of my interest in forming the Latin American Subaltern Studies Group. I was determined that "subaltern" not be conflated with the Marxist idealization of the "working class" that dominated leftist thought at the time the group was founded. Beverley remarks on "the persistence of male chauvinism and violence against women in many, perhaps all, subaltern groups" ("The Im/possibility of Politics", 59). I would not be so totalizing about "all" subalterns as a matter of definition, but I would also remark that male chauvinism and oppression of women are only the beginning of unravelling the complexities of subalternity and human rights, and the civic debates, subaltern and official, as I argue here. My attempts to unravel the layers of subalternity within subalternity are also dramatically abbreviated.

32. See Laurie Gunst, *Born Fi' Dead: A Journey through the Jamaican Posse Underworld* (Edinburgh: Payback Press, 1999).

33. See Carr, *Black Nationalism,* chapter 6.

34. Gray, "Rethinking Power".

35. Spivak, *Critique of Postcolonial Reason.*

36. See Craig Calhoun, ed., *Habermas and the Public Sphere* (Cambridge, Mass.: Massachusetts Institute of Technology Press, 1994).

37. Spivak, *Critique of Postcolonial Reason,* 373.

38. In this sense the interest in subaltern studies that has been shown in Latin America, in the Caribbean, in North America, and in Africa is interesting as it lays fertile ground for looking at and addressing the issues of those excused from the benefits of the process of globalization, which is much of the population of the periphery.

39. See Lloyd Barnett, "Civil Society and Human Rights" (paper presented at the Human Rights Day Roundtable, UNDP, Kingston, Jamaica, 7 December 2001); and Vasciannie, "Human Rights".

22

The Word in Cyberspace
Constructing Jamaican Identity
on the Internet

Bernard **Jankee** |

Introduction

Edward Kamau Brathwaite's project of empowerment through *nation language* articulates oral and scribal traditions in an attempt to deal with the complex problematic of establishing a distinct contemporary identity while repossessing significant aspects of the history of Caribbean people, "grounded in the idea of a 'nation' or national mode of expression".[1] This liberating thrust is mirrored at the popular level through a variety of communicative genres, the most evident being, perhaps, the lyrical strength of Caribbean music. Grounding in the idea of the nation has transcended the spatial confines of the nation state. Caribbean people, not least among them Jamaicans, have inserted themselves in transnational, transborder realms of existence. Nevertheless, there has been a striving to maintain a sense of national identity wherever persons nominally regarded as Caribbean, or more specifically Jamaican, are physically located.

Consciously or unconsciously, Brathwaite's notion of nation language has found popular ground in the practices of maintaining a sense of national identity. In this regard, the technologies of cyberspace and the Internet have provided opportunities for facilitating this process of maintaining notions of self. Through these technologies, what Griffith identifies as "the particularity of *nation language* in the complexity of West Indian registers and dialects" is given new space for expression.[2]

This chapter sets out to conduct an examination of the Internet as a site for the construction of self and community. The notion, I propose, embodies a considerable degree of flexibility and fluidity, in that assumptions of self are not by any means static, neither are they of necessity unstable. Rather, they reflect a constant engagement with wider environments in which people find themselves, and the resulting attempts to comprehend and position themselves within those environments. This chapter represents a preliminary, and provisional, analysis of the ways in which Jamaicans, as Caribbean people, present themselves and are themselves presented in cyberspace. It further speaks to the notion of a particular grouping of diaspora peoples creating space for themselves at the frontier of Internet technology, and using it to maintain and extend their cultural identity/ies as they see it/them. In some ways it is an extension of what Brathwaite addresses through his poetry and historical analysis, but occurring in a new dimension. It is, nevertheless, essentially framed around discourses of self and identity, utilizing in practical ways the technology of cyberspace to create, and recreate, ground for Caribbean voices to be heard.

What I intend is to offer an overview of the Internet as a means of computer-mediated communication, embodying a set of cultural practices in which its users constantly engage, and to progress to an analysis of how this plays out in the specific set of cases selected for review. In exploring the central purpose of this undertaking, I propose to bring a number of the issues raised above into focus. The ultimate intention is therefore to examine cyberspace and its attendant technologies as facilitators of this process of social engagement, highlighting similarities and points of divergence in the way that various individuals and groups constitute themselves and others as Jamaicans on the Internet.

Overview

Internet use has gained extraordinary popularity in the wake of its launch on the world scene, and has come to embrace a diversity of applications encompassing the areas of business, education, politics, leisure and pleasure. In 1998 there were some 320 million Web pages in existence,[3] making it not merely an enormous database, but more fundamentally, the epitome of the information society. By 2004 over 30 billion Web pages were listed in one archive alone (www.web.archive.org).

Activity online is now being regarded as part of a range of cultural practices in which millions of people engage on a daily basis. Far from being merely the technology of bandwidth, keyboards and screens, fibre-optic cables and satellite transponders, the Internet is a means of providing opportunities for, among other things, social engagement. Internet use has become a way of life, extending the boundaries of human interaction, and for many who connect to it, the Internet is a means of transcending previously constructed borders of state and nation. The Internet has become, for the millions of people who use it, an essential means of communication and connectedness with the world around them. It has spawned a range of attitudes and practices, and has consequently created new epistemological dimensions, giving new agency to the concept of cyber – hence the entry of the terms *cybersociety* and *cyberculture,* among others, into the popular lexicon. It has become, in essence, a terrain for facilitating interaction, mediated on one level by technology, but more fundamentally by human interaction.

One further issue that needs to be raised is that of the Internet as a faceless mass of data, residing on computer hard drives in various undescribed places. The way in which the term has come to be used certainly can lead to the impression of a vast, overwhelming space, one in which people can get lost. This parallels the view, prevalent in fifteenth-century Europe, of a flat world whose edges, if transgressed, would send the poor unfortunates headlong into an eternal abyss. This view is countered, however by the assertion that cyberspace is really a network of lived, shared spaces that become familiar to individual users. While, as Miller and Slater declare, the Internet represents a "symbolic totality", it has also come to represent a way in which technology becomes rooted by its use in particular circumstances.[4]

Against this backdrop, therefore, the potential for understanding these still-evolving phenomena of the Internet and cyberspace was hardly overstated by those who saw them as worthy candidates for scholarly investigation in a range of disciplines, and who saw the capacity of the new information and communication technologies, of which the Internet is at the cutting edge, to transform modern society and culture.[5] These debates are quite relevant to the Caribbean, in that they reflect the dialectics that have been very much a part of the region's historical experience.

History, Identity and Representation

In looking at the Internet, there is a strong temptation to see its advent and development as a radical departure from the way in which the world had previously functioned. Technology-based society appears to establish new paradigms of existence and interaction. While not wishing to discount the notion entirely, I would like to proffer the view that the Internet, for all its contributions to transformation, is fundamentally rooted in a much older notion of globalization, the basis of which lay in colonial expansion and domination. This is noted by Said, who states that "this pattern of dominions or possessions laid the groundwork for what is in effect now a fully global world".[6] What this points to is a historical continuity of a process of bringing the world together, certainly in the period of colonial domination for purposes of enriching and enabling European control of the world's resources. In the contemporary situation, while that objective might not have been entirely removed from the agenda, other items of concern, as played out on the Internet, also have a space. What is important to underscore here is that there is a longstanding predisposition to globalization, of which colonialism was an earlier manifestation. Cyberspace, while opening up several new lanes on the information superhighway, and thereby giving agency to a broader diversity of views, does not entirely transcend the deeper roots of its history. There is indeed, in the words of the late Errol Barrow, some "loitering on colonial premises after closing time".[7]

As with any other means of communication, the Internet has the potential of being seen as another means of facilitating the cultural dominance of the industrial and, more relevantly, technologically advanced countries of the North, following from the point made above. Indeed, a significant volume of the information available via the Internet emanates from these countries. However, and far more so than has hitherto been the case with earlier technologies of communication, the Internet also holds great possibilities for giving agency to forms of expression from outside of the economically advanced countries of the world, as evidenced by the sites examined in the course of my research. In the current era of globalization, the interactivity of the Internet holds out far greater prospects for wide access to information and also the ability of different peoples to make their voices heard. The issue of perpetuating domination is real if most of the information is generated externally to the country of the user. On the other hand, access to information created extranationally is not necessarily a bad thing, as it increases access to other information and other points of view.

While Internet use has allowed for great advances in educational, business, military and government communication, the technology has also facilitated new ways of interaction, new possibilities for people outside of these arenas to make contact and to keep in touch. This has given rise to new communities of interest, appropriately labelled *cybersociety(ies)*, and to various notions of cyberculture. While postmodernist theories eschew notions of culture and question the adequacies of ideas of society, these notions have persisted, been adopted and co-opted into the arena of cyberspace. The notion of cyberspace itself has been the subject of many debates: does it lead to the end of society as we know it, in the postmodern vein, or does it reinforce and create new opportunities for society to renew itself?

Identity is a contested notion, and one which has figured prominently in consideration of the new parameters of cyberspace. This can be related to the varying strands of approach, such as the ability of cyberspace to reflect identity, or the agency it gives to the creation of new or other identities. Also to be considered is the very concept of identity itself: What is it, and how does it advance our understanding of human situatedness? Identity has been defined in some quarters as a relatively stable and enduring sense that a person has of himself or herself.[8]

Is identity a useful analytical category or is it problematic? It is problematic in the sense that, in some views, it is seen a static concept. While notions of identity might seem to fix a definition of who a person is in some kind of limiting, bounded description, I regard it to be a dynamic phenomenon, problematic but nevertheless an important frame of reference to employ in understanding constructions of persona, collective or individual. My use of the term therefore recognizes the fluidity and indeterminacy of the concept.

Closer to home, in the situation of a society like Jamaica, emerging from its particular experiences with transatlantic slavery and colonial domination spanning over four centuries, the issue of identity strikes a particular resonance. In a country entering the world of postcolonialism in 1962, the issue of identity was the focus of considerable attention. Identity was also an issue in the movement towards independence itself.[9] The presence of identity on the agenda for debate underscored the polemics of the issue, and this was certainly recognized and articulated: "It is indeed difficult to determine what exactly is meant by the term the 'Jamaican' identity. It is variously expressed as 'things Jamaican' or 'the Jamaican image'."[10] This difficulty sought resolution in appeals to analyses of race, ethnicity and class, among other concepts. One avenue of resolution proposed by Nettleford to this thorny issue was to appeal to conceptual unity between internal perceptions of Jamaica and Jamaicanness, and external conceptions of Jamaica as a national entity. This approach, however, is fraught with the pitfalls of closure, and dangers of an overbearing and unrealistic conformity. What this does is to underscore the issue of identity as a problematic one, and point to the need to be mindful of closing doors to broader understandings and possibilities.

Similarly, representation comes with its own considerable theoretical baggage. I do not propose to engage in a lengthy debate, within the confines of this undertaking, concerning the value of representation. Suffice it to say that, like its philosophical companion identity, representation is a contested notion. However, it does offer some useful means of understanding the construction, reconstruction and performance of self and community, and particularly so in the worlds of cyberspace. While there is undoubtedly merit in the view that identity and representation are problematic as analytical categories, the notions continue nonetheless to be omnipresent in debates surrounding social interaction, and do offer some ways of examining social phenomena.

Internet Use in Jamaica

Technologically, Jamaica is very much travelling on the information superhighway. The first Internet service provider (ISP) was the University of the West Indies, which established the service to facilitate scholarly communication, much in the same way that Internet use evolved in other places. Within a relatively short time Internet use spread to wider communities of interest, and the landscape, or more appropriately the cyberscape, mushroomed. The Internet infrastructure now reflects a situation in which there are approximately sixty-seven ISPs serving nearly a hundred thousand registered clients.[11] These figures are conservative, however, and do not reflect the level of multiple users who do not themselves have personal Internet accounts. It is also not unusual for registered users to have multiple accounts, although figures relating to this are virtually impossible to come by. In addition to established Internet accounts, there are approximately nine cybercafés in operation throughout the country.[12]

There is significant public and private sector interest in further extending the availability of Internet services. Plans exist, and have to some extent been put into operation, for the service to be made available via Internet kiosks. These are to be established within the network of some seven hundred post offices throughout Jamaica, with no end-user charges, giving various communities access to the World Wide Web and other Internet services. This is a joint initiative by the government and the country's sole telecommunications service provider, Cable and Wireless. Other similar though smaller-scale projects are also in train to provide access to communities and individuals who would otherwise not have access to the service. One such community kiosk has been established in the National Library of Jamaica, and an initiative by non-governmental organizations has spearheaded a network of focal points for Internet access in a number of locations across the island.[13] Increasingly, schools at all levels in the education system are logging on to the Internet. The potential for widespread use of this means of communication is therefore great. This takes care of the technology side, to some extent. On the information side, there is the concern that information on and about Jamaica should be readily available online.[14]

There is evidence, however, that this is taking place. Over the course of my research, I conducted several online searches, using the words and phrases "jamaica", "jamaican identity" and "jamaican culture". The number of hits over the period has been, on average, in the region of seven hundred thousand.[15] Taking into account the duplication of results that often occurs on search engines, the figures still represent a considerable amount of data concerning Jamaica available in various forms on the Internet. The sites themselves have been quite varied, ranging from government and other official sites, to academic, entertainment, personal, and business sites.

The Internet and the Construction of Self/Others: A Selection of Sites

From the range of sites viewed during the course of this project, three were eventually selected for analysis. These were www.jamaicatravel.com, the site of the Jamaica Tourist Board;[16] www.jamaicans.com, an independent site giving information about many aspects of Jamaican life; and www.afflicted yard.com, also private and purporting to deal with matters Jamaican, but from a completely different perspective.

Of the three sites, www.jamaicans.com was by far the most sophisticated, boasting an extensive list of links, followed by the Tourist Board site, and lastly Afflicted Yard, which appears to be a fairly small operation, though not by any means amateurish in its site design. I propose to look at each site separately at first, specifically for purposes of doing a brief description of the stated aims and objectives of each and a summary of its content. Following this will be an analysis of their constructions of personas, with a view to identifying variations or similarities between the three.

Jamaicans.com is not as explicit as the other two in its aims and objectives. There was no statement of purpose evident on the site's home page. However, it gives the appearance of being geared towards providing a variety of information on Jamaica relevant to four broad categories of persons:

- tourists
- Jamaican nationals intra- and internationally
- businesspersons
- persons with an interest in things Jamaican.

The domain is registered in Hollywood, Florida. In terms of physical design and layout, it is evident that considerable effort has gone into making the site extremely navigable, in the sense that it has a multiplicity of links carrying visitors to different parts of the site. Among the main information pages are ones labelled "geography", "people", "economic indicators", "climate", "currency", and "Jamaican culture". There is also a page devoted to information on Jamaicans considered to have made significant contributions to the arts, culture, sports, business and religion at home or abroad. In its description of the people of Jamaica, it portrays them as having "emerged from a historical process in which peoples of all the continents were brought together within a well defined social hierarchy". One of the features of the site is a community discussion board, in which a broad range of issues is debated, by an apparently large list of users. From the user profiles it appears as if the composition of the list is varied, including persons who are Jamaican by birth or connection and those who are not. It includes among its membership persons living in Jamaica, North America, Europe and, in one case noted, Turkey. Topics include nostalgic visions of Jamaica, gossip, news and current affairs, exchanging of recipes, and making contact with friends and acquaintances not heard from in a while. It is supported to some extent by advertising, and conducts e-commerce through the sale of a variety of Jamaican merchandise. The site also hosts links to other Jamaican Internet connections in other parts of the world.

Jamaicatravel.com, the Jamaica Tourist Board site, introduces potential visitors to Jamaica, enticing them to buy holidays there. It is primarily a promotional site, and contains similar, though not as extensive, categories of Web pages to those at Jamaicans.com. This approach is aimed at presenting its product, Jamaica commodified, in what it considers the best possible light. The site has seven major pages, all in colour, which compartmentalize the information into such areas as travel planning, history and culture, activities, and frequently asked questions. The front page is visually strong, with photographs of various scenes, including sea, beach and people, over which the Tourist Board's jingle, adapted from Bob Marley's "One Love", is played. The presentation of images is maintained on the other pages on the site as well. The domain is registered in New York.

Afflictedyard.com, in contrast to the other two, is a stark, dark site. It is also the only one which clearly articulates its aim and intent (although in the case of the others, their purpose emerges clearly enough). The purpose, it states, is to present a view of Jamaica that differs in style and content from the other two sites in this study. The author of the site states in his introduction that he is trying to "provide a Jamaican-based Web site that isn't operated by the Jamaican Government or a bunch of romantic-minded farts in Miami [a reference to Jamaicans.com]. A website that has nothing to do with recipes, tourist information or content based solely on the life of Bob Marley." The site bills itself as media terrorism at its finest, a claim it certainly tries to live up to in terms of its coverage of issues, which often borders on libel. It obviously manipulates many of the images on the site, and makes statements that appear calculated for their shock value. One can navigate ten pages at Afflictedyard.com, which include the purpose of the site, information on the creators, links to reggae and dancehall music, a series of charities it considers worthy of support in addition to its own charity initiative, and a discussion list. Afflictedyard.com is registered in Toronto.

In reviewing these sites against the backdrop of their constructions of personas, it is fairly clear that Jamaicans.com is the one that most completely creates a space, or more correctly several spaces, for the articulation of identity built around varying notions of what is considered Jamaicanness. This is most strongly manifested in the discussion list, appropriately labelled as the site's community noticeboard. It provides an interactive space, a forum, for engagement with these constructions of persona, which are expressed through language including inflections, vocabulary and syntax. Immediately upon entering the discussion group there is the recognition of being in a conversation with other Jamaicans or people who identify with Jamaicans. There is a banter that is familiar, the foods discussed are familiar, the music, news and current affairs all evoke a strong sense of engagement in face-to-face interaction. The site is not constructed as a closed community, but appears to welcome participation. It is definite in its Jamaicanness. The very names of some of the participants, which range from "Ackee" (a savoury fruit eaten primarily in Jamaica) to "Mi Granny", indicate an anchoring to some concept of and identification with Jamaica. Anyone familiar with Jamaican parlance entering the discussion list on any of the topics at Jamaicans.com will have the immediate feeling that they are at home.

This should not be construed as an attempt at establishing some kind of monolithic Jamaican culture or persona; there is far too much variety within the social hierarchy for that to become possible. What I would like to put forward, instead, is the proposition that even if people do not share the same class background in Jamaica, there is some degree of commonality of referents, and consequently shared understandings, that transcend class or ethnic backgrounds within Jamaica. This also reinforces a critical point made earlier in the chapter: that people use the technologies available to them to facilitate their social existence, and that while these technologies can and do perform some mediating role, they are ultimately tools created to perform particular functions. The use of the Internet in this example practically recreates and maintains what, for at least some of the people who use it, is a sense of self. This is by no means a static or unified self, as a perusal of the various discussion topics reveals. For some, the engagement is one serving the purpose of nostalgia, recreating a sense and feeling of Jamaica that existed many years ago for that particular person or group of persons. Others plant their feet in the here-and-now, and their conversations reflect this, inquiring about purchasing land, what's in the news, and have you heard the latest?

Jamaicatravel.com evokes a somewhat different reading. In packaging Jamaica for sale it creates what I suppose are necessary myths for fulfilling its purpose, creating a delicate balancing act between gilding the natural assets of the country and sanitizing the people. Jamaicans are constructed as warm, friendly, smiling natives, in a typically stereotyping project that renders the island a paradise on earth. There is, of course, the music: Bob Marley, no less. Women and children predominate in the photographs that illustrate the site, a scenario ripe for serious gender analysis that falls outside the scope of this study. Dreadlocks are present, but on a child. What is also different about Jamaicatravel.com is that the personas, where they exist, are predetermined by the creators of the site. They have no agency, and are metaphorically frozen in time. While Jamaicans.com does devote a considerable amount of space to a similar type of traditional approach to constructing the tourism product, which of course includes a presentation of the natives of the country, this is counterbalanced by the strength of its interactive community noticeboard. This example using the Jamaica Tourist Board site probably comes closest to the concerns discussed above, about identity evoking the limitations of closure. It must be noted, however, that there is the possibility that this representation inadvertently reflects the strong tendency towards packaging tourism, with the all-inclusive offerings being at the top of the pile.

Of the three sites surveyed, Afflictedyard.com represents a strong divergence from the more mainstream approaches of the other two. Whereas the Jamaicans.com and Jamaicatravel.com sites are essentially upbeat, Afflictedyard.com, in direct contrast, projects a much less sanguine persona. The areas of divergence include, first, a construction that is more singular and individualistic, with much less community participation and mediation – although the site does have a message board page, in which messages are actually posted. While it is available on the World Wide Web and easily accessed technologically, Afflictedyard.com is not a welcoming site. The author has constructed a persona that is fundamentally different from the images of Jamaicans presented on either of the other sites. There is no docility – though I would hasten to add that the community board at Jamaicans.com doesn't come across as docile either. Instead, what confronts the visitor to the site is the apparent unwelcome of an antisocial person, who throws out abuse on virtually every page. The author is not reclusive, however. The pages on the site are filled with stories purportedly penned by him, and we are regaled with cynical accounts of his international travels and resulting experiences, all told with a wry humour that I personally found quite funny.

Another element of the site is the author's references to disability and other afflictions in very disparaging terms, which would elicit very negative reactions in many quarters. As an example, he speaks of taking photographs of people who have lost limbs as something he enjoys. He also claims that he and his partner laughed when the US space shuttle *Challenger* blew up shortly after taking off. Listed among the people he holds in high esteem are the photographers who "ran Lady Diana off the road", a reference to the ill-fated journey of Diana, Princess of Wales. At the same time, however, he displays a concern for the less fortunate in some of his social commentary, as well as by hosting information about charities on his site. These statements present a construction of a persona which also lays claim to being Jamaican – a far cry from the warm, even feisty representations found on the other sites, but essentially no less true. In fact, Afflictedyard.com is aware of these other representations of Jamaicanness and deliberately sets out to counter these images. Instead of being a community, this site establishes for itself a soapbox from which to comment stridently on social realities as perceived by the author.

Summary and Conclusions

The analysis of three Web sites has been conducted against the backdrop of the initial proposition that the Internet gives agency to the construction of identity. This examination has been bracketed by an exploration of the evolution of the Internet as a facilitator of social construction and interaction. The very notions of identity and representation have been examined to determine their value in exploring the broader issue.

In each of the three Internet sites examined, notions of Jamaicanness have been constructed and presented for anyone with access to the World Wide Web to see and also to engage with. What has emerged from this preliminary examination is an indication that identities are constructed around words and word-images that are owned or co-opted by particular communities of interest, and that these evoke a certain familiarity. These words and word-images are by no means uniformly or uncritically accepted within the universe of Jamaicanness, as highlighted by the representations made on the three sites analysed.

The examination also points to a greater sense of the possibilities presented by the technologies available to enable this process of engagement with notions of self and others. I would not go so far, however, as to close the curtains on the issue. It is far from being fully resolved; further work in the area certainly needs to be done. There is certainly scope for other avenues, not pursued here, to be explored in order to throw more light on the potential and limitations of these technologies as facilitators of agency in the continuous project of defining, redefining, performing and presenting notions of self, particularly in the era of computer-mediated technologies embedded in the Internet.

Acknowledgements

This chapter is based on research conducted during the period October 2000 to March 2001. Some revision and updating of information relative to Internet use was done in early 2004.

Notes

1. Glyne A. Griffith, *Deconstruction, Imperialism and the West Indian Novel* (Kingston, Jamaica: The Press, University of the West Indies, 1996), 11.
2. Ibid., 12.
3. K. Reymers, *Identity and the Internet*, 1998, 1, available at http://www.acsu .buffalo.edu/-reymers/identity.html.
4. Daniel Miller and Don Slater, *The Internet: An Ethnographic Approach* (Oxford: Berg, 2000), 16, 4.
5. Arturo Escobar, "Welcome to Cyberia: Notes on the Anthropology of Cyberculture", *Current Anthropology* 35, no. 3 (June 1994): 211–31.
6. Edward Said, *Culture and Imperialism* (London: Vintage, 1994), 4.
7. Statement made by the late Errol Barrow, former prime minister of Barbados, at the Barbados Constitutional Conference, London, 1966, in relation to Barbados's then impending independence from Britain. Quoted in C.R. Gooch, "Loitering on Colonial Premises after Closing Time: An Analysis of Television Programming Policy in Barbados", in *Globalization, Communications and Caribbean Identity*, ed. H. Dunn (Kingston, Jamaica: Ian Randle, 1995), 98.

8.   S.J. Frosh, "Identity", in *Fontana Dictionary of Modern Thought* (London: Harper
     Collins, 1999), 413.
9.   Rex M. Nettleford, *Mirror Mirror: Identity, Race and Protest in Jamaica* (1970;
     reprint, Kingston, Jamaica: Kingston Publishers, 1998), 19.
10. Ibid.
11. Jamaica Information Service (JIS), http://jis.gov.jm, accessed in 2004.
12. Ibid., accessed in 2000.
13. V. Heron-Gordon, "Strategic Alliances for Community Information Networks:
     The Case of Jamaica" (paper presented at the conference Islands of the World,
     Isle of Skye, 2000), 5–8.
14. J. Aarons, "The Role of Public Authorities in Access to Information:
     Democratising Access to Information Services and Networks with Special
     Reference to the Caribbean" (paper presented at conference Infoethics 2000, Rio
     de Janeiro, Brazil, 2000), 5.
15. A similar search conducted in May 2004 achieved the following: for "jamaica",
     10.3 million hits; for "jamaican identity", 31,300 hits; for "jamaican culture",
     142,000 hits.
16. This site was revamped by the Jamaica Tourist Board and relaunched under the
     URL www.visitjamaica.com. I have been unable to determine, at the time of
     writing, where the domain is currently registered.

Contributors

Annie Paul is a writer and critic based at the University of the West Indies, Mona, Jamaica, where she is publications officer at the Sir Arthur Lewis Institute of Social and Economic Studies. She is a founding editor of *Small Axe* and associate editor of the Cultures and Globalization series published by Sage, London. Paul is the recipient of a grant from the Prince Claus Fund (Netherlands) in support of her book project, "Suitable Subjects: Visual Art and Popular Culture in Postcolonial Jamaica". She was one of the founding editors of the original *Caribbean Review of Books* and has been published in international journals such as *Art Journal, Wasafiri, South Atlantic Quarterly, Callaloo* and *Bomb*.

Kofi Anyidoho is a poet, literary scholar and cultural activist, professor of literature, head of the Department of English and director of the African Humanities Institute Programme at the University of Ghana, Legon. Among his many special awards and distinctions are Visiting Distinguished Cornell Professor (Black Studies, Theatre, English), Swarthmore College; Visiting Distinguished McLean Professor of English, Colorado College; and an honorary fellow of the International Writing Programme, University of Iowa.

Robert Carr is currently director of the Caribbean Centre for Communication for Development and director of graduate programmes at the Caribbean Institute of Media and Communication, University of the West Indies, Mona, Jamaica, and co-chair of the Caribbean Vulnerable Communities Coalition. He is the author of *Black Nationalism in the New World: Reading the African-American and West Indian Experience.*

J. Edward Chamberlin is university professor of English and comparative literature at the University of Toronto. His books include *Come Back to Me My Language: Poetry and the West Indies; If This Is Your Land, Where Are Your Stories? Finding Common Ground;* and *Horse: How the Horse Has Shaped Civilizations.*

Douglas B. Chambers is associate professor of history and editor of *Southern Quarterly*. His publications include *Murder at Montpelier: Igbo Africans in Virginia*.

Jeanne Christensen is professor of history at the University of Colorado, Boulder. Her publications include articles on Rastafarianism in *Archaeology Jamaica* and the *C.L.R. James Journal: A Review of Caribbean Ideas*.

Yacine Daddi Addoun is currently completing his doctorate at York University, Toronto, on the history of slavery in Algeria in the nineteenth century. He has conducted archival and fieldwork in France, Algeria and Mali. In addition to his translation of *Kitb al-Salt*, he has also translated *Musalliyat al-gharb of 'Abd al- Rahmn al-Baghdd*, a text on the Muslim community in Brazil.

Elizabeth DeLoughrey is assistant professor of English at Cornell University. She has published articles on Caribbean and Pacific Island literatures in journals such as *Ariel, Interventions, Thamyris* and the *Journal of Caribbean Literatures*. With Renée Gosson and George Handley, she has edited the forthcoming *Caribbean Literature and the Environment: Between Nature and Culture*.

Hubert Devonish is professor of linguistics at the University of the West Indies, Mona, Jamaica. He has written widely on the structure, form and politics of Caribbean Creole languages, and his publications include *Language and Liberation: Creole Language Politics in the Caribbean* and *Talking Rhythm, Stressing Tone: The Role of Prominence in Anglo-West African Creole Languages*.

Nadi Edwards is senior lecturer in the Department of Literatures in English at the University of the West Indies, Mona, Jamaica. His scholarly interests include popular culture and nationalism, Caribbean cultural criticism, and travel writing. He is the author of a number of scholarly articles in such journals as *Found Object, Studies in Travel Writing*, and the *Journal of West Indian Literature*, and is currently completing a book on anglophone Caribbean poetics.

Cecil Gutzmore lectures in the Institute of Caribbean Studies at the University of the West Indies, Mona, Jamaica. He is engaged in research and writing on Caribbean folk/popular culture, creolization, pan-Africanism, the history of race and racism, and the debate generated by Eric Williams's

Capitalism and Slavery. He has published articles in a number of journals including *Black Liberator, Marxism Today, Race and Class* and *Interventions.*

Donna P. Hope is an adjunct lecturer in philosophy and politics at the University of the West Indies, Mona, Jamaica, and the University College of the Caribbean, and host of the daytime radio talk show *Disclosure.* She is the author of *Inna di Dancehall: Popular Culture and the Politics of Identity in Jamaica.*

Bernard Jankee is the director of the African-Caribbean Institute of Jamaica/Jamaica Memory Bank, a division of the Institute of Jamaica. He is a graduate of the University of the West Indies and the University of London, and he is presently completing his doctorate in anthropology and media studies at the School of Oriental and African Studies, University of London.

Linton Kwesi Johnson is the author of numerous poetry books, the most recent being *Selected Poems.* He has also released fifteen albums, many on his own record label, LKJ Records. His latest CD, also the title of his first DVD, is *LKJ Live in Paris with the Dennis Bovell Dub Band.*

Paul Lovejoy is distinguished research professor and a fellow of the Royal Society of Canada, and he holds the Canada Research Chair in African Diaspora History at York University, Toronto. He is also director of the Harriet Tubman Resource Centre on the African Diaspora (www.yorku.ca/nhp) and a member of the UNESCO Slave Route project. His publications include *Transformations in Slavery: A History of Slavery in Africa* and (with Jan S. Hogendorn) *Slow Death for Slavery: The Course of Abolition in Northern Nigeria, 1897–1936*

Lilieth H. Nelson is head of international programmes at the University of the West Indies, Mona, Jamaica. She is a science educator with vast experience in the performing arts in Jamaica.

Marie-José Nzengou-Tayo is senior lecturer in French and head of the Department of Modern Languages and Literatures at the University of the West Indies, Mona, Jamaica. Her most recent publications are "La Diffusion de la littérature haïtienne en France: Quelle reconnaissance?" and "Bay kou blye, Pote mak sonje: Le Massacre de 1937 dans les romans haïtiens".

Glen Richards is lecturer in the Department of History, University of the West Indies, Mona, Jamaica. He is co-editor (with Verene Shepherd) of *Questioning Creole: Creolisation Discourses in Caribbean Culture* and (with Kathleen Monteith) of *Jamaica in Slavery and Freedom: History Heritage and Culture.*

Ileana Rodríguez is distinguished professor of Spanish at Ohio State University. Her publications include *Transatlantic Topographies: Islands, Highlands, Jungles; Women, Guerrillas, and Love: Understanding War in Central America;* and *House/Garden/Nation: Space, Gender, and Ethnicity in Post-Colonial Latin American Literatures by Women.*

Leah Rosenberg is assistant professor of English at the University of Florida. She teaches Caribbean studies and is the author of *Nationalism and the Formation of Caribbean Literature.*

Veront M. Satchell is senior lecturer in the Department of History, University of the West Indies, Mona, Jamaica. He is the author of *From Plots to Plantations.*

Verene A. Shepherd is professor of social history at the University of the West Indies, Mona, Jamaica. She is president of the Association of Caribbean Historians, chair of the Board of the Jamaica National Heritage Trust and chair of the Jamaica National Bicentenary Committee. Her most recent book is *I Want to Disturb My Neighbour: Lectures on Slavery, Emancipation and Post-Colonial Jamaica.*

Maureen Warner-Lewis is emeritus professor of African-Caribbean Language and Orature, Department of Literatures in English, University of the West Indies, Mona, Jamaica. Her research on African cultural and linguistic retentions in the Caribbean has resulted in the publication of *Guinea's Other Suns; Yoruba Songs of Trinidad; Trinidad Yoruba;* and *Central Africa in the Caribbean.*